PROCEEDINGS OF THE SECOND EUROPEAN CONFERENCE ON COMPUTER-SUPPORTED COOPERATIVE WORK – ECSCW '91

Proceedings of the Second European Conference on Computer-Supported Cooperative Work

ECSCW '91

Edited by

LIAM BANNON and MIKE ROBINSON
Centre for Innovation and Cooperative Technology,
University of Amsterdam, The Netherlands

and

KJELD SCHMIDT
Cognitive Systems Laboratory,
Risø National Laboratory, Denmark

SPRINGER-SCIENCE+BUSINESS MEDIA, B.V.

ISBN 978-0-7923-1439-4 ISBN 978-94-011-3506-1 (eBook)
DOI 10.1007/978-94-011-3506-1

Printed on acid-free paper

ECSCW '91 Organization

Conference Committee

Conference Chair: Mike Robinson, The Netherlands
Conference Vice Chair: Kjeld Schmidt, Denmark
Treasurer & ECSCW '89 Past Chair: Paul Wilson, UK
Conference Office Executive: Andrei Roussakov, USSR
Local Arrangements Chair: Erik Andriessen, The Netherlands
Demonstrations Chair: Tom Rodden, UK
Procedures Chair: Pål Sørgaard, Norway
Delegate Pack Chair: Steve Benford, UK
Program Chair: Liam Bannon, The Netherlands
Proceedings Chair: John Bowers, UK
International Committee Chair: Steve Scrivener, UK
USA Publicity Chair: Charles Grantham, USA
SIGCHI Liaison: Brad Hartfield, USA
COSCIS '91 Liaison: Ronald Stamper, The Netherlands
CSCW '90 Liaison: Tora Bikson, USA

Program Committee

Liam Bannon (Chair), University of Amsterdam, Netherlands
Susanne Bødker, Aarhus University, Denmark
John Bowers, University of Nottingham, UK
Claudio Ciborra, Theseus, France
Peter Docherty, Institute for Management of Innovation & Technology, Stockholm, Sweden
Charles Grantham, University of San Francisco, USA
Riitta Hellman (Vice Chair to Feb.'91), Postdirektoratet, Norway
Hiroshi Ishii, NTT, Japan
John King, University of California at Irvine, USA
Klaus Kreplin, Triumph-Adler Research, Germany
Wanda Orlikowski, MIT, USA
Mike Robinson, University of Amsterdam, The Netherlands
Tom Rodden, University of Lancaster, UK
Kjeld Schmidt, Risø National Laboratory, Denmark
Pål Sørgaard, Norwegian Computing Centre, Norway
Lucy Suchman, Xerox PARC, USA
Michel Tueni, IFATEC, France
Ina Wagner, Technische Universität Wien, Austria
Gerard de Zeeuw, University of Amsterdam, The Netherlands
Heinz Züllighoven, GMD, Germany

International Committee

England: Steve Scrivener
The Netherlands: Erik Andriessen
USA: Brad Hartfield
Japan: Hiroshi Ishii
Poland: Bernard Kubiak
Germany: Henrik Lewe, Wolfgang Prinz
Canada: Marilyn Mantei
Spain: Leandro Navarro
Finland: Markku Nurminen, Kari-Jouko Raiha
Brazil: Christianne Ferreira Ribeiro
USSR: Andrei Roussakov
Italy: Thomas Schael

Sponsors of ECSCW '91

Rank Xerox EuroPARC, Cambridge, UK

Kluwer Academic Publishers, Dordrecht, The Netherlands

University of Amsterdam, The Netherlands

City of Amsterdam, The Netherlands

Commission of the European Communities (General Directorate XIII)

Computer Sciences Company Europe, London, UK

Koninklijke Nederlandse Akademie van Wetenschappen, The Netherlands

Foundation for Cooperative Work Technology

Gesellschaft für Mathematik und Datenverarbeitung (GMD), Bonn, Germany

Apple Computer, Inc., Cupertino, California, USA

Philips, The Netherlands

From the Conference Chair

It gives me great pleasure to welcome all the participants at ECSCW '91 to the city of Amsterdam. I trust the beauty of this city, and the long cooperative tradition of The Netherlands will inspire our debates.

It is a hope of the Conference Committee to help develop a distinctively European profile within CSCW. While the official language of the Conference is English, we are addressing a multi-disciplinary, multi-cultural, and multi-lingual ensemble, whose socio-political context is undergoing unprecedented, large scale, rapid change. Our differences in language reflect differences in work practices, social traditions, and emotive imagery which cannot simply be translated, transferred, or transplanted. Contradictions and conflicts at many European levels give the "cooperative" in CSCW special significance and magnetism. The emphasis within the worldwide CSCW community on understanding the specifics of practical, situated action before embarking on computer interventions has a special relevance, far wider than our own research field. As several of the authors remark, the combination of social theory with system design as CSCW intervention may signal the emergence of new paradigms. Their nature and methodologies will be debated furiously. But it seems certain they will be more humble: the old emphasis on canonical forms will be displaced by works in which "many voices" are heard.

At a practical level, we have planned for a small conference in which dialogues and debates are supported and encouraged. There will be ample time and space for meetings and encounters within the formal program, in the Trippenhuis, and in pleasant local cafes and bars. We believe the formal program is exciting. There are at least three invisible influences on its quality that should be mentioned.

First, there is a special "thank you" to those at the conference whose papers were not accepted. They contained many thought provoking and interesting studies and ideas. These efforts, while not on "public display", will surely benefit the level of informed debate within the conference and within the field of CSCW generally.

The second invisible influence is the European Commission CO-TECH program. This has encouraged and supported the emergence of a network of European researchers stretching from Finland and Scotland to Spain and Yugoslavia. Without this support the fragmentations of language and geography would have prevented the mutual learning and friendships that have made CSCW as a field, and both the '89 & '91 conferences possible.

Third and last, there is the invisible work of the Conference, Program, and International Committees. Their members reflect the real geography of CSCW, stretching from Russia and Japan through Europe to California and Brazil.

I would like to thank all those on the committees who have spent much of their own time and energy in preparing for the conference, all the authors, and the participants who made ECSCW'91 possible.

Enjoy the conference, enjoy Amsterdam.

Mike Robinson

From the Program Chair

It is a pleasure to welcome participants to ECSCW '91. I hope that you find the Program we have put together for the Conference stimulating and informative. The field of CSCW has been evolving and developing rapidly since its formal inception in the mid-eighties. While debates about the very nature of the field continue to rage, both technical and empirical work has broadened and deepened our understanding of cooperative work and how we can support it through computing. This common concern with the support requirements of cooperative work has helped focus the efforts of people from a wide variety of disciplines, one of the hallmarks of the emerging CSCW community. We hope that we have captured some of the excitement of the field, with its interdisciplinary commingling, its prototype systems, and its analyses of actual use of systems in these Proceedings.

This is only the second European CSCW Conference, yet in the intervening years since the 1989 Conference in Gatwick, UK, we have witnessed an explosion of interest within Europe. Special interest groups, international projects, newsletters, books, and journals on the topic are being set up. For this Conference, 88 manuscripts from 16 countries together with a number of panel proposals, were submitted to the Program Committee. Each paper was blind reviewed by several members of the Program Committee. Once again, we decided to maintain a single-track Program for the majority of the Conference. This has undoubted benefits in terms of ensuring a shared view on the issues raised at the Conference, and as a focus for ongoing discussion. However, it has also required the Committee to make very difficult choices in the selection process. Many papers of interest were not able to be accommodated in the Program. We hope that you find the papers selected to be of interest, and to reflect diverse aspects of this inter-disciplinary field. In an effort to provide a forum for additional voices, the Program Committee encouraged a number of authors to organize small parallel workshops for a short period during the Conference. While this idea has been acted on by some, it generated a number of organizational problems, and future Program Committees will need to address this problem of encouraging wider participation without losing the common focus that has been at the heart of CSCW Conferences to date.

In conclusion, I would like to thank the members of the Program Committee and their colleagues for their hard work in reviewing the large number of manuscripts and providing feedback to authors, to the authors who submitted manuscripts for review, and to all you participants who will make this Conference a living affair. We are particularly keen to make this Conference one where there is adequate time for questions and comments around the presentations, and this has been a factor in the choice of a relatively small venue for the meeting, and the small number of papers accepted for presentation. We hope that the papers in this volume, together with the panels and informal discussions that will take place over the next few days in Amsterdam, will stimulate you and contribute to the continued growth of the CSCW field. Enjoy!

Liam J. Bannon

Special Thanks

Chairing the ECSCW '91 Program Committee over the past year has been problematic given my lack of an institutional base, and so I would like to especially thank people at Amsterdam, Mike Robinson and Andrei Roussakov, for handling additional work on my behalf. I would also like to thank Kjeld Schmidt for his excellent work on producing the Proceedings. Finally a number of institutions helped me in a variety of ways: Computing Services, University College Dublin; Institute for Computer & Systems Sciences, Copenhagen Business School; Dept. of Information Processing, University of Umeå; and the Center for Innovation & Cooperative Technology in Amsterdam.

Table of Contents

Proceedings of the Second European Conference on Computer-Supported Cooperative Work
Bannon, L., Robinson, M. & Schmidt, K. (Editors)
September 25-27, 1991, Amsterdam, The Netherlands

Riding a Tiger, or Computer Supported Cooperative Work

Kjeld Schmidt
Risø National Laboratory, Denmark

Abstract: The idea of supporting cooperative work by means of computer systems raises, inter alia, the problem of how to model cooperative work and incorporate such models in computer systems as an infrastructure of the work organization. Cooperative work arrangements should be conceived of as emerging formations that change dynamically and involves distributed decision making. Thus, modelling cooperative work and incorporating such models in CSCW systems is a precarious undertaking. The paper explores the dynamic and distributed nature of cooperative work and discusses the implications for CSCW systems design.

The idea of supporting cooperative work by means of computer systems - the very idea! - can be compared with riding a tiger. Cooperative work may seem familiar and tame. And in fact, a plethora of languages and schemes has been furnished that confidently claim to provide reliable models of organizational roles and patterns of communication.

The innocence and familiarity of cooperative work is deceptive, however. Cooperative work is difficult to bridle and coerce into a dependable model. And anyone trying to incorporate a model of a social world in a computer system as an infrastructure for that world is as reckless as a daredevil mounting a Bengal tiger.

The apparent stability of organizational roles and patterns of communication is a superficial hide beneath which a capricious beast is hidden. Cooperative work arrangements should rather be conceived as emerging formations that change dynamically in accordance with the requirements of the situation, and cooperative work involves, inescapably, the vicissitudes of distributed decision making. These characteristics have important implications for CSCW systems design.

The emergent nature of cooperative work

In his concise way, Montesquieu stated that "Man is born in society and there he remains." In the same vein, Marx (1857) posited that

> "Individuals producing in society - hence socially determined individual production - is, of course, the point of departure. The individual and isolated hunter and fisherman, with whom Smith and Ricardo begin, belong among the unimaginative conceits of the eighteenth-century Robinsonades."

Marx' critique of the Robinson Crusoe metaphor is rooted in a conception of work as an intrinsically social phenomenon:

> "Production by an isolated individual outside society - a rare exception which may well occur when a civilized person in whom the social forces are already dynamically present is cast by accident into the wilderness - is as much of an absurdity as is the development of language without individuals living *together* and talking to each other." (Marx, 1857).

Society, that is, is ubiquitous. Work is always immediately social in that the object and the subject, the end and the means, the motives and the needs, the implements and the competencies, are socially mediated. The social character of work is not a static property, however; it develops historically. With the the ever deeper and increasingly comprehensive social division of labor, the subject and object of work, etc. become increasingly social in character. Hunter-gatherers, for instance, work in an environment that is appropriated socially and yet to a large extent naturally given, whereas, in the case of operators in modern chemical plants, every aspect of work is socially mediated - to the extent that it is conducted in an 'artificial reality'.

While work is always socially organized, the very work process does not always involve multiple people that are mutually dependent in their work and therefore required to cooperate in order to get the work done. We are social animals, but we are not *all* of us *always* and in *every* respect mutually dependent in our work. Thus, in spite of its intrinsically social nature, work is not intrinsically cooperative in the sense that workers are mutually dependent in their work.

The essence of the notion of mutual dependence *in work* is not the negative interdependence among workers using the same resource. They certainly have to coordinate their activities but to each of them existence of the others is a mere nuisance and the less their own work is affected by the others the better. The time-sharing facilities of operating systems for host computers cater for just that by making the presence of other users imperceptible. Being mutual dependent *in work* means that 'A' relies positively on the quality and timeliness of 'B's work and vice versa. 'B' may be 'down stream' in relation to 'A' but in that case 'A' nonetheless will depend on 'B' for feedback on requirements, possibilities, quality problems, schedules etc. In short, mutual dependence in work should primarily be conceived of as a positive, though by no means necessarily harmonious, interdependence.

Due to their being interdependent in conducting their work, cooperating workers have to articulate (divide, allocate, coordinate, schedule, mesh, interrelate, etc.)

their respective activities. Thus, by entering into cooperative work relations, the participants must engage in activities that are, in a sense, extraneous to the activities that contribute directly to fashioning the product or service and meeting the need. The obvious justification of incurring this overhead cost and thus the reason for the emergence of cooperative work formations is, of course, that workers could not accomplish the task in question if they were to do it individually, at least not as well, as fast, as timely, as safely, as reliably, as efficiently, etc. (Schmidt, 1990). For example, in a study of the impact of technology on cooperative work among the Orokaiva in New Guinea, Newton (1985) observes that technological innovations for hunting and fishing such as shotguns, iron, torches, rubber-propelled spears, and goggles have made individual hunting and fishing more successful compared to cooperative arrangements. As a result, large-scale cooperative hunting and fishing ventures are no longer more economical or more efficient and they are therefore vanishing. Likewise, the traditional cooperative work arrangements in horticulture for purposes such as land clearing and establishment of gardens have been reduced in scope or obliterated by the influence of the steel axe. A similar shift from cooperative to individual work can be observed wherever and whenever new technologies augment the capabilities of individual workers to accomplish the task individually: harvesters, bulldozers, pocket calculators, word processors, etc.

Cooperative work relations emerge in response to the requirements and constraints of the transformation process and the social environment on one hand and the limitations of the technical and human resources available on the other. Accordingly, cooperative work arrangements adapt dynamically to the requirements of the work domain and the characteristics and capabilities of the technical and human resources at hand. Different requirements and constraints and different technical and human resources engenders different cooperative work arrangements.

As befits an emergent phenomenon, cooperative work develops historically. For example, agricultural work and craft work of pre-industrial society was only sporadically cooperative. Due to the low level of division of labor at the point of production, the bulk of human labor was exerted individually or within very loosely coupled arrangements. There were, of course, notable exceptions to this picture such as harvest and large building projects (e.g., pyramids, irrigation systems, roads, cathedrals), but these examples should not be mistaken for the overall picture.

Cooperative work as a systematic arrangement of the bulk of work at the point of production emerges in response to the radical division of labor in manufactories that inaugurated the Industrial Revolution. In fact, systematic cooperation in production can be seen as the 'base line' of the capitalist mode of production. However, cooperative work based on the division of labor in manufactories is essentially amputated: the interdependencies between the specialized operators in their work are mediated and coordinated by means of a hierarchical systems of social control (foremen, planners etc.) and by the constraints embodied in the layout and mode of operation of the technical system (conveyer belt etc.). In Marx' words:

> "To the workers themselves, no combination of activities occurs. Rather, the combination is a combination of narrow functions to which every worker or set of workers as a group is subordinated. His function is narrow, abstracted, partial. The totality emerging from this is based on this partial existence and isolation in the particular function. Thus, it is a combination of which he constitutes a part, based on the his work not being combined. *The workers are the building blocks of this combination*. The combination is not their relationship and it is not subordinated to them as an association." (Marx, 1861-63, p 253).

The societal precondition for the prevalence of this 'fetishistic' form of cooperative work is that manufacturing and administrative organizations are in control of their environment to the extent that they can curtail its complex and dynamic character. By severely limiting the range of products and services offered and by imposing strict schedules and procedures on their customers and clientele, organizations in branches of mass production and mass-transactions processing were able to contrive synthetic work settings where activities, for all practical purposes, could be assumed to be subsumed under preconceived plans.

In view of the fundamental trends in the political economy of contemporary industrial society, the 'fetishistic' form of cooperative work is probably merely a transient form in the history of work. Comprehensive changes of the societal environment permeate the realm of work with a whole new regime of demands and constraints. The business environment of modern manufacturing, for instance, is becoming rigorously demanding as enterprises are faced with shorter product life cycles, roaring product diversification, minimal inventories and buffer stocks, extremely short lead times, shrinking batch sizes, concurrent processing of multiple different products and orders, etc. (cf. Gunn, 1987). The turbulent character of modern business environments and the demands of an educated and critical populace, compel industrial enterprises, administrative agencies, health and service organizations, etc. to drastically improve their innovative capability, operational flexibility, and product quality. To meet these demands, work organizations must be able to adapt rapidly and diligently and to coordinate their distributed activities in a comprehensive and integrated way. And this requires horizontal and direct cooperation across functions and professional boundaries within the organization or within a network of organizations.

In short, the full resources of cooperative work must be unleashed: horizontal coordination, local control, mutual adjustment, critique and debate, self-organization. Enter CSCW.

In order to support and facilitate the articulation of distributed and dispersed work activities, modern work organizations need support in the form of advanced information systems. This is illustrated by the efforts in the area of Computer Integrated Manufacturing to integrate formerly separated functions such as design and process planning, marketing and production planning, etc., and by the efforts in the area of Office Information Systems to facilitate and enhance the exchange of information across geographical distance and organizational and professional boundaries. Common to the efforts in these very different areas are the issues explored by CSCW: How can computer systems assist cooperating ensembles in developing and exercising horizontal coordination, local control, mutual adjustment, critique and debate, self-organization?

These issues all revolve around the problem of the distributed character of cooperative work.

The dialectics of cooperative work

Cooperative work is, in principle, distributed in the sense that decision making agents are semi-autonomous in their work.

Situated action. Reality is inexhaustible. The contingencies encountered in any human action - " in the fog of war," as Clausewitz aptly put it - invariably defeat the very best plans and designs. As pointed out by Suchman (1987), "the relation of the intent to accomplish some goal to the actual course of situated action is enormously contingent." Plans may of course be conceived by actors prior to action but they are not simply executed in the actions. Action is infinitely rich compared to the plan and cannot be exhausted by a plan.

Since the circumstances encountered in human action defeat the very best plans and designs, each individual encounters contingencies that may not have been predicted by his or her colleagues and that, perhaps, will remain unknown to them. Each participant in the cooperative effort is faced with a - to some extent - unique local situation that is, in principle, 'opaque' to the others and have to deal with this local situation individually. For example: misplaced documents, shortage of materials, delays, faulty parts, erroneous data, variations in component properties, design ambiguities and inconsistencies, design changes, changes in orders, cancellation of orders, rush orders, defective tools, software incompatibility and bugs, machinery breakdown, changes in personnel, illness, etc.

No goal or criterion applies to all contingencies. In order to handle local contingencies effectively, actors may have to apply criteria that violate even putatively global criteria such as corporate policy. In fact, on closer examination the putative global goals and criteria are also local in the sense that they are formulated in specific contexts as answers to specific questions.

Thus, due to the 'situated' nature of human action, cooperative work arrangements take on an indelible distributed character. No agent in the cooperative ensemble is omniscient.

Incommensurate perspectives. Reality is inexhaustible in another sense too. The world defies unitary and monolithic conceptualizations. As pointed out by Gerson and Star (1986), "no representation of the world is either complete or permanent."

A representation is a "local and temporary closure." Accordingly, a multiplicity of distinct perspectives is required to match the multiplicity of the field of work. A perspective, in this context, is a particular - local and temporary - conceptualization of the field of work, that is, a conceptual reproduction of a limited set of salient structural and functional properties of the object, such as, for instance, generative mechanisms, causal laws, and taxonomies, and a concomitant body of representations, e.g., models, notations, etc. Thus, to grasp of the diverse and contradictory aspects of the field of work as a whole, the multifarious ontological structure of the field of work must be matched by a concomitant multiplicity of perspectives on the part of the decision-making ensemble (Schmidt, 1990). Accordingly, the cooperative ensemble reproduces the multiplicity of its environment in the form of the multiplicity of 'small worlds' of professions and specialities.

There are two aspects to the multiplicity of perspectives.

First, as demonstrated by Rasmussen in a number of studies (e.g., 1979, 1985), a stratified structure of conceptualizations is characteristic of a number of work domains. In technical domains, for example, Rasmussen has identified five levels of abstraction in a *means-end hierarchy.*

Second, perspectives are not always related to conceptual *levels* in the sense of a stratified order, however (Rasmussen, 1988). In addition to conceptualizations as different levels of generative mechanisms or means-end relationships, conceptualizations may reflect *different functional requirements* that are contradictory in the sense that efforts directed at solving one functional problem interfere with efforts directed toward the others. That is, contradictory ends divides the field of work into distinct object domains, orthogonal to the levels of abstraction of the means-end hierarchy.

An omniscient and omnipotent agent to match the multifarious environment of modern work does not exist. The application of multiple perspectives - whether stratified conceptualizations such as means-end relationships or the orthogonal conceptualizations of distinct object domains - will typically require the joint effort of multiple agents, each attending to one particular perspective and therefore engulfed in a particular and parochial small world. So, in addition to the distributed character of cooperative work stemming from the contingent nature of work, cooperative work in complex settings is distributed in the profound sense that the cooperative ensemble is divided into myriads of small worlds with their own particular views of the world.

This dissolution must be overcome, however. The cooperative ensemble must interrelate and compile the partial and parochial perspectives by transforming and translating information from one level of conceptualization to another and from one object domain to another (Schmidt, 1990). Again there is no omniscient and omnipotent agent to perform these transformations and translations. Rather, the transformations and translations are performed in the context of specific situations, to solve particular problems. The generalizations by means of which the partial perspectives are integrated are not globally valid; they are merely satisfactory to solve the problem at hand. They are local and temporary closures.

Bucciarelli (1984) has provided an excellent example of this aspect of cooperative work. In a study of cooperative work in engineering design he observed that

> "different participants in the design process have different perceptions of the design, the intended artefact, in process. What an engineer in the Systems Group calls an interconnection scheme, another in Production calls a junction box. To the former, unit cost and ease of interconnection weigh most heavily; to the latter, appearance and geometric compatibility with the module frame, as well as unit cost, are critical.
>
> The task of design is then as much a matter of getting different people to share a common perspective, to agree on the most significant issues, and to shape consensus on what must be done next, as it is a matter for concept formation, evaluation of alternative, costing and sizing - all the things we teach."

This also applies to the the propagation of goals and criteria from one level of conceptualization to another. Propagation of goals and criteria within a cooperative ensemble is not a simple 'decomposition' or a syllogistic inheritance operation but involves a conceptual translation and a transformation of representations (Rasmussen, 1988). Again, there is no omniscient and omnipotent agent to perform these transformations and translations.

An interesting issue, raised by Charles Savage in a 'round table discussion' on Computer Integrated Manufacturing, illustrates this issue quite well:

> "In the traditional manual manufacturing approach, human translation takes place at each step of the way. As information is passed from one function to the next, it is often changed and adapted. For example, Manufacturing Engineering takes engineering drawings and red-pencils them, knowing they can never be produced as drawn. The experience and collective wisdom of each functional group, usually undocumented, is an invisible yet extremely valuable company resource." (Savage, 1986)

This fact is ignored by the prevailing approach to CIM, however:

> "Part of the problem is that each functional department has its own set of meanings for key terms. It is not uncommon to find companies with four different parts lists and nine bills of material. Key terms such as *part, project, subassembly, tolerance* are understood differently in different parts of the company."

The problem is not merely terminological. It is the problem of multiple incommensurate perspectives. The effort to 'design for assembly,' for example, requires an 'iterative dialogue' involving guardians of incommensurate perspectives: Assembly, Subassembly, Parts Processing, Process Planning, Design, Marketing, etc. The issue raised by Savage is rooted in the multiplicity of the domain and the contradictory functional requirements. In Savage's words: "Most business challenges require the insights and experience of a multitude of resources which need to work together in both temporary and permanent teams to get the job done".

In sum, in complex work settings the multiplicity of the field of work is matched by multiple 'small worlds', each specialized in applying a particular perspective.

There is no omniscient and omnipotent agent to match the multifarious environment or to integrate the specialized and local knowledge.

Incongruent heuristics. In complex environments, decision making is performed under conditions of excessive complexity and incomplete, missing, erroneous, misrepresented, misunderstandable, incomprehensible, etc. information and will thus require decision makers to exercise discretion. In discretionary decision making, however, different individual decision makers will typically have preferences for different heuristics (approaches, strategies, stop rules, etc.). Phrased negatively, they will exhibit different characteristic 'biases'. By involving different individuals, cooperative work arrangements in complex environments are arenas for different decision making strategies and propensities (Schmidt, 1990). Thus, the decision making process of the cooperating ensemble as a whole is distributed in the sense that the agents involved are semi-autonomous in selecting their heuristics.

However, in order to ensure a satisfactory degree of consistency and objectivity in the performance of the ensemble as a whole and thus to meet the requirements of the environment in terms of product quality, reliability, safety etc., the different heuristics must be integrated. To ensure this integration of heuristics, the different decision makers subject the reliability and trustworthiness of the contributions of their colleagues to critical evaluation. This way they are able, as an ensemble, to arrive at more robust and balanced decisions.

For example, take the case of an "experienced and skeptical oncologist," cited by Strauss and associates (1985):

> "I think you just learn to know who you can trust. Who overreads, who underreads. I have got X rays all over town, so I've the chance to do it. I know that when Schmidt at Palm Hospital says, 'There's a suspicion of a tumor in this chest,' it doesn't mean much because she, like I, sees tumors everywhere. She looks under her bed at night to make sure there's not some cancer there. When Jones at the same institution reads it and says, 'There's a suspicion of a tumor there,' I take it damn seriously because if he thinks it's there, by God it probably is. And you do this all over town. Who do you have confidence in and who none."

This process of mutual critical evaluation was described by Cyert and March (1963) who aptly dubbed it 'bias discount.' Even though dubious assessments and erroneous decisions due to characteristic biases are transmitted to other decision makers, this does not necessarily entail a diffusion or accumulation of mistakes, misrepresentations, and misconceptions within the decision-making ensemble. The cooperating ensemble establishes a negotiated order.

Incongruent interests. Any cooperative work arrangement is a tricky - or, in the terminology of 'dialectical logic', 'contradictory' - phenomenon in so far as it is a phenomenon of *individuals working together*. On one hand, since the individuals are mutually dependent in their work, the work of the individual is a particular functional element of the concerted effort of the cooperating ensemble as a totality. But on the other hand, work is an individual phenomenon in so far as labor power happens to be tied to individuals and cannot be separated from the individuals. That is, a cooperative work process, is performed by individuals with individual interests and motives. Because of that, cooperative ensembles are coalitions of diverging and even conflicting interests rather than perfectly collaborative systems. Thus, in the words of Ciborra (1985), the use of information for "misrepresentation purposes" is a daily occurrence in organizational settings. The Russian proverb saying that 'Man was given the ability of speech so that he could conceal his thoughts' applies perfectly to the use of information in organizations.

In sum, then, cooperative work in complex settings is, in principle, distributed in the sense that decision making agents are semi-autonomous in their work in terms of: goals, criteria, perspectives, heuristics, and interests and motives. There is no omniscient and omnipotent agent.

The design of CSCW systems is therefore faced with the challenging problem of supporting the exchange and integration of information within a self-organizing cooperative ensemble of decision makers that have a high degree of autonomy in their cognitive strategies and conceptualizations.

This makes the question of modelling cooperative work and the incorporation of such models in computer systems come to the fore.

The precarious use of models in CSCW

A computer system embodies a model of another system in the 'real world', e.g., in the simple case of a payroll system, a model of the wage calculation system (tariffs etc.) and the staff of the company (names, positions, account numbers etc.).

Models, however, are limited abstractions; they are only valid within a limited area of application. Thus, a computer system will inevitably encounter situations in which the underlying model of the world is no longer valid. With simple systems the user is normally able to know immediately if and when the system's world model does not apply and to take the necessary corrective measures. However, the more complex the system, the more obscure the validity of the system's performance. Thus, as pointed out by Roth and Woods (1989), a "critical element for effective intelligent systems is that they provide some mechanisms to facilitate the detection and resolution of cases that fall outside their bounds." This facility is rarely provided, however: "One of the major failure modes that we have observed in AI systems is to not provide support for the human problem-solver to handle cases where the AI system is beyond its bounds."

Like any other computer system, a CSCW system is based on a model of an aspect of the world, in this case a model of a social world. And like any other model, a model of a social world has an application area within which it is a valid - abstract and limited - representation of the world. That is, there is a boundary beyond which the model is invalid. Thus a CSCW system is inevitably placed in a situation beyond the bounds of the underlying model. The critical question is what happens to the cooperating ensemble using this system when the underlying model of cooperative relations is beyond its bounds? Unlike a typical expert system, a CSCW system is not controlled by a single agent in a position to switch the machine off if its performance is blatantly unsatisfactory. A CSCW system is part and parcel of the infrastructure of the cooperating ensemble it supports. Thus, with the conventional 'automation' paradigm, CSCW systems are disasters to come. Therefore, CSCW systems should not be designed on the assumption that the system will automate the functions of articulation work. UTo the contrary, users should be in full control of the system so that they are able to know and maintain control when the system is beyond its bounds.

Let us therefore look into the problems of modelling cooperative work in CSCW design.

Different aspects of the social world is modelled in the different approaches to CSCW systems design. For example, even a CSCW facility as 'generic' as a shared view system, must provide a floor-control protocol for managing turn-taking. Of the more elaborate approaches to modelling cooperative work, two categories are of particular here: models of organizational structures and models of conceptual structures.

Models of organizational structures: In the Office Automation tradition, systems incorporated a model of a canonical allocation of tasks and responsibilities or prescribed patterns of communication (e.g., Zisman, 1977; Hammer and Sirbu, 1980; Hammer and Kunin, 1980; Ellis, 1982; Ellis and Bernal, 1982). Although this approach has been stubbornly perpetuated under the CSCW label (e.g., Sluizer and Cashman, 1984; Victor and Sommer, 1989; Smith, Hennesy, and Lunt, 1989), it was critiqued accurately in 1983 by Barber, de Jong, and Hewitt:

> "In all these systems information is treated as something on which office actions operate producing information that is passed on for further actions or is stored in repositories for later retrieval. These types of systems are suitable for describing office work that is structured around actions (e.g. sending a message, approving, filing); where the sequence of activities is the same except for minor variations and few exceptions. [...] These systems do not deal well with unanticipated conditions." (Barber, de Jong, and Hewitt, 1983, p. 562).

In the dynamic environments characteristic of modern work settings, work articulation by means of execution of preestablished schemes of task allocation, procedures, plans, and schedules is no longer adequate. Rather, the radical transformation of work and its organization calls for an 'open systems' approach. In the words of Gerson and Star (1986):

> "Every real-world system is an open system: It is impossible, both in practice and in theory, to anticipate and provide for every contingency which might arise in carrying out a series of tasks. No formal description of a system (or plan for its work) can thus be complete. Moreover, there is no way of guaranteeing that some contingency arising in the world will not be inconsistent with a formal description or plan for the system. [...] *Every real-world system thus requires articulation* to deal with the unanticipated contingencies that arise. Articulation resolves these in-

consistencies by packaging a compromise that 'gets the job done,' that is, closes the system locally and temporarily so that work can go on."

In the analysis of conventional mass-production and mass-transaction processing organizations a cautious and guarded abstraction from the 'open' nature of the system is legitimate and provides valuable insight. The current transformation of work, makes a complete inversion of perspective mandatory. Instead of conceiving of the work organization as a closed and stable system, subject to local and temporary disturbances, a work organization under contemporary conditions should be conceived of as an open system that reduces complexity and uncertainty by local and temporary closures. Thus, in view of the dynamic nature of the environment facing modern work organizations, patterns of cooperative work relations should be conceived as being, in principle, ephemeral.

An alternative approach to the OA tradition, suggested and explored by Barber and Hewitt, posited that systems should embody an explicit representation of the goal structure of the organization: "This builds a teleological structure of the office work within the computer" (Barber and Hewitt, 1992; Barber, 1983). Thus the system provides a resource to handle unexpected contingencies. However, as pointed out by Woo and Lochovsky (1986), while such systems (for instance, Barber's OMEGA) may be useful for office applications that are *logically centralized* and involve only a single user in performing the work, they do not support the *distributed nature of cooperative work*: "Supporting distributed, yet cooperative, office activities by providing a logically centralized office system (i.e., gathering the knowledge of all office workers involved in performing a task into a global and consistent knowledge base) creates a number of problems." First, cooperative work in complex environments involves integration of specialized conceptualizations, and "converting specialized, yet cooperative, office procedures to fit an integrated environment will not be easy since it requires the integrator to have knowledge of all the different kinds of specialization." And second, "In a logically centralized office system, inconsistent office procedures, specified by different office workers, are not allowed." In spite of intentions, the approach suggested by Barber and Hewitt assumes the intervention of an omniscient and omnipotent agent.

Models of conceptual structures: Even in systems that do not prescribe procedures for human interaction but, rather, provide facilities for a community to cooperate via a common information space (Schmidt and Bannon, 1991), the conceptual structure of that space is in itself a model of aspects of a social world. A taxonomy, for instance, is a negotiated order.

Engelbart and Lehtman (1988) have outlined an ambitious vision of a "system designed to support collaboration in a community of knowledge workers." Such a system should support the creation, modification, transmission etc. of messages, as well as cross-referencing, cataloging and indexing of the accumulating stock of messages. With services such as these, they claim, "a community can maintain a dynamic and highly useful 'intelligence' database." And they propose extending this facility toward

> "the coordinated handling of a very large and complex body of documentation and its associated external references. This material, when integrated into a monolithic whole, may be considered a 'superdocument.' Tools for the responsive development and evolution of such a superdocument by many (distributed) individuals within a discipline- or project-oriented community could lead to the maintenance of a 'community handbook,' a uniform, complete, consistent, up-to-date integration of the special knowledge representing the current status of the community.
>
> The handbook would include principles, working hypotheses, practices, glossaries of special terms, standards, goals, goal status, supportive arguments, techniques, observations, how-to-do-it items, and so forth. An active community would be constantly involved in dialogue concerning the contents of its handbook. Constant updating would provide a 'certified community position structure' about which the real evolutionary work would swarm."

While this 'community handbook' effectively addresses the issue of supporting cooperation via a common information space, there is no omniscient and omnipotent agent to ensure that the special and local knowledge of the different semi-autonomous agents is integrated in "a uniform, complete, consistent, up-to-date" way. A "uniform, complete, consistent, up-to-date" community handbook is simply a chimera.

First, the data incorporated in the community handbook will be incomplete. It is simply a question of the benefit versus the cost of entering or capturing 'all' data, whatever that may mean. In fact, the community handbook will be a coarse representation of the diversified and multifarious reality of the community.

Second, the data incorporated in the community handbook will not be indexed consistently. The system would of course provide a global classification scheme to support the distributed indexing of information items to be included in the database, for example, taxonomies and thesauri. Such a classification scheme is itself an partial and temporary conceptualization, however. In order to include an information item in the database, an agent needs to *interpret* the conceptual structure of the classification scheme, *relate* it to the specialized conceptualizations of his or her particular perspective, and *translate* it to local circumstances. That is, the scheme will not be applied uniformly, and the database will over time become inconsistent.

And third, the conceptual structure of the community handbook as embodied in the classification scheme is itself of local and temporary validity. The semantics of categories will change and new categories will emerge. In order not to deteriorate, the scheme must evolve with the conceptual evolution of the community it is a reflection of. Integration of the diversified work activities of modern organizations requires that actors from the different subdomains and specialties involved negotiate a shared understanding. Because of the incommensurate perspectives involved, a shared understanding is a local and temporary closure destined to break down in face of a diversified and dynamic environment. To support the ongoing integration work, then, the taxonomies and classification schemes embodied in and supporting company-wide databases and other integrated business systems must be maintained, reinterpreted, adapted, etc. by means of an ongoing cooperative effort. That is, the conceptual structure of the 'community handbook' is itself subject to the vicissitudes of distributed decision making and it will thus itself be incomplete and inconsistent.

In short, irrespective of the approach taken to modelling cooperative work for CSCW systems design, it is a precarious undertaking.

We do not have to despair, though.

The problem with incorporating models of plans (established procedures, organizational structures, or conceptual schemes) in computer systems is not that plans are fictitious. Rather, plans serve a heuristic function in action by identifying constraints, pitfalls and strategic positions in the field of work. As observed by Suchman (1987), in order to serve this heuristic function "plans are inherently vague". Thus, in Suchman's conception,

> "plans are resources for situated action, but do not in any strong sense determine its course. While plans presuppose the embodied practices and changing circumstances of situated action, the efficiency of plans as representations comes precisely from the fact that they do not represent those practices and circumstances in all of their concrete detail."

In fact, 'plans' may serve different functions. Consider organizational procedures, for example: Procedures may of course codify 'good practice,' recipes, proven methods, efficient ways of doing things, work routines. In flexible work organizations such procedures are of little value and may actually impede flexibility. However, a procedure may also convey information on the functional requirements to be met by the process and the product; it may highlight decisional criteria of crucial import; it may suggest a strategy for dealing with a specific type of problems (e.g., which questions to address first?); it may indicate pitfalls to avoid; or it may simply provide an aide de memoir (such as a start procedure for a power plant or an airplane). And third, a procedure may express some statutory constraints in which case disregard of the procedure may evoke severe organizational sanctions. More often than not, a particular procedure will express, in some way, all of these different functions. Whatever the function, however, organizational procedures are not executable code but rather heuristic and vague statements to be interpreted and instantiated, maybe even by means of intelligent improvisation

Therefore, instead of pursuing the elusive aim of devising models that are not limited abstractions and thus in principle brittle when confronted with the inexhaustible multiplicity of reality, models of cooperative work in CSCW systems (whether procedures, schemes of allocation of tasks and responsibilities, or taxonomies and thesauri, etc.) should be conceived of as *resources* for competent and responsible workers. That is, the system should make the underlying model accessible to users and, indeed, support users in interpreting the model, evaluate its rationale and implications. It should support users in applying and adapting the model to the situation at hand; i.e., it should allow users tamper with the way it is instantiated in the current situation, execute it or circumvent it, etc. The system should even support users in modifying the underlying model and creating new models in accordance with the changing organizational realities and needs. The system should support the documentation and communication of decisions to adapt, circumvent, execute, modify etc. the underlying model. In all this, the system should support the process of negotiating the interpretation of the underlying model, annotate the model or aspects of it etc.

An approach similar to this has been explored in some 'shared view' systems. Cooperative work in real world settings is characterized by immense flexibility because people proficiently utilize the rich resources of everyday conversation to handle contingencies. It has therefore been argued (Greenberg, 1989) that 'shared view' systems should provide support for a broad variety of modes of interaction (turntaking protocols etc.) and, most importantly, provide support for users to control the choice of mode of interaction.

Likewise, in the case of models of organizational structures, CSCW systems to support flexible work organizations should not impose prescribed or preestablished patterns of cooperative work relations. Rather, CSCW systems should provide facilities allowing users to interpret and explore prescribed procedures and formal structures as well as conventional patterns of communication, and leave it to the users to abide by or deviate from norm and practice according to their professional judgment of the contingencies of the current and local situation. That is, in CSCW systems, models of organizational structures should be presented as heuristic information that users can appropriate, explore, modify, negotiate, reject, circumvent, or execute according to the contingencies of the situation.

Similarly, in the case of models of conceptual structures, a CSCW system should provide facilities supporting users in appropriating, exploring, modifying, negotiating etc. - cooperatively and yet distributed - 'community handbooks' that are openly incomplete and inconsistent.

Providing support for distributed cooperative appropriation, circumvention, modification of the system is, perhaps, the toughest challenge in designing computer systems for cooperative work. Is it possible to formulate general principles of the design of the functional allocation between humans actors and a CSCW artifact so that the cooperating ensemble can maintain control of the situation when the underlying model is beyond its bounds? Which aspects of social systems are suitable for being modelled in CSCW systems? Roles, procedures, rules of conduct, patterns of communication, conceptual structures? What are the specific problems and limitations of different kinds of models? How can users be supported in designing models of their world for incorporation in CSCW systems? How should the underlying model of the system be made visible to users? How should different users perceive the model? How and to which extent can it be made malleable? Should all users really be allowed to circumvent all constraints of the system? Is it possible to support users in anticipating the consequences of a circumvention or modification under consideration? Should a circumvention affect other users? How should a circumvention of the model be logged, reported, and presented to other users? And so forth. Questions such as these are still open issues in research and development of computer systems for cooperative work in complex and dynamic settings.

Acknowledgments

The study has been supported by the CEC ESPRIT Basic Research Action under the MOHAWC project (Modelling Human Activities in Work Context, Basic Research Action no. 3105) and by Danish Technical Research Council, under the FTU Programme (Project Number 5.17.5.6.07.). My ideas of the basic issues in the design of computer systems for support of cooperative work have been developed in ongoing discussions with Liam Bannon, Mike Robinson and other members of WG4 of "CoTech" (COST Action 14).

References

Bannon, L., and K. Schmidt (1991): "CSCW: Four Characters in Search of a Context", in J. Bowers and S. Benford (eds.): *Studies in Computer-Supported Cooperative Work: Theory, Practice and Design*, North-Holland, Amsterdam, 1991, pp. 3-16.

Barber, G. R. (1983): "Supporting Organizational Problem Solving with a Work Station", *ACM Transactions on Office Information Systems*, vol. 1, no. 1, January 1983, pp. 45-67.

Barber, G. R., and C. Hewitt (1982): "Foundations for Office Semantics", in N. Naffah (ed.): *Office Information Systems*, INRIA/North-Holland, Amsterdam, 1982, pp. 363-382.

Barber, G. R., P. de Jong, and C. Hewitt (1983): "Semantic support for work in organizations", in: R.E.A. Mason (ed.): *Information Processing 83. Proceedings of the IFIP 9th World Computer Congress. Paris, France, 19-23 Sept. 1983*, North-Holland, Amsterdam 1983, pp. 561-566.

Bucciarelli, L. L. (1984): "Reflective practice in engineering design," *Design Studies*, vol. 5, no. 3, July 1984, pp. 185-190.

Ciborra, C. U. (1985): "Reframing the Role of Computers in Organizations: The Transaction Costs Approach," *Proceedings of Sixth International Conference on Information Systems, Indianapolis, December 16-18, 1985*.

Cyert, R. M., and J. G. March (1963): *A Behavioral Theory of the Firm*, Prentice-Hall, Englewood Cliffs, N.J.

Ellis, C. A. (1979): "Information Control Nets", *Proceedings of the ACM Conference on Simulation, Measurement and Modeling, Boulder, Colorado, August 1979*.

Ellis, C. A. (1983): "Formal and Informal Models of Office Activity," in R.E.A. Mason (ed.): *Information Processing 83. Proceedings of the IFIP 9th World Computer Congress. Paris, France, 19-23 Sept. 1983*, North-Holland, Amsterdam 1983, pp. 11-22.

Ellis, C. A., and G. J. Nutt (1980): "Office Information Systems and Computer Science," *Computing Surveys*, vol. 12, no. 1, marts 1980, pp. 27-60.

Engelbart, D., and H. Lehtman (1988): "Working together," *Byte*, December 1988, 245-252.

Gerson, E. M. and S. L. Star (1986): "Analyzing Due Process in the Workplace," *ACM Transactions on Office Information Systems*, vol. 4, no. 3, July 1986, pp. 257-270.

Greenberg, S. (1989): "Sharing Views and Interactions with Single-User Applications", *Proceedings of the ACM/IEEE Conference on Office Information Systems (COIS), April 1990*.

Gunn, T. G., 1987, *Manufacturing for Competitive Advantage. Becoming a World Class Manufacturer*, Ballinger, Cambridge, Mass.

Hammer, M., and J. S. Kunin (1980): "Design principles of an office specification language", *Proceedings. AFIPS National Computer Conference, May 1980*, pp. 541-547.

Hammer, M., and M. Sirbu (1980): "What is Office Automation?", *Proceedings. First Office Automation Conference, Atlanta, Georgia, March 1980.*

Marx, K. (1857): "Einleitung", MEGA, vol. II/1.1. (English transl. by Nicolaus, in Marx: *Grundrisse*, Pelican, Harmondsworth, 1973).

Marx, K. (1861-63): *Zur Kritik der politischen Ökonomie (Manuskript 1861-63)*; MEGA, vol. II/3.1

Newton, J. (1985): "Technology and Cooperative Labour Among the Orokaiva," *Mankind*, vol. 15, no. 3, December 1985, pp. 214-222.

Rasmussen, J. (1979): *On the Structure of Knowledge - a Morphology of Mental Models in a Man-Machine Context*, Risø National Laboratory, November 1979. [Risø-M-2192].

Rasmussen, J. (1985): "The Role of Hierarchical Knowledge Representation in Decisionmaking and System Management", *IEEE Transactions on Systems, Man, and Cybernetics*, vol. SMC-15, no. 2, March/April 1985, pp. 234-243.

Rasmussen, J. (1988): "A Cognitive Engineering Approach to the Modelling of Decision Making and Its Organization in Process Control, Emergency Management, CAD/CAM, Office Systems, Library Systems," in W. B. Rouse (ed.): *Advances in Man-Machine Systems Research*, vol. 4, JAI Press, Greenwich, Conn., 1988, pp. 165-243.

Roth, E. M., and D. D. Woods (1989): "Cognitive Task Analysis: An Approach to Knowledge Acquisition for Intelligent System Design", in G. Guida and C. Tasso (eds.): *Topics in Expert System Design. Methodologies and Tools*, North-Holland, Amsterdam, 1989, pp. 233-264.

Savage, C. M. (ed.) (1987): *Fifth Generation Management for Fifth Generation Technology (A Round Table Discussion)*, Society of Manufacturing Engineers, Dearborn, Michigan.

Schmidt, K. (1990): *Analysis of Cooperative Work. A Conceptual Framework*, Risø National Laboratory, June 1990. [Risø-M-2890].

Schmidt, K., and L. Bannon (1991): "CSCW, or What's in a Name?" (submitted for publication).

Sluizer, S., and P. Cashman (1984): "XCP. An experimental tool for supporting office procedures," *Proceedings. First International Conference on Office Automation*, IEEE-CS Press, December 1984, pp. 73-80.

Smith, H., P. Hennessy and G. Lunt: "And Object-Oriented Framework for Modelling Organizational Communication", in J. Bowers and S. Benford (eds.): *Studies in Computer-Supported Cooperative Work: Theory, Practice and Design*, North-Holland, Amsterdam, 1991, pp. 145-158.

Strauss, A. (1985): "Work and the Division of Labor," *The Sociological Quarterly*, vol. 26, no. 1, 1985, pp. 1-19.

Suchman, L. A. (1987): *Plans and situated actions. The problem of human-machine communication*, Cambridge Univ. Press, Cambridge etc..

Victor, F., and Sommer, E. (1991): "Supporting the design of office procedures in the DOMINO system", in J. Bowers and S. Benford (eds.): *Studies in Computer-Supported Cooperative Work: Theory, Practice and Design*, North-Holland, Amsterdam, 1991, pp. 119-130.

Zisman, M. D. (1977): *Representation, Specification and Automation of Office Procedures*, Ph.D. diss., Dept. of Decision Sciences, The Wharton School, Univ. of Pennsylvania, PA.

Proceedings of the Second European Conference on Computer-Supported Cooperative Work
Bannon, L., Robinson, M. & Schmidt, K. (Editors)
September 25-27, 1991, Amsterdam, The Netherlands

Personalizable groupware: Accommodating individual roles and group differences

Saul Greenberg
Department of Computer Science, University of Calgary, Canada T2N 1N4

Abstract—For groupware to be considered successful, it must be usable and acceptable by most, if not all, members of the group. Yet the differences present between group members—their varying roles, needs, skills—and the differences between groups as a whole are a serious obstacle to achieving uniform acceptance of the groupware product, especially when the product treats all people and groups identically. This paper raises several consequences of not accommodating individual differences, and then offers a possible solution to the problem. First, instances of groupware failure are described: the inability of the group to reach a critical mass; the unequal accessibility of the groupware by participants; the failure to accommodate the different roles participants may play; the failure to balance the work done against the benefits received; and the failure of groupware to evolve with the needs of the group. Second, the notion of *personalizable groupware* is proposed, defined as a system whose behaviour can be altered to match the particular needs of group participants and of each group as a whole. Finally, the paper presents SHARE, a working example of personalizable groupware. SHARE is a shared screen system that offers its users a flexible choice of floor control models to help them mediate their interactions with the shared application.

1. Introduction

Design teams now build single user systems with good interfaces suitable for selling to the mass market. While the product may not be to everyone's tastes, the vendor's goal is to have it acceptable to enough customers to make its production an economically worthwhile venture. Those customers with differing requirements or preferences simply go to another product, or do without.

Designers of groupware face more rigid criteria. Of course, the product must satisfy enough groups to be commercially viable. But unlike single user software, the product chosen by the group should almost by definition be acceptable and usable by almost *all* its members. While this may seem a strong claim, experience has revealed conditions of groupware failure due to its inability to satisfy all its supposed users.

Consider the following issues and instances of groupware failures.

a) *A critical mass of system adopters may not be reached if too many people opt out of using the groupware product.* A new feature-rich asynchronous conferencing system was introduced at a work site to replace an old but still usable one. Although the new product had a strong champion and was used heavily by 20% of the departmental community (predominantly upper management), a good number of the staff resisted switching to it mostly due to the overhead of learning and using the new system's primitive user interface. Conference activity dwindled as contributors realized they were not reaching the majority of the intended audience. The new system was eventually shelved until a better interface could be developed. (See also Markus and Connolly's 1990 discussion of payoff criteria for adopting technology).

b) *Participants who cannot or will not use the technology face the danger of becoming second class citizens within their own group.* Participants of CAPTURE LAB face-to-face meetings can access a large public screen through their personal computers (Mantei 1988). Austin, Liker and McLeod (1990) noticed that CAPTURE LAB participants who rated themselves as less than 25% proficient with its computer technology were unlikely to use it. Those with greater proficiency were equally likely to use or not use it. Austin et al suggest the existence of a "proficiency floor", above which an individual would perceive themselves as having sufficient competency to use the technology. Those below the floor would avoid its use.

Our similar observation concerned face to face meetings whose members had shared access to a spreadsheet program being projected at the front of the room. Participants who were not familiar with the spreadsheet package or who were not adept typists were inhibited from adding to the model being displayed.

c) *New people joining an established but evolving group must be able to use the system adeptly, otherwise cliques of expertise may evolve.* The initial joining period is critical for new members to assert themselves into the established group. In the spreadsheet case above, we observed that the complex uses made of the spreadsheet package by the already adept but established group made the system almost unreachable by new participants. The newcomers, although familiar to some extent with the technology, were unfamiliar with the ways it had been applied. Unconsciously, the established group became a clique of elite controllers.

d) *Participants in a group may have quite different roles that are not recognized by the groupware product.* Consider a screen sharing package that enforces a pre-emptive floor control protocol (ie anyone can pre-empt control away from anyone else). We have observed one interacting team of a senior and junior person, where the junior person was quite uncomfortable and almost unwilling to take control away from the senior person.

Another effect of role differences was noticed in the CAPTURE LAB study mentioned above. Austin et al (1990) write that use of the public screen technology was proportionally higher by influential group members when contrasted to members with less influence, and by males when compared to females. They suggest that some group members perceived the public screen as a means of influencing other group members. The CAPTURE LAB technology does not recognize these effects; unequal use of the technology is neither encouraged nor guarded against.

e) *There is often disparity between who does the work and who gets the benefit when using groupware.* Grudin (1988) argues that groupware applications often fail because they require that some group members do additional work even when they are not the ones who perceive or receive a direct benefit. A familiar example is a group appointments scheduler that requires all members to do the extra work of keeping their on-line calendars up to date for the benefit of the person (usually the manager) who schedules most of the meetings (Grudin 1988; Bullet and Bennett 1990).

f) *Group needs evolve rapidly, not only from meeting to meeting but within the course of a meeting. The Groupware must keep pace.* Users of COGNOTER, a multi-user idea organizer, would often split into multiple sub-groups to work on ideas raised in the brainstorming session (Foster and Stefik 1986; Tatar, Foster and Bobrow 1991). An early COGNOTER design created a formal division of the sub-groups into "rooms" (Stefik et al 1987). However, these formal boundaries did not reflect the evolving sub-group membership or interactions between them. As a result, Stefik et al conjectured that formation and dissolution of subgroups would be inhibited.

We believe that a prerequisite to successful groupware is that it must be acceptable by most or all members of the group. This can be accomplished in several ways. First, groupware use can be so generic or transparent that almost anyone can use it. For example, tele-conferencing requires only normal interaction skills of participants, while vanilla electronic mail requires mostly familiarity with an editor of choice. Second, the service provided could be so valuable or so entrenched in the organization (perhaps politically) that all users are effectively "forced" to accommodate to it.

This paper raises a third possibility: that groupware be *personalizable* so that it can accommodate individual roles and group differences.

2. Personalizable Groupware

Personalizable groupware is defined as groupware whose behaviour can be tailored to match the particular needs of group participants (ie each member of the group may observe a different behaviour), and the particular needs of the group as a whole (ie each group may observe a different collective behaviour). Illustrating the first point, suppose that a small group of three people, say two architects and a client, are in a remote real time meeting consulting over blueprints displayed through a shared computer aided design (CAD) package. Depending upon personal needs and tastes, each participant may require a slightly or even completely different style of user interface. For instance, the senior architect may have complete access to the controls in the CAD package, while the apprentice architect may only be able to observe the drawing. The CAD-naive client may still be able to gesture and sketch around the existing drawing through a very simple graphics pencil. Illustrating the latter point about between-group differences, the same groupware tool may be used by a group of contractors to implement the blueprint. In this case, the contractors may only be able to annotate that part of the drawing that they are responsible for, perhaps to indicate deviations they had taken from the design.

Although this paper names and champions the concept of personalized groupware, it is not a novel idea. A handful of groupware systems incorporate some level of personalization. Consider QUILT, a computer-based tool for collaborative document production (Leland, Fish and Kraut 1988). A person's ability to manipulate a document is tailored to one's position in a permission hierarchy. Some positions are readers, commentors and co-authors, each with greater powers of annotation and revision. Another example is INFORMATION LENS (Malone et al 1987), an information manager for mail and news. Here, users can construct their own semi-structured templates representing particular types of mail they wish to compose, can create their own rules to filter incoming information in quite sophisticated ways, and can create custom views that summarizes selected information (see also OBJECT LENS, Lia and Malone 1988). A third example is CRUISER, a video-based "virtual hallway" system that facilitates casual interaction (Root 1988; Fish 1989). People in the CRUISER network can control privacy by setting a variety of personal permissions that limit how others can observe and/or interact with them. Finally, the VIRTUAL LEARNING COMMUNITY (Johnson-Lenz and Johnson-Lenz 1991) is an asynchronous conferencing system that lets a conference facilitator tailor the groupware to support the purpose and the variety of the group's activities. For example, the boundaries that define group membership can be adjusted to either enforce equal participation of all group members, or to allow "lurkers"—people who follow the group's discussion but who never express themselves.

Aside from these four and a few other notable exceptions, personalization is usually ignored—sometimes intentionally—in groupware design. Consider at the extreme the point of view of "groupware as mechanism", where the computer's role is to provide a single well-defined mechanism that incorporates some social model of interaction (Johnson-Lenz and Johnson-Lenz 1991). Here, the social model enforced by the system and imposed on its users is an explicit attempt by the designer to provide methods to help keep the group on task, enforce roles and commitments, and make the group efficient and productive (a common goal of group decision support systems). While such systems certainly have a positive role in some settings, the Johnson-Lenzs argue that inflexible structures may trigger organizational and individual resistance, and that flexible patterns encouraging personal initiative are just as important as well-defined group procedures. The negative outcome of mis-matched groupware as mechanism may well be inflexible systems that force its users to do things in undesirable and unproductive ways, where people must change their behaviour to match the machine's model, rather than vice versa. At their worst, users will perceive such systems as "fascist software" and will avoid their use (for example, see Bair and Gale's 1988 report on the COORDINATOR).

Yet we do not advocate the chaos of a completely customizable and unstructured interface, for these will often leave its users at a lost of what to do (Johnson-Lenz and Johnson-Lenz 1991; Thimbleby 1980; but see Dykstra and Carasik 1991 for another point of view). We see personalizable groupware as a way to soften the negative effects of groupware as mechanism by offering a range of structures that reflect a complementary range of the group's requirements. The groupware designer's job is to determine what parts of the groupware system should remain immutable and what part personalizable, and then to set reasonable constraints on the personalization allowed.

3. A working example of personalizable groupware

3.1 Shared window systems and floor control.

"Collaboration aware" groupware for real-time sharing of work explicitly recognizes the existence of each participant in the collaboration (Lauwers and Lantz, 1990). For example, a collaboration-aware sketchpad can be designed to support what people actually do in collaborative design (Tang 1991) eg gesturing by displaying multiple cursors, and concurrent work by allowing participants to sketch simultaneously into a common shared workspace (Greenberg and Bohnet 1991). It is unlikely, however, that collaboration aware systems will have a major impact on the market in the next few years. Not only are they technically difficult to build, but the prerequisites for design are lacking—we really know very little about how people work together.

An alternate approach stems from the old idea of taking a single-user application and sharing it between participants of an on-line meeting through a "shared screen" or "shared window" (Engelbart and English 1968; see Greenberg 1990 for a survey). Each participant would have an identical view of the running application and an opportunity to interact with it. Special "view-sharing" software would allow *any* unaltered single-user application to be brought into a meeting; the application itself would have no awareness that more than one person was using it. This scheme is usually implemented by merging all participants' inputs into a single stream sent to the application, and by sending a copy of the application's output stream to every participant's workstation[1]. While limited in power, shared views are a logical and reasonable "stepping stone" to true collaboration aware systems (Johansen 1989).

A catch of sharing single-user applications is that users must take turns; attempts at simultaneous activity would have the input to the application garbled (eg two people typing at the same time would have their input merged into a nonsense sentence; simultaneous attempts to move the single cursor would result in "cursor wars"). Consequentially, most shared view systems enforce serial turntaking through some type of explicit floor control mechanism (see Table 1 for a brief summary of several floor control protocols and some systems that implement them). For example, the CAPTURE LAB, the face-to-face meeting room that allows participants to share a single large screen, forces a *pre-emptive protocol* where one can pre-empt the floor away at any time from the current floor holder (Mantei 1988). The commercial TIMBUKTU product offers a *free floor*, where any participant can enter any input at any time—turntaking must be mediated out-of-band (Farallon 1988). In contrast, CANTATA uses a first in, first out *queue with explicit release*, where the current floor holder must release the floor before the next person in line gets it (Chang, Kasperski and Copping 1987).

While existing shared view systems usually offer one particular style of protocol for floor control, no literature provides justification as to why that style was chosen. Is there, in fact, a "best" general floor control policy? We believe there is not, for

[1]While simple to do in shared terminal systems (eg by using pseudo-tty filters to trap i/o in UNIX), the technology of sharing windows is far more complex and is fraught with many technical issues and difficulties (Lauwers, Joseph, Lantz and Romanow 1990; Greenberg 1990).

groups will differ in how its members interact with each other. As Lauwers writes (the designer of the technically sophisticated DIALOGO view sharing system) "...the only certainty [about floor control] is that no one policy will suffice for all groups, in all situations" (Lauwers 1990 p97).

We can easily envision situations where groups desire different policies. A small group of practised collaborators may prefer the free floor, choosing to mediate interaction by voice alone, while a larger cooperating group may employ pre-emptive control to avoid accidental input merging. As a case in point, programmers using the SharedX shared window system (Garfinkle, Gust, Lemon and Lowder 1989) reported the need to alternate between free floor when brainstorming to system-controlled one-person-at-a-time when wanting to make sure a particular piece of code was coded correctly (reported in Lauwers 1990). In distance education, a seminar presenter or teacher may use a "central moderator" approach to hand off and take back control from members of the audience who are posing questions. In a formal meeting context, a group decision support system may enforce a round-robin or queue policy.

Protocol	Description	Where implemented
Free floor	Any participant can enter input at any time, with floor control mediated out of band usually through a voice channel. Accidental mixing of multiple input streams is possible.	TIMBUKTU (Farallon 1988) SHARE (Greenberg 1990)
Pre-emptive	Any participant can pre-empt control away at any time from the floor holder.	CAPTURE LAB (Mantei 1988) DIALOGO (Lauwers 1990) SHARE (Greenberg 1990)
Explicit release	The floor holder must explicitly release the floor before another participant may claim it.	CANTATA (Chang et al 1987) SHARE (Greenberg 1990)
First in, first out queue with explicit release.	Participants line up to take turns, where the floor, once explicitly released by the floor holder, is given to the person at the front of the line.	CANTATA (Chang et al 1987) VCONF (Lauwers 1990)
Central moderator	A moderator oversees all activity and decides who should hold the floor, usually by monitoring requests for the floor by other participants.	RTCAL (Sarin & Greif 1985) SHARE (Greenberg 1990)
Pause detection	The floor is made available to any participant only after the system detects a suitable pause of activity by the floor holder.	EMCE (Garcia-Luna-Aceves et al 1988) SHARE (Greenberg 1990)

Table 1. Some floor control protocols that have been implemented in view-sharing systems

Lauwers (1990) suggests that even aspects of the operating environment—the availability and quality of an audio/video channel, the length of communication delays—will also influence the choice of policy. For example, a group preferring to use out-of-band traditional social protocol (ie voice, gestures) to mediate a free floor may suffer increasing accidental input collisions as a function of lengthening the communication delays and degrading the audio/video channel.

3.2 Personalizable floor control in SHARE

Lauwers (1990) recommends that an ideal shared window system should "support a broad range of [floor control] policies... in an architecture capable of switching between different policies depending on user preferences and the operating environment". We have taken up this challenge. Based on the belief that no single policy can address adequately all groups, we have designed and implemented SHARE, a view-sharing system that supports personalizable floor control.

SHARE is a "policy free" view-sharing system whose kernel supports primitives upon which one can build a broad range of policies to manage floor control (Greenberg 1990). Its architecture is comprised of four entities (Figure 1).

a. The *Registrar* is a daemon process responsible for initiating the shared view conference set up and tear down, the selective entry and departure of participants while the conference is in progress, and feedback of the conference's current status. One or more conferences may be established via the Registrar, and participants may join as many of the running conferences as they wish. There is one Registrar daemon for the entire network
b. The *View Manager* is the technical heart of the system, a process responsible for synchronizing and transmitting the shared views between participants. There is one View Manager per conference. In the current implementation, the View Manager provides only rudimentary shared views of a text-based terminal window running UNIX applications (eg UNIX SHELL, the GMACS editor, etc), and cannot share views of graphical mouse-based applications. While this limits the true usability of SHARE, we avoided the extremely time-consuming implementation of a graphics-based window-sharing system[2], allowing us to concentrate on other design aspects such as floor control.
c. The *Chair Manager* process is responsible for interpreting (but not setting!) a floor control policy. It receives directions from the Turntaker (see next point) on what *observe* and *write* permissions it should set on each participant's view into the application. There is one Chair Manager per conference.
d. The *Turntaker* process sets a particular floor control policy and presents the interface to it. User interactions are interpreted and translated into protocol primitives, which is sent to the Chair Manager. There is usually one Turntaker per participant.

When a person asks for a new shared view meeting, the Registrar will create instances of the View Manager and Chair Manager processes. A fully interactive and sharable UNIX SHELL window will then appear on the person's workstation.

---

[2]SHARE was up and running within two man-months of work. In contrast, the technically sophisticated SHAREDX (Garfinkel et al 1989) and DIALOGO (Lauwers 1990) systems required several man-years to implement.

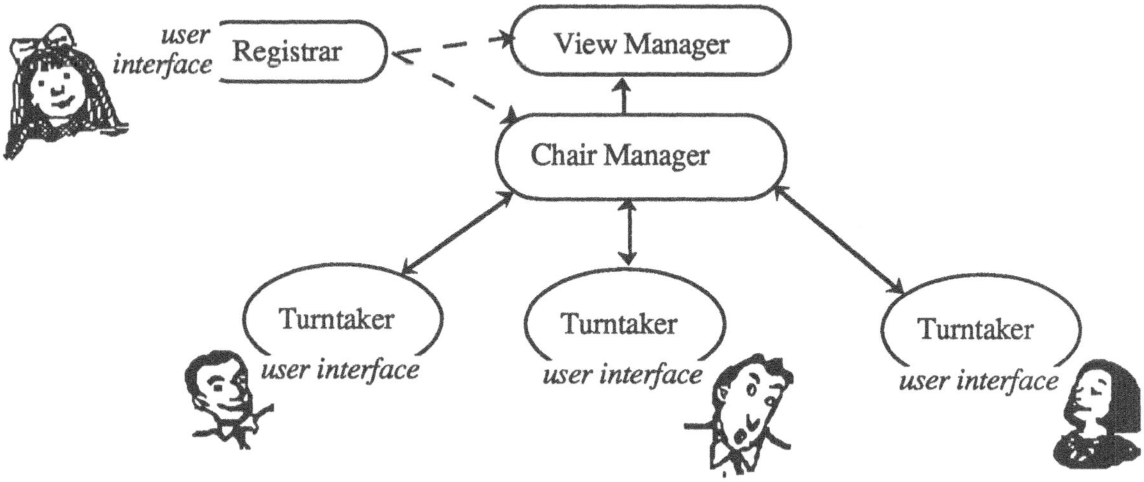

Figure 1. Main architectural components of *Share*

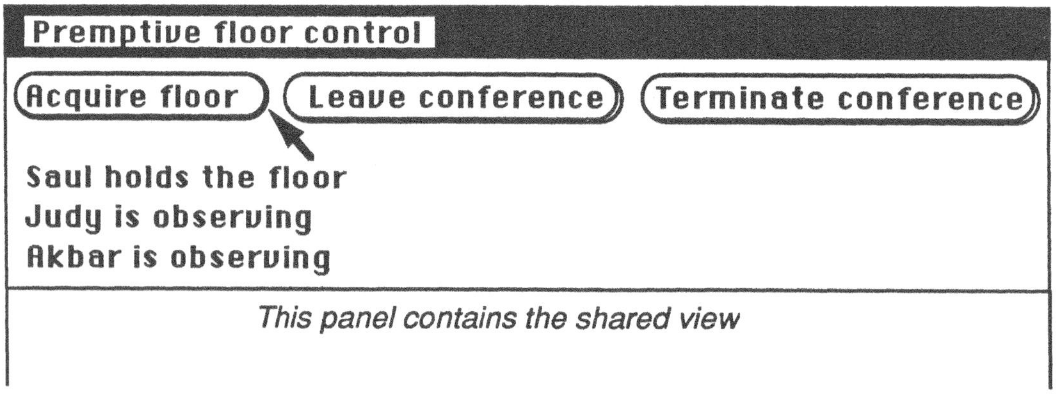


```
ForEach participant
    if participant[i].id = self
        SendToChairManager (SETFLOORPERMISSIONS, participant[i].id, "Write")
    else
        SendToChairManager (SETFLOORPERMISSIONS, participant[i].id, "Observe")
```

Figure 2 Pre-emptive floor control: the interface and the protocol sent for pre-empting control

Other people may now join the meeting, which will cause a copy of the UNIX window to appear on their workstations.

At this point, no floor control policy has been specified. The Chair Manager will by default allow only the original meeting creator to enter input into the shared view. Others can observe but not interact with the application. The actual floor control policy resides in the Turntaker processes—one activated for each participant—that presents its users with an interface to a particular floor control scheme and converts a user's request into a set of primitive messages sent to the Chair Manager (as listed in the Appendix). These primitives include asking the Chair Manager: to set any participant's *observe* and *write* status; to get information about other participants; and to forward messages to other Turntakers. The result is that different floor control policies are easy to implement. Each participant's Turntaker and its interface may be specialized to reflect one's specific political role in the meeting, and floor control policies can even be switched on the fly. The Appendix gives detail on the sequence of events that occurs between the Turntaker and the Chair Manager.

Figure 2, for example, illustrates a simple pre-emptive floor control interface supported by SHARE. Here, all participants have invoked the Turntaker process that enforces the pre-emptive policy. When a user selects the "Acquire floor" button, the Turntaker requests the Chair Manager to assign *write* permission for that person, and *observe-only* status to all other meeting participants (bottom of Figure 2, Appendix). The Turntaker also tells its user who is in the meeting and who currently holds the floor.

In contrast, Figures 3a and 3b illustrate the more complex "central moderator" protocol (Table 1) used by a seminar presenter and by the audience respectively. This scheme requires two different (but coordinated) styles of Turntaker processes representing the roles of the presenter and of the seminar participants. The single presenter would invoke the Presenter Turntaker, while each audience member would invoke their own copy of the Participant Turntaker. In Figure 3a the presenter sees: a list of all participants who desire the floor (the raised hands); who currently holds the floor (the writing hand); and who is just observing (the eyes). The presenter can assign or take away interaction permission by selecting the icon portraying the chosen participant. In Figure 3b participant Ruth has requested the floor by selecting her single icon (selecting it again will put her back to observer status). She also sees that participant George is the current floor holder. It is worth noting that the presenter and the participant also have different controls affecting conference departure. While the presenter can terminate the conference for all participants by pressing the "end conference" button, participants can only leave (which does not affect any other participants).

Another floor control policy we have implemented is pause detection (Table 1). If there is a pause in input activity of the current floor holder for several seconds, the floor becomes free. The floor is then automatically assigned to the next participant that attempts to interact with the application (eg by typing). Because a short pause is required before the floor is freed (we use a delta of 2 seconds), the accidental overlap of input commonly seen with a free floor policy is eliminated. We have found this method effective for general use by small cooperating groups as it reflects a person's natural and implicit way of mediating turntaking in conversation, unlike the other methods mentioned here that require one to explicitly request a turn.

Some shared view architectures have similarities to SHARE. We are aware of two other systems—DIALOGO (Lauwers and Lantz, 1990) and SHAREDX (Garfinkle,

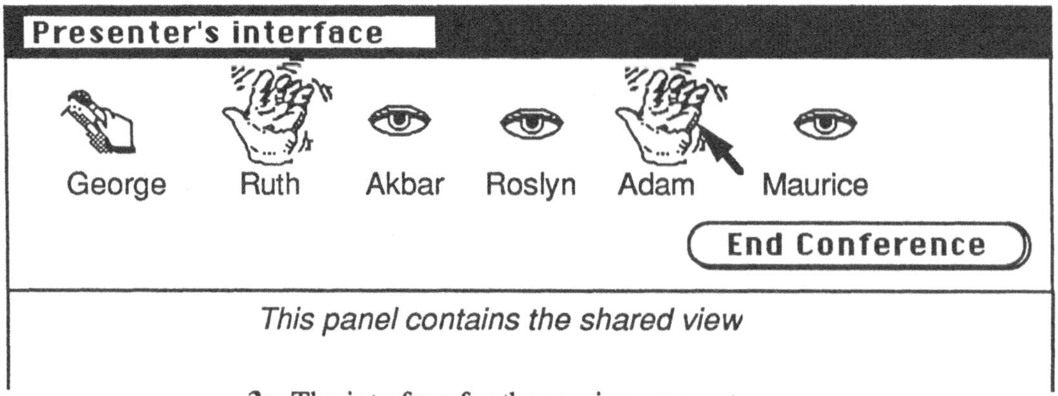

3a. The interface for the seminar presenter

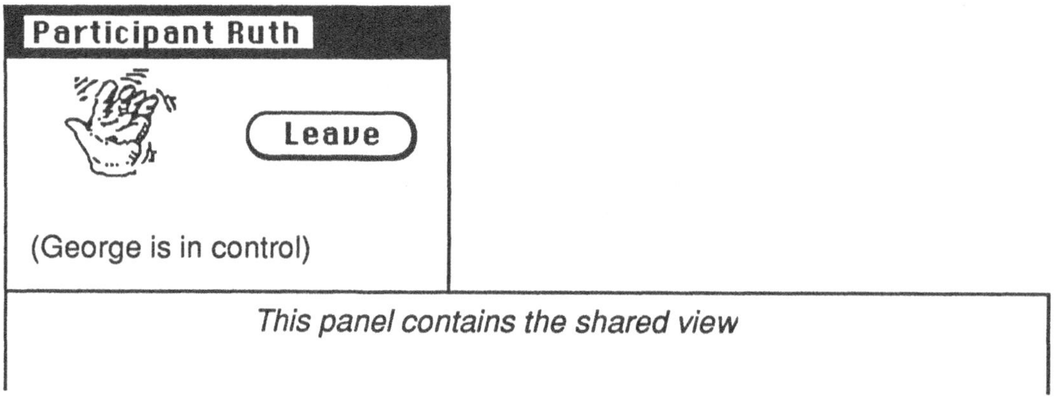

3b. The interface for a participant who can only request the floor

Figure 3. Two roles for participants in a centralized floor control interface.

Gust, Lemon and Lowder 1989)—that have the same potential in its architecture for flexible floor control. What is novel is that we have striven to give the power of this flexibility directly to the end users. Additionally, SHARE has an extensible open architecture. Given the protocol primitives understood by the Chair Manager (as mentioned in the Appendix), a programmer should have little trouble designing new Turntakers. Access to SHARE's source is not required, and the kernel does not need recompilation[3]. In the current version of SHARE, people and groups personalize their system by selecting the desired floor control policy from a library of policies—the library is extended only by programming new Turntakers. We foresee providing end users with the power to construct and/or extend a floor control policy through a prototyping tool or through a scripting language.

4. Summary

In spite of individual differences and preferences between group members and between groups, most groupware now available requires its users to conform to a single model of use. As a consequence, people may opt out of using the product, which seriously threatens the potential benefit the system can offer to the group as a whole. This paper argued that personalizable groupware can lead to wider acceptance of the product by offering a system that conforms to the individual needs of participants and of groups.

We have presented SHARE, a shared view system, as a simple example of personalizable groupware. As these systems allow only serial interaction with the running application, floor control must be mediated. SHARE supports between group differences by providing an extensible library of floor control policies for groups to chose from. Within-group differences are managed as well, for a particular policy may provide several roles appropriate to a participant's position within the group (as in the seminar presenter/student case).

Programming the differet policies proved both easy and quick. What is missing is an end user evaluation. Although we have our own successful experiences using SHARE's various floor control policies, it remains to be tested in an unbiased environment, preferably by tracking its long term use by people requiring desktop conferencing capabilities in real settings. This will be difficult to do in practice, for it demands the costly process of bringing Share to near-product functionality and reliability.

Personalizable groupware has a long way to go. On the social side, we must understand how group participants vary and how groups differ. This is fundamental if we are to supply appropriate flexibility to handle that diversity. On the technical side, we must provide not only architectures appropriate to personalization (an interesting possibility is a self-adaptive interface; Greenberg 1985), but also the means to allow the participant and the group to select the method the best fits their needs.

---

[3]We recently discovered that the ASPECTS, a commercial groupware product, allows a single group mediator to select three floor control levels: free floor, serial, and central moderator (Group Technologies 1991). Unlike SHARE, however, ASPECTS is a closed system. Policies are hard wired and can only be extended by altering the source code.

Appendix. Protocol primitives used between the Turntaker and the Chair Manager

This appendix describes the protocol primitives transmitted between the Turntaker and Chair Manager processes and gives examples of their use. The Chair Manager and the View Manager form the kernel of SHARE, with participants creating, entering and leaving conferences through the Registrar. The Turntaker process, which implements a particular floor control policy, may be created and destroyed by the participant at any time. When a Turntaker is created, it establishes a UNIX socket connection with the Chair Manager and then presents an interface to the user (as in Figures 2 and 3). The Turntaker then embodies the particular floor control policy by sending message primitives to the Chair Manager and to other Turntaker processes. The list below describes most of the primitives exchanged. The <id> field indicates the identification of the participant. The '|' is used as a field delimiter.

Protocol	Explanation
TURNTAKERREGISTER <id>	The Turntaker registers with the Chair Manager. If the participant id is specified, the Chair Manager will signal the Turntaker when that participant leaves the conference, upon which the Turntaker will usually destroy itself.
REGISTERUSER <id>	The Chair Manager informs the Turntaker that a new participant has connected to the conference.
UNREGISTERUSER <id>|<id>|...	The Turntaker requests the Chair Manager to unregister the participants specified by their id's from the conference. This will delete that user's shared view from their workstation.
ENDMEETING	The Turntaker requests the Chair Manager to terminate the entire conference. This will unregister all participants and destroy the meeting's Chair and View Manager processes.
SETFLOORPERMISSIONS <id><permission>| <id><permission>|...	The Turntaker requests the Chair Manager to assign *observe-only* or *write* permission to the participants listed.
SETMETAFIELD <id>|message|<id>|message|...	The Turntaker requests the Chair Manager to attach a message to a participant's id and then forward it as a STATUSCHANGED message to all other Turntaker processes. Usually used to define a protocol between Turntakers.
GETINFORMATION <bit mask>|<id>|<id>|...	Turntaker requests information on some or all participants (this information is stored by the Chair Manager). The bit mask indicates the information desired, which includes: •the participants login name, •the host and port number of the participant's machine, •the participant's pseudo-terminal containing the shared view •the message (meta) field associated with the participant •the current *observe/write* status of the participant.
STATUSCHANGED <bit mask>|<id>|message|...	When a participant's status information is changed, the Chair Manager broadcasts the particular change to all Turntakers. The bit mask is as noted in GETINFORMATION.
TIMERCHANGE <seconds>	Turntaker specifies a time delay value for pause detection.

Consider a meeting implementing the simple pre-emptive floor control policy shown in Figure 2. When the Turntaker process is started, it does the following.

1. Register with the Chair Manager via the TURNTAKERREGISTER request.
2. Ask the Chair Manager for all it knows about the other conference participants via the GETINFORMATION request; this will include who is in the conference, who holds the floor, and so on.
3. Present the user interface, listing the current status of other participants (eg "Judy is observing").
4. When a message is received from the Chair Manager indicating a change of status of any of the participants (the STATUSCHANGED message), then update the status information on the display.
5. When the user selects the 'Acquire Floor' button, tell the Chair Manager to change the permissions to *write* for self, and *observe* for all others via the SETFLOORPERMISSIONS message. The Chair Manager acknowledges via a STATUSCHANGED message.
6. If the 'Leave Conference' button is pressed, the Turntaker notifies the Chair Manager via the UNREGISTERUSER message. When the Chair Manager acknowledges the request, the Turntaker will destroy itself.
7. Alternatively, if the Terminate Conference button is pressed, the Turntaker will send the ENDMEETING message to the Chair Manager.

Changing this floor control policy to explicit release (explained in Table 1) is fairly straight forward. Substituting for step 5 above:

5a. Alter the "Acquire Floor" button so that it is enabled only when no participants hold the floor (ie have *write* permission), and dimmed otherwise. When enabled and selected, the Turntaker requests the Chair Manager to set *write* permission for self. The button's label is then changed to 'Release Floor'. Other Turntakers will be informed of the change in status and will dim their 'Acquire Floor' buttons.

5b. When 'Release Floor' is pressed, the Turntaker tells the Chair Manager to change the permission of self from *write* to *observe*. A status message indicating that floor permissions have changed is sent automatically by the Chair Manager to all Turntakers, who in this case react by enabling their "Acquire Floor" button.

A more complex example is the centralized floor control interface shown in Figure 3, where a participant may request the floor from the presenter. As the Chair Manager has no primitive that directly supports a 'floor request', this must be implemented as a protocol between cooperating Turntakers. In our implementation, Turntakers attach a "raised hand" and "lowered hand" message to a participant id and transmit status changes to each other. To illustrate, when the participant requests the floor by selecting the icon (Figure 3b), the Turntaker sends the Chair Manager the SETMETAFIELD primitive along with the participant's id and the message "raised hand". This is then forwarded by the Chair Manager to the presenter's Turntaker (Figure 3a), which will interpret the message and change the appropriate icon on the display. The important point here is that this extended protocol is implemented completely within the Turntakers; no change had to be made to the code in the Chair Manager. The rest of the centralized floor control interface is straight forward. When the presenter assigns the floor to a participant, the appropriate permission fields are set and sent via the SetFloorPermissions message. When the Turntaker of the participant chosen receives its StatusChanged message, it will change the icon being displayed to a writing pen.

As a final twist, we can implement a selective free floor policy in the above centralized floor control scheme. All that is required is to set write permission for the presenter, which is maintained even when a student has write permission.

Acknowledgements. The Alberta Research Council sponsored part of this research during my position there as a National Science and Engineering Research Council Industrial Research Fellow. Many thanks to Ralph Bohnet, who was instrumental in implementing SHARE.

References

Austin, L. C., Liker, J. K. and McLeod, P. L. (1990) "Determinants and patterns of control over technology in a computerized meeting room." In *Proceedings of the Conference on Computer Supported Cooperative Work (CSCW '90)*, p39-52, Los Angeles, California, October 7-10, ACM Press.

Bair, J. H. and Gale, S. (1988) "An investigation of the Coordinator as an example of computer supported cooperative work." Hewlett Packard Laboratories, California, Unpublished.

Bullen, C. V. and Bennett, J. L. (1990) "Learning from user experience with groupware." In *Proceedings of the Conference on Computer Supported Cooperative Work (CSCW '90)*, Los Angeles, California, October 7-10, ACM Press.

Chang, E., Kasperski, R. and Copping, T. (1987) "Group co-ordination in participant systems." Technical report, Department of Advanced Computing and Engineering, Alberta Research Council, Calgary, Alberta, Canada, September.

Dykstra, E.A. and Carasik, R.P. (1991) "Structure and support in cooperative environments: The Amsterdam Conversation Environment." In S. Greenberg (ed.):*Computer Supported Cooperative Work and Groupware*, Academic Press, London. Originally published in *Int J Man Machine Studies*, **34**(3), March.

Engelbart, D. and English, W. (1968) "A research center for augmenting human intellect." In *Proceedings of the Fall Joint Computing Conference*. Montvale, NY, Fall, AFIPS Press.

Farallon (1988) "Timbuktu user's guide." Manual, Farallon Computing Inc., Berkely, California,

Fish, R. S. (1989) "Cruiser: A multi-media system for social browsing." *The ACM SIGGRAPH Video Review Supplement to Computer Graphics*, **45**(6). ACM Press, Baltimore, MD. Videotape.

Foster, G. and Stefik, M. (1986) "Cognoter: Theory and practice of a Colab-orative tool." In *Proceedings of the Conference on Computer-Supported Cooperative Work (CSCW '86)*, p7-15, Austin, Texas, December 3-5, ACM Press.

Garcia-Luna-Aceves, J.J., Craighill, E.J. and Lang, R. (1988) "An open-systems model for computer-supported collaboration." In *Proceedings of the IEEE Conference on Computer Workstations*, p40-51, March.

Garfinkel, D., Gust, P., Lemon, M. and Lowder, S. (1989) "The SharedX multi-user interface user's guide, version 2.0." Research report STL-TM-89-07, Hewlett-Packard Laboratories, Palo Alto, California, March.

Greenberg, S. (1990) "Sharing views and interactions with single-user applications." In *COIS '90: Proceedings of the Conference on Office Information Systems*, Boston, April.

Greenberg, S. and Bohnet, R. (1991) "GroupSketch: A multi-user sketchpad for geographically-distributed small groups." In *Proceedings of Graphics Interface '91*, Calgary, Alberta, June 5-7. Also available as Reseach report 90/414/38, Dept of Computer Science, University of Calgary, Alberta, Canada.

Greenberg, S. and Witten, I. H. (1985) "Adaptive personalized interfaces -- a question of viability." *Behaviour and Information Technology*, **4**(1), pp. 31-45, January.

Group Technologies (1991) "Aspects: The first simultaneous conference software for the Macintosh, Version 1." Manual, Group Technologies Inc, Arlington, Virginia.

Grudin, J. (1988) "Why CSCW applications fail: Problems in the design and evaluation of organizational interfaces." In *Proceedings of the Conference on Computer-Supported Cooperative Work*, pp. 85-93, Portland, Oregon, September 26-28, ACM Press.

Johansen, R. (1989) "User approaches to computer-supported teams." In M.H. Olson (ed.): *Technological Support for Work Group Collaborations*, p1-32, Hillsdale, New Jersey, Lawrence Erlbaum Associates.

Johnson-Lenz, P. and Johnson-Lenz, T. (1991) "Post-mechanistic groupware primitives: Rhythms, boundaries and containers." In S. Greenberg (ed.): *Computer Supported Cooperative Work and Groupware*, Academic Press, London. Originally published in *Int J Man Machine Studies*, **34**(3), March.

Lauwers, J. C. (1990) "Collaboration transparency in desktop teleconferencing environments." PhD Thesis, Available as Technical Report CSL-TR-90-435, Stanford University, Computer Systems Laboratory, Stanford, CA, July.

Lauwers, J. C. and Lantz, K. A. (1990) "Collaboration awareness in support of collaboration transparency: Requirements for the next generation of shared window systems." In *Proceedings of the ACM/SIGCHI Conference on Human factors in Computing*, Seattle, April, ACM Press.

Lauwers, J. C., Joseph, T. A., Lantz, K. A. and Romanow, A. L. (1990) "Replicated architectures for shared window systems: A critique." In *Proceedings of the Conference on Office Information Systems*, p249-260, Boston, April 25-27.

Leland, M. D. P., Fish, R. S. and Kraut, R. E. (1988) "Collaborative document production using Quilt." In *Proceedings of the Conference on Computer-Supported Cooperative Work*, p. 206-215, Portland, Oregon, September 26-28, ACM Press.

Lia, K.-Y. and Malone, T. W. (1988) "Object Lens: A 'spreadsheet' for cooperative work." In *Proceedings of the Conference on Computer-Supported Cooperative Work*, p. 115-124, Portland, Oregon, September 26-28, ACM Press.

Malone, T. W., Grant, K. R., Lai, K.-Y., Rao, R. and Rosenblitt, D. (1987) "Semi-structured messages are surprisingly useful for computer-supported coordination." *ACM Trans Office Information Systems*, **5**(2), p115-131, April.

Mantei, M. (1988) "Capturing the Capture concepts: A case study in the design of computer-supported meeting Environments." In *Proceedings of the Conference on Computer-Supported Cooperative Work*, 257-270, Portland, Oregon, September 26-28, ACM Press.

Markus, M. L. and Connolly, T. (1990) "Why CSCW applications fail: Problems in the adoption of interdependent work tools." In *Proceedings of the Conference on Computer Supported Cooperative Work (CSCW '90)*, Los Angeles, California, October 7-10, ACM Press.

Root, W. R. (1988) "Design of a multi-media vehicle for social browsing." In *Proceedings of the Conference on Computer-Supported Cooperative Work*, p. 25-38, Portland, Oregon, September 26-28, ACM Press.

Sarin, S. and Greif, I, (1985) "Computer based real-time conferencing systems." *IEEE Computer*, **18**(10), p33-45.

Stefik, M., Bobrow, D.G., Foster, G., Lanning, S. and Tatar, D. (1987) "WYSIWIS revised: Early experiences with multiuser interfaces." *ACM Trans Office Information Systems*, **5**(2), 147–167, April.

Tang, J. C. (1991) "Findings from observational studies of collaborative work." In S. Greenberg (ed.): *Computer Supported Cooperative Work and Groupware*, Academic Press, London. Originally published in *Int J Man Machine Studies*, **34**(2), February.

Tatar, D. G., Foster, G. and Bobrow, D. G. (1991) "Design for conversation: Lessons from Cognoter." In S. Greenberg (ed.): *Computer Supported Cooperative Work and Groupware*, Academic Press, London. Originally published in *Int J Man Machine Studies*, **34**(2), February.

Thimbleby, H. (1980) "Dialogue determination." *Int J Man Machine Studies*, **13**.

Proceedings of the Second European Conference on Computer-Supported Cooperative Work
Bannon, L., Robinson, M. & Schmidt, K. (Editors)
September 25-27, 1991, Amsterdam, The Netherlands

Office systems development and gender: Implications for computer supported co-operative work

Eileen Green, Jenny Owen and Den Pain
Sheffield City Polytechnic, UK.

Abstract

We present new UK research (1987-90) in the area of gender and office information systems design. Our paper will contribute to the CSCW debate in two areas. Methodology, where we use our case-study experiences to reflect upon the traditional computing approaches to office systems design. Secondly, participatory design, through our active involvement in the work-place we consider a gender perspective on obstacles and opportunities for involvement in the design process. We open by briefly discussing the range of current UK office systems design methods, contrasting these with more innovative approaches developed in Europe. Secondly we focus upon clerical work as a major area of women's employment concentrating on the relationship between technical and organisational aspects of systems development. In section three we present the outcome of our own case-study research. We worked in collaboration with staff in a large public library, where management envisaged the acquisition of a new integrated system to link previously discrete services. Our aim was to develop techniques and strategies through which women staff could intervene in the evaluation of systems and suppliers. In conclusion, we identify a number of factors within public sector office work, which affect opportunities for a proactive role for clerical workers and their trade unions, in the design and implementation of office information systems.

The authors wish to acknowledge the research contribution made by Ian Franklin to this paper.

This research was funded by the Joint Committee of the UK Economic & Social Research Council, and Science & Engineering Research Council from 1984-1990. Current grantholders are Eileen Green and Den Pain.

Introduction - links with concerns within CSCW

In his introduction to a special issue of the international journal of man-machine studies S Greenberg (1991) provides a loose categorisation of concerns within CSCW. We feel our work can contribute to the debate under two of these headings. Firstly, methodology, in section one we take a theoretical look at approaches to office systems development, examining both the current dominant techniques and new, more cooperative ways. Secondly, participatory design, we adopt a gender-perspective on this concern in our section on clerical work and information technology providing detailed examples from our case-study work.

Another of the main issues for CSCW is the bringing of technology into particular organisational contexts and the need to analyse the socio-political dimensions associated with the development of information systems in the workplace (Bannon, Bjorn Andersen, Due-Thompson 1988). We address this issue in section 2.1. technology and organisation: links and definitions.

A theme of cooperative work underlies our chosen case-study. Integrated library management systems focus on a shared common database and there is considerable emphasis on mechanisms for improved communications both formal (through designed procedures) and informal (through the presence of electronic mail). Finally the development of large integrated software systems to support work within the office environment is increasingly (within the U.K.) being achieved through the acquisition of highly parameterisable packages. Hence approaches and techniques that help to evaluate such systems will be intensifying in importance, our case- study (section 3.2) provides some interesting ideas in this area.

1. Gender, computerisation and 'user relations'

The phase of computerisation since the 1980's has been described as one dominated by a concern with 'user relations'. (Friedman and Cornford, 1989). In contrast, Friedman and Cornford identify two earlier phases in the history of computerisation: the first characterised by hardware constraints, and the second by difficulties with software production.

In the UK at least, women continue to be defined largely as the end-users or operators of computerised systems, even where their work may in practice include an increasing range of systems-related or technical aspects. Women still occupy a relatively marginal position both within computing, and at the senior management levels where strategic decisions on information technology are taken. Therefore we need to know how far this suggested shift in focus within computing, away from hardware and software constraints and towards user relations, may present women with changing issues and opportunities. It is possible, for instance, to envisage the creation of jobs which combine clerical and technical elements; this could open up new forms of access to computing, and to better-paid work, for women office workers (see for instance Hales, 1989). Such developments could build on, and enhance, the informal patterns of cooperation and communication which are an integral but unrecognised part of many clerical jobs (Olerup et al, 1985; Green et al, 1991). However, to date there has been little exploration of these possibilities, in the UK context. A brief examination of the systems development literature shows that in the UK, many systems development methodologies and approaches now claim to involve 'the user'. But in many cases, this appears to be an ambiguous response to the large number of failed or inadequate computerised systems - not a significant move towards empowering users.

'Structured' systems analysis and design methodologies, for instance, are widely used, especially in the public sector. They claim to provide 'a lot of interaction with the user' (LBMS, 1986). However, in practice the emphasis here is only on the manager as user; and priority is given to analysing formal data flows and relationships, not organisational processes, or 'user' interests in any broad sense. These approaches have been criticised for implying a functionalist and deterministic model of social relations: structure and consensus are taken as the norm, while change and conflict or inequality within the workplace are largely ignored. Our own previous research has illustrated the ways in which this specifically undermines progressive initiatives on equal opportunities and job design, (Green et al, forthcoming). It is clear that these dominant ideas and practices are not compatible with the notion of cooperative work nor the participatory methods required to develop appropriate support systems.

Other methodologies do address the issue of user relations in greater depth. Both the Socio-Technical Systems and Soft Systems approaches are examples (Mumford, 1983; Checkland, 1981). Neither, however, deals adequately with issues of power and inequality within the workplace. Mumford, for instance, suggests that the goals of increased job satisfaction and increased productivity can be pursued largely without conflict. Checkland does identify the existence of different 'stakeholders' or sets of interests within an organisation but his response is a liberal and idealist one, envisaging the resolution of differences through discussion among equals. Neither approach puts forward thorough analyses of conflict and inequality within organisations, or practical approaches through which the least powerful systems users could address these.

In contrast, scope for more radical initiatives has been shown both by the Scandinavian 'Collective Resource' approach, and by UK initiatives in the area of 'human-centred' systems design. (Ehn, 1988, Gill, 1990). These initiatives have sought to develop computer systems which protect or enhance the skills of, and exercise of control and discretion by, workers who conform to the ideal underlying Braverman's original 'deskilling' thesis: male craft workers, who possess not only skilled status, but also a high degree of union organisation. Within the field of CSCW there are particular instances of cooperative approaches to systems development see for example Bodker and Gronbek (1991). These approaches have related workplace experience to a wider concern with trade union and democratic rights: that is, within the terms of the relations between capital and labour. However, neither the choice of which groups of workers to involve, nor the analyses of skill or of workplace relations, reflect any concern with women workers or with broader gender issues.

First funded by two UK Research Councils in 1984, our own research project has focussed on a major area of women's employment: office work, which has also been the subject of much intense and contradictory speculation, in relation to automation.

The limitations of existing human-centred design perspectives, with the emphasis on class rather than gender relations, soon became apparent. In connection with technology in particular, feminist analyses have revealed the enduring nature of gender divisions. These are not explained by women's real or assumed domestic responsibilities; and far from withering away, gender inequalities continue to be reproduced through distinct material and ideological practices, within the workplace itself. But these patterns have become visible largely through feminist perspectives. Social theory, however radical, has failed to address such issues. (Cockburn, 1985).

In connection with systems design, feminist initiatives have begun to challenge the gender-blindness which has characterised both conventional methodologies and the range of more radical, interdisciplinary projects. Systems development methodologies tend to reproduce the gendered dichotomies embedded in Western natural science traditions: categories such as 'hard' and 'soft', thought and emotion, objective and subjective, are treated as opposed rather than interdependent. Greater status is accorded to 'hard', quantifiable data than to workers' own accounts of priorities or procedures. (Greenbaum 1987). Research such as Greenbaum's offers a potentially important link between feminist perspectives on epistemology and the 'human-centred systems' emphasis on human diversity and on the interdependence of subjective and objective knowledge (Gill, 1990). In Europe and in Scandinavia in particular, research has begun to explore innovative systems design approaches, within which women's skills and working knowledge can become central. (Olerup et al, 1985; Tijdens et al, 1989).

Drawing on these perspectives, our own research initially analysed a range of conventional approaches to the design of office information systems. We then moved on to assess the scope for women clerical workers to intervene in processes of office systems development, in the context of the UK public sector. In section two we turn to a consideration of the themes addressed in this recent research and in section three we briefly discuss some of the techniques adopted during our case-study.

2. Clerical work and information technology:

Clearly, IT can be introduced into office work as part of a wider restructuring which does result in job losses, and in worsening working conditions. However, neither the 'optimistic' forecasts of the early 1980s (the 'paperless office'), nor the 'pessimistic' ones (large-scale job losses) have been fulfilled. Both may be seen as implying a degree of technological determinism, as well as over-estimating the homogeneity and coherence of management strategies. Office work remains a major area of employment for women and recent research indicates that the technical and organisational skills, the range of tasks and the relative stability which characterise many clerical jobs, also make it a primary rather than a secondary labour market for women.

Surveys and case-studies also illustrate the complexity of women clerical workers' experience of computerisation. In connection with typing and word-processing, Webster (1989) demonstrates how strongly pre-existing forms of work organisation shape and limit office applications of IT, resulting for instance in substantial under-use of word processing technology. Women report a range of positive and negative experiences, regarding office computerisation: increased job satisfaction, and the development of some new skills and opportunities; but also increased stress, intensification of work, health and safety problems, and a general absence either of consultation or of adequate training, (Liff, 1990). In the UK, very little research exists at all on the subject of clerical workers' formal or informal participation in processes of systems planning and design, as distinct from implementation.

2.1. Technology and organisation: links and definitions:

In much systems development literature, 'social' or 'organisational' factors remain ambiguous. The terms may be used to refer to individual user needs, to organisational processes, or to the ways in which these reflect wider social and economic relations. In contrast, technological aspects in systems development may appear to be fixed or well-defined and apparently neutral ground. This leaves intact the 'hard'/'technical' versus 'soft'/'non-technical' dichotomy referred to above (Greenbaum op.cit.). In contrast, a growing body of social science research points to complexity and interdependence, in the relationship between technology and organisation:

> "Technologies are patterned by, and in turn, condition the development of organisations... the boundary between the two is obviously far from clear."
>
> (Williams, 1990, p.12-13)

From a gender perspective, we need to explore how this interdependence may be manifest in specific situations. Can systems development techniques be adopted, through which women workers may influence the ways in which organisational and technical factors are defined and negotiated? In the next section we investigate this issue within the context of our case- study.

3. Case-study research

The case-study organisation is 'City Libraries', the public library department of a major, Northern City Council in the UK. With a workforce of 32,000, the City Council is by far the largest local employer. Most manual, administrative and clerical staff are women, concentrated in the lower grades. Within City Libraries, virtually all the 400 staff on clerical, 'library assistant' grades are women; but men outnumber women at senior professional and management levels.

Within the organisation, management and staff share the view that previous phases of library automation were 'disastrous'. When our case-study began, in 1986, a piecemeal, technology led process of computerisation had taken place over a ten year period. However staff found that the delays associated with a batch-processed, mainframe-based system made these facilities less satisfactory than previous manual systems. There was, therefore, a common desire to find a new approach to further phases of computerisation. At the same time, City libraries as a whole had moved towards an outward- looking, active and community-oriented model of library provision. As part of this, management accepted a trade union based equal opportunities proposal to expand the pay and career opportunities for library assistants on clerical grades. In addition to dealing with routine tasks - issuing, shelving and repairing books, processing catalogue and borrower records - many library assistants deal with complex public enquiries. Through new grading arrangements, management began to acknowledge and reward this overlap between professional and non-professional or clerical roles.

In 1986, management had begun to discuss the need for a new computerised library system, probably to be based on one of the integrated library systems then becoming available from a range of suppliers. However, the management team had not been able to complete a new systems specification, nor to develop proposals for staff involvement. They therefore welcomed our research approach. Following discussions both with management and the trade union branch, we were able to reach an agreement to collaborate, based on three principles. Firstly, a view of library automation as enhancing jobs and services, not replacing staff; secondly, a view of the systems planning and development processes as embracing both technical and organisational aspects; and thirdly, a commitment to exploring new forms of consultation or involvement for library assistants on clerical grades, in connection with computerisation. The notion of the 'quality of service' was an important unifying one in this context and helped to provide some semblance of cooperative work. That is the workers in different sections and at varying levels in the hierarchy saw themselves cooperating to provide an improved quality of service to their community-based clients. The new computer system was generally regarded as providing a significant means to this end.

Responsibility for managing this process remained with City Libraries' management team. Our research role included facilitating meetings and other activities, as well as analysing outcomes on the basis of observation and of in-depth interviews. Below we discuss major aspects of this collaborative work:

3.1. Planning for a New System: Women's Study Circles

Technical and organisational issues and boundaries.

Within City Libraries and in the City Council more generally, a large gap exists between policies on Information Technology and organisational policies, including those on gender and equal opportunities. The former tend to be debated in depth by senior staff within the Computer Services Division: people with technical computing skills, who then advise City Councillors. Councillors have tended to lack the background knowledge, and perhaps the political perspective, required in order to broaden the terms of the debate, beyond narrow technical concerns. Equal opportunities policies, on the other hand, have been pursued particularly by women, inside and outside the City Council, with very uneven support at senior levels.

Both management and trade union representatives at City Libraries welcomed our research interest in inviting staff to discuss computerisation. Management, however viewed women library assistants as dominated by their bad experience of current computerisation, and thought them unlikely to respond enthusiastically. This is an interesting instance of the ways in which a 'sympathetic' male view of women, as passive victims of badly-designed (past) technologies, can operate to reproduce the effective marginalisation of women from active intervention in connection with IT. In this context, we organised a series of study circles for women library assistants. We aimed firstly, to invite them to share their experience and their views on computerisation; and secondly, to invite them to put forward specific ideas regarding the selection and implementation of a new system. This study circle process is discussed in detail in Green et al (1991).

3.2. Developing systems evaluation techniques within a mixed design team

Informal Communication versus 'increased efficiency' ?

Study circle reports proposed a design team structure, with members drawn from all levels of the library staff, including library assistants. Reassured by this expression of staff interest, management agreed, and this group was convened in 1988, with the initial brief of completing a specification for a new library system.

Early discussions in the City Libraries Design Team provided some vivid examples of the different experiences and perspectives of the group's members, some of which are related to gendered work experience. At this stage, the group was preparing a draft specification for the new system. Apparently simple issues often revealed radically different assumptions about how a balance should be struck between making the best use of the latest technical options and facilities, and providing the best service and working conditions. In the following extract from one such discussion, group members are debating whether letters requesting borrowers to return overdue items should be processed centrally or in local branches. As things stand, this is a very sensitive issue for women library assistants, who are often on the receiving end of complaints when borrowers are sent reminders for items already returned, but not processed by the current, batch-supported system. 'CDL', the male professional computer development librarian, is responding to various library assistants ('LA'), who want a distributed system under branch control, rather than a centralised one:

CDL: Why send overdue letters from each service point?

LA: The currency of reminders is important; overdue letters can be a source of friction now.

CDL: But you could put a disclaimer in the letter, in case a book had been returned already.

LA: But for instance, elderly people do get very upset; lots of people get upset.

CDL: But they are a small percentage. You could have a facility to suppress overdues. It's not just a question of automatic printing; it can also collate and stamp, it's all automatic... There are cost implications. Having a large enough stock of good quality paper at each service point would cost a lot of money; and paper might run out in branches.

For the women library assistants, the quality of social interaction with library users is the priority; the number of people likely to be upset by late reminders may be 'a small percentage' for the computer development librarian, but it has a large effect on library assistants' day-to-day working relationships. The computer development librarian appears to give this scant consideration; he enthuses about the image of a streamlined, centralised system, and resorts in the end to an incongruous argument - the suggestion that paper may run out, at local branches. As this discussion proceeded, the women library assistants ceased to take part, exchanging exasperated glances. After further discussion, however, their contribution was recorded in the completed specification, in the form of a compromise: a facility for branch staff to over-ride centrally-processed letters quickly and easily.

This extract, then, brings to life some aspects of the gendered dichotomies referred to above. Library assistants' concerns arose in the context of daily routines with 'caring' or 'social' aspects which have historically become defined as 'women's work'. As such, these concerns were very vulnerable to being marginalised, by the assumption that the most sophisticated technical solution was the obvious one. The stress levels arising from public complaints left no formal, statistical trace, to set against the computer development librarian's references to percentages. This example underlines the general importance of ensuring that 'end-user' concerns - spanning technical and organisational issues - are addressed clearly at the earliest stages of systems development. It also illustrates the pressures and the obstacles faced by junior women staff, in moving towards new forms of cooperative systems planning and design with male technical and professional colleagues. We now turn to a short account of one set of techniques adopted in our case-study: the development of criteria and methods for evaluating existing integrated library systems, by the mixed Design Team.

Developing Systems Evaluation Techniques

Integrated library automation packages are now available from at least eight major suppliers. City Libraries, therefore, did not regard the development of a system 'in-house' as a feasible economic proposition. However, the available systems and suppliers display significant differences; these systems are also designed to operate according to locally set parameters. Selecting a system and a supplier is usually the prerogative of a small number of key senior managers and computing staff, for whom systems suppliers have a repertoire of demonstration modules. Available literature on library automa tion, in the UK, includes a range of checklists for use in these contexts; however, these are brief, and not adapted for cooperative or in-depth use by a broader range of prospective systems users. In City Libraries, therefore, the Design Team needed both to plan a programme of evaluation events, and to devise a method of recording and analysing staff assessments of the available systems.

In October 1989, outline plans were made for a series of Design Team visits to libraries already using the systems under consideration; in parallel, each supplier was invited to provide an on-site demonstration within City Libraries, extending over at least one week, and open to all library staff to attend. The Design Team began to draft questionnaires to record the assessments made by participants in visits and demonstrations. The women library assistants on the team compiled an initial set of questions; these were then debated, edited and supplemented by the whole group, in a process that extended over a six month period. Increasingly drastic budget cuts, within the City Council as a whole, obliged the Design Team to cut short its planned programme of visits to working library systems; the demonstrations therefore proved to be the main focus of the team's evaluation effort, on the basis of which available systems were shortlisted in December 1990.

How far can the evaluation exercise briefly summarised here be said to have succeeded in making 'technical' and 'organisational' aspects of systems development more readily available for discussion and negotiation, by women clerical users and their professional and technical colleagues and managers? In common with the study circle process referred to above, the evaluation process did open up systems selection and development issues to basic-grade women library staff, in an unprecedented way. Suppliers and end-users met face to face, without the usual technical or managerial intermediaries. Comparing the different questionnaire sections produced by the Design Team is also instructive: technical or 'systems management' questions - often jargon laden, and requiring translation for most Design Team members - make up about one eighth of the total; the rest are phrased to directly reflect staff and library borrower needs. In the absence of junior women on the Design Team, we would have expected these proportions to have been reversed.

As anticipated, the Design Team did experience difficulties in seeing through the evaluation work. Firstly, drafting the questionnaires proved stressful and time-consuming for the women library assistants, who contributed the initial versions. The Study Circles had established a strong, informal basis for cooperation and mutual support, based on exchange of personal experience and on practical activities. In contrast the Design Team came to base its discussions increasingly on written documents: the draft specification, the questionnaires. That is, the Design Team sometimes appeared to drift back into some of the bureaucratic, inhibiting patterns, characteristic of City Libraries, which the Study Circles had successfully challenged. Draft questions, put forward tentatively by library assistants in good faith, were sometimes torn apart or rejected - with little positive recognition of the effort put into the drafting process. In a mixed- gender, mixed-status forum, this placed considerable strain on the library assistants. On occasion this was deflected with a humorous comment:

"Here I am sitting next to my boss - he gets up and contradicts what I've just said. What am I supposed to do about it?"

(Tina, Clerical Assistant)

Considerable tensions emerged in connection with the detailed organisation of the visits and demonstrations. It also proved impossible to hold the suppliers themselves to the exact demonstration format originally proposed by the Design Team. The latter had proposed that flexible 'hands-on' sessions should make up the larger part of each session. In practice, most suppliers kept to a conventional pattern of talks or lectures, followed by questions and a restricted period of practical work at terminals. This limited the scope of the evaluation questionnaires, in many respects. Clearly, within the confines of a particular market, system suppliers still wield considerable influence in their own right. We found that some suppliers were not sensitive to the concept of cooperative work nor were they keen on dealing with mixed groups of users selected on a non-hierarchical basis. One representative suggested: -

"....once you start introducing democracy into a thing, it opens up the whole thing, and they never decide on specification they'll never decide what they want and it just won't happen".

4. Discussion

The Study Circle process made positive gains for the women concerned at a number of different levels. In particular, their interests as major users of the new system are now represented. However, although both management and the trade union have ostensibly welcomed this involvement, they are uneasy about the broader implications of changes to the organisation's personnel structure and associated work cultures. At a formal level, all parties have accepted that library assistants are equal members of all the groups involved in the systems development process. But in practice, many of the bureaucratic changes needed to sustain that involvement have been either delayed or not delivered, as promised e.g. provision of stand-by relief to cover the work of the assistants involved in the Design Team. Explanations for this lack of support involve both economic issues, such as resourcing of staff time during a period of cut-backs, and the reluctance of relevant line-managers (mostly male) to release the women from public duties. Both responses, although justified on certain levels, serve to reinforce the status quo and confirm the library assistants' position as low status, women workers, marginalised from decision-making processes. Similarly, the trade union involved is supportive in theory of the women's involvement, but has not found the resources to either follow up the specific issues raised by the women, or change their stance on negotiations with management. The union has found it difficult to recognise that the formal union strategy on new technology is viewed as less relevant by many women library assistants than the study circle and design team processes.

At a broader level, the evaluation work is more difficult to analyse and assess. Mixed gender groups are obviously desirable in theory; in practice they present problems, since gender inequalities have become entrenched in the divisions between professional (including technical) and non-professional jobs (Davies and Rosser, 1985). These tensions are manifest in the relative status of the contributions made by different members of the design team. The technical computer support staff involved in the process are male, and in permanent posts, confident of their abilities as 'experts': overseers of the current system (inadequate though it is) and midwives of the new one. In addition the majority of the professional librarians and senior managers are also male and largely at ease with the technical jargon and associated cultures surrounding IT. In contrast, women library assistants were conscious of tensions and ambiguities surrounding their participation. Day-to-day experience enabled them to make practical contributions, for example to the systems specification, on issues not easily visible to managers or systems designers. However, many of these issues had links with broader areas of library policy, which, as library assistants were very aware, remained the prerogative of senior management. In a period of cutbacks and organisational transition, resources such as training were not readily available to support library assistants in expanding their role. In the library context, key members of the senior management group favour a view of IT as promoting organisational flexibility, enhanced access to information and increased mobility of staff. This informal but powerful view is regarded with suspicion by library assistants, who fear that the new system will be used to justify cuts in staffing. Indeed most recently, some senior managers have begun to refer to the proposed new system as potentially facilitating substantial job losses which the recent budget crisis has made inevitable. Although previously opposed to the view that computers can or should replace staff, when faced with the problem of implementing budget cuts they struggle with the concept of protecting the library service through prioritising the new system, even though it may be accompanied by a reduction in staffing:

> "...if the choice is between having the computer and not having it at all, and if we have it with a slight staff reduction, I think initially that might be acceptable, as a shorter term strategy. And then we would have to review whether or not staffing was right."
>
> (Chair of Design Team)

The considerable unease with which the woman manager concerned made this comment demonstrates the contradictions experienced by managers, caught between a managerial ideology which prioritises the interests of the organisation and its 'duty' to offer a service to customers, and a personal commitment to preserving jobs and job satisfaction.

Although this managerial view implies that the library assistants are justified in being cynical, at another level it captures the effects of a widespread dislocation between IT strategy and equal opportunities policies. Junior clerical workers with few line-management responsibilities are freer to innovate in the area of job design; they have much to gain from linking computerisation with challenges to gendered hierarchies in the work place. Similarly the confusion of senior managers about the potential connections between computerisation, staffing levels, and job satisfaction is intensified by the separation of technical and social/organisational issues characteristic of computer experts' jargon. Technical and scientific knowledge is commonly viewed as 'authoritative' and legitimate (Suchman & Jordan 1989). This knowledge also becomes 'concrete' and reassuring when it apparently gives rise to computer hardware. More at risk in times of economic constraint are innovative, 'soft' areas such as creative and informal work on job design; this is easily seen as dispensable. This gendered and problematic dichotomy, between technical and organisational factors, contributes to the continuing marginalisation of the interests of the women clerical users of office information systems.

Conclusion

Where the goals of an information system include substantial integrated or cooperative elements then this has particular implications for the way the system should be developed. The chosen methodology must reflect these aspects of cooperation (across functional areas or within the organisational hierarchy) and demands some form of participatory approach. Cooperative aims such as the quality of service provision become paramount in this situation. The required methodology must include techniques which empower the participants and recognise their differences such as gender and status.

At the beginning of this paper, we referred to the suggestion that 'user relations' issues characterise the current phase of computerisation (Friedman and Cornford, op.cit.). Our own case-study data does confirm this suggestion. User relations, and more specifically basic-grade staff involvement and consultation, were the major priority for both management and workforce in the organisation concerned. From the earliest stages of planning and discussion, both perceived 'user-involvement' not only as desirable within a framework of generally progressive employment policies, but also as crucial to the success of a new phase of computerisation. As discussed above, this new phase of computerisation was to be based around the selection and local 'tailoring' of an existing, integrated information system: not around an in-house, one-off process of systems development. This pattern is increasingly common, in the areas of clerical work and other service sector employment for women. It is essential therefore, that we begin to map out the positive and the negative factors influencing women's opportunities for cooperative intervention and improved working conditions in this context.

At a general level, our case-study confirms that the advent of large-scale, integrated information systems increases managerial reliance on the skills and cooperation of 'users' at all levels (Williams op.cit.) and in particular women clerical workers. In our example, managers were prepared to resource an unprecedented level of clerical worker involvement, as they could not envisage the successful development and implementation of a more sophisticated information system without it. Within a public sector context, there is scope to make links between this increased management recognition of clerical skills in relation to information systems development, and broader, prior commitments to facilitating equal opportunities. In this situation, structures such as the study circles and the mixed gender and status 'Design Team' were able to retain a considerable degree of initiative. They established new forms of cooperative decision making; they sustaind a focus on both technical and organisational aspects of systems development, and they retained maximum scope for negotiating with systems suppliers over systems features and implementation. However, the case-study also illustrates a range of complex and difficult issues. Paradoxically, close collaboration between women clerical workers and their technical and professional colleagues, mostly male, made more visible the informal patterns of male 'tenure' of IT, for instance the ways in which male computing professionals spontaneously asserted the benefits of a 'state of the art' system, rather than stopping to listen to arguments about staff-client relationships. Challenging this traditional, patriarchal, hierarchy, in which 'the technical' takes precedence, proved intensely difficult and stressful in practice, especially for the women library assistants.

Lastly, it is important to acknowledge the political and economic climate of the case-study: an intensifying crisis in the UK public sector, and the slide into another major economic recession, with the associated threats to employment levels and to hard-won rights and opportunities. Looking ahead to further rounds of central government cutbacks, some managers in City Libraries visualise a 'transformed' public library service, operating perhaps with 30% fewer staff. However, the ground gained through clerical worker involvement in planning for further automation has not been lost. Even in such an unfavourable climate, it is no longer possible for computerisation to be viewed simplistically as a solution to the problem of maintaining service delivery with a drastically-reduced workforce. Through intervention at the systems planning and design stages women clerical workers, and their union representatives are in a stronger position to expose and challenge this assumption, and to negotiate over technical and organisational alternatives.

References

Bannon L, Bjorn-Anderson N, Due-Thomsen B (1988). 'Computer support for cooperative work: An appraisal and critique.' In H J Bullinger, *(Ed.) Eurinfo '88. Information Systems for Organizational effectiveness.* North-Holland, Amsterdam.

Bodker S, Gronbek K (1991) 'Cooperative prototyping: users and designers in mutual activity.' *The international journal of man-machine studies* Vol.34. (1991)

Checkland P (1981) *Systems Thinking, Systems Practice,* Wiley, London.

Cockburn C (1985) *Machinery of Dominance: Women, Men and Technical Know-How,* Pluto, London.

Davies C & Rosser J (1985) 'Gendered Jobs in the Health Service: a Problem for Labour Process Analysis'. *In Knights & Wilmott (eds) Gender and the Labour Process,* Gower, Aldershot.

Ehn P (1988) *Work-Oriented Design of Computer Artifacts.* Swedish Centre for Working Life, Abelistraum, Stockholm.

Friedman A with Cornford D (1989) *Computer Systems Development: History, Organisation and Implementation,* Wiley, Chichester.

Gill K S (1990) *Summary of Human-Centred Systems* Research in Europe. Research paper, SEAKE Centre, Brighton Polytechnic.

Green E, Owen J and Pain D (eds) (forthcoming) *Gender, Information Technology and the Design of Office Systems.* Falmer Press.

Green E, Owen J, Pain D (1991) *Developing computerised office systems: a gender perspective in UK approaches.* Paper to IFIP Conference, Finland (1991).

Greenbaum J (1987) *The Head and the Heart: Using Gender Analysis to Study the Social Construction of Computer Systems,* Computer Science Dept. Aarhus University, Denmark.

Greenberg S (1991) 'Computer-supported cooperative work and groupware: an introduction to special issues. *In The International Journal of Man-machine studies.* Vol.34.

Hales M (1989) *Women: the Key to Information Technology,* London Strategic Policy Unit, Barefoot Documents, Brighton.

LBMS (1986) *Introduction to LSDM,* Learmonth and Birchett Management Systems, London.

Liff S (1990) 'Clerical Workers and Information Technology: Gender Relations and Occupational Change' *New Technology, Work and Employment,* 5.1.1990.

Mumford E (1983) *Designing Human Systems,* Manchester Business School Publications, Manchester.

Olerup A, Schneider C and Monod E (eds) (1985) *Women, Work and Computerization: Opportunities and Disadvantages,* North-Holland, Amsterdam.

Suchman L and Jordan B (1989) Computerization and Women's Knowledge in Tijdens K et al(eds) *Women, Work and Computerization: Forming New Alliances,* North-Holland, Amsterdam.

Tijdens K et al (1989) *Women, Work and Computerization: Forming New Alliances* North-Holland, Amsterdam.

Webster J (1989) *Office Automation: The Labour Process and Women's Work in Britain, Harvester* Wheatsheaf, Hemel Hempstead.

Williams R (1990) 'Participation and New Technology: *Theoretical Framework and Research Hypotheses' in Attitudinal Survey Working Paper No. EF/WP/90/30/EN,* European Foundation for the Improvement of Living and Working Conditions.

Proceedings of the Second European Conference on Computer-Supported Cooperative Work
Bannon, L., Robinson, M. & Schmidt, K. (Editors)
September 25-27, 1991, Amsterdam, The Netherlands

CSCW and Distributed Systems: The Problem of Control

Tom Rodden Gordon Blair
Lancaster University, U.K.

The user-centred philosophy of CSCW challenges the established principles of many existing technologies but the development of CSCW is dependent on the facilities provided by these technologies. It is therefore important to examine and understand this inter-relationship. This paper focuses on distributed computing, a technology central to the development of CSCW systems. The nature of both CSCW and distribution are compared by using a common framework. In this discussion, control emerges as the major problem in supporting CSCW systems. It is argued that existing approaches to control in distributed systems are inadequate given the rich patterns of cooperation found in CSCW. A number of recommendations are made for improving distributed support for CSCW.

1. Introduction

Computer support for cooperative working (CSCW) has emerged over the last five years as a research discipline in its own right (Bannon, 1991). The growing interest in CSCW reflects the demands of industry for improved tools to aid the coordination and control of group activities. The majority of CSCW applications are fundamentally distributed and are dependent on the facilities provided by existing distributed systems platforms. It is therefore important to assess the support that such systems provide.

The aim of this paper is to evaluate distributed system support for CSCW. In particular we wish to consider the particular requirements of CSCW and the interaction between distributed systems and CSCW. To achieve this two dimensions of CSCW are introduced in section 2. These dimensions provide a basis for the our discussion. This is followed in section 3 with an examination of distributed system support for CSCW based on the above dimensions. Control, an additional and important feature of both CSCW and distributed systems, is introduced in section 4. The impact of control on distribution is examined and techniques to support control are also discussed. Distributed transactions are presented in section 5 as an illustrative case study of the problem of control. Finally some concluding remarks are presented in section 6.

2. Dimensions of CSCW

A wide variety of CSCW systems have been developed reflecting the many different views of cooperation. The nature of cooperation has been an on-going debate within the CSCW community (Schmidt, 1989). Two principal characteristics have emerged from this debate *the form of cooperation* and *the geographical nature*. We shall use these characteristics as the basis for examining both CSCW systems and the underlying support provided by distributed systems.

2.1 The Form of Cooperation

CSCW systems are primarily concerned with supporting a number of users cooperating to address a particular problem, or range of problems. People cooperate in a variety of ways depending on a range of circumstances. The nature of this cooperation can be distinguished by the way in which the group members interact. People can either interact and cooperate *synchronously* or *asynchronously*. Synchronous interaction requires the presence of all cooperating users while asynchronous cooperation occurs over a longer time period and does not require the simultaneous interaction of all users.

Figure 1 shows how a number of classes of CSCW systems fit into this division.

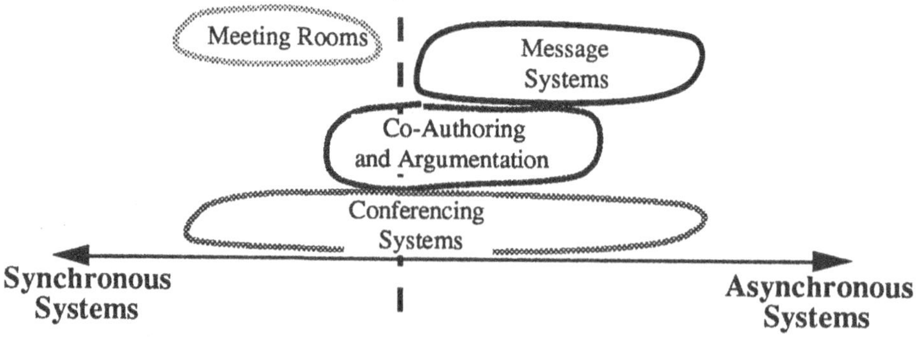

Figure 1 Forms of cooperation in CSCW systems

From this classification three general classes of CSCW system can be highlighted.

i) Purely synchronous systems

Purely synchronous systems need the simultaneous presence of all users. This general class of system is used for investigative and creative problems. Systems which typify this approach include real-time conferencing systems (Lauwers, 1990) using shared screen techniques (Stefik, 1987b) and the brainstorming tools found in meeting rooms (Stefik, 1987a)

ii) Purely Asynchronous systems

Asynchronous systems are designed to allow cooperation without the simultaneous presence of all group members. Cooperative message systems are a primary example of this type of system where users take on independent roles which produce and consume messages. Similarly, traditional conferencing systems assume an asynchronous mode of cooperation with users reading and adding articles to conferences independently of other users.

iii) Mixed Systems

Mixed systems contain elements of support for both synchronous and asynchronous cooperation. They allow real-time synchronous cooperation to take place within the same framework as time-independent asynchronous working. The primary examples of this type of systems are computer conferencing and co-authoring and argumentation systems. Modern computer conferencing systems provide a central asynchronous conferencing systems often augmented with facilities such as real-time conferencing (Sarin, 1985).

2.2. Geographical Nature

Computer support for group interaction has traditionally considered the case of geographically distributed groups who work asynchronously to each other. More recent research (Stefik, 1987a) has complemented this emphasis by considering the support of face to face meetings. As a result cooperative systems can be considered as being either *remote* or *co-located*. In this classification the division between remote and co-located is as much a logical as a physical one and is concerned with the accessibility of users to each other rather than their physical proximity. A range of CSCW systems are divided in terms of their geographical nature in figure 2.

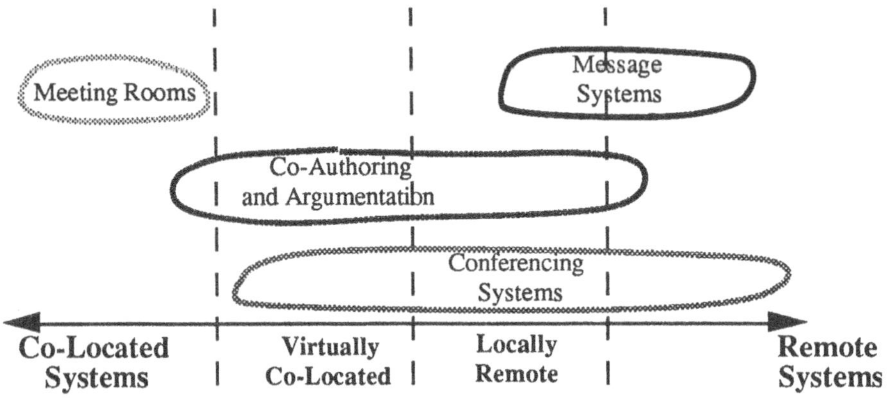

Figure 2 Geographical nature in CSCW systems

Four general divisions can be highlighted.

i). Co-Located.

Purely co-located systems require the local presence of all users. This class of system normally takes the form of a purpose built meeting room with a large projected computer screen and a number of personal computer linked by a local area network (Kraemer, 1988).

ii) Virtually co-located

Systems which are virtually co-located are similar to co-located systems but do not have the requirement that participants need to be in one room. This is often achieved by the use of Multimedia technology, allowing real-time audio and video links to be maintained. Systems in this class include real-time multimedia conferencing systems such as those been developed for MMConf (Crowley, 1990) and Mermaid (Watabe, 1990).

iii) Locally Remote

Locally remote systems are those systems which provide high-bandwidth real time accessibility between users often using shared screen techniques.. Argumentation and co-authoring systems such as CoAuthor (Hahn, 1991) or gIBIS (Conklin, 1987) and real-time conferencing facilities such as RTCAL (Sarin, 1985) can be considered in this way.

iv) Remote

Remote cooperative systems are those that assume the existence of only minimal accessibility between users. These include message systems which assume only the simplest of communication systems and computer conferencing systems which assume only rudimentary "dial-in" mechanisms.

3. CSCW and Distributed Systems

Distributed systems have been one of the major growth areas in computing over the past decade. Products such as ETHERNET (Shoch, 1982) and MACH (Jones, 1986) are available in the market place and standards to provide open communications are generally agreed.

It can be argued that distributed systems are entering a period of consolidation with techniques for implementing distributed systems relatively well understood, and that emphasis should be placed on issues such as promotion of standards, large scale experiments, and gaining of experience. However, a major problem in distributed systems is a lack of existing applications of the technology leading to technological solutions to technological problems.

Until recently, this feature of distributed computing has not posed many problems. However, the emergence of CSCW has led to more sophisticated demands on the underlying technology. This section reviews the ability of existing distributed system technologies to support the wide range of CSCW systems.

3.1. The Form of cooperation

Distributed systems have traditionally being viewed in terms of support for cooperation between a number of computers connected by a network. It is important to note that the term cooperation is used in this context to refer to how closely related the computers within the distributed systems are to each other, rather than the more general application of the term in section 2. This interpretation is used throughout this section.

The nature of support for cooperation varies greatly from system to system. A traditional problem with cooperation in distributed systems is the need to recognise autonomy of individual sites in a network. Indeed, full cooperation and full autonomy are actually two extremes in a spectrum of possibilities with most practical systems found between these two extremes.

Increasing the autonomy of a system inevitably decreases the support for cooperation and vice-versa. Much of the research in distributed systems has been concerned with resolving this design tension and establishing a compromise between the two extremes. A number of distinct classes of system, each taking a particular approach to this issue, have been developed:-

i) autonomous systems with mailing capabilities

This is an important class of system where personal computer environments are interconnected by electronic mail allowing users to interact asynchronously via (usually) text based messages.

ii) resource sharing systems

Resource sharing systems allow resources to be accessed whether they are local or remote to a workstation. The motivation for resource sharing systems is that many resources are expensive and hence it is economical to share such resources across a network.

iii) distributed operating systems

Distributed operating systems are operating systems which manage resources across a distributed environment (Tanenbaum, 1985). They provide global management of such resources with the consequent loss of node autonomy. Most distributed operating systems are based on the *client-server* model of interaction with clients requesting remote operations from *servers* on other nodes.

More recent distributed operating systems have also tended to provide more sophisticated support for interaction. For example, several systems have developed protocols to provide general group interaction (e.g. ISIS (Birman, 1989)) as opposed to the one to one patterns encouraged by the traditional client-server model.

The need to support autonomy has proved to be more important than the support for cooperation. Most commercially available computer systems support a mailing capability and this has become accepted as a standard means of cooperation in a distributed system and provides adequate support for the development of asynchronous cooperative systems.

Systems with resource sharing capabilities provide access to networked resources such as printers and remote files. More sophisticated resource sharing systems will provide the user with a global file system accessible from anywhere in the network. Resource sharing systems provide an ideal platform for developing *mixed cooperative systems* with asynchronous cooperative working as the norm and rudimentary synchronous support being provided as an expensive shared resource.

There has been much less commercial interest/ exploitation of distributed operating systems. Distributed operating systems have been an area of intense research activity (Mullender, 1986); however, this has yet to be mapped on to a real demand for the technology.

Distributed operating systems represent the maximum support available for cooperation. They support reasonably sophisticated modes of interaction and often mask out the problems of distribution (e.g. locating objects and handling failure). However, most distributed operating systems allow some recognition of the autonomy of individual nodes and the cooperative end of the spectrum has not been explored fully. There are a few notable exceptions , for example, the work of the ISIS project on group interaction could be viewed as supporting more sophisticated levels of cooperation.

This spectrum of support corresponds quite closely to the forms of cooperation described in section 2.1. Synchronous systems require highly cooperative distributed systems while asynchronous systems tend to be much more autonomous in nature. Basic asynchronous cooperative systems need only the facilities provided by electronic mail systems, the most autonomous of distributed systems. Fully synchronous systems test the facilities provided by the most cooperative of distributed operating systems. Most distributed systems are found at the lower end of the spectrum, i.e. supporting a high degree of autonomy. This may account for the lack of highly interactive synchronous cooperative systems. The two views of a cooperative system are shown together in figure 3

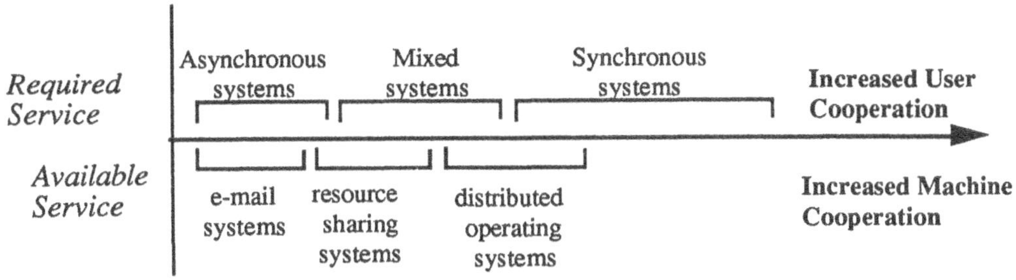

Figure 3 Comparison of Models of Cooperation

A strong correspondence can be seen between the two categories in figure 3. However, there appears to be a gap when considering more sophisticated forms of synchronous working. It is not clear how best to support highly synchronous cooperative systems such as meeting rooms and real time multimedia conferencing with existing distributed technology.

3.2. Geographical Nature

As discussed in section 2.2, the geographic nature of CSCW systems is concerned with the *logical* concept of co-location. In contrast, distributed computing has been solely concerned with the *physical* transmission and processing of specialised, computer-oriented, media such as numerical and textual data. Most distributed computing environments have been connected by a range of local or wide area networks providing a reasonable handling of such media types. The characteristics of each type of network is summarised in figure 4.

Network	Throughput	Classification
Ethernet	10 Mbits/Sec	Local Area Network
1Base5 CSMA/CD	1 Mbits/Sec	Local Area Network
PSS (UK)	64 KBits/Sec	Wide Area Network
Arpanet (USA)	64 KBits/Sec	Wide Area Network

Figure 4 Local vs Wide Area Networks

The performance characteristics listed above have proved sufficient to support a range of distributed computing environments. The table also highlights the quantitative difference that currently exists between local and wide area technologies. Local area networks have been used to implement the full range of systems described in section 4.1 including distributed operating systems supporting varying degrees of cooperation. Wide area networks have generally been restricted to mailing systems and, occasionally, resource sharing systems.

Recently, there has been great interest in high speed networks and, in particular, their capability to handle a greater variety of media types. The capabilities of these multimedia networks are summarised in figure 5.

Network	Throughput	Classification
FDDI	100 Mbits/Sec	Local Area Network
DQDB	upto 100 Mbits/Sec	Metropolitan Area Network
Basic Rate ISDN	64 KBits/Sec	Wide Area Network
Primary Rate ISDN	2 MBits/Sec	Wide Area Network
Broadband ISDN	155 MBits/Sec	Wide Area Network

Figure 5 High Performance Networks

Networking technology is increasing at a rapid rate but there is still a long way to go before such networks can provide support for sophisticated forms of multimedia cooperation. The problems are most acute when considering the group interactions demanded by CSCW. Considerable research is also required in issues such as synchronisation of different multimedia channels and the integration of high performance protocols into multimedia workstations (Hopper, 1990).

The existing spectrum of communications technologies in distributed systems can be compared directly with the geographical nature CSCW systems (figure 6)

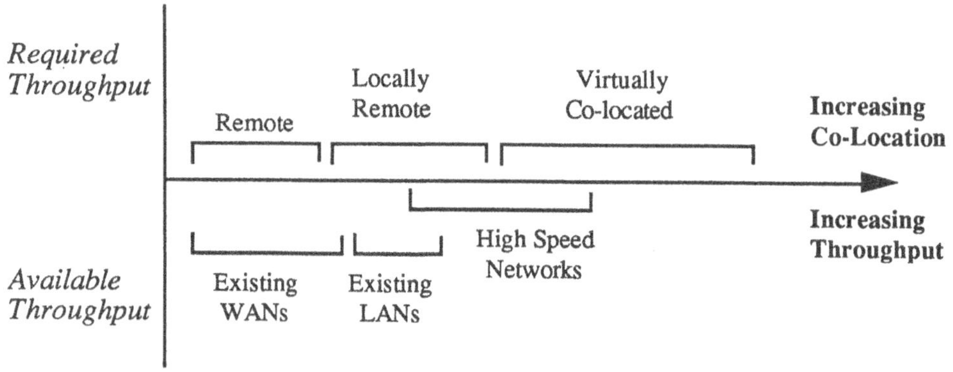

Figure 6 Geographic Dispersion Comparison

As in the case of cooperation distributed systems seem to provide good support for asynchronous cooperative systems. However, there are limitations with existing technology in supporting more synchronous styles of work. This is particularly true in CSCW applications supporting a high degree of co-location. Communication networks simply cannot cope with the logical 'bandwidth' demanded by this class of application. It is likely that high performance multimedia networks will have some impact on CSCW systems. The extent of this impact will depend on the development of protocols suitable for CSCW systems.

4. The Importance of Control

The previous sections have examined the styles of interaction and the geographical nature of both CSCW and distributed systems. However, a critical element is still missing from our discussion. The distinguishing feature of CSCW systems is their approach to representing and controlling cooperation. This section examines this issue in more depth. In effect, the authors see this issue as crucial to future success of CSCW systems.

4.1 CSCW and Control

People work together to solve a wide variety of problems using different forms of cooperation for each class of problem. Cooperative problems can be though of as existing at some point on a spectrum ranging from *unstructured* problems at one end to *prescriptive* tasks at the other. Unstructured problems are those requiring creative input from a number of users which often cannot be detailed or described in advance; software design is a good example of such an activity. Prescriptive tasks, on the other hand, represent the routine procedural cooperative mechanisms used to solve problems which have existing group solutions. Prescriptive tasks respond well to detailed control of cooperation while unstructured problems require a significant degree of freedom to be exercised by the cooperative system.

The amount of control provided by cooperative systems is an additional means of classifying cooperative systems. This classification is significant in that it highlights the level of automation each cooperative system provides.

CSCW systems exhibit two major forms of control, *explicit* or *implicit* control. In systems which provide explicit control users may both view and tailor group interaction and cooperation. In contrast, systems exhibiting implicit control provide no techniques for representing or coordinating group interaction. These systems dictate cooperation by the styles of interaction they allow.

A simple classification of the representation and control of cooperation in CSCW systems yields five classes of system.

i) Speech act or conversation based systems

Speech act systems apply a linguistic approach to computer supported cooperation based on speech act theory which considers language as a series of actions. Cooperation is represented and controlled within this class of system using some form of network structure detailing the patterns of message exchange. Speech Act theory has been forms the basis of several computer systems including the Coordinator system (Winograd, 1987) and the CHAOS project (De Cindio, 1986).

ii) Office procedure systems

Office procedures describe tasks performed within an office in terms of the combined effect of a number of small sub-tasks or procedures. Research has concentrated on developing languages which allow the specification of office procedures and a description of their interaction. This class of system is characterised by the use of a procedural language to describe and control cooperation by defining roles and activities.Approaches of this form include the AMIGO (Danielson, 1986) and COSMOS (Wilbur, 1988) projects.

iii) Semi-formal active Message systems

Semi-formal or active message systems provide supportive mechanisms for automatic message handling including the concepts of roles and autonomous agents. Systems of this form include the OBJECT LENS (Malone, 1988), the Strudel project (Sheperd 90), and the ISM system (Rodden, 1991)

iv) Conferencing systems

Conferencing systems provide basic control mechanisms which are minimal and fixed within applications. In traditional conferencing systems this takes the form conferences and moderators who control the addition of information to these topics. In real time conferencing systems control centres around the floor control mechanism imbedded in the conferencing application which dictates who has access to a shared conference space at any given time.

v) Peer- group meeting or Control free systems

Peer meeting systems such as the Colab system (Stefik, 1987a) deliberately do not provide any control mechanisms and rely on the meeting participants to formulate their own meeting protocols. All users have equal status and may amend and use the systems freely. In turn the systems keeps no track of the nature or form of group work being undertaken and provide limited support for these work processes.

The first three classes listed above are all examples of systems which exhibit *explicit* control allowing the representation and editing of control information. In contrast, conferencing and control free systems are *implicit* control systems which contain no representation of control.

4.2 Control requirements for CSCW

CSCW encompasses a wide range of control techniques. In many ways this is to be expected; CSCW is essentially about supporting the rich patterns of inter-personal cooperation. This richness should be reflected in the provision of control within CSCW systems, and the underlying technology should support rather than constrain this process.This latter point highlights the importance of the relationship between CSCW and distributed systems design. It is difficult to derive precise requirement from the list of control techniques presented above. However, some important observations can be made:

- The organisational context of the work needs to be captured.
- The many different forms of cooperation need to co-exist.
- The structure and organisation of groups need to be explicitly recognised.
- Groups work in dynamic and unexpected ways and are themselves dynamic
- Control should be enabling rather than constraining

Collectively these issues demand a *user-centred* approach to the control of cooperation within CSCW systems. This poses fairly fundamental questions for distributed system designers and highlights significant deficiencies in existing technology.

4.3 Supporting Control in Distributed Systems

Traditionally, distributed systems have taken a *systems-oriented* approach to control. They view control as dealing with the problems of distribution and masking such problems from applications (*distribution transparency*). Unfortunately this focus on transparency has tended to re-inforced the bottom-up development of distributed systems. For example, consider the problem of shared access to resources. In most distributed systems this is dealt with by masking out the existence of other users. Hence sharing is transparent with each user unaware of the activity of others. This clearly contradicts the needs of CSCW.

Recent work on distributed systems has clarified the meaning of the term distribution transparency (ANSA, 1989). Distribution transparency is now seen as a collective name for the masking out of various features of a distributed computation. In effect, there are a number of individual transparencies corresponding to each of these features(figure 7).

Transparency	Central Issue	Result of Transparency
Location	The location of an object in a distributed environment	User unaware of the location of services
Access	The method of access to objects in a distributed system	All objects are accessed in the same way
Migration	The re-location of an object in a distributed environment	Objects may move without the user being aware
Concurrency	Shared access to objects in a distributed environment	Users do not have to deal with problems of concurrent access
Replication	Maintaining copies of an object in a distributed environment	System deals with the consistency of copies of data
Failure	Partial failure in a distributed environment	Problems of failure are masked from the user

Figure 7 The Forms of Transparency in Distributed Systems

The prevalent view in distributed computing is to implement each of these transparencies to mask out *all* the problems of a distributed system. This is particularly true in the distributed operating system community. The problem with this approach is that presumed control decisions are embedded into the system and hence cannot be avoided or tailored for specific classes of application. This is the root of the problem in supporting CSCW. Because of the dynamic requirements of CSCW applications, it is very unlikely that such prescribed solutions will be suitable.

It is important to consider alternatives to this complete distribution transparency. System designers are currently aware of the problems that can be caused by full distribution transparency. Consequentially, a number of alternative approaches have already been explored:

i) Non-transparency

In non-transparent systems, all the features of distribution are visible to the programmer. They must therefore deal directly with issues such as failure and migration. This allows more flexibility since individual applications can deal with the management of objects in a distributed environment. However, the handling of distribution can become an intolerable burden on the programmer.

ii) Selective Transparency

Selective transparency allows the application developer to opt for transparency or non-transparency for each of the issues in distributed computing (figure 7). It is therefore possible to have location and access transparency, for example, but request non-transparency for the other issues. This approach provides some of the flexibility required for CSCW applications, however, existing solutions do not include user selection.

None of these provide complete solutions to the problem of controlling CSCW applications. The option of transparent control is too prescriptive for the needs of CSCW applications. However, the alternative of non-transparency imposes too high a burden on application developers. Selective transparency does appear more promising but does not address the fundamental user issues within control in cooperative working. CSCW demands a fresh approach to control which is specifically tailored for cooperative working. There has been very little work in this area. However, it is possible to identify a number of features of such an approach.

i) Clean separation of mechanisms and policies

The first requirement for control in CSCW applications is that there should be a clean separation between the mechanisms required for distribution management and the policies which govern the use of these mechanisms. To appreciate this distinction, consider the case of migration. There is a clear distinction between the ability to move an object (the mechanism) and the decisions about when the object should be moved and to which site (the policy). Distributed systems can provide the mechanisms required to manage distribution leaving higher level authorities to impose the policy. This separation of concerns is implicit in both non-transparency and selective transparency.

ii) Tailored Mechanisms

Current mechanisms have been developed in the classical bottom-up tradition of distributed systems. Such mechanisms may not be suitable for the particular semantics of CSCW applications. It is therefore important to consider existing mechanisms for the various transparencies and whether they are suitable for the demands of CSCW. Returning to the discussion of section 4.1 mechanisms delimit the *implicit control* exhibited by CSCW systems. A single set of mechanisms is unlikely to be suitable for all manifestations of implicit control in CSCW applications and the co-existence of a range of mechanisms needs to be considered.

iii) Tailored Policies

Distribution policies provide the representation necessary for *explicit control* in CSCW systems. It is important that these policies meet the control requirements identified in 4.2. It is equally important that policies can be tailored to allow support across the range of explicit control techniques identified in section 4.1. The provision of the policies will require input from all areas of CSCW. It is important to avoid these policies overly inhibiting the cooperation of users. As described in (Armstrong, 1990) when considering good practice in management science: "Policies are both restrictive and permissive at once. They spell out the limits to actions, but at the same time they give freedom to act within the limits specified".

5. A Case Study in Control: Distributed Transactions

Transaction mechanisms are concerned with the maintenance of consistency in a distributed system (Spector, 1989). In particular, they deal with concurrent access to data and partial failure of the system. Traditional approaches to transactions typify the *transparent* approach to distributed computing. More specifically, transaction mechanisms realise both concurrency and failure transparency, masking out problems associated with these features of a distributed system. Transparency is achieved by *prescribing* the following principles:-

i) serialisability

Transactions handle concurrent access to shared information by enforcing a regime where concurrent operations are allowed only if their combined effect is equivalent to a serial sequence of operations.

ii) recoverability

Systems recoverability is supported by the creation of a set of consistent *snapshops* which can be returned to in the event of failure. Effectively, this allows transaction to be undone if an error occurs.

The provision of both serialisability and recoverability has been examined in detail and a wide range of algorithms have been proposed (Kohler, 1981). The general approach adopted is to restrict access to data by *locking* out other operations. This gives the impression of shared access being carried out in isolation. The problem with this approach is that it embeds one particular view of cooperation. This is unacceptable for CSCW giving the rich patterns of cooperation identified above (section 4.1). For example, consider the case of a co-authoring system. If a group member is updating a section of text, then it might make sense for an interested colleague to "read over their shoulder". This would not be supported by a simple locking strategy.

Several researchers have started to focus on transactions for group working (Ellis, 1989). This research is still at an early stage. However, some interesting results are starting to emerge. For example, a paper by Skarra (Skarra, 1988) challenges traditional transaction models and proposes an alternative approach more closely tailored for group work. They explicitly identify the notion of a *transaction group* which co-ordinates access to shared data for a number of co-operating members. Within a transaction group, the notion of serialisability is replaced by access rules based on the semantics of the cooperation. Access rules provide the *policy* of cooperation as discussed in the previous section. Policies can thus be *tailored* for a particular application by amending access rules.

Transaction are symptomatic of the mismatch between distributed systems platforms and CSCW systems. It is clear that traditional approaches to transactions are not well suited to group work and hence many group applications have chosen to by-pass the system support. This places unacceptable burdens on developers of CSCW systems. It is therefore important to continue the work on group transactions and to identify suitable user-centred mechanisms and policies. Similar examinations are required across the field of distributed systems.

6. Concluding Remarks

Existing distribution technology currently has shortfalls in supporting CSCW systems both in terms of the cooperation between users and the geographic nature of these users. However, it is possible to see how particular shortfalls can be overcome by current developments in technology, e.g. high speed networks. More seriously, the traditional approach to control in distributed systems seems to be inadequate. It is difficult to foresee how distribution transparency can provide the highly flexible and tailorable facilities needed to represent the process of cooperation within CSCW applications.

The provision of appropriate facilities will almost certainly require a careful re-examination of distributed systems architectures and the provision of control within these architectures. It is important to avoid prescriptive and often unsuitable solutions to issues such as migration, concurrency and failure. Rather, both the mechanisms and policies of distribution should be tailored more closely to the demands of group working. This raises some fundamental and, as yet, unresolved questions:-

i) what are the most suitable *mechanisms* to support group working,
ii) what are the appropriate control *policies* for CSCW, and
iii) how are cooperation and control *represented* in CSCW systems?

A solution to these problems will require a detailed understanding of *both* the behaviour of distributed systems and the behaviour of interacting user groups. This problem therefore illustrates the inherently cross-disciplinary nature of CSCW research. The problem compounded further by the fact that existing distributed systems already provide adequate support for a range of applications. It is important that distributed systems continue to support these applications and any mechanisms for supporting CSCW systems need to smoothly integrate with these existing distributed applications.

7. References

ANSA (1989): *ANSA: An Engineer's Introduction*, Release TR.03.02, Architecture Projects Management Limited. November 1989.

Armstrong, M (1990): "Management Processes and Functions", in Armstrong, M., Farnham, D. (eds): *Management Studies Series*, ISBN 0 85292 438 0.

Bannon, L., Schmidt, K (1991): "CSCW: Four Characters in Search of Context", in J.M. Bowers and S.D. Benford (eds): *Studies in Computer Supported Cooperative Work. Theory, Practice and Design*, North-Holland, Amsterdam, 1991, pp 3-17.

Birman, K., and K. Marzullo.(1989): "ISIS and the META Project." *Sun Technology* No.: Summer, Pages: 90-104.

Conklin, J (1987): "gIBIS: A Hypertext Tool for Team Design Deliberation", *Proceeding of Hypertext 87*, November 1987,pp 247-251.

Crowley, T., Milazzo, P., Baker E., Forsdick H., Tomlinson R.(1990):"MMConf: An Infrastructure for Building Shared Multimedia Applications", *in proceedings of CSCW* 90, Los Angeles, CA, October 7-10 1990, ACM press , ISBN 0-89791-402-3.

Danielson, T., Panoke-Babatz, U., et al. (1986): "The AMIGO project: Advanced Group Communication Model for Computer-based Communication Environment", *in proceedings of CSCW 86*,Austin,Texas,December 1986.

De Cindio, F., De Michelis, G., et al (1986): " CHAOS as a Coordinating Technology", *in proceedings of CSCW 86*, Austin, Texas, December 1986.

Ellis, C.A., Gibbs.S.J. (1989): "Concurrency Control in Groupware Systems." *ACM SIGMOD International Conference on the Management of Data*, SIGMOD Record, Pages: 399-407.

Hahn, U., Jarke, M., Kreplin, K.et al.(1991): "CoAuthor: A Hypermedia Group Authoring Environment", in J.M. Bowers and S.D. Benford (eds): *Studies in Computer Supported Cooperative Work. Theory, Practice and Design*, North-Holland, 1991, pp 79-100.

Hopper, A. (1990): "Pandora - An Experimental System for Multimedia Applications", *ACM Operating Systems Review*, Vol. 24, No. 2, April 1990.

Jones, M.B., and R.F. Rashid. (1986): "Mach and Matchmaker: Kernel and Language Support for Object-Oriented Distributed Systems." *Proceedings of the Conference on Object-Oriented Programming Systems, Languages and Applications (OOPSLA '86):*, Portland, Oregon, 1986. Editor: N. Meyrowitz, Special Issue of ACM SIGPLAN Notices, Vol: 21, Pages: 67-77.

Kohler, W.H (1981): "A Survey of Techniques for Synchronisation and Recovery in Decentralsied Computer Systems", *ACM Computer Surveys*, Vol. 13, No. 2, June 1981.

Kraemer, K L, Kling, J L (1988): "Computer Based Systems for Cooperative Work and Group Decision Making" , *ACM Computing Surveys*, Vol 20, No 2, June 1988.

Lauwers, J.C., Lantz, K.A. (1990): "Collaboration Awareness in Support of Collaboration Transparency: Requirements for the Next Generation of Shared Window Systems", *Proceedings of CHI '90* Seattle, Washington April 1-5, 1990, ACM press, ISBN-0-201-50932-6.

Malone, T W, Lai, K (1988): "Object Lens: A Spreadsheet for Cooperative Work", in *proceedings of CSCW'88*, Portland, Oregon, September 1988.

Mullender, S.J., and A.S. Tanenbaum. (1986): "The Design of a Capability-Based Distributed Operating System." *The Computer Journal* Vol: 29 No.: 4, pp 289-299.

Rodden T., Sommerville I. (1991): "Building Conversations using Mailtrays", in J.M. Bowers and S.D. Benford (eds): *Studies in Computer Supported Cooperative Work. Theory, Practice and Design*, North-Holland, Amsterdam, 1991, pp 79-100.

Sarin, S., Grief, I.(1985): "Computer-Based Real time Conferencing Systems", *IEEE Computer* October 1985, pp 33- 45.

Schmidt, K. (1989): "Cooperative Work: A Conceptual Framework", FCI Publication #89-1, The Informatics Centre of the Danish Trade Union Movement, June 1989, ISBN 87-89369-00-9.

Sheperd A, Mayer N., Kuchinsky A. (1990): "Strudel- An Extensible Electronic Conversation Toolkit", *in proceedings of CSCW 90*, Los Angeles, CA, October 7-10 1990, ACM press , ISBN 0-89791-402-3.

Shoch, J.F., Y.K. Dalal, D.D. Redell, and R.C. Crane.(1982): "Evolution of the Ethernet Local Computer Network." *IEEE Computer*, August 1982. Pages: 10-26.

Skarra, A.H. (1988): "Concurrency Control for Cooperating Transactions in an Object-Oriented Database." *Proceedings of the ACM SIGPLAN Workshop on Object-Based Concurrent Programming*, San Diego, September. Editor: Gul Agha, Peter Wegner and Akinori Yonezawa, SIGPLAN Notices, Pages: 145-147.

Spector, A. (1989):"Distributed Transaction Processing Facilities", in Mullender, S. (ed):, *Distributed Systems*, Addison-Wesley, New York, 1989.

Stefik M., Bobrow D.G., et al. (1987b): "WYSIWIS Revised: Early Experiences with Multiuser Interfaces", *ACM transactions. on Office Information Systems*, Vol 5, No 2, April 1987, pp 147-168.

Stefik M., Foster G., et al. (1987a): "Beyond the Chalkboard: Computer Support for Collaboration and Problem Solving in Meetings", *Communications of the ACM* Vol 30, No 1, January 1987.

Tanenbaum, A.S., and R.V. Renesse. (1985): "Distributed Operating Systems." *ACM Computer Surveys* Vol: 17 No.: 4, December 1985, Pages: 419-470.

Watabe K., Sakata S, Maeno K et al. (1990): ' Distributed Multiparty Desktop Conferencing System: MERMAID', *in proceedings of CSCW 90*, Los Angeles, CA, October 7-10 1990, ACM press , ISBN 0-89791-402-3.

Wilbur S.B., Young R.E.(1988): "The COSMOS Project : A Multi-Disciplinary Approach to Design of Computer Supported Group Working", in R. Speth(ed): *EUTECO 88: Research into Networks and Distributed Applications*, Vienna, Austria, April 20-22,1988.

Winograd T. (1987): "A Language/Action Perspective on the Design of Cooperative Work", Stanford University Department of Computer Science Technical Report, STAN-CS-87-1158.

Proceedings of the Second European Conference on Computer-Supported Cooperative Work
Bannon, L., Robinson, M. & Schmidt, K. (Editors)
September 25-27, 1991, Amsterdam, The Netherlands

Collaborative Activity and Technological Design: Task Coordination in London Underground Control Rooms

Christian Heath Paul Luff

United Kingdom

Despite technical advances in CSCW over the past few years we still have relatively little understanding of the organisation of collaborative activity in real world, technologically supported, work environments. Indeed, it has been suggested that the failure of various technological applications may derive from its relative insensitivity to ordinary work practice and situated conduct. In this paper we discuss the possibility of utilising recent developments within social science, and in particular the naturalistic analysis of organisational conduct and interpersonal communication, as a basis for the design and development of tools and technologies to support collaborative work. Focussing on the Line Control Rooms on London Underground, a complex multimedia environment in transition, we begin to explicate the informal work practices and procedures whereby personnel systematically communicate information and coordinate a disparate collection of tasks and activities. These empirical investigations form the foundation to the design of new tools to support collaborative work in Line Control Rooms; technologies which will be sensitive to the ordinary conduct and practical skills of organisational personnel in the London Underground.

Introduction

Recently there are been significant developments in technologies to support the work of groups of users: shared text editors have been designed to assist people write documents at the same time while using computers at different locations (e.g. Olson, Olson, Mack and Wellner 1990), shared drawing tools have been developed for groups of designers (e.g. Bly 1988), systems have been built so that groups can represent and structure arguments, ideas and designs (Lee 1990), and others aim to support group meetings, group decision making and group communication (Winograd and Flores 1986, Cosmos 1988). These technological developments incorporate innovations in computer architectures, computer networks, audio and video communications. Yet. despite all of these developments, the application of the technology often fails (Grudin 1988, Markus and Connolly 1990). As Galegher and Kraut (1990) outline in the introduction to a recent book on CSCW the technology often 'fails to reflect what we know about social interaction in groups and organizations' (Galegher and Kraut p6). To cope with this problem they call for social scientists to become involved in the design of tools for CSCW.

It may appear strange that such a call is made, given the significant amount of work on social aspects of communication and collaboration that is addressed to a CSCW audience. Although some of this work has described abstract properties of groups there have been several detailed empirical studies set in real-world environments. For example, Linde (1986) has explored the communicative work that takes place in a helicopter cockpit, Hutchins (1990) has described the collaborative use of charts, range-finders and other artifacts to navigate a large vessel and Nardi and Miller (1990) have shown the collaborative aspects of working with computer spreadsheets in an office environment. Though this work has revealed some of the organization of collaborative work implications for the development of technology appear to be difficult to draw. The reasons behind this appear to be in the nature of the technology rather than the results of the study. The technology used in the settings studied by social scientists is usually of quite a different nature to that being currently developed in CSCW and it is often not possible to put the new technologies into real-world, naturalistic settings. This has meant that evaluations of CSCW systems have mostly been carried out as experiments in laboratory settings.

This paper attempts to bridge this gap by describing the details of communicative and collaborative work in a real-world environment which incorporates technology similar to that being developed in the field of CSCW. In common with Suchman and Trigg's (1989) study of communication in an airline terminal operations room this paper aims to show that social scientists can be involved in the design of tools for CSCW. Focusing on the social organisation of cooperative work in a control room, the ways in which various personnel coordinate multiple tasks and utilise a complex array of tools and technologies are explored. This begins to reveal the nature of the interaction between the controllers and their work practices. In particular, the ways in which they collaborate and mutually monitor each others work and communication has implications for the design of further developments to the technology in the control room and to the general design and implementation of shared tools.

Methodological background

The investigation of cooperative work supported by complex technologies demands a rather different conceptual and methodological orientation than that commonly found within research on human-computer interaction. The analysis is no longer primarily concerned with the individual and the system, but rather the interaction between different personnel as they coordinate a range of tasks and utilise various tools. The ability to coordinate activities and the process of interpretation and perception it entails, inevitably relies upon a social organisation; a body of skills and practices which allows different personnel to recognise what each other is doing and thereby produce appropriate conduct. Following recent developments in the psychology of work, we might conceive of this organisation as a form of 'distributed cognition'; a process in which various individuals develop an interrelated orientation towards a collection of tasks and activities (cf. Hutchins 1989, Olson 1990, and Olson and Olson 1991). Yet even this relatively radical reconceptualisation of the relationship between the individual, his activity and the system does not capture the situated and socially organised character of cooperative work. It is not simply that tasks and activities occur within a particular cultural framework and social context, but rather that collaboration necessitates a publicly available set of practices and reasoning which are developed and warranted within a particular setting, and which systematically inform the work and interaction of various personnel.

Whether one subscribes to a theory of distributed cognition or a more sociological conception of cooperative work, it is clear that we need to move away from laboratory studies of cognition, "which have deliberately stripped away the supporting context of the everyday world, in an effort to study 'pure' internal processes" (Olson 1990) and begin to explore task coordination and computer support in real world, everyday work settings. Fortunately, recent developments in social science, namely ethnomethodology and conversation analysis, provide a methodological framework with which to begin to explore the situated and social character of collaborative work. Utilising audio and video recordings, augmented by field observation the process of coordinating multiple activities whilst utilising various tools and technologies can be subjected to detailed and systematic analysis. Drawing on this naturalistic framework, it is hoped that we will not only begin to generate findings concerning the social and interactional organisation of collaborative work, but provide a distinctive method for user-centered design.

The technology in the control room

The Bakerloo Line, London Underground is currently undergoing extensive modernisation. By 1991 signalling will be fully computerised and monitored from the Line Control Room at Baker Street. At the present time, the Bakerloo Line Control Room houses the Line Controller, who coordinates the day to day running of the railway and the Divisional Information Assistant (DIA) whose responsibilities include providing information to passengers through a public address (PA) system and communicating with station managers. Figure 1 shows the general layout of the Control Room.

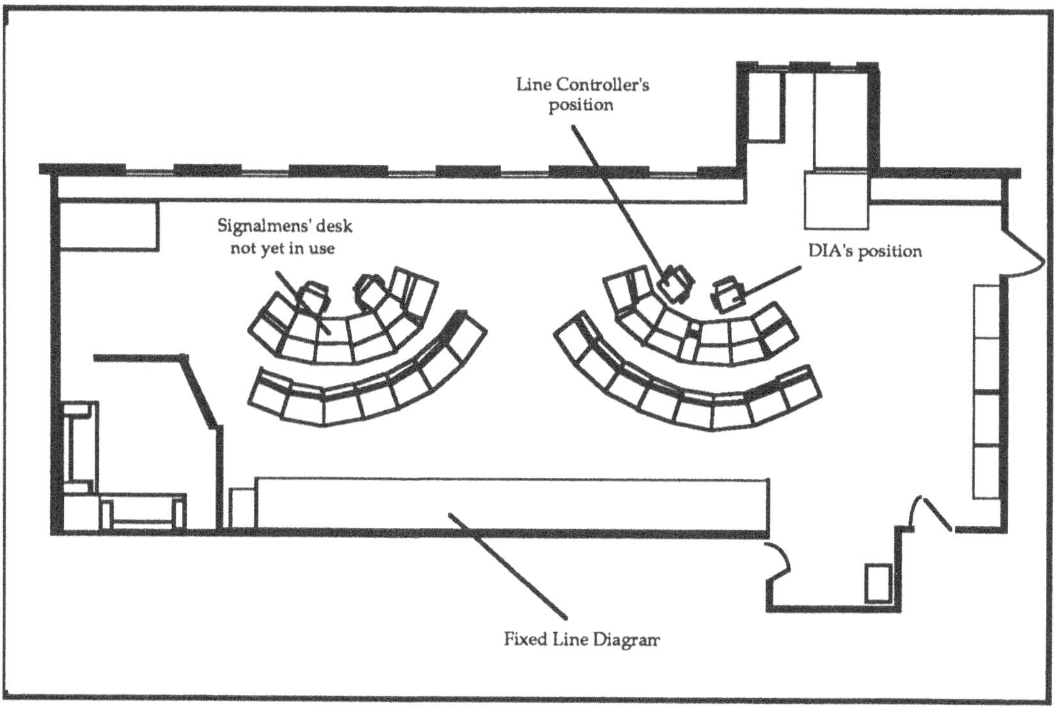

Fig. 1. The Bakerloo Line Control Room

The Controller and DIA sit together at a semicircular console which faces a tiled, real time, hard line display which runs nearly the entire length of the room and shows traffic movement along the Bakerloo Line (from the Elephant and Castle to Queens Park). The console includes touch screen telephones, a radio system for contact with drivers, the PA control keys, and close circuit television (CCTV) monitors and controls for viewing platforms (see Figure 2). Occasionally a trainee DIAs (tDIA) or a second controller will sit at this console. In the near future, two or three signal assistants will sit at a similar console next to the Controller and DIA (see Figure 1) and personnel will also have access to monitors showing real time graphic display of the line. Therefore, the Controller and DIA use a range of devices similar to the technologies being developed in CSCW; they use audio and video channels of communication, a shared display, various keypads and monitors. Revealing some of the practices of the personnel as they utilise these tools, should inform both the further development of technology in the control room and have implications for the design of similar technology elsewhere.

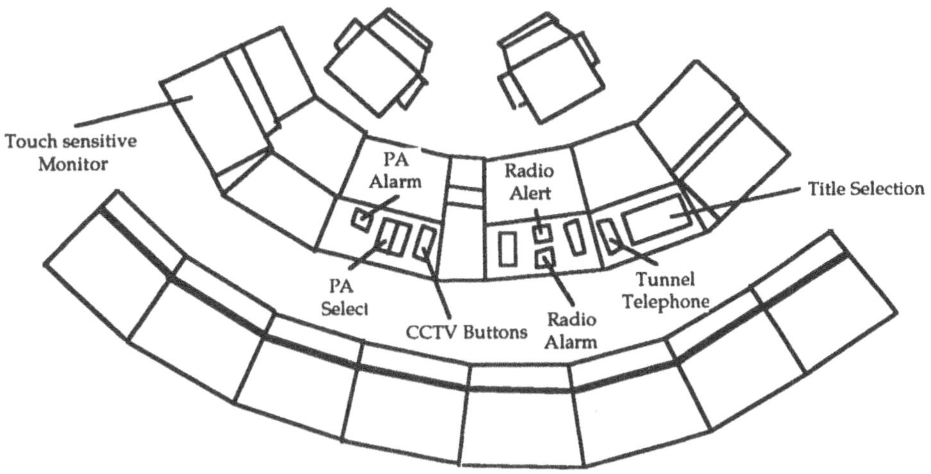

Fig. 2. Line Controller's and DIA's Desk

The Underground service is coordinated through a paper timetable which specifies; the number, running time and route of trains, crew allocation and shift arrangements, information concerning staff travel facilities, stock transfers, vehicle storage and maintenance etc. Each underground line has a particular timetable, though in some cases the timing of trains will be closely tied to the service on a related line. The timetable is not simply an abstract description of the operation of the service, but is used by various personnel including the Controller, DIA, Signalmen, Duty Crew Managers, to coordinate traffic flow and passenger movement. Both Controller and DIA use the timetable in conjunction with their understanding of the current operation of the service to determine the adequacy of the service and if necessary initiate remedial action. Indeed, a significant part of the responsibility of the Controller is to serve as a 'guardian of the timetable' and even if he is unable to shape the service according to its specific details, he should, as far as possible, attempt to achieve its underlying principle; a regular service of trains with relatively brief intervening gaps.

The timetable is not only a resource for identifying difficulties within the operation of the service but also for their management. For example the Controller will make small adjustments to the running times of a particular train to cure a gap which is emerging within the running of the service. More severe problems such as absentees, vehicle breakdowns or difficulties with the electric current, which can lead to severe disruption of the service, are often successfully managed by reforming the service. These adjustments are marked in felt pen on a polythene coated timetable both by the Controller and communicated to Operators (Drivers), Signalmen, the Duty Crew Managers and others when necessary. It is critical that the DIA and others receive the information and make the relevant changes to their timetable otherwise their understanding of the service and their consequent decisions will be incorrect.

Despite important differences in the formal specification of the responsibilities of the Controller and DIA, the various tasks they undertake rely upon extremely close collaboration. Indeed, control room personnel have developed a subtle and complex body of practices for monitoring each other's conduct and coordinating varied collection of tasks and activities. These practices appear to stand independently of particular personnel, and it is not unusual to witness individuals who have no previous experience working together, informally, yet systematically coordinating their conduct. One element of this extraordinary interweaving of often simultaneous responsibilities and tasks is an emergent and flexible division of labour which allows the personnel to manage difficulties and crises.

Public announcements : coordinating passenger movement

The DIA makes public announcements when problems emerge within the 'normal' operation of the service. In particular, they provide information and advice in circumstances in which they envisage that certain passengers may experience difficulties in using the service. So for example, unlike others forms of transport, urban railway systems such as the Underground do not provide a timetable to the public, rather passengers organise their travel arrangement on the assumption that trains will pass through particular stations every few minutes. When such expectations may be broken, or travellers are unable to change at certain stations, or have to leave a train because the line is blocked, then the DIA should provide information and advice. The nature of the announcement varies with the circumstances, though they do tend to some recurrent characteristics. Consider the following instance.

Fragment 1 (Abbreviated and simplified)

DIA: Hello and good afternoon Ladies an Gentlemen. Bakerloo Line Information.

DIA: We have a slight gap in our south bound Bakerloo Line service^ towards the Elephant an Castle. Your next south bound train, should depart from this station in about another three minutes.

DIA: The next south bound train, should depart from this station in about another three minutes.

.........a related announcement follows a couple of minutes later.........

Even though it is a public announcement, apparently addressed to a generalised audience, it achieves its performative force, its relevance, by virtue of its design for a specific category of passenger; its 'recipient design' (cf. Sacks 1966, Sacks, Schegloff and Jefferson 1974). In the case at hand, the information is only delivered to passengers who are are waiting on a particular station and who potentially suffer a slight delay before the next train arrives. The announcement 'fits" with their potential experience of the service at this moment in time and gains its relevance by virtue of that experience. To produce timely and relevant information for passengers, the DIA systematically monitors the service and the actions of his colleagues and transforms these bits and pieces into announcements for passengers using the service at particular moments in time.

Surreptitious monitoring and interrelating tasks

In the space provided· it will be impossible to describe in any detail the interaction between Controller and DIA the foundation to passengers receiving timely information concerning the operation of the service. However, we will try to provide a flavour of the complex skills which underlie their cooperative work. It is perhaps best to begin by mentioning that it is relatively unusual for either the Controller or the DIA explicitly to give information to one another. Rather they rely upon their ability to overhear each other's conversations and mutually monitor their actions even though they may be simultaneously engaged in distinct and apparently unrelated tasks. Through his subtle yet systematic monitoring of the Controller, the DIA can track the operation of the service and design information for passengers. Returning to fragment 1, we can see how the announcement(s) emerge in the light of actions undertaken by the Controller. We enter the scene as the Controller calls a driver.

Fragment 1 Transcript 2 (Abbreviated and simplified)

.............calls driver.............

C: Control to the train at Charing Cross South Bound, do you receive?

............C. Switches monitor to the platform...

C: Control to the train at Charing Cross South Bound, do you receive?

Op: Two Four O Charing Cross South Bound

C:	Yeah, Two Four O. We've got a little bit of an interval behin:nd you. Could you take a couple of minutes in the platform for me please?
Op:	(( )) Over
C:	Thank you very much Two Four O.
	(5.2)
DIA:	Hello and good afternoon Ladies an Gentlemen. Bakerloo Line Information...............

The announcements therefore emerge in the light of the DIA overhearing the Controller's conversation with the driver and assessing its implications for the passengers expectations and experience of the service. He transforms the Controllers request into a relevant announcement, by determining how and who the decision will effect, namely the passengers at Embankment, the station beyond Charing Cross whose next train is delayed as a result of the Controller's request. The subsequent announcement (not included in the above transcript) is designed for those at Charing Cross who now find their train held in the station.

The DIA does not wait until the completion of the Controller's call before preparing to take action. Indeed in some cases its critical that the announcement is delivered as adjustments are being made to the service. In the case at hand, as the call is initiated, we find the DIA progressively monitoring its production and assessing the implications of the Controller's request for his own conduct. The technology, and in particular the hard line display, provides resources through which the DIA can make sense of the Controller's actions and draw the necessary inferences for his own conduct. For example, at the onset of the call he scan's the hard line display to discern why the Controller might wish to speak to the operator. Even by the second attempt to make contact with driver, the DIA is already moving into a position where he will be able to make an announcement. At the word "couple" he is able to infer exactly what's happening and grabs the microphone to inform the passengers of the delay in the service. By the completion of the call, the DIA has set the Public Address system and is ready to make the announcement.

To enable him to provide information to passengers, the DIA monitors the actions of the Controller, using the hard line display and the station monitors to account for his colleague's interventions in the running of the service. The common availability of the same sources of information, allows the DIA and Controller to assume that they can both independently draw similar inferences concerning the operation of the service, and they can witness each other's use of the available systems.

Certain phrases or even single words addressed to an operator or signalman, implicate action for the DIA by virtue of transforming the service for certain passengers. For example, in the following instance, the DIA who is apparently engaged in making changes to his own timetable, suddenly grabs the phone to call a station manager on over hearing the word "reverse".

Fragment 2 (Abbreviated and simplified)

C: Controller to South Bound Two Three Three, do you receive

Op: Two Three Three receiving over.

C: Yeah ,Two Three Three (.) I'd like you to **reverse** at Piccadilly, and you'll also be reformed there. I'll come back to you when you get to Piccadilly. Over?

: *...call continues. Some seconds later the DIA reaches*

: *the station manager at Piccadilly Circus.........*

DIA: Two Three Three is going to reverse with with you, South to North.

Rendering tasks visible

Whilst relying on the DIA's ability to overhear his conversations and draw the necessary inferences, the Controller employs various techniques to keep his colleague informed of various changes to the operation of the service. For example, the Controller frequently 'rewrites' part of the timetable whereby he reschedules particular trains and their crews; a process known as 'reformation'. It is critical that the DIA and other organisational personnel outside the Control Room, know the precise details of any reformations which have are being undertaken. Without these details they will not only misunderstand the current operation of the service, but also in the case on the DIA. provide incorrect information to passengers and staff. The Controller needs to make relevant information available to the DIA, but often, especially during crises in the operation of the service, does not have the time to abandon his various tasks to explicitly inform the DIA of the various changes. Consequently, whilst reforming the service, it is not unusual to find the Controller talking aloud to himself; a technique which allows him to undertake quite complex changes to timetable, whilst simultaneously passing information to the DIA. Interestingly this 'self talk', not only provides the DIA with the details of reformations, but also the reasoning used by the Controller in making the particular changes. Details of which can be crucial for the DIA in deciding how to handle certain problems. Whilst the Controller's talking to himself, it is not unusual for the DIA successively glance at the hard line display and station monitors to determine exactly which trains at which locations are being reformed.

On occasions, it is necessary for the Controller to draw the DIA's attention to particular events or activities, even as they emerge within the management of a certain task or problem. For example, as he is speaking to an operator or signalman, the Controller may laugh or produce an exclamation and thereby encourage the DIA to monitor the call more carefully. Or, as he turns to his timetable or glances at the hard line display, the Controller will swear, feign momentary illness or even sing a couple of bars to a song to draw the DIA's attention to an emergent problem within the operation of the service. The various objects used by the Controller and DIA, to gain a more explicit orientation from the other towards a particular event or activity, are carefully designed to encourage but not demand the other's attention. They allow the individual to continue with an activity with which they might be engaged, whilst simultaneously inviting them to carefully monitor a concurrent event.

In accomplishing various activities therefore, whether its undertaking a reformation or contacting signals to reschedule various changes, the Controller designs his actions so that they simultaneously address various purposes. So for example, on the one hand he will gearing his talk with his co-interactant in the signal box or on the station, whilst at same time design his talk so that its available to, and possibly, structures the participation of his colleagues in the Control Room. The production format (cf. Goffman 1981) of the activity is sensitive to multiple, simultaneous demands, coordinated with the actions of the 'primary recipient' outside the Control Room, whilst being available for and implicating action for the DIA and even a second DIA or Controller. The same activity is produced to organise participation and implicate action both in and outside the Control Room; the activity and the participation framework it generates merge, momentarily, different ecologies within the organisational milieu.

Overseeing the local environment

On occasions the Controller has to explicitly draw the DIA's attention to a particular event. In the following instance, an emergency has arisen at Baker Street and trains have not been stopping at the station. As the DIA provides information to Bakerloo Line passengers, the Controller receives a call giving the 'all clear'.

Fragment 3 (Abbreviated and simplified.)

DIA: Hello and Good Morning Ladies and Gentlemen.

....C answers the phone and begins conversation...

DIA: At Baker Street, Circle, Ham'smith and City, and Metropolitan Line trains, are not stopping at the station as the London Fire Brigade are investigating a report of emergency.

C: *.....puts receiver down, and snaps fingers....*

C: All clear

tDIA: All clear

C: Yep

DIA: Hello Ladies and Gentlemen, a correction to our last message all (........ ......) and Circle Line trains are now stopping at Baker Street Station, this follows London Fire Brigade investigating reports of emergency at that station. All trains on all lines, that includes the Bakerloo Jubilee Metropolitan, Ham'smith and City and Circle Line are now:stopping at Baker Street. Interchange facilities are now ....

Despite receiving information which contradicts the announcement, the Controller avoids interrupting the DIA. As the DIA begins to reach the first possible completion of the announcement, and before it is recycled, the Controller turns towards his colleagues, snaps his fingers and on the possible completion of the utterance, mentions it sis 'all clear'. The trainee DIA responds, but the DIA himself maintains contact with the passengers, forestalls his earlier message, and immediately delivers a modified announcement.

Even in relatively extreme circumstances, the Controller and DIA rarely interrupt each other's activities, but provide overlaying information which will inform how they see the service and the actions they will undertake. There are of course a complex graduation of such objects; moving from the most unobtrusive, to actions which almost demand the attention of the other.

The flow of information between Controller and DIA is not simply one way. Just as the Controller assumes responsibility for keeping his colleague informed, so the DIA will monitor the operation of the service and draw the Controllers attention to any problems which might arise. Consider the following instance. The Controller finishes a conversation on the phone and the DIA attempts to draw his attention to a problem which appears to be emerging at Baker Street on the southbound. Rather than explicitly mentioning the problem to the Controller, the DIA initially successively glances at the hard line display and the station monitor attempting to delicately have his colleague notice, independently, that a problem may be emerging. His glances pass unnoticed and as the Controller begins a new activity, the DIA gently queries the signalman's conduct.

Fragment 4 (Abbreviated and simplified)

...........The Controller puts phone down.....
...DIA successively glances at the hard line display and station monitor, and as the C. returns to read the timetable utters....

DIA: Is he holding that train at Baker in the South?

.....Phone rings: Cii goes to answer: query from shunter and then takes a second call; a query from signals. Throughout the calls the DIA continues to glance at the hard line display and station monitor.......
...........37 seconds later...........

Cii: Controller calling the train Baker Street on the South Bound platform?

:

Cii: Oh I see I just wondering because we are blocking back behind you at the moment......

:

...........Now speaking to signals....

Cii: No no no it's nothin between you an him an they're all piling up behind him. (2.8) Yeh, well let him go at Baker Street please....

((30.00))

DIA: Hello Ladies and Gentlemen Bakerloo Line Information. The next South Bound train just now leaving Ba:ker Street, an will be with you shortly.........

Before the Controller is able to deal with the potential problem, he is interrupted by a couple of phone calls. During these calls the DIA begins once more to make successive glances between the hard line display and the station monitor and shows to the Controller that the problem has not been solved and delay is becoming increasingly severe. As soon as the second call finishes, the Controller attempts to speak to the driver at Baker Street and the DIA quietly returns the activity in which he was engaged before noticing the problem. The hard line display and monitor not only provide the DIA with the possibility of noticing the problem which is emerging within the operation of the service, but also provide for the ability to display the difficulty through his particular use of the system to his colleague. The public availability of the technology's use provides a range of resources for rendering actions visible and coordinating an individual's tasks with colleagues.

The Controller contacts the operator and finding no reason for the delay speaks to the signalman, who is mistakenly holding the train. So, the DIA monitors the operation of the service 'for' the Controller and draws his attention to a potential problem, which implicates various actions for both participants; the remedial activities of the Controller and the public announcements by the DIA rely upon close, moment by moment, cooperation.

The continual flow of information between the Controller and DIA and their ability to monitor, and if necessary correct, each others' actions, are essential features of work in the Control Room. The constant updating of information, coupled with ability and responsibility to make make it 'publicly' available within the Control Room, provides the Controller and the DIA with resources with which to make sense of the operation of the service. Without knowledge of the current circumstances, the timing and movement of vehicles on this occasion, the development of the service and any difficulties on this particular day, Controller and DIA would be liable to draw the wrong inferences from the various sources of information that they have available and risk the possibility of making incorrect decisions. The intelligibility of the scene, the possibility of coordinating tasks and activities, rests upon these communicative and socially organised practices.

An essential feature of these practices are the ways in which the accomplishment of specific tasks and responsibilities are interweaved with an interactional organisation. For example, the ways in which the DIA participates in conversations with Station Managers and the like and accomplishes various activities is not only geared to demands of the particular phone call, but also may simultaneously be designed to monitor a separate conversation between his colleague and a train driver. The accomplishment of one task being embedded within the interactional constraints of simultaneously participating in an unrelated activity. Similarly, for example, in producing an activity such as requesting a driver to 'take a couple of minutes in the station', a Controller is not only sensitive to the overt task at hand and the conduct of his 'primary' recipient, but is also simultaneously designing the activity so that in some part it is available to the DIA and perhaps other's within the Control Room. The accomplishment of specific tasks are embedded within interactional organisation and an overarching responsibility to distribute certain information. The production format of tasks and activities is interweaved with various forms of participation framework.

The usefulness of the hard line display, the CCTV system, and the accompanying tools, relies upon a collection of informal practices through which Controller and DIA coordinate information flow and monitor each others' conduct. Without the information continually being made public and exchanged between the various personnel, the DIA or Controller's interpretation of the scenes presented by the various technologies would be wrong and thereby lead to mistakes and errors. The technology and the information it provides, does not stand independently of the various practices in and through which personnel exchange information and coordinate their actions, rather the use of the various systems is thoroughly dependant upon a current version of train movement, running times and changes to the timetable which are currently being undertaken.

The technology provides individuals with the ability to assess the state of the current operation of the service and undertake specific tasks such as remedial activities and the provision of public information. More importantly perhaps, the hard line display and the station monitors provide the foundation to collaboration between the DIA, Controller and other personnel who may be 'helping out' in the Control Room. We have noted already how the various displays may be used to make sense of a colleague's actions, such as an intervention in the particular running time of a train, or the ways in which the CCTV may be used as an 'objective' source of information concerning the presence of a particular train at a certain station. The technology does not simply provide the resources through which assessments of the state of the service are produced. Rather it provides a set of tools through which the sense of the activities of an individual and his colleagues can be unpicked, placing a single action within the framework of the overall appearance of the traffic. Moreover, the visibility of the use of the technology by a colleague within the Control Room, whether its simply glancing at a particular Station on the hard line display or looking at a platform at a certain station, provides others within the local environment of action to draw various inferences and assess their implications for their own responsibilities and obligations. The technology provides a keystone to the collaboration within the Control Room, not only a source interrelated bodies of information, but critically a medium through which particular activities become visible or publicly available within the local ecology.

Implications for design

The analysis of work practice and interpersonal communication in the Control Room has begun to generate various implications for the design of the current systems and the socio-ergonomic framework of the various interfaces and layout of the technology. More interestingly perhaps, it has begun to identify innovative tools which will support the various responsibilities of Controller, DIA and others within the Control Room and the forms of collaboration that we have begun to discover. One such tool is a real time, screen based timetable, and we are currently exploring the possibility with London Underground of developing an intelligent system which will provide conventional timetable information and the possibility of undertaking complex changes.

In the first instance, the design of the system will be based upon detailed analysis of the conventional use of the current timetable and the type of information which is exchanges between Controller, DIA and others concerning moment by moment changes to the schedule. At the present time, Controller and DIA cover their paper timetables with cellophane sheets which allows them to mark changes and add details with a felt pen and later to remove the various arrows, figures and notes. As noted, the various changes undertaken by the Controller are rarely explicitly told to DIA or others, rather as colleagues pick up the various changes being made they sketch in the reformations and adjustments on their own timetable. By simulating these processes and providing information which is necessary to running the service, we can build a tool which will support the various tasks undertaken with the timetable and the necessary indirect communication which occurs within the Control Room.

It is envisaged that the interface will consist of a screen which presents pages of the timetable which running times alongside scheduled times. The screen will be embedded in the console at various positions so as to allow Controllers, DIA and in the future Signal Assistants direct access. The timetable can be overwritten through the use of electronic pen, and the changes represented in a similar way to that of marking a document. In undertaking reformations and making adjustments, the Controller then sends these changes to his colleagues and they appear on the screen in just the way they were drawn. Besides various other facilities, we plan build in increasing intelligence to the system, initially for example, allowing the Controller to test the consequences of candidate reformations before they are confirmed. Over time, of course, as the system builds up a substantial data base of changes and decisions made by Line Controller's, it will be possible to elicit conventional and candidate solutions from the system to specific problems faced in the operation of the service.

The provisional design of the system therefore is not simply sensitive to the conventional uses of the paper document, but the forms of collaboration undertaken by Controller, DIA and others. It supports the current forms of information exchange, and, by providing running times alongside scheduled times, allows Control Room personnel to identify problems in parallel. The system complements rather than replaces current technologies, but more particularly provides a secure foundation to current informal processes of communication and collaboration. In the long term, it is envisaged that such a tool will help merge the various organisational ecologies within the real time management of the service, communicating timetable changes and adjustments to staff at different locales. For example, within the Control Room the system will prove invaluable to the collaboration between Signal Assistants and the Controller and outside to Duty Crew Managers involved in rearranging crews and their allocation to particular trains.

In designing collaborative tools for the Control Room which are based upon an understanding of current work practice, it should be possible to avoid some of the pitfalls which frequently arise in the introduction of 'inappropriate' systems into a real-world environment. An approach to user-centred design has been outlined that by detailed analysis of the collaborative work of people using various tools and technologies begins to imply appropriate developments to that technology. In the case at hand tools are being designed that facilitate, rather than undermine, the systematic, yet informal, process of collaboration between personnel which forms the foundation to control and passenger information and which also provide for a safe and reliable service.

Acknowledgements

We would like to thank Jens Rasmussen, John Gardner, Bernard Conein and Isaac Joseph for discussions concerning a number of the issues addressed in this paper.

References

Bly , S. A. (1988): "A Use of Drawing Surfaces in Different Collaborative Settings", in *Proceedings of CSCW '88*, 26th-28th September, Portland, Oregon, pp. 250-256.

Cicourel, A. (1973): *Cognitive Sociology: Language and Meaning in Social Interaction*. Penguin, Harmondsworth.

Cosmos (1988): "Specification for a Configurable, Structured Message System", Cosmos Report 68.4 Ext/ALV, Queen Mary College, London.

Galegher, J. and Kraut, R. E. (1990): "Technology for Intellectual Teamwork: Perspectives on Research and Design", in J. Galagher, R.E. Kraut, and C. Egido (eds.):*Intellectual Teamwork: The Social and Technological Foundations of Cooperative Work*, Lawrence Erlbaum Associates, Hillsdale, New Jersey, pp. 1-20.

Garfinkel, H. (1967): *Studies in Ethnomethodology*, Prentice Hall, Englewood Cliffs, N.J.

Goffman, E. (1967): *Interaction Ritual*., Doubleday, New York .

Goffman, E. (1981): *Forms of Talk*, Blackwell, Oxford.

Grudin, J., (1988): "Why CSCW Applications Fail: Problems in the Design and Evaluation of Organizational Interfaces", in *Proceedings of CSCW '88*, Portland, Oregon, 26th-28th September, pp. 85-93.

Gumperz, J. J. (1982): *Discourse Strategies*, Cambridge University Press, Cambridge.

Hutchins, E. (1989): "A cultural view of distributed cognition", Unpublished Manuscript, University of California, San Diego.

Hutchins, E. L. (1990): "The Technology of Team Navigation", in J. Galagher, R.E. Kraut, and C. Egido (eds):*Intellectual Teamwork: The Social and Technological Foundations of Cooperative Work* 191-221. Lawrence Erlbaum Associates, Hillsdale, New Jersey.

Kendon, A. (1977): *Studies in the Behaviour of Social Interaction.*, Peter de Rider Press, Holland (second edition forthcoming with Cambridge University Press).

Lee, J. (1990): SIBYL: "A Tool for Managing Group Decision Rationale", in *Proceedings of CSCW '90,* Los Angeles, California, 7th-10th October 1991, pp. 79-92.

Linde, C. (1986): "Who's in charge here? Cooperative work and authority negotiation in police helicopter missions", in *Proceedings of CSCW '88,* Portland, Oregon, 26th-28th September, pp. 52-64.

Markus, M. L. and Connolly, T. (1990): "Why CSCW Applications Fail: Problems in the Adoption of Independent Work Tools", in *Proceedings of CSCW '90,* Los Angeles, California, 7th-10th October, pp. 371-380.

Moran, T. P. and Anderson, R. J. (1990): "The workaday world as a paradigm for CSCW design", in *Proceedings of the Conference on Computer Supported Collaborative Work.* Los Angeles, California, 7th-10th October, pp. 381-393.

Nardi, B. A. and Miller, J. R. (1990): "An ethnographic study of distributed problem solving in spreadsheet development", in *Proceedings of CSCW '90,* Los Angeles, California, 7th-10th October, pp. 197-208.

Olson, G. M. (1990) "Collaborative Work as Distributed Cognition", Unpublished Manuscript, University of Michigan

Olson, G. M. and Olson, J. S. (1991): "User-Centered Design of Collaboration Technology", *Organisational Computing,* Vol 1, No. 1, pp. 61-83.

Olson, J. S., Olson, G. M., Mack, L. A. and Wellner, P. (1990): "Concurrent editing: the group interface", in *Proceedings of Interact '90 - Third IFIP Conference on Human-Computer Interaction,* Cambridge, 27th - 30th August 27-30, pp. 835-840.

Rasmussen, J. (1989): "Coping with human errors through system design: implications for ecological interface design", *International Journal of Man Machine Studies,* Vol. 31, pp 517-534.

Rasmussen, J., Pejtersen, A. and K. Scmidt (1990): *Taxonomy for Cognitive Work Analysis,* Riso National Laboratory, Roskilde.

Sacks, H. (1966): *Unpublished Transcribed Lectures,* transcribed and indexed by Gail Jefferson. University of California at Irvine.

Sacks, H., Schegloff, E. A. and Jefferson G. (1974): "A Simplest Systematics for the Organisation of Turn Taking in Conversation", *Language,* Vol. 50, pp. 696-735.

Suchman, L. A. and Trigg, R. H. (1989): "Understanding Practice: Video as a Medium for Reflection and Design", Paper prepared for the 12th IRIS Conference, Skagen, Denmark, 13th-16th August 1989.

Winograd, T. and Flores, F. (1986): *Understanding Computers and Cognition: A New Foundation For Design,* Addison-Wesley, Norwood, NJ.

Proceedings of the Second European Conference on Computer-Supported Cooperative Work
Bannon, L., Robinson, M. & Schmidt, K. (Editors)
September 25-27, 1991, Amsterdam, The Netherlands

The Group Facilitator: A CSCW Perspective

Stephen Viller
Department of Computation, UMIST, United Kingdom.

What unites CSCW research is the need to help people work together (Greif, 1988) or, to be more precise, "...the support requirements of cooperative work." (Bannon & Schmidt, 1989). An important contribution to the understanding of these requirements, therefore, are the results from research into group working, its structure, and dynamics. A well recognised concept in group work is the role of the group facilitator; someone who's responsibility it is to assist the group in achieving its objectives. This recognition, however, is not yet reflected by work published under the CSCW banner. This paper aims to take a first step at addressing this omission.

1 Introduction

CSCW is a subject that draws on research in numerous disciplines, such as computer science, psychology, sociology, and artificial intelligence. What distinguishes it from these other areas is that whilst group work may be considered a special interest for them, the provision of computer-support for groups of people working together is central to CSCW (Greif, 1988). Group work itself is a much longer established discipline which can be traced back to the beginnings of sociology and social psychology at the turn of the century (McGrath, 1984). Over this period, a number of concepts have become established in the wealth of research that has been undertaken. For example, the group's task - its reason for existence - can be divided into its content (what is to be achieved) and process (how it is to be achieved). Furthermore, the group process may be divided into task behaviours - aimed at achieving the group's task; and maintenance (or socio-emotional) behaviours - aimed at maintaining the group as a cohesive unit. These two types of behaviour are antagonistic, and group members must engage in both types as they progress towards fulfilment of the task (Smith, Beck, Cooper, Cox, Ottaway & Talbot, 1982). It is in smoothing out the problems in group process that the skills of a facilitator become important. Someone who understands group processes and can therefore assist a group to understand its problems, and find solutions for them, is a valuable asset to any group.

When group interaction takes place via computers, then CSCW is the relevant discipline for its study. The role of the facilitator, however, has been largely neglected by CSCW research, despite the importance of such a role in improving the effectiveness of group work. The need for the facilitator's role to be discussed in the context of CSCW systems is the motivation behind this paper.

In what follows, a description of the facilitator's role is given, and the effects of communication via computer on this role are considered. Four 'CSCW scenarios' are identified, and the facilitator's role is examined in two of them. Finally, the extent to which the role should be supported and/or automated is discussed.

2 The Role of the Facilitator

Research and practice in group work use a multitude of terms for the person who has the facilitating role within a group. In social work and psychotherapy for example, the group may have a *worker* (Douglas, 1970), or *therapist* (Whitaker, 1985). Another major application of group work is in the management sciences, where groups have much clearer defined tasks in terms of furthering the aims of the organisation concerned. These groups are typically made up of members who already exist within some other organisational structure and therefore have an established relationship between one another. These groups will usually have a *leader* (Smith *et al.*, 1982), who will also quite often be the most senior member of the group in terms of the organisational structure.

A feature common to these group situations is the notion of someone who's role is to assist the process of group working, generically referred to as a facilitator. The term facilitator itself denotes a set of skills and behaviours that may be applied by a group-worker, teacher, manager, therapist, coordinator, and so on. The application of these skills may be different in the various contexts. Nevertheless, "facilitator" is a readily identifiable, common 'core' of skills and behaviours that may be used by any of the above.

The Shorter Oxford English Dictionary defines facilitate as "To render easier; to promote, help forward". The role of a group facilitator, therefore, is concerned with assisting the other group members in performing their collective task as a group.

2.1 The 'Central Person'

Early work on the role of the group facilitator introduced the concept of the *central person* (Redl, 1942). This person is so named because s/he evokes a common emotional response in the other group members, and the group formative processes take place through her/him. Redl defined this person as someone who provides an object of identification, an object of drives, and an ego support for the other members of the group. Douglas (1970) states that this role definition is not very useful in itself because of the static nature in which it treats groups. Heap (1968) noted, however, that the static description of the central person applies very well to the initial stages of a group's development, and can therefore be modified to take into account the dynamics of group work.

At the initial stages in a group's lifecycle, the relationship towards the facilitator may be all that is common to the other group members, and thus the facilitator becomes the group's central person. A facilitator, with their knowledge of group process, can utilise this position to improve group cohesion, and for the setting of group norms. As a group develops, individuals will identify themselves more as group members, and the common relationship of everyone towards the central person will become less important (Douglas, 1970). During these middle stages of the group's lifecycle, the central person's role is much more that of enabler, sitting back from the group and only intervening when necessary. Finally, as the group nears its end, the role of the central person becomes more important again, as s/he assists the other members through the process of winding-up the group. The precise role played by the facilitator at this stage will depend upon the circumstances in which the group is breaking up; for example, whether or not the group has fully achieved its purpose (Douglas, 1970).

2.2 Membership Status

Opinions differ on the facilitator's status within a group. Some of this difference can be explained by the 'bias' of the source. For example, if the facilitator is to perform some leadership function for the group - as in management situations - then s/he will be in a position of power over the other group members. Conversely, if s/he is someone who is brought in from outside of the group as a professional facilitator, then her/his function will be more of an assistant to the group, helping the other group members to achieve their objectives without having any stake in the outcome. This second example describes the facilitator's role in its generic sense, the key factor being that the facilitator is concerned with enabling the *process* of the group achieving its aims, whilst having no stake in the *content* of these aims. Three different views of this relationship between facilitator and group are presented in figure 1, which is adapted from Douglas (1970). The first viewpoint is the status of the facilitator when a group is first set up, the second illustrates the status of the facilitator in its generic sense, whilst the third represents when a member of the group performs the role of the facilitator (as in management situations).

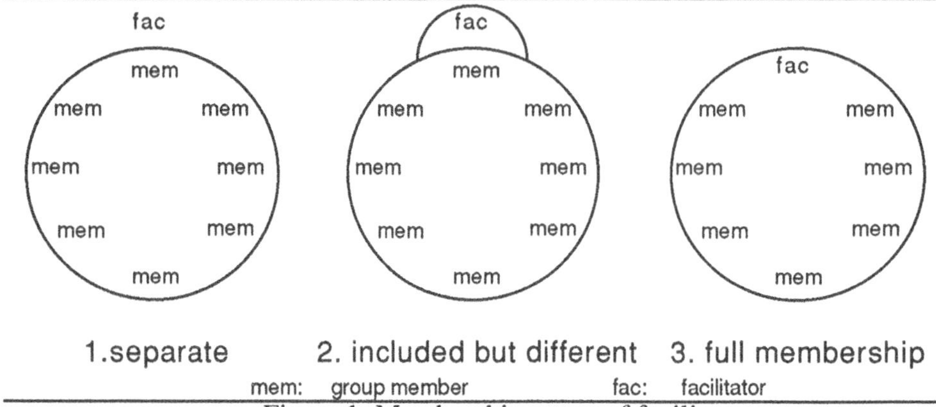

Figure 1: Membership status of facilitator

2.3 Intervention strategies

The role of the facilitator described so far is open to criticism for its relatively static nature. A group working environment is by no means static, with participation by, and relationships between, the various members changing throughout a group's life. Whilst the dynamic aspect of group work is one of its advantages, problems can develop, and when they occur the facilitator's role takes on greater importance. It is necessary for any facilitator to be able to recognise when a problem is developing, and to also have the skill and knowledge of how to enable the group to deal with it. Any action that a facilitator takes to 'correct' group process problems is known as an *intervention.* Five *Generic Problem Syndromes* (along with their symptoms, possible causes, and possible interventions) have been identified by Westley & Waters (1988) - presented in table I - along with two intervention methods: *Interpretation*; and *Direct Action.*

2.3.1 Interpretation Method

This type of intervention involves the facilitator shifting the focus of the group away from task-content to process in two steps. First of all, after a process problem has been diagnosed, the facilitator articulates the observed cues to the group in as neutral a manner as possible. Descriptive language is used, whilst avoiding over-generalising and being evaluative. Subsequently, the group is directed to focus on the process problem that has been identified. If the facilitator has a clear picture of the problem, then a diagnosis can be proposed to the group. Alternatively, s/he can invite the group to discuss the problem as a result of her/his reporting it. The following discussion in the group should aim at solving the identified problem. For this, it is essential that the facilitator is capable of suggesting a *design* for the solution - how the group can solve its problem and return to the content of its task - otherwise a breakdown in the group is inevitable.

'Multi-Headed Beast' syndrome

SYMPTOMS	Digressions; interruptions; multiple topics; no listening; no integration of ideas.
POSSIBLE CAUSES	No agreement on agenda; no process design; mixing problem-solving strategies.
POSSIBLE INTERVENTIONS	• Suggest round robin to clarify task • List perceptions of task • Seek synthesis (rephrase, find continuities, categories) • Formulate/reformulate agenda

'Feuding Factions' syndrome

SYMPTOMS	Repetitious arguments; open attacks, anger.
POSSIBLE CAUSES	Hidden agendas/power struggles; fear of change.
POSSIBLE INTERVENTIONS	• Stop action: "we're having difficulty agreeing on a solution..." • Allow individual to privately list criteria • List criteria independently of alternatives • Measure alternatives against criteria.

'Dominant Species' syndrome

SYMPTOMS	'Plops'; 'unequal air-time'; passive/aggressive body language; withdrawal
POSSIBLE CAUSES	Dominance: not heard, frustrated Withdrawn: afraid, frustrated, insulated
POSSIBLE INTERVENTIONS	**Direct:** question/poll under-participators; thank/limit over-participators **Interpretative:** At end of meeting, share perceptions on levels of participation • self rating • round robin on views • solicit norms on participation

'Recycling' syndrome

SYMPTOMS	'Broken record' behaviour; irritation with lack of progress; failure to gain consensus.
POSSIBLE CAUSES	Ideas not being recorded; confusion about problem-solving process.
POSSIBLE INTERVENTIONS	• Introduce/reintroduce problem-solving steps • identify which issues belong to which steps • identify 'where we are, where we've been, where we're going'.

'Sleeping Meeting' syndrome

SYMPTOMS	Long silences; absence of energy/ideas; withdrawal.
POSSIBLE CAUSES	Fear of volatile issue; hostility; depression, fatigue.
POSSIBLE INTERVENTIONS	• Describe observation - 'blocked condition of meeting' • Suggest mood-check • Then: - take a break - address underlying problem - decide on action plan to rectify • and/or - return to task, allotting time to address the problem at end of meeting.

Table I: Generic Meeting Problem Syndromes

2.3.2 Direct Action Method

As opposed to the above method, where the flow of the meeting is suspended to deal with a process problem. This method directly manipulates the processes of the group, for example: preventing interruptions until the current speaker finishes; or encouraging a hesitant participant by giving positive feedback to their contribution. This type of intervention is not suited to all situations, or to all individual facilitation styles. It would be unsuitable, for example, if the problem is part of an underlying trend that would be better dealt with explicitly through the use of an interpretative intervention.

The choice of intervention method made by the facilitator will depend upon both the nature of the problem, and on the facilitator's personality and experience of group working. The interpretative method is more likely to be successful for a facilitator who is not very experienced or who is not sure how to solve a particular problem. Either method may be resisted by the other group-members, although the interpretative method is less likely to be seen as manipulative.

3 Face-to-Face versus Computer-mediated Communication

Having introduced the facilitator's role in its traditional sense, this section will give a brief comparison of face-to-face and computer-mediated communication, prior to investigating 'electronic' facilitators, and their role in CSCW.

Face-to-face communication can be broken down into audio and visual channels, with each being decomposed further, as shown in figure 2 (Hiltz & Turoff, 1978). This model of face-to-face communication illustrates the richness of the medium, thus allowing a facilitator many ways of monitoring, and intervening in the group process, in a face-to-face meeting.

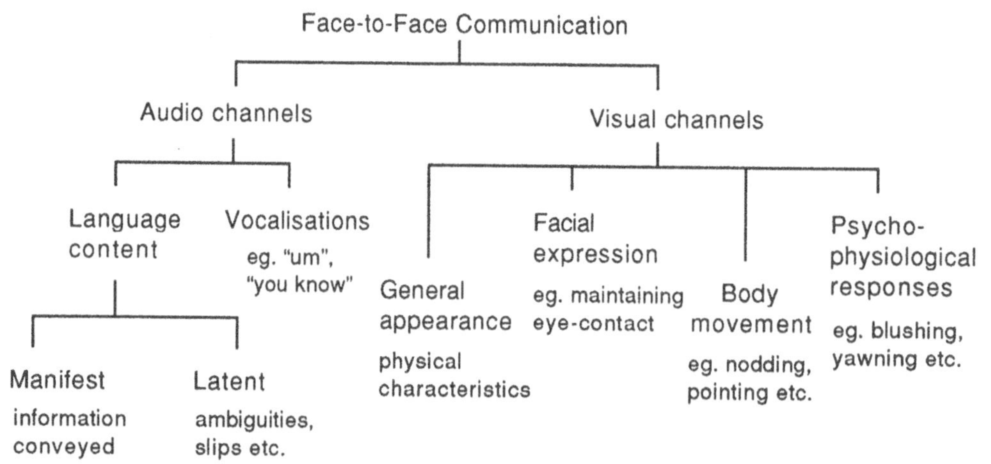

Figure 2: Face-to-face Communication Model

Communicating via computers replaces the above channels with (usually) a single visual channel conveying the language content. This can have a number of effects on the quality of communication, and obviously has implications for the facilitator's role in the group. Some of the differences are outlined below.

3.1 Extra Visual Channel

The written form of computer mediated communication provides an additional visual channel for participants to utilise. The use of indentation, numbering, capital letters, and spacing enables individuals to structure their communication, thus aiding comprehension by the message's recipients.

3.2 Expression

The visual channels convey information about the speaker and hearer's feelings as well as enabling the use of gestures to reinforce what is being said. Without this information, participants can only use the structure of their text to provide emphasis; and they can only treat messages on 'face value', being without access to any signals that may indicate deliberate misinformation, for example, on the part of the 'speaker' (eg. lack of eye contact).

3.3 Precision

Not only are individuals able to structure their messages, they can take as long as they wish to do so, taking time to ensure that what they write is expressed correctly. This leads to more organised communication than is usually observed in a face-to-face situation.

3.4 Participation

Without the information about people's general appearance etc. being conveyed, individuals from the groups in society that are traditionally discriminated against (eg. women, disabled people, or people of different ethnic origin), stand more chance of being treated according to what they say rather than what they look like.[1]

3.5 Turn-Taking

In face-to-face communication, the cues governing turn-taking in conversation are usually conveyed as vocalisations, through body language, and by facial

---

1 This could only now be said to apply to the more primitive mailing systems that provide very little information about the sender. It also assumes that the sender does not, intentionally or unintentionally, reveal the information, eg. in their message style.

expression (Levinson, 1983). Therefore, the removal of the audio and visual channels in computer-mediated communication interferes with the normal turn-taking mechanisms. This affects synchronous, rather than asynchronous communication, with messages in the latter mode potentially taking up more than one turn in a conversation (Bowers & Churcher, 1988).

4 The Facilitator in CSCW

A broadly accepted framework for the study of CSCW systems classifies the type of work according to its temporal and geographical distribution (eg. (Cook, Ellis, Graf, Rein & Smith, 1987), (Ellis, Gibbs & Rein, 1991)). In this two-dimensional space, four types of cooperative working can be identified (see figure 3). These working types correspond to four different meeting types, or scenarios, in which the cooperative work is supported by computers. The remainder of this section will concentrate on two of these scenarios, and the implications on the role of a group facilitator in each one is discussed.

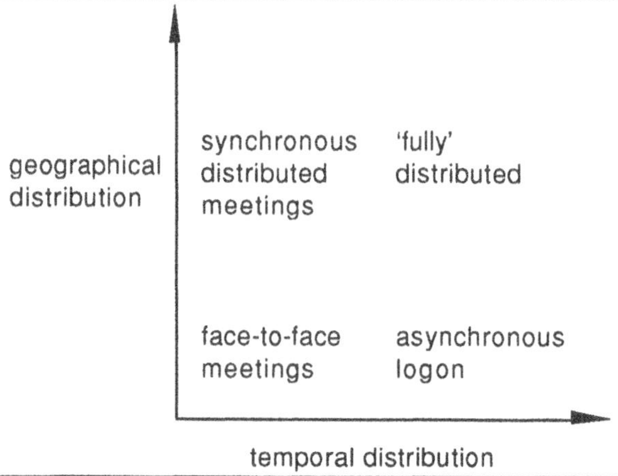

Figure 3: CSCW Scenarios

4.1 'Fully' Distributed

This is the longest established type of computer-mediated communication, and (probably because of this) the only scenario for which specific research on the facilitator's role was found (known usually in this context as the *moderator* (Brochet, 1985), (Feenberg, 1986), (Kerr, 1986)). Computer Conferencing systems, or Bulletin Board systems, have been in use since the late 1960's, and numerous examples exist in both academic and industrial contexts (Quarterman & Hoskins, 1986), encompassing early systems, such as EIES (Hiltz & Turoff, 1978) through to recent Computer-Based Messaging Systems, such as COSMOS (Young, 1988).

Facilitating (moderating) computer conferencing systems is seen as a means of reducing communication problems that are due to the lack of the face-to-face communication channels. Whilst it is acknowledged that a conference can be successful in the absence of a facilitator, this is the exception to the rule (Brochet, 1985). Feenberg (1986) outlines seven functions that characterise the role of the facilitator in computer conferences, these are: Setting the contexts, setting the norms, setting the agenda, recognition, prompting, weaving[2], and meta-commenting.

If the last four of the above items are shared by other members of the group, the conference is likely to be more successful, in fact, Feenberg (1986) states that they are listed as functions of the moderator more to ensure that they are carried out, rather than being exclusive to the facilitating role.

Brochet (1985) gives a different classification in terms of what stage the conference is at. The stages given are:

- Successful beginnings;
- Nurturing the introductory stages;
- Maintaining the mature conference; and
- Wrapping up the conference.

Successful beginnings is concerned with the setting up of the conference - deciding on the topic, setting an agenda, inviting potential participants, etc. Also included at this stage are activities such as organising training on the system to be used; introductory 'parties', where participants may meet face-to-face; and maybe also organising an initial face-to-face meeting to get the conference started. Kerr (1986) also encourages the setting-up of a face-to-face training session to assist group cohesion.

The introductory stages require nurturing on three levels: firstly, the facilitator must ensure that both system hardware and software are available and serviceable; secondly, the facilitator needs to set ground-rules and norms regarding, for example, defining success for the group, group decision-making process(es) used, and copyright issues; finally, the facilitator is responsible for stimulating discussion and identifying new topics.

During the 'mature' stages of the conference, the facilitator plays a number of roles to maintain participation and cohesion amongst the members of the conference. Brochet (1985) gives these roles as: organiser; goal-setter; discriminator[3]; host; explainer; and entertainer. The facilitator must ensure that discussion does not stray off the agreed topic of the conference, if necessary highlighting the need for a separate conference to be set up for the discussion of matters arising from the present topic.

---

2 This function in particular illustrates an effect of the communication medium on the facilitator's role. Here, the phenomena of multiple turns in messages (Bowers & Churcher, 1988) necessitates the 'weaving' together of threads of one conversation across many messages.

3 As in discriminating between useful and useless ideas, and in helping to make complex matters simple.

It is helpful to announce the 'wrapping-up' of a conference well in advance, as this type of announcement can quite often lead to a flurry of last-minute contributions. The facilitator should close the conference down in two stages: firstly making it into a 'read-only' conference, allowing participants to copy any information they wish to keep; then finally 'purging' the conference from the system.

In this scenario, the facilitator must assist the group as in a face-to-face meeting, whilst working via a modified communication medium as described in section 3. Important cues used by the facilitator in face-to-face settings are now missing, and the asynchronous nature of this scenario requires her/him to work with the group over days or weeks rather than minutes or hours. Support for the facilitator in this scenario, therefore, must compensate for these aspects of the communication medium that make her/his job harder. Without specific support, for example, the facilitator will not know how much the different members are participating, other than through the number and length of messages transmitted. The system, however, is able to monitor such things as login frequency, messages that have not been read by individuals, activity on text editors etc. This information can be provided to the facilitator in such a way as to supplement her/his 'picture' of the group's performance, and to enable her/him to facilitate more effectively.

4.2 Computer-Supported Meetings

Participants in this type of meeting are able to use all of the usual face-to-face channels, in addition to the extra visual channel provided by computer-mediated communication. It is unlikely, however, that both types of communication will be used simultaneously to their full; experiences indicating that participants will switch between the two (see, eg. Foster & Stefik (1986)). The facilitator, therefore, will also need to switch to whichever means of communication the other group members are using at the time.

This type of cooperative working is the focus for a growing number of research projects and systems, with more established examples being Colab at Xerox PARC (Foster & Stefik, 1986), (Stefik, Bobrow, Foster, Lanning & Tatar, 1987), and Project Nick at MCC (Cook *et al.*, 1987). Of the two projects, Colab appears to 'hard-wire' the role of the facilitator by incorporating it into the processes of its tools. For example, the Cognoter tool (Foster & Stefik, 1986) structures a group's efforts in collaboratively organising their thoughts for the purpose of making a presentation. With this tool, the process is supported in three stages: *brainstorming*; *ordering*; and *evaluation*, with the participants guided through the process by the tool. Whilst noting the danger of the tool being too prescriptive, they also recognise that a 'funneling' environment would assist group-members to achieve their goals in a more efficient manner. In other words, the tool implements some aspects of the facilitator's role and 'imposes' this facilitation through the structuring of the process.

Project Nick (Cook *et al.*, 1987), however, supports a human facilitator with the provision of the following features: there is a means for the facilitator to record the group-process activities using minimal keystrokes/mouse movements; in addition to this, there is an allowance for other group-members to communicate comments about the group-process to the facilitator. The facilitator is thus able to keep a record of, for example, how much time is spent participating in the group process by the various individual members, and therefore monitor over or under participation, as well as keep an overall record of the time taken for different agenda items etc. Furthermore, explicit comments on members' feelings about the group process (eg. boredom, need to push on, etc.) can be received by the facilitator to enhance the information that s/he has collected through her/his participation in the group session. This information can be used to facilitate the group in a more effective manner and will supplement the facilitator's impressions of the group process obtained through observing the members' interactions, as in face-to-face communication.

In this scenario, therefore, the facilitator has a larger choice of communication channels to use for monitoring the group process. At the same time, s/he has the same increased choice of channel to use when making interventions. For example, eye contact can be utilised to prevent an interruption with less distraction for the other group members. Similarly, there is less need to prevent sub-groups or side-discussions from forming since these also can take place, to a large extent, without distraction for the other members of the group.[4] Means to monitor such communication, that is potentially detrimental to the group's working together as a unit, should be provided for the facilitator. The extent to which such monitoring could take place - should facilitators be allowed to 'tap' private conversations, or should they only be provided information regarding who is talking to whom, and how often? - is an area for debate, dependant upon how much 'power' is desirable for a facilitator to have over other group members.

5 Allocation of Tasks

When allocating tasks for a computer system between the computer and its user(s), the extent to which the tasks are automated can be looked at as a continuum between no support (a completely human system) through to full support (a completely automated system). These two extremes, however, will not be considered here. Considering the importance of the facilitator's role, to provide computer support for a group without specifically supporting the facilitator is to make the task of facilitating the group harder, and less effective. Furthermore, group facilitation is an essentially human task, which if carried out by computer

4 There are obviously limits to this as a sub-group or side-discussion could take over the discussion for the whole group, with those not involved unaware except for their knowledge of keyboards being used without any resultant messages appearing on their screens.

alone will not be fulfilled sufficiently. This section will consider, therefore, how computer support can augment the role of the facilitator in terms of her/his individual tasks, and group tasks.

5.1 Support for Individual Tasks

The individual tasks referred to here are the tasks that a facilitator carries out when working with a group, that are private to the facilitator. Over and above the tools that each member of the group will possess to support their tasks (for example, word processing facilities, 'notebook', graphics generation, database access etc.), there are tasks specific to a facilitator that must also be supported. These facilitator support tools should be aimed at supporting the tasks that are seen as the facilitator's responsibility, and will include: time-keeping aids; monitoring of the group in terms of degree of participation of each member; creation and maintenance of an agenda; and support for administrative tasks.

These support tools are therefore aimed at the level of collecting and structuring information about the group to enable the facilitator to make 'better informed' decisions and to facilitate more effectively. For example, an agenda creation and maintenance tool could be combined with a time-keeping aid in order to set points in the agenda that should be reached by a certain time (in order to coordinate with another group working on a related task perhaps). These times should be agreed upon by the whole group during its initial stages and the tool can then keep the facilitator informed as to how well the group is running to schedule. The emphasis here, then, is that any such tool is providing information, not directives, and how the group is conducted is still down to the judgement of the individual facilitator. In a similar vein, providing a monitoring tool will enable a facilitator to have a clear picture of which group-members are monopolising the discussion, or conversely, which members are under-participating. Once again, the tool should be aimed at providing the facilitator with structured information that can be acted upon, or not, as decided by the individual facilitator.

5.2 Support for Group Tasks

In contrast with the above, this allocation of tasks sees the computer taking a more 'active' role in group facilitation. In essence, this is an extension of the above allocation, with the computer automating part of the facilitator's role, rather than just supporting it. Obviously, it would be easy to propose that the tools required in such a system would simply continue with the information as structured by the tools mentioned above, and act upon it according to some heuristics. Whilst this sounds fine in theory, decisions would have to be made in practice as to whether group members will find computer-made interventions desirable. Similarly, the parts of the facilitator role that are automated should not require other members of the group to modify the way in which they interact with each other, as this would almost certainly be resisted (Grudin, 1988).

Another aspect of the facilitator's role that could be automated is the support of decision-making procedures. Kraemer & King (1986), review a number of group-support technologies and includes three methods of automating the group decision-making process. These *structured group process* methods are: social judgement analysis, delphi technique; and nominal group technique.

In reviewing the above, McGrath (1984) notes that when compared with interactive groups (as opposed to structured), all the methods perform better than the average, but significantly worse than the 'best individual' performance (they actually perform at about the same level as second best individual). It can be seen, therefore, that whilst they can all potentially be automated, they are by no means perfect.

One further area that has potential for automation is the monitoring of over and under participation of the group-members. This monitoring would take different forms dependent upon the scenario in which it is used. Essentially, this would go one step further than the supported individual task of reporting the amount of participation to the facilitator by the system. Rather than structuring the information to enable the facilitator to make better informed interventions, the system itself would make the interventions, perhaps by informing participants of the proportion of group participation they 'are responsible for', if they exceed or fall below certain limits. As mentioned above, the way in which system interventions are made will have to be decided upon carefully to avoid putting off people from becoming members of the group.

6 Conclusion

The omission, to a large extent, of any consideration for the role of the facilitator in CSCW systems was the impetus for the work presented in this paper. The facilitator is a well established and important role in 'traditional' group work, existing to enable the other members of a group to achieve the group's objectives by assisting them in negotiating any problems that may occur.

Communicating via computer has a number of effects on the interaction between members of a group, and therefore on the actions undertaken by the facilitator when performing her/his duties. These effects differ depending upon the 'scenario' in which the interaction takes place, but are primarily due to the removal of the face-to-face channels of communication, the addition of a new computer-mediated channel, and interaction between usage of the two types of channel.

To provide support for a group without also supporting the group's facilitator is an omission which inevitably will be detrimental to the effectiveness of the group. Therefore, support for the facilitator's role must be considered when designing CSCW systems. How the role could, or should, be supported is a matter for further research. The extent to which the role is supported, or automated, in particular CSCW systems will depend on the application concerned. Consideration must be given, however, to the effect that this support will have on the facilitator, and especially on the other members of the group.

Acknowledgements

I would like to thank Martin Lea (Department of Psychology, University of Manchester) and Linda Macaulay (Department of Computation, UMIST) for their encouragement and assistance throughout the production of this paper. This paper is the result of work funded by a SERC Advanced Course Studentship at the University of Manchester Department of Psychology.

References

Bannon, L.J. & Schmidt, K. (1989): "CSCW: four characters in search of a context", in J.Bowers & S.Benford (ed.): *EC-CSCW'89: Proceedings of the First European Conference on Computer Supported Cooperative Work*, Computer Sciences Company, Gatwick, UK, pp. 358-372.

Bowers, J. & Churcher, J. (1988): "Local and global structuring of computer mediated communication: developing linguistic perspectives on CSCW in COSMOS", in I.Greif (ed.): *CSCW'88 Proceedings of the Conference on Computer-Supported Cooperative Work*, ACM, Portland, Oregon, pp. 125-139.

Brochet, M.G. (1985): "Effective moderation of computer conferences: notes and suggestions", in M.Brochet (ed.): *17th Ontario Universities Computing Conference Proceedings*, pp. 123-130.

Cook, P., Ellis, C., Graf, M., Rein, G. & Smith, T. (1987): "Project Nick: meetings augmentation and analysis", *ACM Transactions on Office Information Systems*, vol. 5, no. 2, pp. 132-146.

Douglas, T. (1970): *A Decade of Small Group Theory, 1960-1970*, Bookstall Publications, London.

Ellis, C.A., Gibbs, S.J. & Rein, G.L. (1991): "Groupware: some issues and experiences", *Communications of the ACM*, vol. 34, no. 1, pp. 38-58.

Feenberg, A. (1986): "Network design: an operating manual for computer conferencing", *IEEE Transactions on Professional Communications*, vol. PC29, no. 1, pp. 2-7.

Foster, G. & Stefik, M. (1986): "Cognoter, theory and practice of a Colab-orative tool", in D.Petersen (ed.): *CSCW'86- Proceedings of the Conference on Computer-Supported Cooperative Work*, ACM, Austin, Texas, pp. 7-15.

Greif, I. (1988): "Overview", in I.Greif (ed.): *Computer Supported Cooperative Work: A Book of Readings*, Morgan Kaufmann Publishers Inc., San Mateo, CA, pp. 5-12.

Grudin, J. (1988): "Why CSCW applications fail: problems in the design and evaluation of organisational interfaces", in I.Greif (ed.): *CSCW'88 Proceedings of the Conference on Computer-Supported Cooperative Work*, ACM, Portland, Oregon, pp. 85-93.

Heap, K. (1968): *The Social Group Worker as Central Person*, Case Conference, Cited in Douglas (1970).

Hiltz, S.R. & Turoff, M. (1978): *The Network Nation. Human Communication via Computer*, Addison-Wesley, Reading, MA.

Kerr, E.B. (1986): "Electronic leadership: a guide to moderating online conferences", *IEEE Transactions on Professional Communications*, vol. PC29, no. 1, pp. 12-18.

Kraemer, K. & King, J.L. (1986): "Computer-based systems for cooperative work and group decision making: status of use and problems in development", in D.Petersen (ed.): *CSCW'86- Proceedings of the Conference on Computer-Supported Cooperative Work*, ACM, Austin, Texas, pp. 353-375.

Levinson, S.C. (1983): *Pragmatics*, Cambridge University Press, Cambridge.

McGrath, J.E. (1984): *Groups: Interaction and Performance*, Prentice-Hall, Englewood Cliffs.

Quarterman, J.S. & Hoskins, J.C. (1986): "Notable computer networks", *Communications of the ACM*, vol. 29, no. 10, pp. 932-971.

Redl, F. (1942): "Types of group formation, group emotion and leadership.", *Psychiatry*, vol. V, no. 4.

Smith, M., Beck, J., Cooper, C.L., Cox, C., Ottaway, D. & Talbot, R. (1982): *Introducing Organisational Behaviour*, Macmillan, Houndmills.

Stefik, M., Bobrow, D.G., Foster, G., Lanning, S. & Tatar, D. (1987): "WYSIWIS revised: early experiences with multiuser interfaces", *ACM Transactions on Office Information Systems*, vol. 5, no. 2, pp. 147-167.

Westley, F. & Waters, J.A. (1988): "Group facilitation skills for managers", *Management Education and Development*, vol. 19, no. 2, pp. 134-143.

Whitaker, D.S. (1985): *Using Groups to Help People*, Tavistock/Routledge, London.

Young, R.E. (1988) (ed.): *Interim Report on the Cosmos Project*, Cosmos Coordinators Office, Queen Mary College, London.

Proceedings of the Second European Conference on Computer-Supported Cooperative Work
Bannon, L., Robinson, M. & Schmidt, K. (Editors)
September 25-27, 1991, Amsterdam, The Netherlands

Idea Management In a Shared Drawing Tool

Iva M. Lu and Marilyn M. Mantei *
Department of Computer Science
University of Toronto
Canada
* also with the Faculty of Library and Information Science

Abstract

The generation of design ideas in group discussion is a complex and dynamic process. Some design ideas are accepted; others are rejected; many others are modified and combined. The fluent expression of ideas and the ability to interact and build on representations created by others contributes significantly to the idea generation process. Computerized shared drawing tools support this fluency and interaction, but such tools need to aid not only the drawing process but also the management of design ideas during group interaction. This paper lays the groundwork for the design of the idea management portion of a shared drawing tool. It presents a taxonomy of group idea management activities, identifies user requirements in support of these behaviours, and illustrates how the user requirements are satisfied by features in CaveDraw, an experimental shared drawing system.

1. Introduction

Because modern technology is complex, it is unusual for an individual to tackle the design of a major project single-handedly. Often, a small team is gathered at the initial stage of the design process introducing problems of organization, coordination and communication. Sketches are an important coordination tool for the shared design process and group communication. This group communication can be faciliated by computerized shared drawing tools which permit simultaneous sketching by team members in different locations. Although these shared drawing tools are exceedingly useful, we believe that the management of multiple inputs remains a significant issue in their design.

Observational studies have identified several critical factors in the design of shared drawing tools. These factors are derived from analyzing and interpreting collaborative workspace activities. Tang and Leifer (1988) point out that different workspace activities occur with different work mediums (e.g., whiteboard, private notebooks), different tasks (e.g., mechanics, architecture), and different time-scale problems (e.g., multi-year versus two-week projects).

We believe that understanding the group process of creating and manipulating task artifacts — sketches in a shared workspace — will allow us to identify user requirements in a shared drawing tool. We focus solely on group behaviours as members manage and manipulate design ideas and ignore variables like cohesiveness and prior design training. Akin (1979) shows that the more imaginative design alternatives and major design conflicts are often recognized while staring at sketches. We believe that supporting group behaviour in manipulating the sketches plays a central role in fostering this creativity. We note that Grudin (1989) has pointed out that lack of understanding of group behaviour is one of the reasons for groupware failure.

In this paper we are concerned with the design of tools that support idea management. Although no direct evidence exists to demonstrate that idea management is an important consideration in the design of shared drawing tools, we suspect this is an important issue based on empirical evidence from studies of individual designers using design aids. Ullman, Stauffer and Dietterich (1987) noted that in an individual design session, designers tended to forget some of the ideas they formulated. Yeomans (1982) discovered similar recall failures. Ullman et al. (1987) also found that a team of designers often worked at different levels of abstraction in their design, making it difficult to integrate the final products.

We also examine studies of group design that did not have the use of shared drawing tools. Rouse and Boff (1987) note the following group design behaviour:

> If an outside observer were to characterize designers' behaviors, particularly for complex domains such as aircraft design, it is quite likely that such an observer would conclude that chaos is the most appropriate characterization of design teams at work.

They explain the chaos as arising from different design philosophies that designers bring to a design team. Scheidel and Crowell (1964) describe group decision making as an idea-in-the-making process wherein one member suggests an idea, another modifies it and a third changes its focus until the final agreed upon solution unfolds. This process of cooperative work in the building of a group decision becomes too complex as more participants are involved. None of the above studies indicate that the outcomes of a design are affected by lack of idea management and no studies have been done on its use in shared drawing tools. However, throughout Section 3, we provide evidence from the literature that strongly suggests that the idea management criteria we propose is valid.

Design ideas are much more than sketches. They also embody task context, conversational exchanges, gestures and the order in which all of these take place. When we use the term "design idea" we loosely refer to the sketches actually laid out on the drawing surface. Thus, we focus on the tasks of choosing, comparing, and integrating multiple design sketches. We use these tasks to classify those areas that would benefit from design idea management tools. We propose a set of user requirements for the design of multi-user shared drawing tools and illustrate the requirements in the design of a prototype, CaveDraw. CaveDraw is a shared tool running within a multi-media environment at the University of Toronto (Mantei, Baecker, Sellen, Buxton, Milligan & Wellman, 1991).

2. The Approach

To develop our user requirements, we studied videotapes of drawing space activities collected by various researchers. We have also drawn on prior research in engineering design studies, group communication and social psychology. We focused primarily on the interactions between collaborators as they manipulate current and previous design ideas. Our research plan is illustrated in Figure 1.

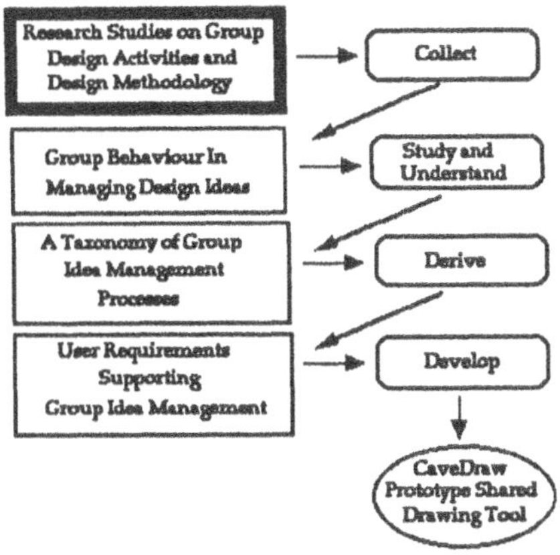

Figure 1. Research focus of this paper

Studying and understanding the scenarios of group behaviour in managing design ideas provides us with constraints on how a tool should be designed to support them. The scenarios presented in the taxonomy lead us to new insights into both shared drawing activity and user requirements for shared drawing tools.

3. A Taxonomy of Group Idea Management Processes

We present our analysis of the design study videos and previous research in the form of an idea management taxonomy. The taxonomy is primarily a listing of the more general levels of group interchanges and idea manipulation decisions made by group members. It is not exhaustive but covers the major behaviours we and others have observed in design activity.

Agree and add on to the suggested idea: A design idea is suggested. One or more collaborators make comments on the design either verbally or by sketching out the alternatives. Additional sketches are performed to further enhance the idea.

Tang (1989) observed this scenario in his studies; for example, one designer (S3) draws a representation of her design idea into the workspace, the other designer (S1) builds on the idea by adding keyhole slots. Tang (1989) points out that this behaviour indicates that initial representations gradually evolve into distinct artifacts, often through modifications and additions made by others.

Agree and subdivide the suggested idea: A design idea is suggested. Participants agree on the idea as a start. They then proceed to break down the idea into sub-tasks or segments and work on them separately.

Breaking up a design idea into hierarchical sub-tasks is a general phenomenon seen in architectural and mechanical engineering design tasks. For instance, in the Office Design Project (Stults, 1988), the architects articulated a shared analysis of the client's needs, formed a concept (an overall design idea) in response to the needs, and summarized the issues (the sub-tasks) underlying the concept. Effective management requires that inter-relationships among solutions for each sub-task be laid out and saved by the group before the group commences work on the sub-tasks (Otto, Riley & Erdman, 1988).

Modify the suggested idea: A design idea is suggested. One or more participants modifies the idea by editing the sketches of the idea or by presenting additional related sketches. Participants may not be notified by others before their sketch is changed.

This scenario occurs in studies using Commune, a three-person shared drawing tool (Minneman & Bly, 1991). One of the participants erases one of the other participant's sketches without requesting prior permission for this action. We observed this in a private viewing of a Xerox PARC design session recorded on videotape. Such behaviour is also observed by Tang (1989). He points out that the change usually addresses a verbal criticism and such criticism often compromises the design idea. In studies of idea development in a small group meeting, Scheidel and Crowell (1964) describe how one idea is progressively remodified in group interaction until the group achieves agreement.

Modify, but preserve the suggested idea: A design idea is suggested, and participants suggest modifications that are distinct from the original idea. These changes can be removed if they don't appear to work.

Although we did not find this behaviour mentioned in the literature, we extrapolate its occurrence from our studies on shared writing (Posner, Baecker & Mantei, 1991). Both ForComment™ (Opper, 1988) and Word 4.0™ (Microsoft Corporation, 1989) permit this type of annotation in a document without the annotation affecting the original text. In the Office Design Project (Stults, 1988), one of the architects is observed to lay tracing paper on top of his tv monitor. Using another architect's sketch displayed on this monitor, he then proceeds to add his own idea on the tracing paper. The original sketch is preserved while the other architects comment on the new suggestion.

Scratch and restart: A design idea is suggested. One or more participants comment on the idea, and the originator admits that there is a problem with the design idea. The idea is discarded and the group searches for another design solution.

Tang (1989) calls this scenario "Admit Problem". He describes it as one of the negotiating patterns in encouraging the group to accept an idea. He notes that this event often encourages others to help resolve the problem and share in developing the idea, but that some groups also use the admitted problem to reject the idea. In fact, the more ideas that members contribute, the more ideas the group will reject (Fisher, 1974). Fisher also points out that the period of idea testing during the conflict phase, involves the rejection of many idea proposals.

Suspend and wait: A design idea is suggested, and one or more participants make comments on the idea. Because the group is unsure about the suggested idea or because the idea is rejected out of hand, the discussion about it is dropped. The suggested idea can be forgotten or later reconsidered in an unrelated context (Tang, 1989).

In Fisher's (1970) study of decision modification processes in small groups, he observes group members introducing a particular decision proposal, discussing it for a length of time, dropping it in favour of another decision proposal and then, re-introducing it later during the group deliberations.

Agree and wait: A design idea is suggested and is well received. The group moves on to the next sub-task on the requirement list to complete the design. The suggested idea is put on hold until all design solutions for the overall design are gathered.

Once a global design idea is agreed upon by participants, it is further broken down into design sub-tasks, as mentioned in "Agree and subdivide the suggested idea". This scenario is shown in the MacViz-A design studies (Tang, 1989) when the participants listed their ideas, one after the other, on the shared workspace. The accepted idea was noted and the group moved on to solving the next design issue.

Compare and consolidate: Multiple design ideas for fulfilling the design requirement are suggested. The group compares and criticizes the solutions, and then consolidates them into one accepted version. In the consolidation process, several design solutions are aborted or modified at the same time.

Fisher (1974) notes from his studies that

> Group members usually focus their attention on various proposals during their interactions and choose from among those alternative proposals the ones which they will accept or reject. The sum of the proposals accepted constitutes the productivity of the group.

This type of activity has been observed to occur iteratively whenever a new design alternative arises during the design process.

Deprivatize design idea: After a design idea is generated, it is sometimes transferred from an individual workspace to a shared workspace.

In studies conducted by Tang and Leifer (1988), one participant was observed to begin drawing privately, producing a graphical object. Other participants noticed the object and began working on it. Tang and Leifer (1988) point out that the migration of this object from a private to a public object illustrates the dual public/private nature of the workspace.

We have identified nine distinct design sharing and modification processes that have been observed in group design. Naturally, the design process has additional complexities and subleties that we have failed to capture. Nevertheless, we believe that we have identified some of the primary behaviour patterns that groups apply in managing their design ideas. We need to incorporate capabilities to support these patterns in shared drawing tools so that they become facile and fluent enough to support this process of developing ideas.

4. A Brief Overview of CaveDraw

Before we use the group idea management taxonomy to generate user requirements, we provide a brief overview of the shared drawing tool under development, CaveDraw. We describe the tool at this point in the paper because we will use examples from CaveDraw to demonstrate the application of the user requirements we have generated.

CaveDraw is a shared drawing package running on Macintosh II workstations. It supports multiple users drawing at the same time. Users working on their workstations, connected through an ethernet, can view and modify shared drawings in their window. Each workstation runs its own version of CaveDraw and communicates with other workstations via a communications manager running on a Sun 3/60 workstation.

CaveDraw differs from other shared drawing software in its support of "transparent layers." A layer is created when a user requests and names a drawing surface. All users can sketch on the layer. Once a workspace is exhausted on the layer, a new layer can be requested. The work on the previous layer dims to a light colour so as not to interfere with the drawing on the new layer. Each participant can create, hide and select any layer. As layers are superimposed on each other, participants can select their own individual layers to work on while drawing activity continues by other participants on other layers. Participants can copy or cut any portion of a sketch on one layer to a desired location on another layer. Sharing a common view of the sketch activity is not automatic in CaveDraw as it is in other shared drawing tools. However, participants in CaveDraw can synchronize their views with another participant.

CaveDraw supports line, rectangle, oval, polygon, text, and freehand (pencil & marker) drawing tools. Users can select and erase drawing segments and can use different coloured markers to identify their own work. CaveDraw shares sketching activities but supports gesture weakly. A coloured telepointer is used for gesturing but its two-dimensionality will never capture the richness of human gestures. CaveDraw is now implemented and is undergoing user testing.

5. User Requirements Drawn From The Group Idea Management Taxonomy

In Section 3, we summarized nine idea manipulation behaviours observed in groups working on design solutions. We now propose user requirements for the design of a shared drawing tool. This tool helps designers manage their design ideas. To build these requirements, we combine the nine idea management behaviours with five critical factors that have been shown to affect group design. As before, our evidence for the importance of these factors comes from prior research on shared drawing environments and from reviews of videotapes of shared drawing activities. Once we have discussed user requirements, we present CaveDraw's solutions to these requirements. We also review the solutions for these requirements in other shared drawing systems and discuss their relative merits.

We focus on five critical factors that support group idea management processes. They are *Work Allocation, Design Integration, Design Ownership, Design Recall* and *Space Sharing. Work Allocation* refers to the split between individual and group work. In group design, participants often work on different parts of the same design. They therefore need a personal design space that can later be *Integrated* into the group's workspace. Conflict can arise in group design sessions if one person's idea is co-opted or erased by another. Thus, *Ownership* becomes an important issue. Drawing space evaporates rapidly as ideas are sketched and discarded. Yet, it is important not to eradicate an idea which could be useful in another context. If *Recall* is hindered by the organisation of a design space, prior ideas can be lost. Finally, group *Sharing of Workspace* can limit the amount of space available and thus, the number of design ideas generated.

5.1 User Requirements Supporting Work Allocation

Table I lists the user requirements for the work allocation factor. The "Agree and subdivide the suggested idea" scenario generates two requirements: Requirement (1.1); to allow participants to select individual segments of the design to work on simultaneously, and Requirement (1.2); to provide mechanisms by which each participant can be kept aware of what the other participants are doing.

Taxonomy Scenarios	User Requirements
"Agree and subdivide the suggested idea"	(1.1) Participants can select individual segments of the design to work on simultaneously. (1.2) Participants are aware of the design activities of others while working on their segment of the design.
"Modify the suggested idea"	(1.3) Participants are able to select and modify all previous design ideas.

Table I. User Requirements Supporting Work Allocation

We believe that offering participants the choice to work on individual design segments simultaneously not only expands the design space for them, but also enhances creativity and reduces the processing time of the design task. Thus, they can select segments that are relevant to their expertise and work with lower communication overhead. Existing instantiations of shared workspaces do not permit group participants to retreat and work on a portion of the drawing without changing the workspace for the rest of the design group. In Commune (Minneman & Bly, 1991), a selection by one participant to move to a previous page of design work causes the screens of all participants to be changed to the previous page.

In a design task, the inter-relationship among design ideas can affect the outcome of the overall design. Ullman, Stauffer and Dietterich (1987) observe that different designers' ideas are sometimes developed at different levels of abstraction. If members in the group were constantly aware of each other's design processes, negotiation and adjustment to an agreed upon standard level of abstraction could go on continuously. Participants could still work on their personal design but would be more likely to make it fit into the greater whole. Requirement (1.2) therefore requests this awareness capability.

The "Modify the suggested idea" scenario generates a third user requirement (1.3); to permit participants to select and modify all previous designs on an individual basis. Manipulating a suggested design idea plays an important role in the design process. In the engineering design world, designers attempt one solution, move on to a second, then a third, etc. With multiple participants, a large number of solution paths are created (Pahl & Beitz, 1984). The group is likely to skip a thorough investigation of prior solutions in the interest of group efficiency, but the ability to access this work on an individual basis can bring up good ideas that would otherwise have been discarded.

We use shared transparent layers in CaveDraw to implement the user work allocation requirements into the design. Their specific relationship to the design requirements is shown in Table II.

User Requirements	CaveDraw's Design Solutions
(1.1) Participants can select individual segments of the design to work on simultaneously.	Participants draw out their design ideas on shared transparent layers. Drawings on the selected topmost layers are the only ones that appear in a brighter colour.
(1.2) Participants are aware of the design activities of others while working on their segment of the design.	The layers are superimposed on each other so that a participant can see other drawing activities taking place in a light grey colour.Participants can synchronize their view with the other participants, also they can find out who is viewing or working on each layer.
(1.3) Participants are able to select and modify all previous design ideas.	Participants can select, create and hide the display of any layer on their screen.

Table II. CaveDraw Design Features Supporting Work Allocation

Each CaveDraw participant can create one or more shared layers. The layers are stacked together and design sketches on the current working layer are displayed in a prominent colour. All the underlying layers are dimmed to a light grey colour. Sketches drawn by others are visible but not intrusive. Figure 2 presents an example of the overlapping layered approach in CaveDraw. In Figure 2a, Designer A is sketching out her idea of a floorplan. The work of Designer B is visible but not prominent on the layer below her layer. Figure 2b shows her co-worker's screen with his layer on top of her layer. He is adding to her work, but on a different layer.

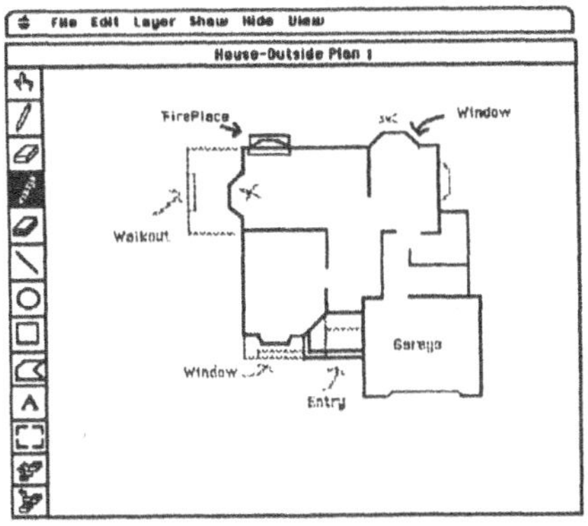

Figure 2a. Designer A chooses to work on the first layer where she put her idea

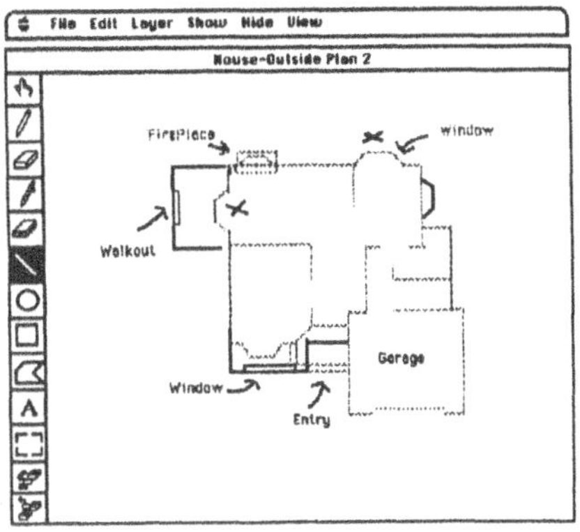

Figure 2b. Designer B chooses another layer to add to Designer A's idea

When participants work separately on different subset of layers, awareness of others' work becomes an essential part of coordinating the collaboration. In CaveDraw, participants can join or view any other participants' work through the View menu. This menu allows participants to view all the selected layers, the top layer or any of the dimmed layers of another participant. Also, participants are able to restore their own view after browsing through another participant's layers or working with another participant. Furthermore, they can find out who is working on each particular layer when they select a layer through the Show menu. Each menu item gives the name of the layer as well as the name of the other participants who are viewing it.

5.2 User Requirements Supporting Design Integration

Table III lists the user requirements that support the critical factor, Design Integration. Requirement (2.1); to allow participants to compare and consolidate modifications to different portions of the original design, while still being able to throw away undesirable changes, is a direct result of the "Compare and consolidate" activity. It is not possible to compare complex design alternatives unless they are equally visible. Group design sessions often involve large amounts of white paper pinned to walls or the use of a large whiteboard for this purpose. Space limitations and the immobility of drawn designs prevent easy comparison of distant designs. Commune requires paging through previous designs and bringing them up one at a time. VideoWhiteboard (Tang & Minneman, 1991) provides a whiteboard sized shared videospace allowing multiple designs to be viewed at the same time, but designs are still immovable. In Ishii's (1990) Teamworkstation, designs can be overlaid and thus, compared, but the technology limits the number of overlays that can be compared in this fashion. Boardnoter in Colab (Stefik, Foster, Bobrow, Kahn, Lanning & Suchman, 1987) supports the reduction of design alternatives into miniature stamp sheets. The stampsheets can be expanded into a full view, but screen space soon exhausts the number of expanded stampsheets that can be viewed at one time.

Consolidating designs is even less easy. Separate designs have to be redrawn and re-merged into a new design requiring a duplication of effort.

Teamworkstation allows participants to overlay video images of separate drawings but the adjustments require fine tuning using video controls. The consolidated design becomes the video sequence stored on videotape.

Taxonomy Scenarios	User Requirements
"Compare and consolidate"	(2.1) Participants can,with little overhead, compare and consolidate modifications to different portions of the original design but still throw out undesirable changes.
"Modify but preserve the suggested idea"	(2.2) Participants can compare different modifications to a design idea at the same time without disturbing the original idea or having to view multiple displays.
"Agree and subdivide the suggested idea"	(2.3) Participants can, with little effort, view both the overall design and its subunits in addition to the design subunit they are working on.

Table III. User Requirements Supporting Design Integration

The "Modify, but preserve the suggested idea" scenario creates Requirement (2.2); to allow participants to compare modifications to a design idea without disturbing the original. In a group design session, participants may have an agreed upon basis for their design, but may be trying out additional ideas to correct some aspect of the design. For example, they may want to design the lighting connections in the trunk of a new car, while retaining the trunk cavity layout design. If they drew over the trunk cavity design on the whiteboard and did not like the design idea, they would need to redraw the trunk cavity.

Requirement (2.3); to allow participants to view both the overall design and all its subunits, is drawn from the "Agree and subdivide the suggested idea" scenario. As participants create their solutions, they move further away from their original plan. Suchman and Trigg (1986) point out that participants relate their ideas to prior ones or to the problem at hand. If the original plan is not viewable from time to time, participants relate their current problem to the most recently solved problem. This eventually places designs far enough away from the overall design that integration could be very difficult. If multiple designers work individually without refering to the overall plan, their designs are unlikely to fit together.

The CaveDraw layer approach allows a form of design integration although it, too, has limitations. Table IV lists the CaveDraw design features that support the user requirements of Design Integration.

User Requirements	CaveDraw's Design Solutions
(2.1) Participants can,with little overhead, compare and consolidate modifications to different portions of the original design but still throw out undesirable changes	Allows the participants to draw alternate design ideas on different layers and superimpose the layers or subsets of the layers in any order selected by the participants. Also allows saving of any of these combinations.
(2.2) Participants can compare different modifications to a design idea at the same time without disturbing the original idea or having to view multiple displays.	Same approach as (2.1). In addition, participants can work on their own layer while the other participants are performing a comparison.
(2.3) Participants can, with little effort, view both the overall design and its subunits in addition to the design subunit they are working on.	Allows each participant to bring up a sublayer showing the connection of all subunits while working on one of the subunits in the previous layer.

Table IV. CaveDraw Features Supporting Design Integration

To support comparison and consolidation activities, CaveDraw permits participants to select a subset of layers to be displayed on their screen. The designs in this subset can be compared and, if desired, consolidated into one design on one layer. Design ideas can be discarded by removing the layer on which they are drawn. Any layer can be brought to the topmost position (brighter colour) by "mouse-clicking" on a pixel located in the layer. Layers below the topmost layer are still visible for the comparison task.

If an overview of the design plan is available, participants can maintain the overview as one of the visible layers on their display. They can refer to it from time to time by bringing it to the topmost layer or simply by looking at it through the other designs showing in the other layers.

Although CaveDraw supports some of the characteristics of Design Integration, it leads to what we call "layer overload." At some point, too many designs with too many different patterns will overlap each other in the layered design space. It will be difficult for users to disambiguate the lines of one layer from that of the other. A feature paralleling Furnas's (1986) fisheye views approach of looking at a design overview would be more useful for this function.

5.3 User Requirements Supporting Design Ownership

Ideas have creators and thus, owners. Any time a sketch is modified by other participants in the group, ownership preservation becomes an issue. The design scenarios, "Add on to," "Modify," and "Deprivatize," represent different ways in which an existing idea can be co-opted by the group. Table V lists user requirements that preserve ownership: Requirement (3.1); to allow participants to declare any portion of a sketch as private and therefore, undeletable, and Requirement (3.2); to allow participants to see who is working on what design.

Taxonomy Scenarios	User Requirements
"Agree and add on to the suggested idea", "Modify the suggested idea", and "Deprivatize design idea"	(3.1) Participants can declare any portion of a sketch as private and not subject to deletion by others. (3.2) Participants can identify, with no additional interaction sequences, who is working on any specific design sketch.

Table V. User Requirements Supporting Design Ownership

Social norms are expected to keep others from erasing our work, but this does not always work. For instance, one dominant participant using Commune was observed to erase the other person's sketches without prior permission. Conflict resolution studies using the University of Minnesota's Group Decision Support System found that asocial acts of removing another participant's ideas were common and disturbed the group process (Poole, Holmes & DeSanctis, 1988).

Ownership prevents undesired deletion of design ideas, but sometimes deletion or permission to copy is desired. If Requirement 3.1 is met, then Requirement 3.2 needs to be in place to identify the owner of the design. Identified owners can then be asked if deletion or duplication is acceptable. Individuals in a design group may also have status. For example, it may not be obvious to other participants that a particularly complex design idea is a good solution, but if it is known that the person who created the idea has a reputation as an extremely successful designer, then evaluation of the design will be more positive. It is also important to know who designed what in a design process to get a measure of the individual contributions of the group members and of their design focus.

Ownership is not a supported concept in most shared drawing tools (e.g., Commune (Bly & Minneman, 1990), GroupSketch (Greenberg & Bohnet, 1991) and BoardNoter (Stefik et al, 1987)). VideoDraw (Tang & Minneman, 1990) uses polarizing filters to fuse two separately drawn video images together making ownership inherent in the technology.

Table VI lists CaveDraw's design solutions for the ownership concerns. CaveDraw supports ownership through the use of colour. Each participant in CaveDraw is assigned a colour that is not currently in use. Participants have two basic drawing tools, a pencil and a coloured marker. If they draw with the pencil, all lines are black and the design they create can be changed by any participant. If they draw with the coloured marker, all lines are in the assigned colour and cannot be erased, only copied. When a user selects the pencil, all associated tools, e.g., "draw circle," generate public drawings. A marker selection makes all tool usage private. Moreover, the use of the public and private markers can distinguish between a tentative and definite idea (Suchman & Trigg, 1986).

User Requirements	CaveDraw's Design Solutions
(3.1) Participants can declare any portion of a sketch as private and not subject to deletion by others.	Allows participants to declare public or personal work by selecting respectively public or personal drawing tools. Work drawn with a personal set of tools cannot be erased by others. Participants are allowed to convert their work from private to public and vice versa through available editing functions.
(3.2) Participants can identify with no additional interaction sequences who is working on any specific design sketch.	Identifies each participant's work or ownership of a design by a specific colour.

Table VI. CaveDraw Features Supporting Design Ownership

Although CaveDraw supports design ownership, its support has some drawbacks. Designers can "sign" their work but the decision to make a particular design private needs to be made at tool selection time. In a creative design session, participants will not always know ahead of time that a particular design is significant. If they choose to personalize all their work, they may quit the design session before it is over, leaving behind a set of undeletable sketches. CaveDraw allows participants to make their design public or private through special cut and paste tools. Also, all their private marks on the shared layers will become public if they quit the design session before it is over. Ownership is only discernible at the topmost layer where colours are displayed. Since lower layers are in light grey, the colouring cue for the other participants' work in those layers is lost.

5.4 User Requirement Supporting Design Recall

In the "Agree and wait" and "Suspend and wait" scenarios, a group defers work on a design and returns to it later. Many other design events occur during the waiting period causing the group to forget the suspended design. Ullman et al. (1987)

found that designers often forgot prior design ideas and Agogino, Cagan and Molezzi (1988) observed design teams covering the same ground and redoing the same design ideas. We call this problem "Design Recall". Coupled with the design suspension behaviour, it generates Requirement (4.1) in Table VII; to allow participants to review prior design ideas with minimum effort.

Taxonomy Scenarios	User Requirement
"Agree and wait" and "Suspend and wait"	(4.1) Participants can review prior design ideas with minimum effort.

Table VII. User Requirement Supporting Design Recall

A large drawing space can support design recall because we have more prior designs visible at once. VideoWhiteBoard takes this approach by projecting a video image of shared drawing spaces on an entire whiteboard-like screen. Leaving the design idea on the video whiteboard has the disadvantage of taking up valuable drawing space. Commune allows users to flip through pages of prior designs, but we believe that users are unlikely to take the time for a serial search. BoardNoter allows users to both have sufficient drawing space and view prior designs by miniaturizing the design ideas. Users cannot view the underlying design idea in the miniature icons and may have to open each one up to recall what they represent.

CaveDraw again relies on its transparent layers to aid users in recalling prior design activity. Table VIII lists the manipulation capabilities that permit access to designs that have been drawn earlier in the design session. The access we refer to is cognitive access, not computer access. We use the layers and the relative ease with which they can be brought up on the display to make participants aware of these prior designs.

User Requirement	CaveDraw's Design Solution
(4.1) Participants can review prior design ideas with minimum effort.	Allows participants to directly select the viewed layers that capture prior design ideas with one mouse click on the dimmed layers. Also allows participants to select layers that have been put away through the pulldown menu.

Table VIII. CaveDraw Features Supporting Design Recall

Design layers which are already on the display but underneath the working layer are in the drawing space where the user can see their dimmed image. They can be brought to the top by a mouse click on a line of the design drawn on that layer. If a layer is not on the display, it can be recalled by its name. A user is required to give each layer a name when it is created. This name is put in a pulldown menu for selecting layers and putting them back on the display. The names in the pulldown menu help the user recall a previously stored design.

CaveDraw's solution does not scale up well. First, since all layers underneath are dimmed, it is difficult to determine if two dimmed lines belong to a particular layer or to two different layers. Second, when too many layers exist in the pulldown menu, it becomes hard to scan the name list or to discriminate between similar names.

5.5 User Requirement Supporting Space Sharing

Suchman and Trigg (1986) point out that participants in a design session often hold different views when interpreting and evaluating a design idea. Misunderstandings are corrected by sketching on a shared drawing surface. Tang (1989) notes that the design process is enhanced if designers can share a common view of the workspace and have a sense of proximity with the ongoing drawing process. VideoWhiteBoard is a good example of this space sharing. The technology permits two users to draw in the same space and have the same view of the design. Table IX lists the user requirement that provides this space sharing. Requirement (5.1); to allow participants to work in their own space yet virtually share the space with other participants.

Taxonomy Scenarios	User Requirement
"Agree and add on to the suggested idea" , "Scratch and restart","Modify the suggested idea", etc.	(5.1) Participants can work in their own space yet virtually share the space with other participants.

Table IX. User Requirement Supporting Space Sharing

GroupSketch, TeamWorkstation and Commune all support shared workspace, but the amount of space is relatively small and quickly fills up with drawings. CaveDraw supports a common view of the work and gives each participant adequate sketching area. Table X lists the features that give this dual capability.

User Requirement	CaveDraw's Design Solutions
(5.1) Participants can work in their own space yet virtually share the space with other participants	Allows participants to generate as many layers of drawing surface as they need.
	Allows participants to select a personal set of layers to work with while retaining elements common with others.

Table X. CaveDraw Features Supporting Space Sharing

Individual layers in CaveDraw can be created, selected, merged with other layers, hidden and cleared. The superimposed visual effect gives each participant a view of the other participants' work. Yet, when a particular drawing is completed, the drawer doesn't run out of drawing space. The drawing is put away and replaced by a blank layer. The drawing space is still constrained because it is on a standard Mac II screen rather than a larger whiteboard.

6. Summary

Tasks carried out by groups can rapidly become overwhelming because of the complexity of the interactions and the amount of information that is generated. We have focused on group design tasks in this paper and mapped a set of group idea management processes against five critical factors that affect group design. The results of this mapping generated a list of design criteria. The list focuses on the task of managing multiple design ideas in shared drawing tools. CaveDraw's solutions demonstrate one software approach for accomplishing the design requirements that have been laid out. Its unique design feature is the use of shared transparent layers to extend the shared workspace. CaveDraw couples this with the use of colour to identify the work of individual participants. The application of these features supports idea management but with limitations especially in terms of drawing complexity. We also discuss the limitations and advantages of other shared drawing packages, most of which have not been designed with idea management in mind. As with most design recommendations, the final proof lies in user testing the next stage in creating CaveDraw.

Acknowledgements

The authors are grateful to Tom Milligan, Jeff Lee, Gifford Louie, Kelly Mawby and Alison Lee for helpful suggestions with this research. Our discussions with Hiroshi Ishii and John Tang have given us insights that have enhanced CaveDraw. The work was supported in part by the Natural Sciences and Engineering Research Council of Canada, IBM Canada Lab Centre for Advanced Studies, Digital Equipment Corporation and ITRC, and through donations to our laboratory by Apple Canada and Alias Research Inc.

References

Agogino, A. M., Cagan, J., and Molezzi, M.J. (1988): "Meta-Design : Reflections on a graduate course in design theory and methodology", in S. Newsome, W.R. Spillers and S. Finger (eds.), *Design Theory '88: Proceedings of the 1988 NSF Grantee Workshop on Design Theory and Methodology*, Springer-Verlag : New York, pp. 18-28.

Akin, O. (1979): "An Exploration of the Design Process", *Design Methods and Theories*, 13(3/4), pp. 189-207.

Bly, S.A. (1988): "A use of drawing surfaces in different collaborative settings", *Proceedings of CSCW'88 Conference on Computer Supported Cooperative Work*, Portland, Oregon, September 1988, pp. 250-256.

Bly, S.A. and Minneman, S.L. (1990): "Commune: A shared drawing surface", *Proceedings of COIS'90 Conference on Office Information Systems*, Boston, MA, April 1990, pp. 184-192.

Fisher, B.A. (1970): "The process of decision modification in small discussion groups", *The Journal of Communication*, 20, March 1970, pp. 51-64.

Fisher, B.A. (Ed.) (1974): *Small Group Decision Making: Communication and the Group Process*. New York : McGraw-Hill.

Furnas, G.W. (1986): "Generalized fisheye views", *Proceedings of CHI'86 Conference on Human Factors in Computing Systems*, Boston, MA, April 1986, pp. 16-23.

Greenberg, S. and Bohnet, R. (1991): "GroupSketch: A multi-user sketchpad for geographically distributed small groups", *Proceedings of GI'91 Conference on Graphic Interface*, Calgary, Alberta, Canada, June 1991.

Grudin, J. (1989): "Why groupware applications fail: Problems in design and evaluation", *Office: Technology and People*, 4(3), pp. 245-264.

Ishii, H. (1990): "TeamWorkStation: Towards a seamless shared workspace", *Proceedings of CSCW'90 Conference on Computer Supported Cooperative Work*, Los Angeles, CA, October 1990, pp. 13-25.

Mantei, M.M., Baecker, R.M., Sellen, A.J., Buxton, W.A.S., Milligan, T. and Wellman, B. (1991): "Experiences in the use of a media space", *Proceedings of CHI'91 Conference on Human Factors in Computing Systems*, New Orleans, LA, May 1991, pp. 203-215.

Microsoft Corporation (1989): Microsoft Word [Computer Program, version 4.0]. Redmond, Wa.

Minneman, S.L. and Bly, S.A. (1990): "Experiences in the development of a multi-user drawing tool", *The 3rd Guelph Symposium on Computer Mediated Communication.* Guelph, Ontario, Canada, May 1990, pp. 154-167.

Minneman, S.L. and Bly, S.A. (1991): "Managing á trois : a study of a multi-user drawing tool in distributed design work", *Proceedings of CHI'91 Conference on Human Factors in Computing Systems,* New Orleans, LA, May 1991, pp. 217-224.

Opper, S. (1988): "A groupware toolbox", *Byte*, December 1988, pp. 275-282.

Otto, K., Riley, D.R. and Erdman, A.G. (1988): "Strategic conceptual design in mechanical synthesis", in S. Newsome, W.R. Spillers and S. Finger (eds.), *Design Theory '88: Proceedings of the 1988 NSF Grantee Workshop on Design Theory and Methodology*, Springer-Verlag : New York, pp. 148-172.

Pahl, G. and Beitz, W. (eds.) (1984): *Engineering Design: A systematic approach*, Springer-Verlag : Berlin.

Poole, M.S., Holmes, M. and DeSanctis, G. (1988): "Conflict Management and group decision support systems", *Proceedings of CSCW'88 Conference on Computer-Supported Cooperative Work*, Portland, Oregon, September 1988, pp. 227-240.

Posner, I. , Baecker, R., Mantei, M. (1991): *"How People Write Together"*. Unpublished manuscript, Department of Computer Science, University of Toronto.

Rouse, W.B. and Boff, K.R. (1987): "Designers, tools, and environments: State of knowledge, unresolved issues, and potential directions", in William B. Rouse and Kenneth R. Boff (eds.): *System Design: Behavioral Perspectives on Designers, Tools, and Organizations*, North-Holland, Amsterdam, 1987, pp. 43-63.

Scheidel, T.M. and Crowell, L. (1964): "Idea development in small discussion group", *Quarterly Journal of Speech*, 50, pp. 140-145.

Stefik, M., Foster, G., Bobrow, D.G., Kahn, K., Lanning S., and Suchman, L. (1987): "Beyond the chalkboard: Computer support for collaboration and problem solving in meetings", *Communications of the ACM*, 30(1), January 1987, pp. 32-47.

Stults, R. (1988): *Experimental Uses of Video to Support Design Activities.* Technical Report No. SSL-89-19. Xerox PARC : Palo Alto, CA.

Suchman, L. and Trigg, R.H. (1986): "A framework for studying research collaboration", *Proceedings of CSCW'86 Conference on Computer-Supported Cooperative Work,* Austin, Texas, December 1986, pp. 221-228.

Tang, J.C. and Leifer, L.J. (1988): "A framework for understanding the workspace activity of design teams", *Proceedings of CSCW'88 Conference on Computer-Supported Cooperative Work*, Portland, Oregon, September 1988, pp. 244-249.

Tang, J.C. (1989): *Listing, Drawing and Gesturing in Design : A Study of the Use of Shared Workspaces by Design Teams*. Technical Report No. SSL-89-3. Xerox Parc : Palo Alto, CA, April 1989.

Tang, J.C. and Minneman, S.L. (1990): "VideoDraw : A video interface for collaborative drawing", *Proceedings of CHI'90 Conference on Human Factors in Computer Systems*, Seattle,Washington, April 1990, pp. 313-320.

Tang, J.C. and Minneman, S.L. (1991): "VideoWhiteBoard : Video shadows to support remote collaboration", *Proceedings of CHI'91 Conference on Human Factors in Computing Systems*, New Orleans, LA, May 1991, pp. 315-322.

Ullman, D., Stauffer, L.A. and Dietterich, T.G. (1987): "Toward Expert CAD", *Computers in Mechanical Engineering*, 6(3), November/December 1987, pp. 56-70.

Yeomans, D. (1982): "Monitoring design processes", in B. Evans, J.A. Powell, and R.J. Talbot (eds.): *Changing Design*, John Wiley & Sons Ltd:Toronto, 1982, pp. 109-124.

Proceedings of the Second European Conference on Computer-Supported Cooperative Work
Bannon, L., Robinson, M. & Schmidt, K. (Editors)
September 25-27, 1991, Amsterdam, The Netherlands

Formalization in CSCW

Elin Rønby Pedersen & Lucy Suchman
Xerox Palo Alto Research Center, U.S.A.

Panelists:

Graham Button, Polytechnic South West, UK
Reinhard Keil-Slawik, Technische Universität, Berlin, Germany
Elin Rønby Pedersen, Xerox PARC, USA
Mike Robinson, University of Amsterdam, The Netherlands
Lucy Suchman, Xerox PARC, USA

A usage perspective on formalization

This panel aims at exploring formalization **in use**, i.e. how people acquire, develop, use, and communicate formalizations.

The notion of formalization applied here emphasizes its situational and historical roots. We would like to take as our point of departure an acknowledgement of well-known obstacles in using formalization, but we want to get further than that, to an acknowledgement of the constructive aspects of using formalization.

The range of formalization issues in typical CSCW situations is wide and includes various activities of description and specification during design and development of an application, procedural structures imposed on those who use the system and representation system and models used in customization and adaption of running CSCW applications.

Three major themes

The panel discussion will be organized around a few selected situations in which formalization - broadly understood as some sort of formality or structure - appears in CSCW related activity:

1. Studying work practice
2. Designing and developing CSCW tools
3. Working with CSCW tools

Reflection on each situation raises a number of questions and issues:

Studying work practice

The attention is here on formal structures used in observing and learning about work situations; the formal structures usually appear in the form of specialized notation.

One area of particular interest is work studies that are done as part of a computer programming effort; formal expressions are mandatory when programming, whereas several other modes of expression are available in human communication.

Some questions to consider are:

Can we assess the role of formal modes of expression relative to, for instance, more narrative means of expression in systems analysis and design? How do the mere formulation and formalization affect or shape our understanding of work situations (as authors as well as readers)? Are other media, e.g., video recordings, different in this regard? And as a very general question: how can we understand the relation between knowledge and certain artifacts, e.g., descriptions, computerized models?

Designing and developing CSCW tools

The attention is here on formal structures that may influence the relevant designers and implementors; the structures may come in the form of expression systems (e.g., specification languages), models of the design area, or as methods for organizing the system development process, and they may be experienced as supporting the process or imposing restrictions on it.

Some questions to consider are:

To what extent can formal structures support collaboration in multi-disciplinary design teams?

To what extent is the analysis and design governed by model-like understandings of the use of the future system (e.g. the seemingly inevitable "models of the user"), and which are the advantages and problems with such models?

Working with CSCW tools

The attention is here on formal structures that are facilitated or required by a running CSCW application; the structures may appear in the form of embedded models and or as prescriptive work procedures, and they may be experienced as supporting the work in the user community or imposing restrictions on it.

Some questions to consider are:

To what extent does the skilful use of a CSCW system rely on the existence of (and the user's awareness of) models in the system?

To what extent can the explicitness of embedded formal models be expected to empower the users, e.g., by making the system accessible and thereby allowing for flexibility and appropriation?

Proceedings of the Second European Conference on Computer-Supported Cooperative Work
Bannon, L., Robinson, M. & Schmidt, K. (Editors)
September 25-27, 1991, Amsterdam, The Netherlands

Experiences with the DOMINO Office Procedure System

Thomas Kreifelts, Elke Hinrichs, Karl-Heinz Klein,
Peter Seuffert, Gerd Woetzel
German National Research Center for Computer Science (GMD), Germany

Abstract: The Domino office procedure system has been equipped with a new user interface, and has been put to use for the support of purchasing. In this paper, we describe the system, the user interface, and the experiences we made during the practical use of the system. We also briefly discuss the consequences for our own research.

1 Introduction

DOMINO is an office procedure system for modelling and monitoring structured office processes in organizations. In this paper we report on the first practical use of the system. Our goal was to test the usability and usefulness of the DOMINO system, to evaluate the applicability of the DOMINO office procedure model, and to learn from this experience for future developments and research into group support systems, e.g. in the form of new requirements.

A first DOMINO prototype had been completed by 1984 (Kreifelts et al., 1984), a second and functionally enlarged version by 1987 (Kreifelts & Woetzel, 1987). The user interface of the first prototype was somewhat primitive (an extended text editor for alphanumeric terminals), the user interface for the second system version was an experiment in end user programming and was implemented on a Lisp machine (Spenke & Beilken, 1989). In 1989, we felt that the development of other systems for group support might benefit from experiences with our (by now) rather stable office procedure system. So we looked for a possibility to try out DOMINO in practice. The user interfaces of the existing prototype systems of DOMINO were not suited for an office environment, so an important prerequisite for a practical test of the system was the development of a new user interface for such an environment.

Since we were interested in a rather quick experimental use of the system, we decided to try it out in our own organization. This is usually not the best decision as far as generalizability of the results is concerned, but one is freed from additional overhead in preparing the implementation of the system. Also, this way the question of the technical environment in which the system had to run was settled: a network of personal computers (Apple Macintoshes) connected to some server machines running Unix (SUN's).

First, we will give a brief account of the assumptions underlying the design of DOMINO, its functionality, and its architecture. We will then highlight the characteristics of the new DOMINO interface. The rest of the paper is concerned with the experimental use of DOMINO, the experiences we made, and the conclusions we have drawn for our further research.

2 The DOMINO System

The application domain of DOMINO are well-structured cooperative processes in the office. There are four assumptions underlying the design of DOMINO:

(a) Every office worker has a private working domain; cooperation takes place by exchanging messages between these working domains (rather than by working on common domains, i.e. by information sharing).

(b) The messages exchanged in a cooperation are regarded as "speech acts" of a conversation concerning a certain task in the sense of Winograd and Flores (1986).

(c) Cooperation in an organizational setting concerning groups of people is organized by specifying the input/output relations of the elementary work steps; an autonomous agent then coordinates the performance of these steps via conversations for action.

(d) The specification of the input/output relations of the steps is regarded as an "ideal" procedure; exceptions from this procedure can be handled within the action conversations and by the mediating agent.

DOMINO is a system for the specification and automation of cooperative office procedures. It is capable of controlling a variety of such processes which are specified in a special, application oriented language. A procedure description specifies which steps ("actions") a procedure consists of, and what dependencies exist between these actions in the form of information ("forms") needed and produced during the execution of the actions. The various actions of the procedure are assigned to "roles" responsible for their performance; at run-time, these roles are assigned to persons making use of an organizational data base. The underlying procedure model is based on Petri nets, and allows for alternative and concurrent courses of action. Procedure specifications have a graphical representation. We give an example in figure 1. Procedure specifications are checked for consistency and translated into executable form by the DOMINO office procedure compiler.

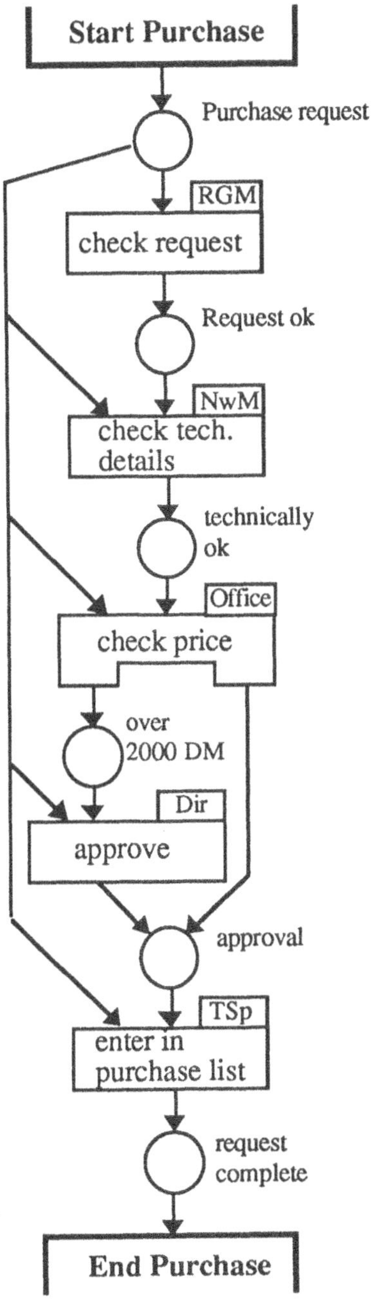

Roles

RGM: Research Group Manager
NwM: Network Manager
Dir: Director of Institute
TSp: Technical Support Person
Office: Pseudo-role for automated actions

Figure 1. A DOMINO office procedure

DOMINO mediates and controls task related communication by notifying the participants about actions due, by providing them with the information needed, and by routing the results of such actions to the parties responsible. Thus, DOMINO coordinates the activity of a group of persons working on a common task. It is able to inform about the progress of task execution, and provides mechanisms for exception handling in office procedures like delegating an action, or setting back a procedure in case of complaints.

The execution of an office procedure is started on request of a user who becomes the initiator of this procedure instance. The communication between the initiator, the other actors of the procedure and the DOMINO system employs message types which are important in the context of procedure processing. The message types "order", "completion", "confirmation" are used for the straightforward course. "Complaint", "forwarding", "cancellation" (and some more) are used for exception handling. The exchange of these messages follows conventions which are summarized in the CoPlanX protocol. The use of this *conversation for action* ensures a consistent view of the procedure state by all participants.

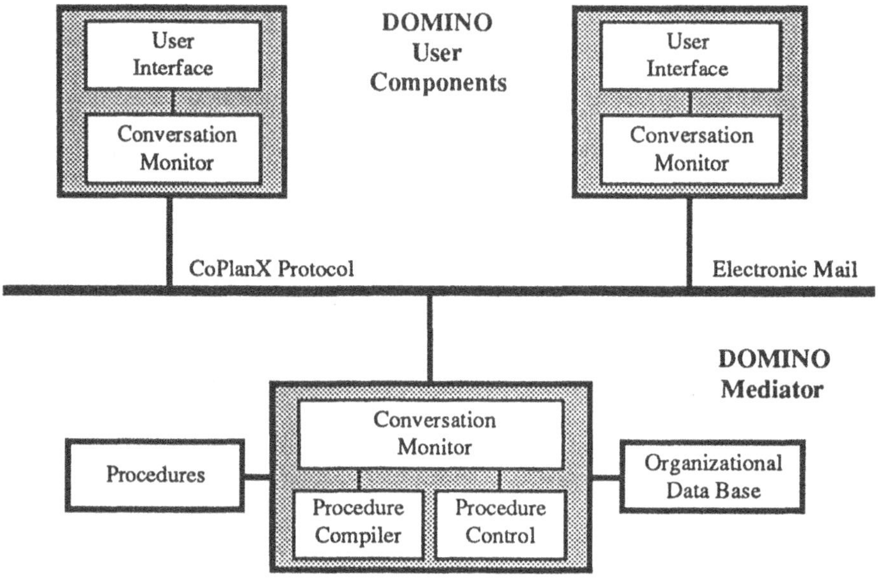

Figure 2. The DOMINO systems architecture

The DOMINO system consists of an automated agent (called "mediator") and user components which communicate via electronic mail using the CoPlanX protocol. The mediator is installed as a fully automated pseudo-user in the mail network. It is responsible for the compilation, installation, and execution of office procedures. It consists of the procedure compiler, the procedure control, and the conversation monitor. All components are implemented in C under UNIX. An experimental organizational data base which is used for role assignment during procedure execution has been realized in Prolog. The overall system architecture is shown in figure 2.

The user components for local user support in procedure processing are installed for every user of the system. They consist of an interface module and the conversation monitor. The implementation depends on the environment in which the DOMINO system is intended to run. In the next section, the user component for our experiment and its development will be described in more detail.

3 The New Interface

3.1 Development

What had to be developed for the new DOMINO version was essentially a way of loosely coupling an office work place equipped with a personal computer (Macintosh in our case) with the central procedure control component. The initial design splitted the user component into a UNIX part and a Mac part and devised a way of communication between the two parts that would ensure a consistent procedure communication even in the absence of a continuous link and with a possible loss of data on the Mac side[1]. The rest of the UNIX components of DOMINO (procedure control, procedure compiler, conversation monitors) remained unchanged.

The initial version of the system concentrated on these technical issues. The user interface design sticked very closely to the original DOMINO concepts, with regard to the procedure model as well as the procedure communication. Although a viable solution for the technical problem of coupling the Macs with the UNIX mediator had been found, this interface was judged as too system-oriented even before completion.

Consequently, the user interface design team was enlarged by a prospective user of the system who is not a computer scientist and who had not been involved in the system development so far. Design work involved many brain storming sessions and screen layouts on paper along with informal descriptions of the functionality of buttons and menus.

The outcome of this phase was a mocked-up user interface. The main characteristics were:

- Form-orientation, i.e. each office procedure type corresponded to an electronic form to be filled in at the various stations it ran through during the procedure execution.
- Inclusion of informal and free format communication, i.e. in addition to the "official" information associated with an office procedure, contained in the form itself, arbitrary enclosures could be added (text documents, drawings, etc.) as well as an informal note sticker (the electronic counterpart to the well known "Post-it" sticker).

---

[1] With the prospect of even smaller and more portable office computer equipment (lap-tops, handhelds, ...) this design may turn out to be also the right choice for future systems.

– Simplification of the original action conversation, i.e. instead of having to handle 13 different message types in dealing with an office procedure form, the user is given essentially three options: send the form to the next station, send it back to a previous station, or send it to a deputy station. In different contexts the meaning of these options (forward, backward, sideways) would change in an obvious way. This decision, along with the forms orientation, also meant in principle that the original procedure model of a net of actions connected by input and output data was transformed by a "migrating form paradigm" on the user level.

The need for early computerized mock-ups led to the use of HyperCard. Consequently, the decision was made to implement the Mac part of the user component completely in HyperCard. In this form, the system was presented at an information technology fair (Systems '89 in Munich, Germany) with a good general response to the user interface and the potential usefulness of the system. After this successful presentation, the interface was slightly improved with regard to graphic quality, layout, and ease of use, the UNIX-Mac communication was based on faster and more reliable protocols (MacTCP, TCP/IP), and it was then decided to engage in the practical test of the system.

3.2 Interface Description

In the following, we will describe the DOMINO interface as it is currently in use. As the typical Macintosh screen is on the small side, the interface is comprised of several full-screen layouts the user may switch between. A screen layout is divided into a menu bar placed across the top, an information window which takes most of the screen, and a bottom row of function buttons for more frequently used functions.

The interface consists of the main screen which gives an overview of the current procedures, a procedure form screen with the data of a single form and several auxiliary screens and dialog boxes, e.g. for tracking procedures, starting a new procedure, entering data in a personal profile, selecting enclosures, etc.

The main screen gives an overview of the procedures the user is currently involved in (see figure 3). The leading character of each entry indicates the state of the procedure from the viewpoint of the user:

(•) form needs to be worked on,
(*) form has changed (new data),
(√) procedure has been successfully terminated,
(†) procedure has been abnormally terminated (e.g. cancelled),
( ) no immediate action is expected from the user, but the procedure is still being processed.

The right part of the screen provides more detailed information when a procedure is selected. The main screen also provides functions such as updating procedure forms when new DOMINO messages have arrived, starting new procedures, saving/

deleting procedures that have terminated,sorting entries and searching for forms. By double-clicking on a procedure entry the associated form is opened.

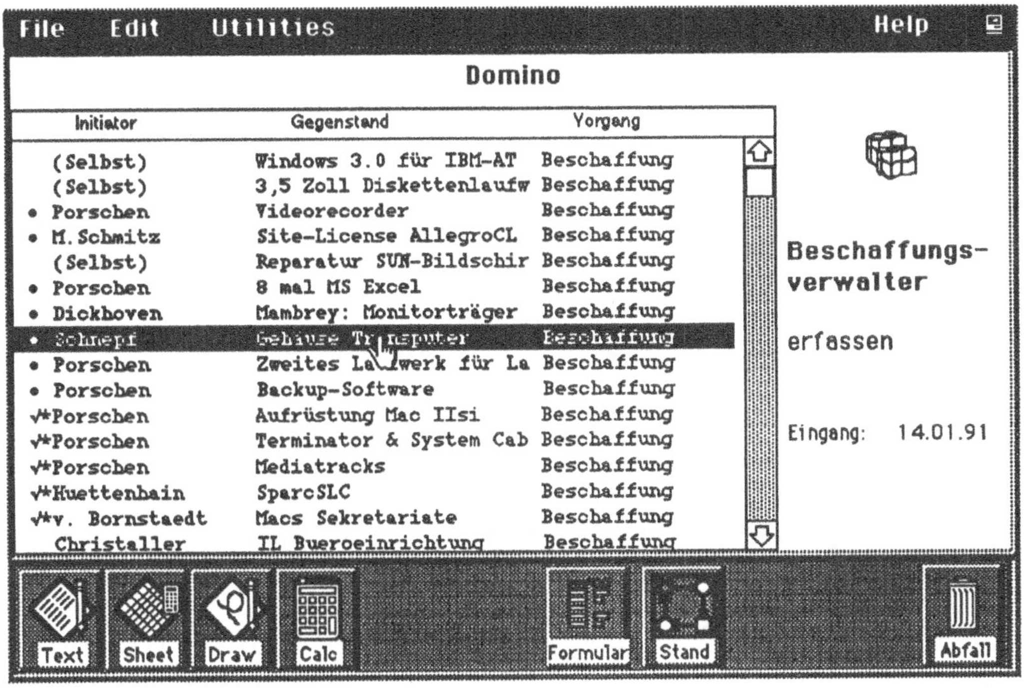

Figure 3. DOMINO interface: The procedure overview

The form screen presents the information relevant to a procedure instance in a forms like interface (see figure 4). It may actually consist of several consecutive screens when the data that have to be displayed do not fit onto one (Macintosh) screen, as is the case with the purchase form of figure 4. The filling in of an empty form is facilitated by automatically using defaults from a user profile, pop-up menus with appropriate choices, automatic calculations, and plausibility checks. Arbitrary enclosures as well as informal note stickers can be added to a form. Complaints may be attached to any field of a form.

The "dispose" menu offers the appropriate choice of actions the user can take in order to deal with the form in the current context; the menu commands are dynamically adjusted to the current status of the procedure. E.g., when a form has come in for approval the user can choose from: approve and pass on the form, or complain and send it back. In order to get more information on the status of a procedure, including a local "history" and — more important — the current location of the form, the "Stand (status)" button can be invoked.

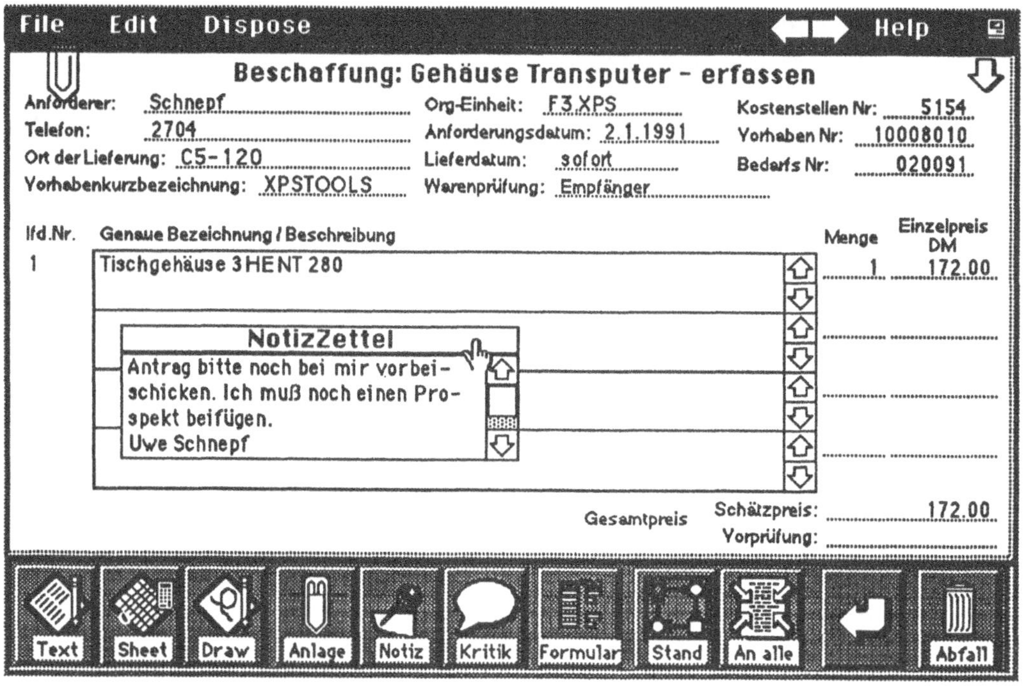

Figure 4. DOMINO interface: A purchase form

4 The Practical Test

Our institute comprises approximately 120 researchers and is divided into 5 research groups. The institute is headed by a director, the groups are headed by research group managers. The candidates for DOMINO were the clerical procedures connected with business trips, purchasing, vacations, etc. Our discussions with the management showed that the purchase procedure would be the most suitable test application, because it involved several steps of processing within the institute. Although DOMINO is meant for modelling and monitoring a variety of procedure types at the same time, the other procedures would have only been useful if the administration department had participated in the test. This turned out to be too difficult for technical reasons (incompatible computer networks and systems).

The internal purchase procedure in our institute consists of four steps. After a purchase form has been filled in by the prospective orderer (the "initiator"), the purchase form has first to be signed by the research group manager who checks with his own budget. Then the form is passed on to the network manager. He is responsible for checking the technical details of a proposed purchase and the compliance with the institute's purchasing policy, e.g., compatibility with existing machinery (network of over 150 machines, personal computers, work-stations and servers). The third step, the final approval by the director of the institute, only becomes necessary if the purchase price exceeds 2000 DM. Otherwise, the signature of the research group manager is sufficient. In the following and last step, the technical support person does the necessary bookkeeping, since he is responsible for the institute's purchase budget and the inventory of the technical equipment. Now the purchase form leaves the institute and is passed on to the purchase department which actually carries out the purchase. The (electronic) DOMINO procedure ends at this point, and the technical support person produces a paper equivalent of the electronic form along with the enclosures, if any. This paper form is then signed by a manager and sent off to the purchase department.

After installation of the procedure itself, a small group for an initial test was selected in which the system would be used only for fictitious purchases. This group consisted of five people who played the roles of the procedure (partly their real life role) with the development team as initiators of purchases. This test phase took approximately three months from June to August, 1990, and resulted in a number of minor modifications concerning technical and organizational details (apart from the identification and elimination of quite a number of bugs).

The official introduction of DOMINO for purchasing in our institute was then discussed with the research groups and the research group managers. Since the majority of employees place orders very seldom or never at all, it was decided to have two to five "purchasers" per research group who could act as initiator on behalf of others. This resulted in a user community of 22 people: six "officials" and 16 "purchasers". This group had the opportunity to play with the system for three weeks, and since mid October, 1990, DOMINO is in official use for purchasing in our institute.

5 The Experiences

In this section, we present our first experiences with the DOMINO system after three months of operation. This does not come near a systematic evaluation of the system (and was not intended as such) since our experimental basis is too narrow: the user community was very limited, we had only one type of procedure and not a variety of procedures, the time period was rather short, and the intensity of usage was quite inhomogeneous within the user group.

But apart from these limitations, we think that the qualitative judgements we have derived from both positive and negative experiences during our current experiment are still quite valuable. They should not be overestimated for the reasons given above, but they still represent first answers to a number of questions we had about the DOMINO system: How good is the user interface? Do the potential advantages of an office procedure system show in practice? Are the DOMINO procedure and process model adequate for practical use? We did not take a systematic quantitative approach to get these questions answered, but rather an informal approach with individual conversations and user meetings. During system installation members of the development team gave a short introduction to the system. We had discussions with users on various occasions (a user had difficulties with the system, a bug turned up, a new system version had to be installed, etc.). Additionally, we had two user meetings where questions, suggestions and experiences were discussed.

Some of the observations we made are DOMINO specific, some are groupware specific, and still others could have been observed with the introduction of any software system in an organization, but are of a specific quality since the software system is a multi-user application.

User interface. In general, the user interface was judged as easy to use and mainly self-explanatory. Sometimes, missing context was criticized: "Who will be at the next station in the procedure?", "Whom does a complaint go to?", "What have I already done with a procedure form?" (the latter especially with people frequently interrupted during their work with the system).

Keeping track of purchases. The better trackability of purchases was appreciated: The person currently processing the purchase order can be looked up any time by the people involved in the procedure. The usefulness of this feature would have been even higher had we succeeded in including the purchase department which is responsible for later stages of a purchase.

Unified treatment of purchases. One of the main benefits of an office procedure system is the unified treatment of all purchases according to the rules laid down in the procedure definition. This also results in a more complete, consistent, and up-to-date budgeting for the institute as a whole as well as for the research groups. However, this can only be achieved if the system is used throughout. In the first months, the use of DOMINO was not strictly enforced so that there were still a number of procedures run with paper forms. The main reason was that paper forms can be run quicker through our institute than their electronic counterparts if the initiator takes the trouble of running around and collecting the necessary signatures on the fly. This mixed mode of operation resulted in extra work (see below) and hampered the advantages of using DOMINO .

Suitability of the DOMINO procedure model. First, the DOMINO procedure model with its net of actions linked together by input/output relations and its potential of mixing parallel and alternative courses of action turned out to be too complex. For the task at hand — purchase procedure processing — which could be characterized as a hierarchical signing process, a simple sequential procedure model would have been sufficient. Secondly, the strict input/output relations between the actions of a procedure do not allow the data produced in one action to be changed in a subsequent action. While this safeguards against unauthorized changing of procedure data, the mechanism is rather rigid in that it requests the procedure to be set back to the person who produced the data to be changed. This was a source of much discussion and we had to employ a work-around for some cases. Of course, this will be different in different application environments.

Suitability of the DOMINO processing model. The conversation-based DOMINO model of procedure processing offers some provisions for exception handling. In addition to the normal course, the processing of a procedure instance can vary in the sense that it may be set back by the procedure control system when one participant complains about, e.g., missing prices, reasons given for purchase, or when the initiator cancels the procedure altogether; however, this exception handling facilities were considered not flexible enough, and there was felt a need for

Integration of informal communication. Especially officials felt themselves "fenced in" by the system features they had to use. The most common complaint was the missing possibility for letting another (arbitrary) person have a look at the purchase form and get it back with her or his comments in an informal way (ad-hoc comment feature). In general, a smooth transition from office procedure processing to more informal ways of communication with respect to the procedure form was missed. This ranged from the possibility of sending forms to other persons just for their information to the before mentioned comment feature.

Grouping procedures. In the DOMINO system, each procedure instance is treated separately. There was, however, the requirement — especially during later stages of the procedure — for grouping procedure forms for further processing: saving them jointly in an archive, dealing with them the same way (e.g., same complaint), or simply creating a local context important for budgeting or tracking purposes.

Lack of integration of other tools. While this seems to be a general problem with CSCW applications, DOMINO users complained particularly about two issues in this area:

(a) A spreadsheet program popular with those concerned with purchasing in our institute could only be "integrated" with purchase procedure processing via a not too comfortable copy and paste mechanism (same would have been true for other programs or procedures).

(b) DOMINO messages are treated separately from ordinary electronic mail — the user has to switch tools to send an e-mail message concerning an office procedure.

Media specific communication problems. The interleaved use of the paper and computer medium turned out to be some problem ("media clash"). The necessity for this mixture arose partly from the limited organizational domain in which DOMINO was in use, and partly from the fact that the provision of paper documents in addition to the purchase form is quite common. When the purchase procedure leaves our institute for the purchase department, a paper version of the form has to be generated, possibly along with enclosures. At the moment, this paper form has still to be signed, and sometimes paper documents, mostly advertisements have to be added. This results in overhead and diminishes the potential benefits of a computerized office procedure system. Possible solutions to this type of problem are the

acceptance of computer generated signatures, a more complete coverage of the organization, and simple-to-use scanners.
A different type of communication problem arises through the use of the computer medium itself. Communication gets more indirect and more explicit at the same time. This tends to result in a certain uneasiness with some users using the system, especially with "negative" communication acts (e.g., complaints). Even in the initial testing phase, users did not very much playfully explore the system as is quite common when trying out other (single user) Macintosh applications. The main reason seems to be that the current system does not give too much cooperative context (no explicit representation of procedures, of people involved) so that users may be in doubt which is the next or previous station, who exactly is receiving their comment or complaint.

Overhead-benefit relation. The question of who is paying for the overhead of a computer group support system and who is going to receive the benefits is crucial for its success (Grudin, 1988). The filling in of the electronic forms was in general not regarded as too much overhead by the initiators when compared with the benefit, i.e. the better trackability of the purchase forms. This may be attributed to the filling-in helps implemented in the user interface (defaults, pop-up menus, automatic calculation). The technical support person, however, complained about an additional workload. The reason was mainly the parallel use of paper forms for purchasing which created two different work modes at his desk. The potential benefit he anticipated — a more accurate budget since no paper form would slip through to the purchase department without passing his desk — could have been only realized by exclusively using DOMINO for purchasing.

6 Conclusion and outlook

We have presented a new version of our office procedure system DOMINO with a form-oriented interface which is running on a network of personal computers and Unix server machines (Macintoshes and SUN's). We have put this system to use for the purchasing process in our institute (as a candidate of a clerical procedure involving more than one step of processing). Comparing the efforts — the development of the new DOMINO interface and the introduction of the system to a user community — with the feed-back we received, we think that the experiment was (and is) a worthwhile exercise.

Our first experiences show that we have succeeded in building an easy-to-use procedure system for an office environment, which is able to demonstrate the potential benefits of such a system. The experiences also exhibited a number of problems. While some of these problems might be attributed to the somewhat limited organizational domain in which DOMINO was used or the initial mixed mode of paper and electronic forms, some of these problems indicate weaknesses of the system, which may be summarized as follows:

- The DOMINO procedure and processing model with its pre-structured net of actions and its given exception handling facilities turned out to be too rigid or ineffective in some respects.
- Easy transition to more informal or simple ways of communication and co-operation was felt to be missing.
- The environment for working on office procedures was lacking tailorability, e.g. individual grouping of procedures, or integration of personal tools.
- The organizational or group context was not or not adequately represented.

Some of these weaknesses may be overcome within or around DOMINO, e.g. the CoPlanX conversation could be extended to include the ad hoc comment feature mentioned above, or e-mail and simpler cooperation support tools could be integrated into the DOMINO environment. We have indeed begun to implement such simple tools like circulation folders and information requests with replies. Circulation folders are sent around in sequential way to a number of persons and can carry any kind of documents[2]. With information requests with replies, the request is posed in parallel to a number of people and the arrival of answers is monitored by the tool. We will integrate these new tools, e-mail and the DOMINO system and put them to use in the same organizational environment.

As a second consequence, we think that more flexible group support tools are needed which complement office procedure systems like DOMINO and lend themselves more easily to serve as a medium for groups as well as individuals to organize their work in areas which are not dominated by pre-structured procedures. Our current research aims at such tools for the coordination of distributed work which are to address the above key issues: flexibility and configurability, easy transition to informal communication, better overview of individual work and its group context. So, our DOMINO experiences have contributed to our direction in CSCW research: from pre-structured cooperation to unstructured or user configurable/modifiable cooperation patterns, from processing of "official" procedures to coordination of day-to-day work in a rich environment allowing for different views on tasks and representing the group context more explicitly, and from a coordination model governed to a large extent by the formalized conversation paradigm to a coordination model where there is still structured interaction but also non-formalized communication, conferencing, and some simple ways of information sharing.

Acknowledgements

We are indebted to our DOMINO users for their readiness to participate in our experiment and their criticism, and especially Peter Hoschka for many valuable suggestions concerning the user interface.

---

[2] We favor an even simpler processing model than that of the circulation folders of Karbe and Ramsperger (1990).

References

Grudin, J. L. (1988): "Why CSCW applications fail: Problems in the design and evaluation of organizational interfaces," in Proc. CSCW '88, ACM, New York, NY, 1988, pp. 85-93.

Karbe, B. H. and Ramsperger, N. G. (1990): "Influence of exception handling on the support of cooperative office work," in S. Gibbs, A. A. Verrijn-Stuart (eds.): *Multi-User Interfaces and Applications*, Proc. IFIP WG 8.4 Conf. on Multi-User Interfaces and Appl., Heraklion, Crete, Greece, Sept. 24 - 26, 1990, North-Holland, Amsterdam, 1990, pp. 355-370.

Kreifelts, Th., Licht, U., Seuffert, P. and Woetzel, G. (1984): "DOMINO: A system for the specification and automation of cooperative office processes," in B. Myhrhaug, D. R. Wilson (eds.): *Proc. EUROMICRO '84*, North-Holland, Amsterdam, 1984, pp. 33-41.

Kreifelts, Th. and Woetzel, G. (1987): "Distribution and exception handling in an office procedure system," in G. Bracchi, D. Tsichritzis (eds.): *Office Systems: Methods and Tools*, Proc. IFIP WG 8.4 Work. Conf. on Methods and Tools for Office Systems, Pisa, Italy, Oct. 22 - 24, 1986, North-Holland, Amsterdam, 1987, pp. 197-208.

Spenke, M. and Beilken, Chr. (1989): "A spreadsheet interface for logic programming," in *Proc. Conf. on Human Factors in Computing Systems (CHI '89)*, Apr. 30 - May 5 1989, Austin TX, ACM, New York NY, 1989.

Winograd, T. and Flores, F. (1986): *Understanding Computers and Cognition: A New Foundation for Design*, Ablex, Norwood NJ, 1986.

Proceedings of the Second European Conference on Computer-Supported Cooperative Work
Bannon, L., Robinson, M. & Schmidt, K. (Editors)
September 25-27, 1991, Amsterdam, The Netherlands

Distributed Computing and Organizational Change Enable Concurrent Engineering

Susan Frontczak, Kathy Miner
Hewlett-Packard Company, U.S.A.

Concurrent Engineering is the latest buzzterm for bringing products to market faster. This paper explores how a distributed computing environment can enable concurrent engineering. The following topics are covered:

- Definition of concurrent engineering and how it applies to non-technical as well as technical companies.
- Case studies of companies who have harnessed their distributed computing environment to foster multi-departmental teamwork and thereby reduce design cycles.
- Suggestions for overcoming organizational and technological barriers to concurrent engineering.

1. Introduction

The purpose of this paper is to illustrate that concurrent engineering is possible through a combination of distributed computing technology and organizational change.

This paper is organized as follows: current industry awareness of concurrent engineering; definition of terms; three case studies of concurrent engineering practiced today; technological and organizational concurrent engineering enablers; and key findings.

1.1 Industry Awareness of Concurrent Engineering

Robert Glasier of Intergraph Corporation defines concurrent engineering as the teamwork approach to engineering that brings all disciplines together from the outset of the project: product development, engineering, purchasing, manufacturing, marketing and finance (Glasier, 1990). It is intended to help product developers consider all elements of the product life cycle, including quality, cost, schedule and user requirements (Edwards, 1990).

An article in the March 22, 1990, issue of Machine Design entitled "Teamwork in Real Engineering" described how concurrent engineering was used to cut the development time on General Motor's LT-5 engine for the ZR-1 Corvette. By involving engineering and other functions concurrently in the development of the engine, GM was able to cut development time from the traditional seven years to four years.

The only collaboration technology enabler described in the Corvette engine article was the use of a FAX machine! It was used for transmitting design changes between the design teams in Detroit, Michigan and Hethel, England, and the manufacturing team in Stillwater, Oklahoma (Stinson, 1990).

Another article on concurrent engineering appeared in the April 30, 1990, issue of Business Week. The article was entitled "A Smarter Way to Manufacture: How 'concurrent engineering' can reinvigorate American industry. The article states:

> "The potential advantages of concurrent engineering have been recognized for decades. But earlier calls for it were thwarted by **middle management fiefdoms** and by the **lack of computerized tools** to spur cooperation between departments. Now that such tools are emerging, top management is cracking down and forcing design and manufacturing, in particular, to collaborate." [empahsis added] (Port, 1990)

1.2 Interaction Between Technology and Organization

Much of the research on concurrent engineering emphasizes organizational issues (Hauser, 1988; Liker, 1986; Takeuchi, 1986; Turino, 1990). This paper explores the interaction between organizational issues and technology issues, especially distributed computing technology. Technological support for the teamwork required by concurrent engineering is highly relevant to the study of computer supported cooperative work.

2. Definitions

2.1 Concurrent Engineering

We define concurrent engineering as: People working in parallel toward a common project goal, who gain productivity by communicating both with each other and through a shared body of data. Our definition is broad to illustrate that concurrent engineering principles apply not only to engineering projects, but also to any product development effort, where the product could be a software package or even a financial portfolio or legal brief.

Literature on concurrent engineering typically describes three major benefits: reduced time to market, higher product quality, and reduced cost (Edwards, 1990). Accompanying these three benefits is the creation of a more innovative product that meets real customer needs. Our case studies describe benefits in terms of time, quality and cost.

2.2 Distributed Computing

Distributed computing is an environment that provides users and applications with transparent access to all resources connected via a heterogeneous network. Resources include data, applications, compute power, I/O devices, services, and knowledge held by other network users (Seybold, 1990).

We identify three levels of communication in distributed computing (see Figure 1): resource-to-resource, person-to-resource, and person-to-person.

At the resource-to-resource level the user need not know that communication is taking place at all. Examples include automatic consistency management of distributed databases, remote procedure calls in distributed applications, and object/agent communications between applications.

Person-to-resource communication implies that all the power on the network is available to the individual user, not just the power of the local terminal or workstation. Example technologies supporting this level are browsers and filters for databases, print spoolers, and compute servers.

Examples of technologies supporting person-to-person communication are electronic mail, electronic conferencing, and group calendars. Transparent access at this level implies that the users can easily reach one another, regardless of hardware or location. Person-to-person communication is addressed by various computer supported cooperative work or groupware products. However, significant strides are being made in enabling concurrent engineering through the use of distributed computing at all three communication levels.

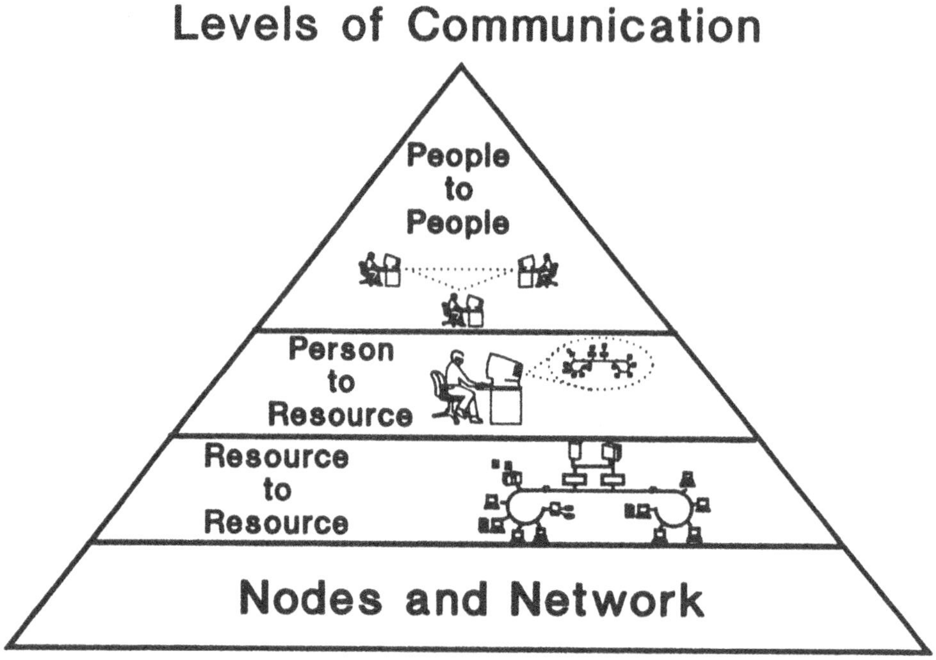

Figure 1

3. Case Studies

Our research includes contacts with 18 project teams at 11 companies that are now practicing concurrent engineering.

We present three case studies here, representing the best examples of concurrent engineering that we found.

3.1 Case Study 1: ME/EE Design

3.1.1 Context

Eight departments participate in mechanical and PC Board design review at HP's Apollo Systems Division. The departments include manufacturing, signal integrity, IC design, components engineering, and mechanical engineering. The team is highly geographically dispersed. For the Series 10000 computer, some parts were designed in Massachusetts, built in Scotland, and assembled in New Hampshire. Furthermore, if expensive ME CAD and EE CAD software are used to view the parts, licenses to this software cost from $40K to $80K per seat.

However, the reviewer of a design does not need to edit it, merely to examine it. Two tools were developed to meet the reviewer's needs: one to view the output from the ME CAD packages (CADACS) and another to view the output from the EE CAD packages (VIEWBOARD). A dialog of comments can be annotated right on the drawing, viewable by all reviewers as well as the originator. These viewing tools have some 'smarts'. For example, VIEWBOARD can highlight the path of a given signal; CADACS can render a 3-D view of a mechanical part.

3.1.2 Benefits Realized

CADACS and VIEWBOARD make information available to reviewers without requiring the expensive licenses needed by the designers who are editing the data. By eliminating the need for eight EE CAD licenses, the Series 10000 development team saved over $400K.

Savings also occur when errors are caught before parts are actually built. A technical writer noticed on one drawing that the front panel logo was upside down on a mechanical part. A simple email message saved many dollars in scrap parts.

There are over 150 active users of CADACS, and 200 active users of VIEWBOARD at Apollo Systems Division today.

3.1.3 Key Technologies

The team identifies DOMAIN's global file system as critical to their success. (DOMAIN is the operating system on HP's Apollo Systems Division computers.) For example, a designer in Massachusetts simply mails an electronic message to a reviewer in Scotland pointing to a drawing in the global file system that is ready for review. The reviewer then accesses the drawing using CADACS or VIEWBOARD as if it were available locally.

The global file system eliminates the need to copy files or worry about whether the most recent version has been sent to the reviewer. It also makes review comments visible to all since comments are recorded on the single copy of the drawing; as contrasted with markups on a copy of a drawing.

With the coming of the ANDREW FILE SYSTEM chosen by the Open Software Foundation for its Distributed Computing Environment (OSF DCE), heterogeneous environments will also enjoy the benefits of a global file system.

3.1.4 Key Organizational Factors

The desire for asynchronous, multi-disciplinary team review formed the impetus for developing CADACS and VIEWBOARD. The charter of Apollo Systems Division's tools development group, allows them to make decisions that enhance communication company-wide.

Also, due to a recent reorganization, the CADACS and VIEWBOARD teams were relocated very near each other. The co-location led to cross-fertilization of ideas. For example, inconsistencies in user interface between CADACS and VIEWBOARD (such as different viewing mechanisms) became apparent. They have recently started an investigation of ways to view EE information (i.e. the ME viewing tool CADACS).

3.2 Case Study 2: Software Development

3.2.1 Context

This is a composite case study of software development projects at HP's Apollo Systems Division, Honeywell, and Motorola.

Software developers need to address concurrency when releasing multiple versions of code. Released versions need to be maintained while, simultaneously, one or more future versions are under development. Fixes need to be incorporated in the future software as well as added to the released software.

DOMAIN SOFTWARE ENGINEERING ENVIRONMENT (DSEE) is a software package developed at HP's Apollo Systems Division. It manages large-scale development projects involving teams of managers, engineers, and technical writers.

DSEE works at all levels of communication described in Figure 1. It supports person-to-person communication through its task manager. DSEE provides resource-to-user communication via automatic triggers that notify people (via electronic mail) about changes to specific files. And DSEE applies resource-to-resource communication by monitoring dependencies between software modules and using all the computers on the network to build the product from its many modules.

3.2.2 Benefits Realized

Developers who use DSEE at Apollo Systems Division report needing fewer face-to-face meetings. Individuals have the power to make decisions that would otherwise require discussion: the software developers know that the tool will automatically notify appropriate team members of changes, and previous versions of the software can be retrieved if necessary.

Honeywell, Motorola, and Apollo Systems Division all report dramatic time savings as a result of using the distributed build capability of DSEE (described above). The IACD division of Honeywell noticed a reduction in build time from six hours for a serial build on a Series 3000 workstation to four hours on two Series 3000's (Merrill, 1990). The build time for a product at Apollo Systems Division decreased from an hour and nine minutes to sixteen minutes (McCourt, 1990).

3.2.3 Key Technologies

DSEE, coupled with the advantages of the DOMAIN global file system and merged account registries, is the key technology used to manage the complexity of simultaneous software development.

3.2.4 Key Organizational Factors

The most important organizational factor reported by Apollo Systems Division developers is trust. Team members have learned to trust each other to make decisions on their own. Each developer is responsible for fully testing his/her own software modules prior to putting them in the pool of modules that is used by other developers. This trust in each other (coupled with trusting the tools ability to reconstruct an earlier development state), increases productivity by maximizing autonomy.

The organization at Apollo Systems Division developed simultaneously with the DOMAIN technology. Therefore the distributed computing environment and the organizational structure were formed together. When existing organizations introduce distributed computing technology, it sometimes forces the organization as a whole to coordinate. In September of 1989 Motorola combined 750 HP Apollo workstations into a network spanning Schaumburg, Illinois, Ft. Worth, Texas, and Plantation, Florida. They report:

> "We formed an active working committee for the Apollo layer to consolidate and unify security policies across the three sites. Conventions such as account creation and deletion, password maintenance, modem access, and group naming needed to be unified and made consistent." (Dolikian, 1990)

3.3 Case Study 3: Rules of Thumb Database

3.3.1 Context

An automotive manufacturer has piloted a database which contains rules of thumb for designing parts of a car. The database contains approximately 30 rules of thumb categories arranged in a hierarchy. For example, a manufacturing process category contains an assembly category.

People in various engineering disciplines enter rules of thumb into the database. An engineer designing a new part can query the database for similar parts developed in the past and discover rules of thumb used and the reasons they were used. (The reasons are important because if the reason changes, a given rule of thumb may no longer apply that may apply to their projects.)

3.3.2 Benefits Realized

Although the database is still being piloted, already it has saved the company time and improved the quality of new parts. The time savings is in reduced think time and reduced communication time. By making the collective knowledge and experience of many engineering disciplines readily available, the engineer spends less time going through the same reasoning process or searching out rules of thumb from co-workers.

The pilot program has also yielded quality improvements. On a particular part, none of the recent design errors were repeated when the rules of thumb database was used.

3.3.3 Key Technologies

The database was originally developed on a host minicomputer but was recently moved to a networked personal computer environment using an off-the-shelf distributed database package.

3.3.4 Key Organizational Factors

A major limitation to the rules of thumb effort is the relatively low priority placed on entering the rules of thumb and keeping the database up to date. It is considered to be 'above and beyond' the engineer's job to enter the data. As the database developer explained, "We tend to put these rules of thumb in our memories. Our memory and experience are valued by co-workers and managers."

3.3.5 Other Observations

Current text-based technology is also limiting the success of the database. The database developer's vision is to be able to easily enter rules of thumb in their most efficient form for information processing: pictures, audio, etc. He is using the video game as a role model for future development efforts: players, from novices to experts, intuitively learn and recall tricks and shortcuts. (Note: no manual needed!) Once they find a trick, they can combine it with other tricks to accelerate through the game.

4. Technological and Organizational Enablers for Concurrent Engineering

These case studies illustrate examples of concurrent engineering practices being implemented with today's technologies and in today's organizations. Companies are realizing concrete benefits even with pilot programs, but it requires a combination of distributed computing and organizational acceptance. Following is a discussion of technological and organizational concurrent engineering enablers.

4.1 Technological Support for Sharing

In our definition of distributed computing, we described resources as including data, applications, compute power, I/O devices, services and the knowledge available on the network. Here we concentrate on two key resources: data and knowledge. We examine how concurrent engineering can be implemented today by sharing data and knowledge.

We differentiate data from knowledge in this way: Data is the representation of the problem to be solved and the solution to the problem, the multiple inputs and outputs of the project. Knowledge is the experience and skill that are applied to solving the problem.

4.1.1 Technologies for Sharing Data

There are several benefits to sharing data, such as:

- Managing the complexity of simultaneous development
- Maintaining a single source of the data
- Widespread access

This section discusses tools and technologies to support each aspect of data sharing.

4.1.1.1 Managing the Complexity of Simultaneous Development

Software tools help manage the complexity of simultaneous development. At the basic level, UNIX provides rcs and/or sccs commands for revision control, and the make command for file dependencies. The DSEE product handles much more complex configuration management for software development.

Some of today's data management systems also handle configuration management. Examples include SHERPA (a stand alone design management system) and HP's mechanical engineering DATA MANAGEMENT SYSTEM (part of the ME10 and ME30 application packages).

4.1.1.2 Maintaining a Single Source of the Data

Sharing data eliminates the dangers and hassles of maintaining multiple copies of the same data. On a small scale, linked directories and the NETWORKED FILE SYSTEM (NFS) support sharing data between a few machines. The DOMAIN file system, and in the future the ANDREW FILE SYSTEM (AFS) support shared access to data on a large scale as well as in the small.

As Motorola reports:

> "Before the [DOMAIN] network, these activities were coordinated 'open-loop', via periodic batch updates of design files via over-night express shipments of cartridge tapes, faxes of documents, and low-speed modem transfers to update changed documents. The process was slow and error-prone, relying on engineers to manually request updates and to propagate these copies to remote sites using brute-force dumping and loading of wbak or tar archive tapes updates were sometimes not done as often as needed, leaving open the possibility of releasing inconsistent versions of software to our customers." (Dolikian, 1990)

Reviewing tools, such as the internal tools CADACS and VIEWBOARD described in the first case study, and commercial tools such as STATION SOFTWARE, allow multiple people to see and comment on a single copy of design drawings.

4.1.1.3 Widespread Access

The combination of a global file system and data management software forms the foundation for making data available to any one who needs it. Availability of data is a prerequisite to empowering individuals to make considered decisions - see discussion of trust, under "Organizational Support for Sharing", below.

But mere access to data is not enough. Some of the issues faced today in exploiting data access are:

- Security. There is always some data for which access should be controlled. This is as much an organizational issue as it is a technological one; policies must be set and specified. Technologies such as Kerberos (as part of OSF's DCE) support security requirements.
- Browsers and Filters. An overabundance of data can be as bad as the lack of data. Technology can help by providing browsers, filters, and other navigational tools to assist the user in acquiring data of interest. Ultimately we predict standards in both database interfaces (based on a Distributed Object Model) and in human navigational interfaces.
- Resource-to-Resource Access. Several application software suppliers, initiatives, and consortia are grappling today with the need to share data between databases, across heterogeneous hardware, between applications, and even across organizational boundaries (such as with vendors). Examples of software supplier solutions include the FALCON framework by Mentor Graphics and the OPUS framework by Cadence for electrical engineering. Examples of industry efforts include the CAD FRAMEWORK INITIATIVE (CFI) for electrical engineering, the PORTABLE COMMON TOOL ENVIRONMENT (PCTE) for software engineering, and the CALS/CE and DICE initiatives for product design.

4.1.2 Technologies for Sharing Knowledge

Knowledge is divided into collaborative and captured knowledge. Collaborative knowledge is knowledge brought to the project team by current team members. Captured knowledge is knowledge and experience that has been accumulated from industry experts and members of past project teams.

4.1.2.1 Collaborative Knowledge

Ideally, the concurrent engineering project team shares knowledge via frequent face-to-face meetings. However, with many of today's project teams being dispersed in time and place, face-to-face meetings are a luxury (Stinson, 1990). Case Study 1 illustrated the use of CADACS and VIEWBOARD, two internally developed distributed computing tools, to share knowledge over time and place at the Apollo Systems Division. Other tools such as electronic mail, electronic bulletin boards and smart meeting rooms make use of distributed computing technology to share collaborative knowledge (I/S Analyzer, 1989).

Hewlett-Packard's SHAREDX is a collaboration tool that extends the industry-standard X WINDOW SYSTEM to enable real-time sharing of X protocol-based applications between two or more remote users using X WINDOW based workstations. Windows can be shared to non-HP workstations running the X WINDOW SYSTEM or to X terminals or PCs running X Window emulation mode (Hewlett-Packard Company, 1991). HP SHAREDX has been used by concurrent engineering teams for consulting on engineering designs, software debugging and joint-authoring of documents. Since HP SHAREDX operates over TCP/IP networks, it takes advantage of distributed computing technology to allow collaborative knowledge sharing.

4.1.2.2 Captured Knowledge

The rules of thumb database in Case Study 2 illustrated the use of relational database technology and distributed computing to capture knowledge of automotive company experts. Expert systems were designed to capture knowledge. Only now are expert systems finding their way into commercial applications. For instance, electrical engineering application supplier Mentor Graphics has developed the CONCURRENT DESIGN ENVIRONMENT. It contains a DECISION SUPPORT SYSTEM that allows individuals who are not programmers to create applications incorporating their design expertise (Mentor, 1990).

A set of prototype software of interest is the Bootstrap Initiative's OPEN HYPERDOCUMENT SYSTEM (OHS). The OHS was developed by Doug Engelbart, a professor at Stanford University. It is designed to capture the knowledge of a project team, much like a lab notebook does. The information is stored in corporate memory and hyperlinked for easy access by current project team members as well as members of future project teams (Engelbart, 1988).

4.2 The Effect of Technology on Communication

Computing technology is changing the way we communicate. For example, automatic bank teller machines alter routine banking transactions from a person-to-person activity to a person-to-resource activity. Essentially this allows the bank client and the bank personnel to "communicate" asynchronously. As another example, telephone switching equipment replaces a person-to-resource activity (where an operator plugs wires into a switchboard) with a resource-to-resource activity (where computers talk to each other).

In general, technology allows activities to occur at lower levels of communication (defined in Figure 1). This has two benefits: it increases the efficiency of the activity and it frees up people to spend their time performing more meaningful, higher quality communication.

Likewise, the distributed computing technologies that enable concurrent engineering support tasks at lower levels of communication (see Figure 2).

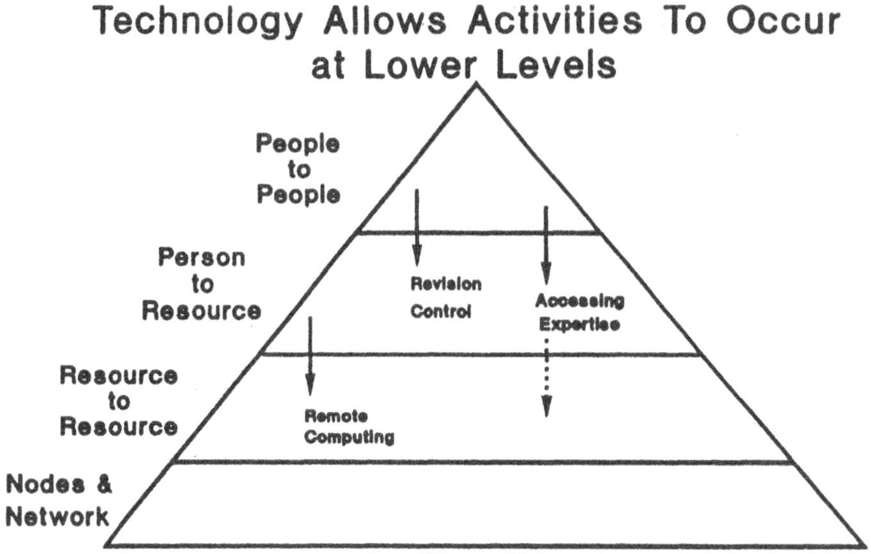

Figure 2

Some examples are:

- Tools that support data sharing, such as RCS and SCCS for revision control, eliminate the need for one person to check with another person prior to editing a jointly authored file. Person-to-person communication is replaced by person-to-resource communication.
- Knowledge sharing tools that capture expertise for later use substitute person-to-resource communication for person-to-person communication. For example, Design for Manufacturability and Design for Analysis tools capture some of the expertise of manufacturing and assembly personnel; the rules-of-thumb database, described above, captures product design expertise.
- Resource sharing tools such as the NETWORK COMPUTING SYSTEM (NCS) eliminate the need for users to learn about networking protocols, processes, etc. They can now tap into the compute resources on the whole network without becoming a computer expert. Resource-to-resource communication supplants person-to-resource communication by transferring to the computer the burden of locating, selecting, and communicating with the remote computer.

The challenge for technology developers is twofold. First, technology needs to support activities at lower levels of communication, in order to free up quality time at higher levels. Second, technology should blend the levels of communication into a seamless continuum so that people have full access to resources as they communicate and work with each other.

4.3 Organizational Support for Sharing

Organizational support can be viewed in terms of sharing data and sharing knowledge.

4.3.1 Sharing Data

Developing a sense of trust among team members is key to data sharing. Individuals need to have the freedom to initiate additions and changes to the project data based on their expertise and roles on the project team. Certainly, computer systems will need to have revision control, notification and archiving mechanisms in place.

4.3.2 Sharing Knowledge

In the area of knowledge sharing, a key enabler is to organize for cross-functional teamwork. At Hewlett-Packard cross-functional product development teams have been the norm for several years (Nevens, 1990). Having participated on cross-functional teams doing concurrent engineering on fast-track projects, we believe that cross-functional team participation is rewarding for individual team members as well as for the company.

Another knowledge sharing enabler is to institute a reward system for recording knowledge for later use. A computerized system for capturing knowledge could easily track the number of times that knowledge is accessed. Management could recognize those people or teams whose knowledge has been accessed most often. Since design re-use reduces duplicated effort, rewards could also be given to teams who re-use designs and concepts.

All of these organizational enablers require management commitment. The organization must be willing to bootstrap itself. Bootstrap is a concept borrowed from the Bootstrap Initiative mentioned earlier. Bootstrapping implies empowering an organization to improve itself. This means setting aside resources and initiating pilot projects for organizational improvement (Engelbart, 1990). In our research we saw many examples of companies bootstrapping themselves.

We heard repeatedly that changing people was more difficult than adopting new technologies. If pilot projects are shown to be successful, people will be much more willing to try new modes of working.

5. Key Findings

There are multiple ways of working in parallel. On one hand, tools can be built and people can be organized specifically to enable synchronous work. Examples include co-location of teams, sharing live screens, and 'smart' electronic meeting rooms. On the other hand, technology can be harnessed to reduce the need for synchronous work. Examples here include electronic mail, voice mail, and tools that migrate communication from the person-to-person level to person-to-resource level.

The challenge is to provide tools that free people to spend their time on the act of communicating and working together, rather than on understanding and managing the processes and mechanics. These tools need to:

- Support communication at a given level with communication at lower levels (Figure 2).
- Blend the communication capabilities of the different levels into a seamless continuum.

From our case studies, DOMAIN users are in the forefront of harnessing their computing environment to enable concurrent engineering. This is especially true at Apollo Systems Division, which grew up along with, and as a result of, the technology. Introducing concurrent engineering is more difficult in an established environment of serial product development and deep management hierarchies.

Frameworks are discipline-specific today. CADACS and VIEWBOARD are facing the need to communicate across the ME/EE boundary. Ultimately, either interfaces between frameworks will need to become standard or the frameworks will need to be unified.

Even with the best tools, humans still benefit from human contact. For example, the co-location of CADACS and VIEWBOARD team members led to unexpected benefits. When co-location is infeasible, as in many development efforts, we recommend that team members meet in person at the outset of the project. Throughout a project, even geographically dispersed teams can strive to maintain a level of informal communication. The promise of multimedia built on distributed computing is that it can promote the kind of communication that occurs in person (e.g., by using desktop video-conferencing and shared workspace).

Evidence of the value of concurrent engineering is being reported in terms of reduced time to market, lower cost of development and production, and improved quality. Perhaps the most important finding is that organizations can take incremental steps today toward developing a concurrent engineering environment. Sharing data and knowledge are the keys.

6. Appendix A - Acronyms

AFS	Andrew File System
ARPA	Advanced Research Projects Agency
CAD	Computer Aided Design
CADACS	Computer Aided Documentation Access System
CALS	Computer-Aided Acquisition and Logistic Support

CE	Concurrent Engineering
CFI	CAD Framework Initiative
DARPA	Defense ARPA
DB	Data Base
DCE	Distributed Computing Environment
DICE	DARPA Initiative for Concurrent Engineering
DSEE	Domain Software Engineering Environment
EE	Electrical Engineering
HP	Hewlett-Packard Company
IC	Integrated Circuit
ME	Mechanical Engineering
NCS	Network Computing System
NFS	Networked File System
OSF	Open Software Foundation
PC	Printed Circuit
PCTE	Portable Common Tool Environment - A CASE framework for data exchange.
RCS	Revision Control System
SCCS	Source Code Control System
UNIX	UNIX is a registered trademark of AT&T in the U other countries.

7. Acknowledgements

We heartily thank the following people and organizations for providing us information and participating in the case studies: Sara Beckman of HP's Product Generation Team (PGT), Tom Bower of HP's Roseville Networks Division, Alexander Cavalli of Microelectronics and Computer Technology Corporation, Dick Collette of HP's Apollo Systems Division (ASY), Ron Collett of Dataquest, Danny Cooper of Texas Instruments, Patrick Fitzhorn of Colorado State University, Takashi Fukuda of ASY, Alfred Gort of HP's Colorado Computer Manufacturing Operation, Chuck Habib of PGT, Paul Johnson of HP's San Diego Division, Steven Levy of Putnam Companies, Larry Mammon of HP, Scott McCourt of ASY, Melanie Merrill of Honeywell, Robert Quist of HP's Fort Collins Systems Division (FSY), Mike Schubert of FSY, Bob Waites of HP's Engineering Applications Group (EAG), Mitch Weaver of EAG, Peter Will of PGT, and others who prefer to remain unidentified. We wish you all the best in your current and future concurrent engineering efforts. We also thank the following reviewers for their clarifying and polishing comments: Jim Borzym, Don Brock, Jim Geer, Terrill Hurst, Rosemary Kramer and Carol McKennan.

8. About the Authors

Susan Frontczak is an R&D Software Development Engineer and Kathy Miner is a Product Manager. They both work in the Collaborative Multimedia Program within Hewlett-Packard's Workstation Group.

9. References

Dolikian, Arman (1990): "Building a cross-country Apollo Network", *ADUS Ring*, May 1990, p.1.

Edwards, Albert (1990): "Concurrent Engineering: The Design Environment for the '90s", *Instructional Television Network Course*, University of Southern California, July 19, 1990, p.1.

Engelbart, Douglas (1990): *Bootstrap Seminar*, Stanford University, June 19-21, 1990.

Engelbart, Douglas and Harvey Lehtman(1988): "Working Together", *BYTE Magazine*, December, 1988, pp. 245-252.

Glasier, Robert A. (1990): "Tying Together Engineering Systems and Data Center", *The Sixth Chautauqua Conference on Computer-Aided Engineering*, D. Brown Associates, Inc., September 10, 1990.

Hauser, John R. and Don Clausing (1988): "The House of Quality", *Harvard Business Review*, May-June, 1988, pp. 63-73.

Hewlett-Packard Company (1990): *HP SharedX Product Data Sheet*, April, 1990.

I/S Analyzer (1990): "Experiences with Workgroup Computing", July, 1990.

Liker, Jeffrey K. and Hancock, Walton M. (1986): "Organizational Systems Barriers to Engineering Effectiveness", *IEEE Transactions on Engineering Management*, Vol. EM-33, No.2, May, 1986, pp. 82-91.

McCourt, Scott (1990): DSEE Product Manager, HP's Apollo Systems Division. Interview August 31, 1990.

Mentor (1990): "Concurrent Design Environment - Design Automation in the 1990s", *Mentor Graphics Press Kit*, p. 5.

Merrill, Melanie (1990): Honeywell Corporation. Interview, September 26, 1990.

Nevens, T. Michael, Gregory L. Summe, and Bro Uttal (1990): "Commercializing Technology: What the Best Companies Do", *Harvard Business Review*, May-June, 1990, pp. 154-163.

Port, Otis, Zachary Schiller, and Resa King (1990): "A Smarter Way to Manufacture: How 'concurrent engineering' can reinvigorate American industry", *Business Week* , April 30, 1990, pp. 110-117.

Seybold, Patricia (1990): "Distributed Computing", *Network Monitor*, January, 1990, p. 2.

Stinson, Terry (1990): "Teamwork in Real Engineering", *Machine Design*, March 22, 1990, pp.99-104.

Takeuchi, Hirotaka and Ikujiro Nonaka (1986): "The New New Product Development Game", *Harvard Business Review* , January-February, 1986, pp. 137-146.

Proceedings of the Second European Conference on Computer-Supported Cooperative Work
Bannon, L., Robinson, M. & Schmidt, K. (Editors)
September 25-27, 1991, Amsterdam, The Netherlands

An analysis of Design and Collaboration in a Distributed Environment

Hans Marmolin and Yngve Sundblad
IPlab, NADA, KTH, S-100 44 Stockholm, Sweden

Björn Pehrson
SICS, Box 1263, S-164 28 Kista, Sweden

The Swedish MultiG program addresses research issues in distributed multimedia workstation applications, including CSCW, and high-speed networks. This report treats some basic CSCW issues in a distributed design environment. We review and analyse relevant literature on system design and computer supported cooperation and discusses the basic issues: What is design? What is collaboration in design? What computer support is necessary for collaboration in a distributed design environment? A task analysis is performed of design and collaboration. Computer support for these tasks in a distributed environment is discussed with emphasis on generic tools for informal collaboration.

Introduction

MultiG is a Swedish cooperative research program on distributed multimedia applications and gigabit networks. It comprises projects from end-user oriented applications to very high-speed fiber optic communications. It has similar goals as the NREN gigabit network testbeds (IEEE Computer, September 1990).

The CSCW project aims at modeling computer supported cooperative design work, and specification of a distributed design environment implementing this model. It is focused on collaborative early design capture of interactive and/or embedded real time systems. The scope of the project is to propose tools for collaboration that enable designers to cooperate in a distributed environment, to specify functional, operational and interface requirements on these tools and to specify the social work situation in which these tools are to be used.

The basis for the specification of the distributed design environment is theoretical and empirical analysis of cooperative system design involving designers working at different workstations distributed geographically and/or contributing at different periods in time. Such studies should answer three questions: What is design? What is collaboration in design? What computer support is necessary for collaboration in a distributed environment? We give a first tentative answer to these questions by reviewing relevant literature on system design and computer supported cooperation and discussing different approaches to CSCW modeling such as the task and the tool approach. We summarize the findings in terms of a set of requirements on computer support for collaboration in a distributed design environment. A coming report uses these results as point of departure for modeling the CSCW environment to be used in MultiG (Marmolin et al 1991).

System design

What is system design? To answer this question we will distinguish between the design task and the design process, i.e between the activities involved in design and how these activities are performed. The design task could broadly be defined as a set of activities aiming at conceptualizing and specifying systems in accordance with the needs and requirements of the users, under existing economical and technological constraints. The design process, on the other hand, could be defined as an iterative problem solving process characterized by intuition, analysis, integration of information, and trade offs in mainly ill-defined situations.

These very broad and general definitions will be further elaborated below, but first the distinction between normative and descriptive models of design should be noted. Normative models attempt to prescribe how design should be performed, while descriptive models describe how design really is performed. Examples of normative models are top-down "structured programming" models, structured Case-methodologies etc. This report addresses only descriptive models. In our view, an understanding of the needs and the requirements on a distributed design environment demands descriptive models, that have to be based both on theoretical analysis of man´s basic capabilities to accomplish the design task and on empirical findings concerning how this task is performed today. The reason for this combined approach is that design is not a static process, but changes continuously over time as new tools and methods are developed. Specific empirical findings are then valid only for a short period of time.

The design task

There are a lot of attempts to analyse the design task into subtasks and subsubtasks or activities, see e.g Rouse and Boff (1987a). They differ in details, but they all agree that the design task includes the set of generic subtasks listed below, although the order of subtasks may differ.

- *Formulation and identification of the design problem*
  Needs, requirements and constraints are identified and the design problem is specified.
- *Understanding the problem*
  Information about the problem and possible solutions is gathered.
- *Generation of alternative solutions*
  Design options are generated and synthesized.
- *Selection and interpretation of alternatives*
  The impact of different design alternatives on the users needs are analysed and evaluated, trade offs and optimization's are made and the most acceptable alternative is selected for implementation.

Rouse and Boff (1987b) suggest that these design subtasks could be further divided into a set of activities. However, their classification is very general, as it is intended to be valid for all kinds of design tasks. A more specific list of activities could be suggested if one limits the scope to design of software systems and to the early stages of this process. Software design can be described as a mapping of the behaviour required of the application (system function, constraints, exception conditions, user actions, etc) on to the computational structure implementing this behaviour (control structures, computer architectures, data structures, algorithms, etc) using knowledge about the application domain and the software domain (Curtis et al 1988). We will use this definition as a basis for our classification of design activities, but we will integrate it with the classification proposed by Rouse and Boff and the result of some empirical studies of software design (Curtis et al 1988, Rosson et al 1988, Meister 1987). We propose that the subtasks listed above are mainly composed of the activities listed in Table I.

Subtask	Activities
Formulation of the design problem	Defining and decomposing the problem Formulating requirements, criteria and constraints Planning and coordinating team activities
Understanding the problem	Learning about the application Mapping application knowledge onto computational structures Building a mental model of the system
Generation of alternative solutions	Reviewing other attempts to solve similar problems Analogizing from earlier experiences Using intuition
Selection of alternatives	Prototyping Logical and/or empirical evaluation, design validation Advocating and reporting the chosen alternative

Table I. A classification of design activities

Many of these activities could be performed either individually or in collaboration. This question will be discussed in detail below. Coordinating team activities concerns planning activities, division of work etc and this activity exists of course only in project teams. The activity learning about the application is composed of many different subactivities such as seeking information, analysing information, integrating information obtained by user interviews, user observations, task scenarios etc. The activity building a mental model of the system is a process that goes on during the whole design phase. The term mental model stands for the way humans integrate new knowledge and earlier experiences in the form of an incomplete, unclear and unspecific but concrete model of the objects and events in question, see e.g. Norman (1983). It functions as a sort of outline of what the designer must do to solve the design problem and what he has accomplished so far (Meister 1987). Reviewing other attempts means to use different kinds of external sources as e.g other systems, literature, research reports etc to get ideas. The activity prototyping means all kinds of prototypes, paper mock-ups etc. Protoyping can of course be used also for understanding the problem and for generation of alternative solutions. Logical evaluation means the use of different kinds of tools for specification and analysis, such as formal languages, simulations etc and empirical evaluation means studies of user performance and satisfaction.

We will use this description as a first tentative model of the design task. Of course, for each design task there will be a mix of the activities listed. Some of the activities may be unconscious, some may be skipped or truncated and some may not be accomplished. In general, however, we will assume that the design task consists of the activities listed above. Although this assumption is based on both theoretical and empirical studies, it has of course to be empirically tested in relevant situations. An on-going study within our project is concerned with this problem.

The design process

As mentioned, the list of subtasks given above does not mean that the design process is a structured process starting with problem formulation, ending with the selection of the best alternative. On the contrary the design process as a whole and each subtask and activity is best described as an unstructured process that varies from designer to designer and from time to time depending on a lot of mainly unknown factors. Thus, it is not possible to describe the design process in terms of a given flow of work. Instead we propose a description in terms of a set of important and interrelated dimensions of the design process.

Design as problem solving

One school of thought describes design as a top-down decomposition of objectives into requirements and physical processes, with cost-performance trade offs. This constitutes what Rouse and Boff (1987b) call the analytic view of design. This view assumes that design is a structured and ordered organized analytic process. Other have observed design as a mixture of top-down and bottom-up processes as an incremental approach. Design is assumed to emerge from bottom-up perceptions of patterns of understanding and experiences of users´ need. This could be called the artistic view of design, characterised as organic growth (Sandewall 1978).

However, design could rather be viewed as a form of problem solving (Rouse 1986). Research in human problem solving (Rouse 1983) indicates that humans approach problems on several levels at the same time moving among recognition, planning and execution activities. Pattern recognition on contextual surface features seems then to be more important than analysis of problem structure. Thus problem representation is of fundamental importance for design. As most design problems are ill-defined at early stages, the goals are unclear and goal clarification occur in parallel with search for solutions, the analytic and artistic approach have to support each other (Klein 1987). That means, that the design process has to start with some definition of the problem, finding tentative solutions, clarifying the problem using these solutions, finding new solutions etc. The design process could then be described as a series of information transactions (Bally 1987). Partial information from the designer´s mind is used as the basis for a first sketch. By externalizing this sketch, the designer can retrieve and accumulate additional information from the task environment as a basis for the next externalization. Design is then an iterative mixture of top-down or bottom-up processes.

For example, Rosson et al (1988) studying 22 design teams at different stages including both business and research teams, found that there were two dominant approaches to design, a phased development approach and an incremental one. The phased approach was characterized by a separation of design, implementation and evaluation, while in the incremental approach these steps occurred simultaneously. The incremental approach was mainly used in research projects, by small teams and in an interpretating programming environment, while the opposite was true for the phased approach. It should be noted that user testing was applied to the same degree in both approaches. Curtis et al (1988) found in a field study of large system design an important reason for applying a mixture of bottom-up and top-down processes: requirements always change during the design process as a result of different and changing needs of the customers, changes in underlying technology, misunderstandings of the application domain and unrequired enhance-ments added by programmers. Although design teams tried to solve this problem by negotiations, it was often difficult to enforce agreement across teams. Thus requirements were not as stable reference for a top-down approach as often assumed. Another possible reason for the different approaches to design can be attributed to individual differences between designers (Rouse 1986). Designers like all humans are different and apply different cognitive strategies to problem solving as serialistic or holistic thinking, impulsive divergent or reflective convergent thinking, etc. Nadler (1984) finds four types of designers, the inactivists that avoid problems, the reactivists that emphasize well proven solutions, the preactivists that designs for the future and the interactivists that emphasize designing of the future.

Design as intuition

Smith (1987) argues that intuition is a fundamental part of design (while others emphasize analytic aspects) and distinguishes two types of intuition of importance for design, generational and judgemental. The former concerns intuitive ideas of new concepts, the latter concerns evaluative judgements about proposed solutions.

Concrete representations play a very important role in intuition (Rouse 1986). As mentioned above the basis for many design decisions are informal experiments as e.g. rapid prototyping, analysis of analogous situations and earlier solutions, concrete representations of alternative solutions such as scenario descriptions, graphical representations, dimensional representations etc. Bally (1987) studying the use of different kinds of representations in design using a hypothetical design task[1], found that the designers use many different representation but one at a time, going back and forth between them and that visual representations were predominant.

The use of concrete representation could be interpreted as an attempt of designers to build a mental model of the system. More seldom is a formal approach applied, in which the designers attempt to find the optimum solution using some decision theory or decision methodology. In this context it should be noted that some argue that design is a question of maximizing system effectiveness within the given constraints, while others view design as a question of producing an acceptable, but not optimal solution (Rouse 1987b). This distinction is important as if the search is not for an optimum or constrained optimal solution, then design support systems based on finding an optimal solution will not be very useful. We will argue that at least in the early stages, the design process could not be described as an optimization process, although later stages may focus on a search for optimal solutions.

Design as information gathering

Rosson et al (1988) investigated how design ideas were obtained and evaluated and found that most ideas were obtained by information gathering techniques such as task/user analysis, analysis of other systems, literature reviews etc. The techniques most used for evaluating ideas were however not the same (see Table II).

Activity	Getting ideas	Testing ideas
Information gathering	53 %	7 %
Creative thinking	16 %	9 %
Group discussions	13 %	14 %
Logical analysis	12 %	46 %
Prototyping	6 %	25 %

Table II. The activities used for getting and testing design ideas[2].

Another important aspect of information gathering concerns the integration of knowledge from different sources into an unified view. This integration could be described as a learning process (Curtis et al 1988). Designers continuously learn about the application domain, about new computational methodologies and about design and implementation decisions made by others. Also the customers undergo a learning process as they begin to understand the implications of their requirements. Curtis found that, although application domain knowledge was necessary for successful design, this knowledge was split among the software development staff. The ability to integrate such knowledge into a unified view and transform it to computational structures characterized the exceptionally good designers they met.

[1]The task was to design a product that allows the payment of credit card bills from home using the telephone.

[2]The figures given represents the percentage of projects in which designers reported the use of a certain technique. The basis for these figures is 21 projects selected by the designers, representing a wide variety of applications and system size. There were seven research projects, seven projects were concerned with site support and seven with product development.

Design as a collaborative process

Many argue that design is collaborative work. Harrison et al (1990) view design as a social construction of a technical reality focused on establishing and maintaining a shared understanding among the participants. Bødker et al (1987) describe design in terms of mutual learning in a design team of computer professionals and end users. Others view design as negotiations. Curtis et al (1988) found that negotiations about requirements and trade off solutions occur throughout the development process. Rosson et al (1988) found that these aspects were the most important and that communication and coordination is especially critical for teams using the incremental approach where system changes occur continuously and unpredictably. Kedzierski (1988) studied the activities of software designers during evolutionary development of a compiler and found that especially during later design stages most time was spent on communication activities as shown in Table III. Norcio et al (1986) conclude from a study of design activities in developing complex software modules, that discussion activities among software designers play a major role in the design process and indicate design progress. Curtis et al found, however, communications outside the team and across organizational levels to be rare and that communication problems often occurred when groups transfer inter-mediate work products and also found documentation to be very ineffective for communication. Instead each team member had several nets of people to talk to for information on issues affecting their work. Sathi et al (1988) point at another communication problem, the problem of identifying the team members that should be informed about changes made to design (in large number) at various stages of development.

Activity	Time spent
Questions to other designers	27 %
Information about changes	25 %
Complaining	13 %
Planning work	14 %
Testing commands, functions	21 %

Table III. The activities if software designers during evolutionary development[3].

Conclusions

This review of descriptive theories and studies of design points to the difficulties in trying to model this very unstructured and complex process in any structured way. The lesson to be learned is instead that any computer support has to be as flexible as the design process itself. However, it points to some important characteristics of the design task and the design process that have to be considered in developing a distributed design environment for early stages of design.

[3]The figures given represents percentage time spent of each activity. The study was based on a small sample of data recorded when the designers used the system they were developing.

Firstly we argue that design is an iterative process in which each activity is characterized by a mixture of analytic, structured, linear, artistic, chaotic and nonlinear behaviour, depending on among other things the design phase, the state of the problem, the size of the design team, the size and kind of the design task etc. Bottom-up approaches seem to be more dominant in earlier stages, in small research oriented design tasks, when the problem is ill-defined, the design teams are small and prototyping is used. Although support for bottom-up processes seems to be very important in the distributed environment that is the concern of this study, both analytic and artistic design have to be supported. More important, the design tools should not be based on any assumptions about how the designers work. That is, they should not impose any restrictions on the design process and they should be available at any time during design.

Secondly, we will assume that earlier stages of design are characterized by intuitive information gathering processes rather than by formal analytic processes and that concrete representations play an important role for understanding and evaluating design ideas. Thus, the support given has to focus on informal cooperation. In addition tools for idea generation as story board facilities and facilities for observing other system, and tools for visualizing and describing ideas are often more valuable than analytic tools.

Thirdly, we adopt the view held by Curtis et al (1988) that good design is characterized by the ability to integrate knowledge into an unified view and transform it into computational structures. The distributed environment has to support integration of knowledge by learning and development of a common frame of reference.

Finally, we regard design as collaborative work. This means that a distributed design environment cannot function without support for coordination, cooperation and communication. Both Curtis et al (1988) and Rosson et al (1988) point to the need for informal and formal collaboration tools for change facilitation, record keeping of ideas and design concepts, for information sharing etc. As collaboration is essential for design ahis support has to be very effective and so easy to use that it does not interfere with the design activities themselves.

Collaboration in distributed design

What is collaboration? As discussed above collaboration is one of the most important components of the design process. Collaboration could be viewed from many different perspectives. Our perspective could best be described as an activity or task perspective, i.e we will focus our analysis on the different activities of collaboration during design and the needs for support that these activities demand in a distributed environment. However, we will start with a more general discussion of some important characteristics of the collaborative process.

The collaborative process

Of fundamental importance for designing usable computerized tools for cooperative work is an understanding of the collaborative process. This section attempts to give a basis for such an understanding by describing central characteristics of the collaborative process and demands that these characteristics put on the computer support.

Collaboration as a social process

Perhaps the most important aspect of collaboration is that it is a social process, controlled by social conventions as Kraut et al (1986) concluded from their study. They interviewed 50 research teams and concluded that the most important aspect of collaboration was the establishment and maintaining of personal relationships. These form the glue that holds together the pieces of collaborative efforts, but also the source of many problems in collaboration. They pointed to the importance of geographical proximity for the development of personal relations and trust, which is crucial for collaborative work. Also Harrison et al (1990) emphasize the social aspects of collaboration. They point out that each participant in a design group becomes part of the group and must maintain working relationship with it throughout the design process and that these social processes constitute the basis for all the negotiations, commitments and responsibilities that control the design process.

Another related aspect of collaboration concerns the establishment of a common frame of reference. Each team member perceives the goals and the design problems differently depending on their knowledge and interests. In order to reach consensus, social processes focused on an understanding of each partner´s real beliefs and motives are necessary. The development of a common framework can also include more formal processes as when a reference model for a project is established. However, the problems with developing a framework is more often related to social factors, than to formal ones. The establishment of a common frame of reference is a necessary base for communication and for the interpretation and integration of information especially in multi-disciplinary design teams where much valuable information is cross disciplinary. Particularly during early phases teams spend considerable time defining terms and common views.

A common frame of reference is usually obtained by having a series of meetings where each partner describe his/her view on the problem. In a distributed environment this could be realized by some kind of electronic meeting room as proposed by Begeman et al (1986).

Collaboration as a communicative process

Another important aspect of collaboration is that it is a communicative process. For example, Johnson (1989) views collaboration as a communication process and argues that the characteristics of human collaboration can be abstracted from examinations of conversations, especially from breakdowns in conversations.

In a distributed environment collaboration has to be accomplished by communication. In any human communication process there are social rules that monitor the communication pattern in terms of social acts like persuasion, negotiation, arguing. In ordinary communication these rules are learned and signaled by a metacommunication language based on gestures, intonation etc. As Danielson et al (1986) point out, in electronic communication, the development of new rules and metacommunication tools are necessary for enabling the participants to monitor the communication process. Winograds Speech Act model (1988) is one example of how conversational structures can be built into a message system. However careful thought should then be given about the effects of the imposed structure on social control. As argued by Harrison et al (1990), communication in design is as ambiguous as the design process itself and ambiguity is a common and healthy characteristic of communication in a design group, a precondition for creativity.

Collaboration as information sharing

Whenever people work together they must share information. In this context we will make a distinction between sharing knowledge and experience among team members as when one asks a team member about some facts, sharing design information and design results as e.g. when one subroutine is passed to another team member, and sharing different sources of background information as research reports, system descriptions etc.

As found by Kedziersky (1988) questions to other designers are an important way of sharing information. In a distributed environment, this points to the need of electronic message systems specially designed to support the search for advice. Information about changes could be supported by some kind of recording device as proposed by Rosson et al (1988). Such recording devices should not only record the decided changes as caused by new requirements, but also the reasons for these changes. Background and design information, relevant research literature and information about similar systems has to be shared and discussed by the team members. This points to the need of a common knowledge basis. However, as documentation is not enough as found by Curtis et al (1988), the knowledge base should also contain information about "who knows what".

Collaboration as knowledge integration

Collaboration could also be viewed as a process of knowledge integration. Integration of knowledge and experience among team members is obtained by collaborative idea generation through discussions and brain stormings etc.

Idea generation refers to activities related to the creation, development, and testing of ideas and proposed solutions to design problems. In an ordinary environment, new ideas are created, developed and tested in mainly informal situations. In a distributed environment this could be supported by electronic multimedia whiteboards in which ideas can be visualized and discussed as in Colab (Stefik et al 1988). Although the study by Rosson et al (1988) did not find group discussions to be very important for getting and testing ideas, we argue that ideas are often informally generated and tested by discussion and explanation o other team members.

Collaboration as co-working

Many emphasize the co-working aspects of collaboration. To support synchronous cooperative work execution such as co-editing or asynchronous such as reviewing, annotating etc have been a challenge for many CSCW projects.

However, with respect to this aspect of the team work, Kraut et al (1988) found that the research teams in their study developed work strategies that reduced the need for co-working and simplified the integration of work results. Examples of such work strategies were division of labour which turns joint tasks into individual ones, encapsulation of subtasks which reduced the information sharing to the sharing of interfaces, and sequential processing which minimizes the need for information sharing to information about the final product. Thus, Kraut et al's study (1986) points to that the preferred work strategy in collaborative work is to avoid working together, i.e to decrease what we will call *the collaboration load.* If this is an effect of basic human capabilities or an effect of missing tools for cooperation could be discussed. However, a lot of groupware, as tools for co-authoring, co-editing, co-drawing (see e.g Beaudouin-Lafon 1990) are built on the assumption that people really want to synchronously accomplish tasks together. A more plausible assumption could be that information sharing is more important for collaboration than to work together on the same task at the same time. This could at least be true for professional routine tasks such as authoring, coding, drawing etc, although it may not hold for highly creative tasks such as problem solving.

Collaboration as management

Dhar and Olson (1989), emphasize the problem solving characteristics of management activities in collaboration, such as planning, monitoring, negotiation, scheduling and decision making. Planning concerns with the coordination of the activities to be performed, which often involves negotiations about commitments. Monitoring concerns decisions about how to achieve the goals.

However, Bally (1987) found that although critical for success, planning and other management activities constitute a small part of the design process (≈ 5%). Most of the efforts were devoted to routine activities as the use of well-rehearsed professional skills. The importance of management activities depend of course on the phase of the design process and the size of the design team. In planning phases and in large design groups management activities will always play an important role. In a distributed environment such activities could be supported by electronic calendars, records of commitments and cooperative project planning tools. applied Such a perspective has been used in cooperative environments for distributed design and development of software by Kurbel & Pietsch (1990), for project management by Bhandary & Croft (1990) and by Sahti et al (1988).

Generic collaborative tasks and tools

The analysis of collaboration presented above could be used as a point of departure for a classification of collaborative tasks in a distributed environment. We will distinguish between the conference task, the coworking task, the information exchange task and the management task. It should be noted that the list presented here is neither intended to be complete nor to be final. It will change as more experience of distributed design is gathered. It represents a first tentative classification based on the studies reviewed above.

The conference task could be defined as any discussion exchange of experience and knowledge between two or more team members. Such discussions could have the form of negotiations, idea generation, problem solving, briefings etc. The task could be asynchronous or synchronous, formal or informal. In a distributed environment it could be supported by electronic conference systems, mail systems etc. Important characteristics of the collaborative process in this task are the social and communicative characteristics and the aspects concerning knowledge integration discussed above. *The co-working task* concerns any activity for synchronous or asynchronous collaborative production of some document or other kind of product. This task could be supported by distributed applications as co-editors, co-authoring and annotating systems etc. *The information exchange task* could be defined as any activity concerning the exchange of documents and other kind of information between two or more team members. In a distributed environment it could be supported by shared databases, hypertext libraries, record keeping tools and other forms of group memories. *The management task* consists of any activities aiming at coordinating and supervising the collaboration within a team. It includes such activities as planning, scheduling etc.

These tasks can be mapped onto the different design tasks listed in Table I. There is of course no perfect mapping, but it is possible to describe the main collaborative tasks during each design task as shown in Table IV

Design Subtask	**Collaborative task**			
	Conference	Co-working	Information	Management
Formulation of the problem	1	4	2	3
Understanding the problem	2	4	1	3
Generation of solutions	2	4	1	3
Selection of alternatives	1	2	4	3

Table IV. The relation between design tasks and collaborative tasks[4].

At this stage of research, Table IV should just be regarded as a set of hypotheses, that have to be tested empirically. According to this table the most important collaborative tasks during design are the conference task and the information exchange task, while less important are the co-working and the management task.

Groupware supporting these tasks could be designed for support of the specific needs of distributed design. However, one then has to model these tasks and build in assumptions about how the task is performed by the users. As little is known about social processes, such models will not be very valid as shown by the many CSCW systems that have failed to be useful. In addition, one then creates a system controlled design environment instead of a user controlled and this is especially dangerous for early design phases that are not very formalized but creative and artistic. To put the user in control means that systems should be designed as toolboxes, as a set of "independent" and powerful tools that the users control and use according to their ideas of how to accomplish the tasks (Bødker et al 1987, Bødker 1989). We therefore argue for a tool-based approach as opposed to the task-based discussed above. Such an approach aims at designing an user controled environment that facilitate for the users to do what they want, without limitations

[4]The figures indicate the importance, in order of priority, of being able to accomplish a certain collaborative task during a certain design task in a distributed environment.

and assumptions imposed by the system (Schneiderman 1989). Instead of designing collaborative tools based on some analysis of the design task or collaboration task to be fulfilled, one could attempt to design very generic collaborative tools (as generic as the telephone), such as the shared folder, the shared window, the video window etc, that the users can use and combine as they want in order to accomplish the collaborative design tasks. Some combination of tools could be used for conferencing, some other for co-working, some for understanding the problem and some other for selection of alternatives etc. In some situations could the tools be used for formal in other for informal collaboration, in some for one-to-one collaboration in other for many-to many collaboration etc. However this set of tools should be designed as an integrated environment. Tools for collaborative work can be isolated both with respect to other collaborative tools and with respect to other application used by the users. Three aspects of integration are important, i.e. user interface integration, flow of control and flow of data. User interfaces to the collaborative tools have to be integrated into the user´s desktop in a consistent way, it must be possible to access functions in other tools from any tool, and one must be able to transfer the results from using one tool to any other tool.

This design paradigm is similar to the paradigm of the Workaday World proposed by Moran and Anderson (1990) as it is not task oriented, but focuses on the social process of collaboration and on giving the users tailorable tools that they can control and attend to according to their needs. According to Moran and Anderson (1990) these tools should not only support the users, they should enhance and encourage people in their work and allow creative deployment and development of job skills. The first problem is then to identify a sufficient and necessary set of basic tools for collaboration. Next each tool has to be designed so that it can be used for different kinds of collaborative tasks in a distributed design environment.

Conclusions

This discussion of collaboration points at some important characteristics that have to be considered when designing groupware for a distributed design environment.

Firstly, the most important form of collaboration in a distributed design environment seems to be informal collaboration. There is a lot of evidence for the importance of informal collaboration in design, especially in early stages (see e.g. Weinberg 1971, Kraut et al 1986). Thus, although both formal and informal collaboration have to be supported in a distributed environment, support for informal cooperation seems to be more important as concluded also in the discussion of the design task. We will assume that the most common form of collaboration in a distributed environment will be asynchronous and synchronous collaboration one toone, but there will also be a need for many-to-many collaboration.

Secondly, there are a lot of different collaborative tasks that have to be supported in a distributed design environment. A set of groupware applications thus has to be designed, where each application is adapted to the characteristics of the corresponding collaborative task. Another solution is to design a few generic tools for collaboration that can be used in different ways. Which approach is to be preferred is an open question that should be further studied, but we will adopt the latter approach. One easons is our belief that a design paradigm as the one discussed by Moran and Anderson (1990) is necessary for creating a user controlled, creative, flexible and tailorable collaborative environment. However, we will use this analysis of the design task and the different collaborative tasks and the results of other on-going empirical studies as a basis for identifying the necessary and sufficient set of generic tools and for specification of the requirements on these tools. In addition we investigate the possibilities to tailor these tools to the more specific needs of the design situation as e.g. the need for some device for recording and communicating design changes, commitments, the need for specific tools for co-working, division of work etc.

Thirdly it can be concluded that computer support for cooperative work should not only facilitate task accomplishment but also support social processes as productive personal relationships, negotiation and the development of a common frame of reference. In addition electronic communication should not only support the transfer of messages, but also the monitoring of the communication pattern by a metacommunication language. Such a language should be able to transfer social communication signals such as gestures.

Finally this discussion indicates that it is not as important to support management activities and collaborative task accomplishment as information sharing and knowledge integration. However, support for the three work strategies for reducing collaboration load discussed above may be of great importance, i.e support for division and integration of work, encapsulation and sequential processing.

General conclusions

What computer support is necessary for collaboration in a distributed environment? We have proposed a classification of generic collaborative tasks that could be used as a basis for the development of groupware applications supporting distributed design. However, we argue that a more tool oriented approach should be tested first. The next step in our project will be to specify in detail the functional, operational and interface requirements on these tools and to model the social work situation in which these tools are to be used. Our analysis of design and collaboration can be summarized in terms of the following set of general functional requirements on groupware support for design in a distributed environment. They are listed in a tentative order of priority.

Support informal collaboration. As discussed above this is perhaps the most important requirement on a distributed design environment, but it is also the one that will be hardest to fulfil. This requirement means that the environment had to support communication of social behaviour patterns, establishment and development of personal relations, drop in meetings etc.

Support sharing and record keeping of design information. As put forward by many researchers in this area, there is really a need for supporting sharing and record keeping of important design information especially in larger teams. Thus a distributed design environment should support record keeping and sharing of requirement-, design- and implementation changes, design results, design ideas and design concepts, commitments, work plans etc.

Support sharing of background knowledge. This requirement points to other important preconditions for cooperation, namely the need for a common frame of reference, for sharing application domain knowledge and for exchanging knowledge about similar systems and other solutions to the design problem.

Support presentations of ideas. As concrete representations are very important in design, the distributed environment has to support different ways of presenting and visualizing ideas for other team members. This could be done different visualization tools, by story board facilities etc.

Support strategies reducing the need for co-working. It may be more important to have efficient tools for reducing the "collaborative load" than tools supporting co-working. Thus one has to support division and integration of work, encapsulation and sequential processing.

Support co-working. Although one supports the strategies mentioned above, there will always be a need for co-working. Especially asynchronous co-working should be supported by annotating and reviewing systems. To support synchronous co-working does not seem to be as important, except for support for distributed interface design together with end-users at other places. For management activities, we will not propose any support, as other projects have shown that tools like electronic calenders etc are not very useful (Grudin and Poltrock 1990).

Although we are concerned with a distributed design environment, we do not assume that groupware will be a substitute for all face-to-face meetings. Galegher argues (1990) that complex collaborative work involves a continuing need for face-to-face meetings, especially in initiating and planning of the collaborative work. We believe that a well designed distributed environment can both reduce the need for face-to-face meetings and offer new and more effective ways of collaboration.

References

Bally J.(1987): "An experimental view of the design process", in W. Rouse and K. Boff (eds.): *System Design*, Elsevier Science Publishing Co, New York, 1987, pp. 65-83.

Beaudouin-Lafon B.(1990): "Cooperative Development of Software", in S. Gibbs and A.Verrijn-Stuart (eds.): *Multi-User Interfaces and Applications.* North-Holland, 1990, pp. 103-115.

Begeman M., Cook P., Ellis C., Graf M., Rein G., Smith T.(1986): "Project Nick: Meetings Augmentation and Analyses", *Proceedings of CSCW'86*, Dec 1986, pp. 1-6.

Bhandary N., Croft B. (1990): "An Architecture for Supporting Goal-Based Coooperative Work", in S. Gibbs and A.Verrijn-Stuart (eds.): *Multi-User Interfaces and Applications*, North-Holland, 1990, pp. 337-355.

Bødker S.: "A Human Activity Approach to User Interfaces". *HCI*, vol. 4, no. 3, 1989.

Bødker S., Ehn P., Kyng M., Kammersgaard J., Sundblad Y.(1987): "A Utopian Experience", in G.Bjerknes , P.Ehn, and M.Kyng (eds.): *Computer and Democracy*, Avebury, Aldershot, 1987.

Curtis B, Krasner H, and Iscoe N.(1988): "A field study of the software design process for large systems", *Communications of the ACM*, Vol 31, no. 11, November 1988.

Danielsen T., Pankoke-Babatz U., Prinz W., Patel A., Pays P., Smaaland K., Speth R.(1986): "The AMIGO project", *Proceedings of CSCW'86*, Dec 1986, pp. 229-246.

Dhar V., Olson M.(1989): "Assumptions underlying systems that support work group collaboration", in M. Olson (ed.): *Technological support for work group collaboration*, Lawrence Erlbaum Ass, Norwood, 1989, pp 33-51.

Galegher J.(1990): "Computer-Mediated Communication for Intellectual Teamwork: A field experiment in group writing", *Proceedings of CSCW'90*, October 1990. pp. 65-78.

Grudin J., Poltrock S.(1990): *Computer supported cooperative work and groupware.* Tutorial at CHI'90, Seattle, April 1990.

Harrison S., Minneman S., Stults B., Weber K.(1990): "Video: A design medium", *SIGCHI Bullentin*, vol, 21, no, 3, January 1990

Ishii H.(1990): "TeamWorkStation: Towards a seamless shared workspace", *Proceedings of CSCW'90*, October 1990, pp. 13-26.

Johansen R.(1989): "User approaches to computer supported teams", in M. Olson (ed.): *Technological support for work group collaboration*, Lawrence Erlbaum Ass, Norwood 1989, pp.1-33.

Johnson B.(1989):"How is work coordinated?Implications for computer-based support", M Olson (ed.):*Technological support for work group collaboration*, Lawrence Erlbaum1989,pp. 51-65.

Kedzierski B.(1988): "Communication and management support in system development environments", in I. Greif(ed.):*Computer-Supported Cooperative Work*, M Kaufman,1988,pp.253-269.

Klein G.(1987): "Analytical versus regognitional approaches to design decision making", in W. Rouse and K. Boff (eds.): *System Design*, Elsevier, New York, 1987, pp. 175-187.

Kraut R., Galegher J., Egido C.(1986): "Relationships and tasks in scientific research collaborations", *Proceedings of CSCW'86*, Dec 1986, pp. 229-246.

Kurbel K., Pietsch W.(1990): "A Cooperative Work Environment for Evolutionary Software Development", in S. Gibbs and A.A Verrijn-Stuart (eds.): *Multi-User Interfaces and Applications.* Elsevier Science Publisher, North-Holland , 1990, pp. 115-131.

Marmolin H., Sundblad Y., Pehrson B.(1991): "TheKnowledgeNet - An Environment for Distributed Design.", IPLab-MultiG Technical Report, 1991. (Forthcoming)

Meister D.(1987): "A cognitive theory of design and requirements for a behavioural design aid", in W. Rouse and K. Boff (eds.): *System Design*, Elsevier, New York, 1987, pp. 29-245.

Moran T. And erson R.(1990): "The Workaday World As a Paradigm for CSCW Design", *Proceedings of CSCW'90*, October 1990, pp. 381-393.

Nadler G.(1984): "System methodology and design", *Proceeding of 1984 IEEE System, Man and Cybernetics Conference*, Halifax, Nova Scotia,, October 1984, pp. 427-437.

Norcio A., Chmura L.(1986): "Design activity in developing modules for complex software.", in B.Soloway and S.Lyenger (eds.): *Empirical studies of programmers*, Ablex , 1986, pp. 99-117.

Norman D.(1983): "Some observations on mental models", in: D. Gentner and A.L. Stevens (eds.): *Mental models.* Hillsdale, New Yersey: Lawrence Erlbaum Associates Inc, 1983.

Rosson M, Maass S., Kellogg W.(1988): "The designer as user: Building requirements for design tools from design practice",*Communications of the ACM*, Vol 31, no. 11, November 1988.

Rouse W., Boff K. (1987a): "Workshop themes and issues: The psychology of system design.", in W.Rouse and K.Boff (eds.): *System Design*, Elsevier, New York, 1987, pp. 7-19.

Rouse W., Boff K. (1987b): "Designers, Tools, and Environments.", in W. Rouse and K. Boff (eds.): *System Design*, Elsevier, New York, 1987, pp. 43-65.

Rouse, W.(1983): "Models of human problem solving: detection, diagnosis and compensation for system failure", *Automatica*, vol. 19, pp. 613-625, 1983

Rouse, W.(1986): "On the value of information in system design: A framework for understanding and aiding designers",*Information Processing and Management*, vol.22, no.2,pp.217-228, 1986

Sandewall E.(1978): "Programming in the Interactive Environment: The Lisp Experience", *ACM Computing Surveys*, vol. 10, no. 1, 1978.

Sathi A, Morton T, Roth S.(1988): "Castillo: An intelligent project management system", in I. Greif (ed.):*Computer-Supported Cooperative Work.* M Kaufman, San Mateo,1988,pp.269-311.

Schneiderman B., Kearsley G: *Hypertext Hands On*, Reading, MA: Addison-Wesley, 1989.

Smith J.(1987): "Intuition by design.", in W. Rouse and K. Boff (eds.): *System Design*, Elsevier , New York, 1987, pp 305-319.

Stefik M., Foster G., Bobrow D., Kahn D., Lanning S., Suchman L.(1988): "Beyond the Chalkboard: Computer support for collaboration and problem solving in meetings", in I. Greif (ed): *Computer-supported cooperative work.* M Kaufman, San Mateo, 1988, pp. 335-367.

Weinberg G.(1971): *The Psychology of Computer Programming*, chapter 4-5, Van Nostrand Reinhold Company, New York, 1971.

Winograd T.(1988): "A language perspective on the design of cooperative work", in I. Greif (ed.): *Computer-supported cooperative work.* M Kaufman , San Mateo, 1988, pp. 623-765.

Proceedings of the Second European Conference on Computer-Supported Cooperative Work
Bannon, L., Robinson, M. & Schmidt, K. (Editors)
September 25-27, 1991, Amsterdam, The Netherlands

ClearFace: Translucent Multiuser Interface for TeamWorkStation

Hiroshi Ishii
NTT Human Interface Laboratories, Japan

Kazuho Arita
NTT Human Interface Laboratories, Japan

Abstract

Through the experimental use of TeamWorkStation, we found the most serious problem is the smallness of the shared screen space. In order to fully use the limited screen space, this paper proposed a new multiuser interface design technique "ClearFace". The face windows are *translucent* and *overlay* the shared workspace window.
We implemented a prototype of ClearFace system on a TeamWorkStation. Several types of face window layout strategies were tested: fixed location windows (right side, left side, top) and movable windows. Through experimental design sessions, we experienced little difficulty in switching our focus between the face images and drawing objects. The theory of selective looking accounts for this flexible perception mechanism. Although users can see draw objects behind a face with little difficulty, we found that users hesitate to draw figures or write texts over face images. Because of this behavior, we concluded that the movable strategy is the best.
TeamWorkStation demonstrated the power of two different usage of translucent overlay technique: *fused overlay* of drawing surface images for seamless shared workspace, and *selective overlay* to save screen space.

1 Introduction

In order to provide distributed users with an "open shared workspace" where every member can see, point to and draw on simultaneously using heterogeneous personal tools, we designed **"TeamWorkStation"** [Ishii90, Ishii91]. TeamWorkStation integrates two existing kinds of individual workspaces: computers and desktops. Because each coworker can continue to use his/her favorite application programs or manual tools simultaneously in the virtual shared workspace, the cognitive discontinuity (seam) between the individual and shared workspaces is greatly reduced.

TeamWorkStation (TWS) provides a "shared screen" in addition to an individual screen. The shared screen supports (1) a shared drawing window for concurrent pointing, writing, drawing, and (2) live face windows for face-to-face conversation.

Through the experimental use of TeamWorkStation (by 2 ~ 3 users at the same time), we found the most serious problem is the smallness of the shared screen space. Because of the limitation of screen size (current prototype uses a 14" screen), it is very hard to secure the space for a shared drawing window large enough for effective use on one screen together with all face windows of the group members. The use of a bigger display or multi-displays is one solution. However, normal desktops are too limited to support these space-consuming solutions. High land and office rental costs in Japan (especially around Tokyo) are the main reasons for this constraint.

This paper proposes a new solution to this problem. We devised the idea of "*translucent*, *movable* and *resizable* live face windows over shared drawing window". We call this new multiuser interface design technique **"ClearFace"**. We implemented a prototype of ClearFace system on a TeamWorkStation.

This paper describes the idea of ClearFace, and some findings through experimental use in design sessions. Several types of face window layout strategies are compared: fixed location windows (right side, left side, top) and movable windows. The effectiveness of ClearFace is also discussed using the theory of "selective looking".

2 Multiuser Interface for a Shared Workspace

White board is the most typical shared workspace in an ordinary face-to-face meeting. Fig. 1 shows a snapshot of shared workspace in a design session. Participants are drawing, writing, pointing, speaking and gesturing concurrently.

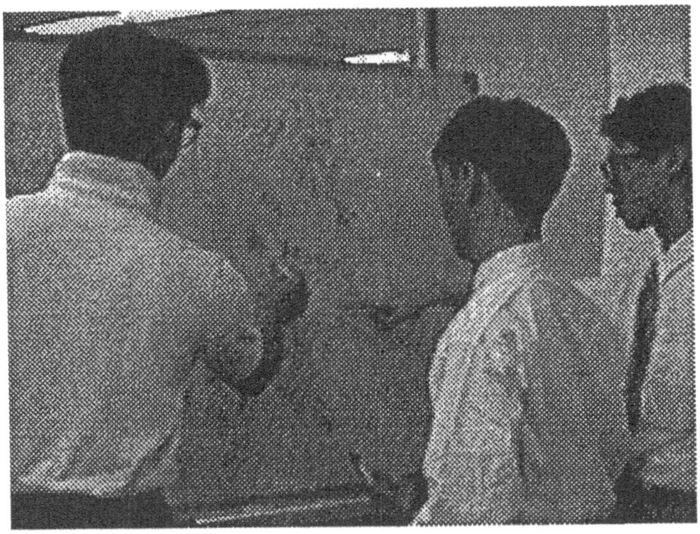

Fig. 1 An example of shared workspace in a design session

People use a white (or black) board as a *shared drawing space* that every member can see, point to and draw on *simultaneously*. Bly, Tang, Leifer and Minneman pointed out that the shared drawing surface plays a very crucial role not only to store information and convey ideas, but also to develop ideas and mediate interaction, especially in design sessions [Bly88, Tang88, Tang90].

At the same time, in the discussion, the participants are speaking to and seeing each other, and using facial expressions and gestures to communicate. In the conversations, it is essential to see the partners face and body. The facial expressions and gestures provide a variety of non-verbal cues that are essential in human communications.

The focus of a design session changes dynamically. When we discuss abstract concepts or design philosophy, we often see each other's face. When we discuss concrete system architectures, we intensively use a white board by drawing diagrams on it. Through the use of TeamWorkStation in design of a video network architecture, we realized that the smooth transition between face-to-face conversation and shared drawing activity is essential for the seamless support of dynamic interaction in design sessions.

All of these dynamic and concurrent activities such as drawing, writing, pointing, speaking, gesturing by each participant form the *shared workspace*. Therefore, when we design the multiuser interface of CSCW environment to provide geographically distributed users with a shared workspace, it is not sufficient to simulate just only the white board function or to provide only a simple picture phone function. It is necessary to integrate a virtual white board with face-to-face communication channels, and users must be able to choose one of them or both channels according to the task contents.

In a face-to-face meeting, the room is perceived as a contiguous space, and there are no physical *seams* between the white board and the participants. By simply moving their eyes, participants can look both other participants and white board. However, in ordinary desktop tele-conference systems, the images of participants and shared document images are usually captured by different cameras, and dealt with separately (displayed in different windows on a screen). Therefore, users must often switch their focus between the face images and shared drawing space.

Previous Approaches: Tiling and Overlapping Windows

A variety of computer-controlled video conference environment, such as Media Space [Webe87, Stul88, Harr90], CRUISER [Root88], TeamWorkStation [Ishii90], MERMAID [Wata90], CAVECAT [Mant91], have been presented. Many of them are designed based on workstations with desktop video communication functions, and live face images are displayed in the windows on a screen. These workstation-based systems take one of the following face image layout strategies:
(1) tiling windows (Fig. 2 (1)), or
(2) overlapping windows (Fig. 2 (2)).

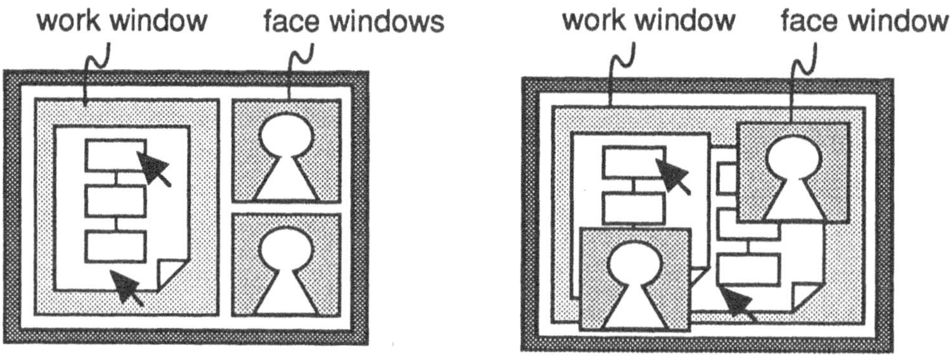

(1) Tiling windows (2) Overlapping face windows

Fig. 2 Two Existing Window Layout Strategies

TeamWorkStation took the tiling approach (1) to layout the windows in a shared screen. Figure 3 shows the appearance of the TeamWorkStation prototype. The individual screen and the shared screen are contiguous in video memory. Two CCD cameras to capture the face image, and the actual desktop image are provided.

Fig. 3 Appearance of TeamWorkStation

Figure 4 shows an example of the original shared screen of TeamWorkStation in a design session. Two users are discussing the system architecture using a draw-editor, a hand-written diagram, pens, and hand gestures simultaneously.

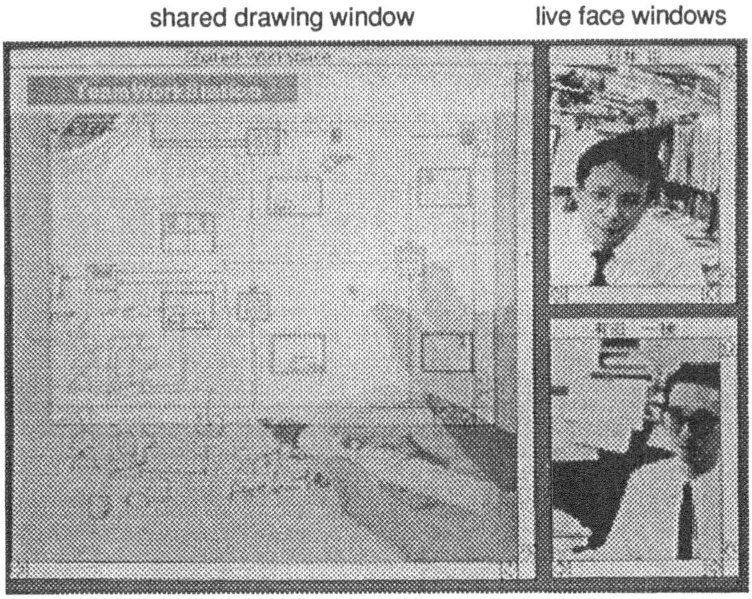

Fig. 4 An Example of Original Shared Screen of TeamWorkStation
(This layout is an example of the tiling window strategy.)

Both approaches, tiling and overlapping windows, must segregate the limited display area into the work window and face windows, and each window is strongly restricted. As a result, users must pay a lot of attention to keep their faces centered in the small face windows, and users must often "scroll" or "refresh" the work space window. Moreover, visually separated windows impose *seams* between faces and drawings to users. Since the goal of TeamWorkStation design is to provide a *seamless* shared workspace, the cognitive seams that exist between spatially separated face and drawing windows motivated us to develop ClearFace.

3 ClearFace: Translucent Face Windows

In order to solve the space problem and decrease the cognitive seams in the shared screen, we devised the idea of "*movable, resizable, and translucent* face windows over work window". The face images are translucent and overlay the shared drawing window. Users can move and change the size of these face windows with mouse operations. We call this new multiuser interface design technique "**ClearFace**".

The idea to superimpose face image over a computer screen image was originally demonstrated by Engelbart and English [Enge68]. However, in their system, the size of all superimposed images were the same. Therefore, it was difficult to show the face images of more than two people on one screen. We overcome this limitation by allowing users to *move* and *resize* the translucent face windows.

Figure 5 and 6 shows an example of ClearFace implemented on TeamWorkStation. These are the snapshots from experimental sessions on icon and screen layout design by the authors.

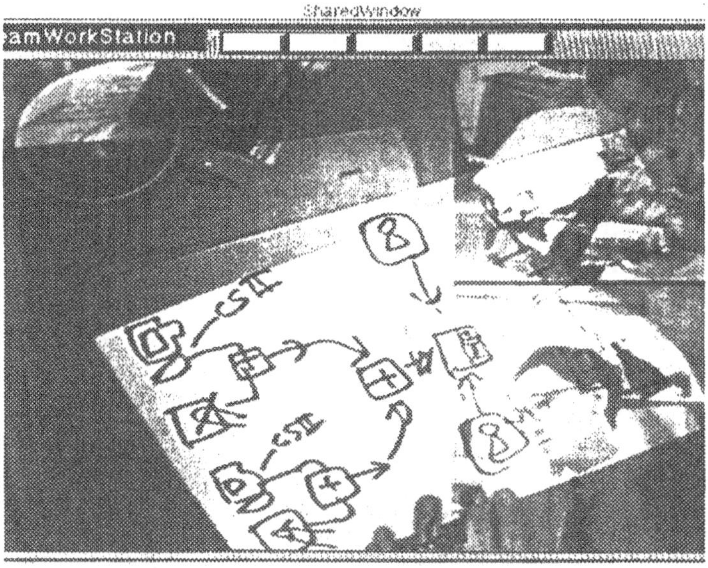

Fig. 5 An example of ClearFace (face images on right side)

Fig. 6 An example of ClearFace (face images at top)

Experimental Use of ClearFace

In order to investigate the usability of ClearFace, we implemented it based on several layout strategies: (1) fixed location windows (right side, left side, top) and (2) movable and resizable windows. Four subjects in our laboratories including the authors used these multiuser interfaces for the collaborative design of icons, prototype system architectures, and the diagrams for technical papers. Each layout was used for about 20 minutes, and the sessions were video-taped.

Until we conducted these experiments, we were unsure about the readability of the overlaid face and drawing surface images. However, the experiments of icon design and system configuration discussions confirmed that there is little difficulty in visually separating the overlaid video layers (face and drawing surface). When a subject looked at one layer, he/she found it is not difficult to ignore the other.

This ability of human perception is accounted for by the theory of "**selective looking**" [Neis75]. Fig. 7 illustrates the selective looking in the use of ClearFace.

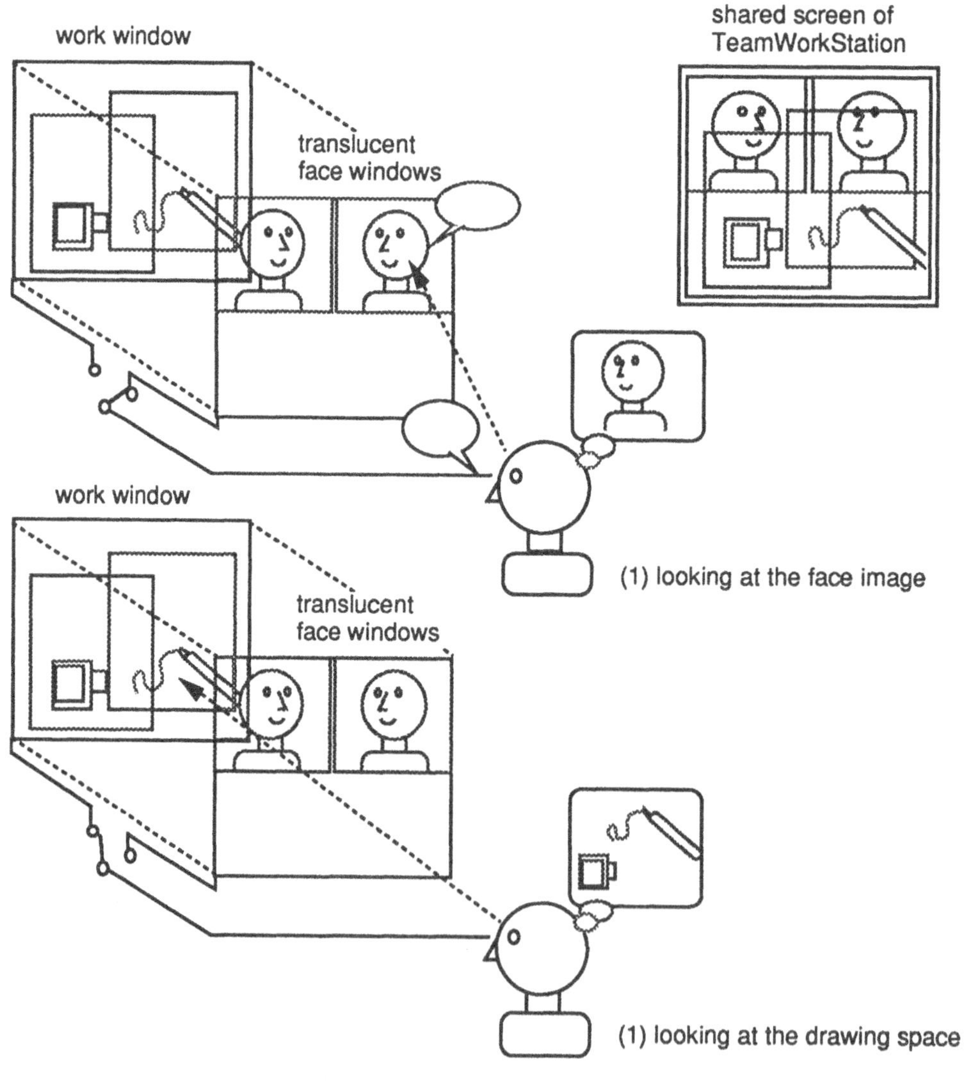

Fig. 7 Selective looking in the use of ClearFace

Neisser and Becklen conducted experiments that investigated the mechanism of "selective looking". In their experiments, the subjects looked at two optically superimposed video screens, on which two different kinds of things were happening. They were required to follow the action in one "screen" and ignore the other. They could do this without difficulty, although both were present in the same fully overlapped visual field. Events in the unwatched screen were rarely noticed. Through these experiments, they found that without any prior practice, it is easy to concentrate one image sequence and ignore another, even when they are overlapped.

ClearFace overlays face images on the drawing surface. Each face looks very different from the marks on desktop documents or hand gestures, and humans have a high sensitivity to recognize a human face. Therefore, because of this selective looking ability, ClearFace hardly confuse the participants.

Neisser and Becklen reported that it was very difficult to monitor *both* screens at once. In design sessions, however, we seldom look simultaneously at faces and drawing objects, but we do frequently switch our focus between them.

Another interesting observation is that all subjects hesitated drawing over the faces. Even though users knew that the entire screen was available for drawing, they tried to use the "free" space. Only when the subjects looked at the actual desktop without looking at the overlaid images on the shared screen, did they freely draw over face images.

When users *looked* at a drawn object behind a face, they did experience little perceptual confusion. However, when they *drew* figures or *wrote* texts on the shared drawing space, they avoided any collision with the face images. Because of this behavior, we concluded that the movable strategy is the best. In the design session, since the drawing on the work window dynamically expands, it is necessary to provide users with the functions needed to move the face images in order to avoid collision.

In the fixed location strategies, we found that "top" is better than right and left side strategies. The reason is because users often use their hands for pointing, drawing and gesturing, and the possibility of blocking the face images with hand images is the least in the "top" strategy. Next best was "left" strategy because all the subjects were right-handed. (Conversely, for left-handed subjects, the next best would be the "right" strategy.)

Another finding is that: to use ClearFace effectively, the background of a face image must be clean. When the face image is surrounded with a visually "messy" background, it makes difficult to distinguish draw objects from the background clutter.

Implementation of ClearFace

Figure 8 illustrates the system configuration for movable ClearFace. Prototype was implemented on TeamWorkStation that is based on Macintosh™ computers connected audio and video network. In order to implement a movable and resizable face windows, we utilized a desktop video board which inserts the live video image into a movable and resizable window. Therefore, users can simply move or resize the face images by dragging or resizing the window at any time in the design session. Special video effectors were also used to overlay video images translucently.

The quality of overlaid video images in this prototype is not sharp enough to support the sharing of drawings, because of the limitation of NTSC video quality. We expect HDTV technologies will overcome this problem in the near future.

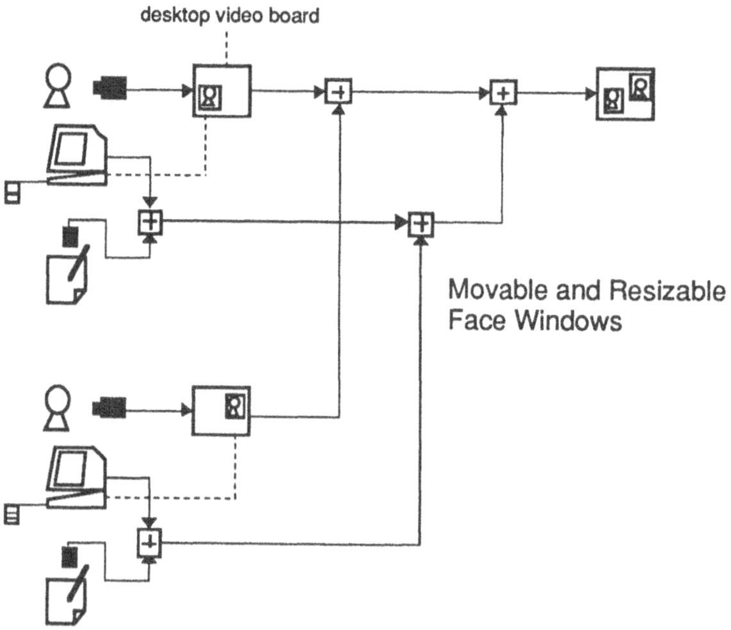

Fig. 8 System configuration of ClearFace prototype

4 Two Translucent Overlay Techniques: Fused and Selective

In contrast to ClearFace, the shared drawing window itself is created by overlaying translucent individual drawing surface images with a different intention. The goal of this overlay is the *fusion* of several images into one. Each video layer is originally physically separated. However, because of the spatial relationships among marks on each layer, the set of overlaid layers provides users with sufficient semantics, fuse them into one image. The usefulness of this *cognitive fusion* was demonstrated through the experiments of remote teaching of calligraphy [Ishii90] and remote instruction of machine operation [Ishii91]. We call this translucent overlay technique "**fused overlay**".

On the other hand, ClearFace demonstrated another technique "**selective overlay**" to use the limited screen space effectively.

TeamWorkStation with ClearFace is the first system that demonstrates two very different effects of translucent overlaid video images: *fused overlay* (for shared drawing window) and *selective overlay* (for face windows over the drawing surface) to create a multiuser interface for remote collaboration. Although the translucent overlay technique itself is very simple, we expect it will provide us with a variety of new research issues in human-human interface design.

5 Conclusion

This paper has proposed a new multiuser interface design technique "ClearFace". In order to fully use the limited screen space, we devised the idea of overlaying translucent, movable, and resizable live face video images over a shared drawing window. Through the informal observations of experimental use in design sessions, we found that we had little difficulty in switching our focus between the face images or drawing objects. The theory of selective looking accounts for this flexible perception mechanism. Although users can see draw objects behind a face without difficulty, we found that users hesitate to draw figures or write texts over face images. Because of this behavior, we devised the "movable" face strategy. However, further empirical evaluations are needed to clarify the usability and limitation of ClearFace approach.

TeamWorkStation demonstrated the power of two different uses of the translucent overlay technique: *fused overlay* of drawing surface images for seamless shared workspace, and *selective overlay* to save screen space. We are going to test ClearFace with a larger variety of tasks and users to investigate the most effective usage of the translucent video overlay technique.

Acknowledgements

The authors would like to thank to Minoru Kobayashi at NTT for his support in the experiments of ClearFace and his valuable discussions. We would also like to thank anonymous reviewers for their invaluable comments on this paper. Thanks are also due to Naomi Miyake for her comments to the draft of this paper, and Yoshio Miyake for introducing us to the research of selective looking of Neisser and Becklen. We would also like to thank Takaya Endo and Gen Suzuki of NTT Human Interface Laboratories for their encouragement.

References

[Bly88] Sara A. Bly, "A Use of Drawing Surfaces in Different Collaborative Settings," Conference on Computer-Supported Cooperative Work (CSCW 88), Portland, Oregon, 1988, pp.250-256.

[Enge68] Douglas C. Engelbart and William K. English, "A Research Center for Augmenting Human Intellect," Proceedings of FJCC, Vol. 33, No. 1, pp. 395-410, AFIPS Press, Fall 1968

[Fost88] Gregg Foster and Deborah Tatar, "Experiments in Computer Support for Teamwork --- Colab (Video)," Xerox PARC, 1988

[Harr90] Steve Harrison, Scott Minneman, Bob Stults, and Karon Weber, "Video: A Design Medium," SIGCHI Bulletin, January 1990, pp. 86-90

[Ishii90] Hiroshi Ishii, "TeamWorkStation: Towards a Seamless Shared Workspace," CSCW '90, Los Angeles, October 1990, pp. 13-26

[Ishii91] Hiroshi Ishii, and Naomi Miyake, "Toward an Open Shared Workspace: Computer and Video Fusion Approach of TeamWorkStation," Communications of the ACM, 1991 (to appear)

[Mant91] Marilyn Mantei, Ronald Baecker, Abigail Sellen, William Buxton, and Thomas Milligan, "Experiences in the Use of a Media Space," Proceedings of CHI '91, New Orleans, May 1991, pp. 203-208

[Neis75] Ulric Neisser and Robert Becklen, "Selective Looking: Attending to Visually Specified Events," Cognitive Psychology, Vol.7, 1975, pp.480-494

[Root88] Robert W. Root, "Design of a Multi-Media Vehicle for Social Browsing," CSCW '88, Portland, 1988, pp.25-38

[Stul88] R. Stults, "Experimental Uses of Video to Support Design Activities," Xerox Palo Alto Research Center, 1988.

[Tang88] John C. Tang and Larry J. Leifer, "A Framework for Understanding the Workspace Activity of Design Teams," Conference on Computer-Supported Cooperative Work (CSCW 88), Portland, 1988, pp.244-249

[Tang90] John C. Tang and Scott L. Minneman, "VideoDraw: A Video Interface for Collaborative Drawing," CHI '90, Seattle, 1990

[Webe87] Karon Weber and Scott Minneman, "The Office Design Project (Video)," Xerox PARC, 1987

Proceedings of the Second European Conference on Computer-Supported Cooperative Work
Bannon, L., Robinson, M. & Schmidt, K. (Editors)
September 25-27, 1991, Amsterdam, The Netherlands

PEPYS: Generating Autobiographies by Automatic Tracking

William M. Newman, Margery A. Eldridge and Michael G. Lamming

Rank Xerox EuroPARC, England

This paper presents one part of a broad research project entitled 'Activity-Based Information Retrieval' (AIR) which is being carried out at EuroPARC. The basic hypothesis of this project is that if contextual data about human activities can be automatically captured and later presented as recognisable descriptions of past episodes, then human memory of those past episodes can be improved. This paper describes an application called Pepys, designed to yield descriptions of episodes based on automatically collected location data. The program pays particular attention to meetings and other episodes involving two or more people. The episodes are presented to the user as a diary generated at the end of each day and distributed by electronic mail. The paper also discusses the methods used to assess the accuracy of the descriptions generated by the recogniser.

Introduction

Human memory is far from perfect. Most people can recount numerous occasions when someone has had to remind them of some of the circumstances of a long-forgotten event. Consider the following scenario:

Person A:	"Do you remember what I said about changing our paper?"
Person B:	"No."
Person A:	"Remember we were working on section two on your workstation?"
Person B:	"No—was John in the office?"
Person A:	"Yes—and you had just had a phone call from the conference organiser."
Person B:	"Oh yes, he said it was too long, and you said....."

and so begins the recall of the main part of the conversation.

All human activities take place in some context: the discussion to which A is referring here took place in a particular room (B's office), in the presence of a third person (John), and after a telephone conversation (from the organiser). Reconstruction of such a context can assist recall of episodes that took place in the context (Smith, Glenberg & Bjork, 1978). The basic hypothesis of the research described in this paper is that if contextual data about human activities can be automatically captured and later presented as recognisable descriptions of past episodes, then human memory of those past episodes can be improved. The collection and analysis of data related to the context of various human activities is a part of a broad research programme into Activity-Based Information Retrieval, or AIR (Lamming & Newman, 1991). The present paper describes one part of the AIR programme which deals with information about the locations of groups and individuals. It describes a program, Pepys, that has been designed to make inferences about collaborative work based on location data. Thus information about meetings and other group activities is combined with information about individual activities, and descriptions of these activities are presented in the form of a personal diary outlining the individual user's day.

Although Pepys presents information to people in the form of a personal diary, it is fundamentally different from other diary management and scheduling systems that have been reported in the CSCW literature. The diary presented by Pepys is *retrospective*, and is not directly applicable to diary management or scheduling meetings (for example, the Visual Scheduler reported in Beard et al., 1990). The system for analysing workstation activity described by Thimbleby, Anderson and Witten (1990) resembles Pepys more closely: one of the aims of their system is to help people recall activities they had previously carried out on their workstations. It does this overnight by performing numerous checks on files that have been created or modified during the day, producing a comprehensive retrospective summary of the day's workstation activity.

A particular emphasis of Pepys is on reconstructing collaborative episodes and including them in the diary. Meetings, hallway discussions, encounters around the photocopier, etc., appear to be particularly valuable as contextual cues for recall. Monitoring workstation activity, as proposed by Thimbleby et al., is also being pursued as part of the AIR project (see Lamming & Newman, 1991), and the aim is to incorporate this information into the diaries generated by Pepys. A wide variety of episodes, many of them collaborative, contribute to the working day and should ultimately find their place in the worker's daily record.

EuroPARC: The Research Site

The AIR project is based at Rank Xerox EuroPARC in Cambridge, England. The EuroPARC building is a multi-media environment, where each office and meeting room contains an audio/video node including a camera, monitor, microphone and speaker (Buxton & Moran, 1990). This system is used to support various multi-media applications, such as video conferencing, video-phones and non-speech audio announcements. The laboratory infrastructure also includes a tracking system that allows people to record their movements automatically. This tracking system, developed at Olivetti Research Labs (Want, 1990), provides location data that serve as a database for the project reported here.

The Active Badge System

EuroPARC shared an interest with Olivetti Research Labs in investigating potential applications of tracking technology, and therefore in 1989 installed the badge system shown in Figure 1. Badges measure about 5 cm square and are worn like normal security tags. Each badge has a different identity code, which it emits approximately every 20 seconds using infra-red signalling similar to the method employed in TV remote controls. This code is picked up by receivers installed in the rooms, hallways and stairwells of the building. Roughly once per second, a polling computer interrogates each receiver for recently detected badge codes. When a badge is detected at a new location, this event is stored in a record that includes the date and time, the badge ID code and the old and new locations. A location server makes these records available to applications that rely on current badge data, including the data logging program that builds log files for Pepys. The data in log files are encoded and are kept secure from unauthorised applications. When decoded, the contents of the files are as shown in Figure 2. Several different types of record may appear in the files: besides the basic records of movement, there may be lost-badge records, where a person has not been detected by the system for several minutes, and attention records, where the person has pressed a button on the

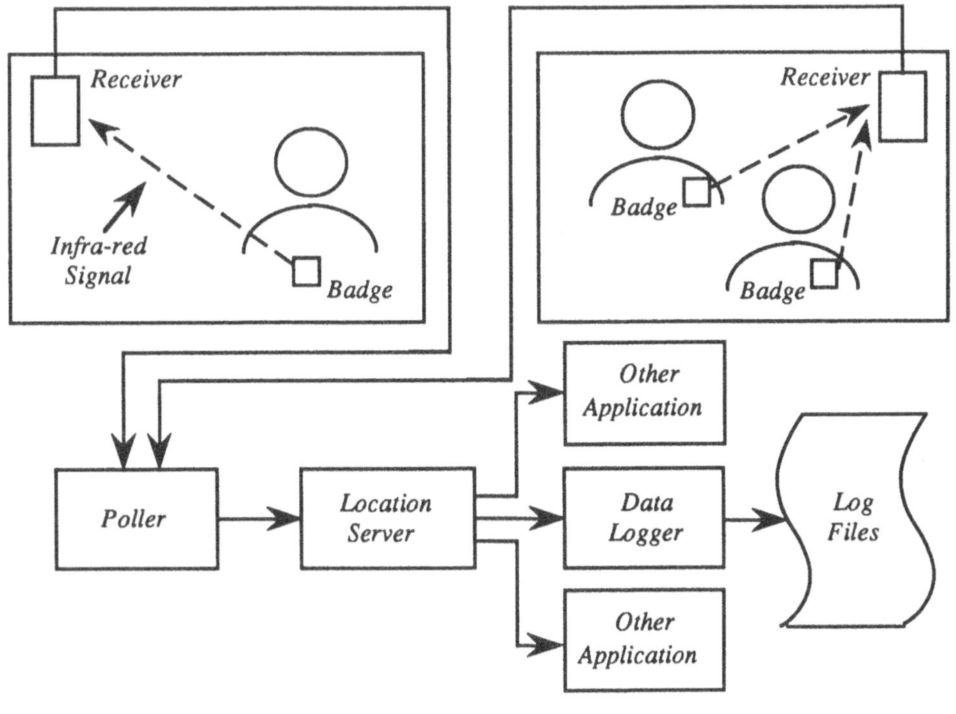

Fig. 1. The Active Badge System

8:26:40 am	30-Oct-90	Morton	move	Commons > Kitchen
8:28:02 am	30-Oct-90	Morton	move	Kitchen > 3rd floor corridor
8:29:05 am	30-Oct-90	Morton	move	3rd floor corridor > Kapp's area
8:29:55 am	30-Oct-90	Morton	move	Kapp's area > Fax/Copier room
8:25:46 am	30-Oct-90	Price	lost	Wilson's office
8:37:30 am	30-Oct-90	Little	attention	Little's office
8:30:18 am	30-Oct-90	Morton	lost	Fax/Copier room
8:41:04 am	30-Oct-90	Little	attention	Little's office
8:42:27 am	30-Oct-90	Morton	move	> Stairwell
8:42:48 am	30-Oct-90	Morton	move	Stairwell > Morton's office
8:45:39 am	30-Oct-90	Morton	move	Morton's office > Reception
8:48:36 am	30-Oct-90	Morton	move	Reception > Morton's office
8:52:09 am	30-Oct-90	Little	move	Little's office > Commons
8:53:27 am	30-Oct-90	Andrews	move	> Rear porch
8:53:27 am	30-Oct-90	Andrews	attention	Rear porch
8:53:38 am	30-Oct-90	Morton	move	Morton's office > Clark's office
8:53:46 am	30-Oct-90	Andrews	move	Rear porch > Stairwell
8:54:24 am	30-Oct-90	Little	move	Commons > Kitchen
8:54:28 am	30-Oct-90	Morton	move	Clark's office > Morton's office
8:54:30 am	30-Oct-90	Morton	move	Morton's office > Kitchen
8:54:35 am	30-Oct-90	Little	move	Kitchen > Stairwell
8:55:02 am	30-Oct-90	Little	move	Stairwell > Little's office
8:55:10 am	30-Oct-90	Andrews	move	Stairwell > Reception

Fig. 2. An example of a decoded portion of a Log File.

badge in a particular location. Each of these records appears in the sample of Figure 2. Pepys takes account of movement and lost-badge records, but ignores all other types of event.

Several other applications have been implemented using the Active Badge system. One system allows the administrative support staff to forward phone calls to EuroPARC personnel by reading their location off a screen (Harper, Lamming & Newman, 1991). Another system allows badge-wearers to gain access to the building by pressing the button on the badge and thus automatically unlocking the main entrance door. These applications have contributed to the Pepys project by encouraging staff to wear badges.

Social Implications of Active Badges

Tracking technologies tend to raise alarms about invasion of privacy. There was considerable concern over the introduction of active badges at EuroPARC, and one of the aims of ongoing research has been to understand these concerns better and to address them. The ultimate goal is to learn how to design and build systems incorporating novel technologies with due attention to their social implications. Many of the technology-based artefacts which support tracking and are now widespread in society, such as credit cards and cellular telephones, have presented similar problems when first introduced. The same problems are now being raised by collaborative technologies used in CSCW, such as video and shared workstation environments. An informed approach to design can avoid the two undesirable extremes of forcing such technologies on an unwilling public or abandoning them altogether in order to avoid a negative backlash.

Preliminary studies of the social impact of badges have helped identify some of the issues at stake. In a study reported by Harper, Lamming and Newman (1991), an application called the Locator was developed at two different sites to enable people to be located more easily, and the outcomes at the two sites were compared. While some of the findings are specific to the Locator application, others can be generalised to apply to other CSCW technologies and applications such as Pepys.

The Locator project raised the issue of what kind of information within an organisation is 'private' and what is 'public'. The balance between these two categories of information is a delicate matter, normally kept at a tacit level. At one of the two sites, system support people felt that their location was public information, since their social role within the organisation depended upon other people being able to find them when needed. In contrast, researchers at this same site, having the freedom to organise their time as they wished, felt that information about their location was not public—their social roles within the organisation did not include being found by others. Introduction of badges appeared to affect the individual's control over the boundary between public and private.

The Locator also showed very clearly the relationship between privacy concerns and utility of technology. Some users found the Locator extremely useful: it meant that they could receive phone calls wherever they were, and that they spent less time answering other people's calls and going in search of them. Administrative staff valued the Locator because it enabled them to do their job better and to respect the individual wishes of staff for privacy or availability. These people seemed relatively unconcerned about the badges' invasive characteristics. Researchers gained little benefit from the Locator, because they worked primarily alone, received few phone calls, and disliked being disturbed. These people tended to view the badges as socially undesirable. There was a strong negative correlation, therefore, between the perceived usefulness of the Locator and concern over the badges' invasiveness: utility appeared to have the effect of attenuating concern. This phenomenon was seen in its most extreme form among researchers who had no access to the Locator, and therefore had no prospect of benefiting from it

A similar comparative study of Pepys at two sites is presently under way. The conclusion of this paper presents some interim observations about possible extrapolations of the Locator results to the Pepys project.

The Design of Pepys

Background

Badges offer a number of possible ways of supporting information retrieval; several of these were investigated before the system described here was built. For example, a simple prototype system was built to demonstrate the feasibility of indexing into recorded audio or video using a database of location data gathered from badges. This was a useful exercise in many ways, helping to identify technically difficult areas and to show where activity-based information retrieval might be most useful. Initially it had seemed that an AIR application, in order to be useful, would need to include at least an interactive user interface and a means of indexing into existing forms of data such as video or electronic documents. The Pepys project showed that neither of these was strictly necessary: that a useful application could consist merely of diaries generated automatically from badge data and issued each day via electronic mail. Indeed, Pepys may be considered an example of an interactive system with an extremely 'low-intensity' user interface (Newman, 1990) requiring almost no effort on the part of the user.

The first stage of the project was to understand how to process badge data into a recognisable reconstruction of the day's events. Part of this stage involved understanding how to organise the data. At first, data were collected in separate files for each user, on the assumption that a fairly simple analysis of each file would yield the events of the user's day. However, the analysis turned out to be far from simple, requiring inspection of all of the users' data together. A different approach was required to data logging, creating a single file for each day's traffic. Although this decision simplified the design, it had some unexpected negative effects on users' attitudes to Pepys, and these are discussed in the Conclusion.

At one stage in this early research, an entire day's badge data were collected and analysed by hand in complete detail. Diagrams were drawn to represent gatherings of several people at one location; from these it was possible to identify the formation and dispersal of meetings at various locations in the building throughout the day. It was possible from the data to recognise journeys made by individuals between events: trips to the coffee pot, tours of the building looking for people, guided tours by visitors. Also recognisable were the periods that users spent alone in their offices. From this analysis it became clear that the program would need to look for three basic types of episode: gatherings of two or more people, travel between locations, and periods spent alone. The analysis also helped in the design of algorithms for automatic recognition of these episodes, which were built into the two principal software modules of Pepys—the so-called Quorum Spotter and Travel Agent.

Quorum Spotter

The Quorum Spotter generates a log of the day's gatherings from the location data log gathered from badges. The term 'gathering' is used in preference to 'meeting' which is inappropriate for casual events. Each gathering is defined in terms of its location, overall start and finish times, and the attendances by the individuals taking part, that is, the periods of time they spent at the meeting. A gathering is normally considered to start when a 'quorum' of two people has formed, and to finish when such a minimal quorum no longer exists. It is necessary, however, for at least one member of the quorum to be a non-resident of the room in which the gathering is taking place; otherwise people sharing offices would appear to be in continuous meetings! Attendances are recognised as periods spent at locations where gatherings exist. It is possible for an individual to make several attendances at the same gathering, and the program identifies these instances so that they can be spelled out in the diary: each attendance record names the gathering involved, by location and start time.

The Quorum Spotter attempts to distinguish between the different types of gathering that may form, and to attach type descriptions appropriate for inclusion in diaries. In particular, it looks for episodes that appear to justify the description 'meeting.' The criteria on which it decides include the length of the episode, the number of people present, speed with which the quorum formed and then dispersed, and the location. Thus it would not apply the description 'meeting' to a gathering in which attendees continually arrived and departed throughout, or to a gathering in a corridor.

Travel Agent

The task of the Travel Agent is to process the data on changes of location and to distinguish between important and unimportant changes. An active user may clock up several hundred such changes during a single day, including many that result in spending only a few seconds at each location. The Travel Agent must discard such transient records, and concentrate on recognising 'stopovers'—significant periods at a single location. Some stopovers are easy to recognise, e.g., lengthy periods in a gathering or alone in the user's office. Others are more subtle, e.g., stopping for three minutes by a photocopier, or spending five minutes in a meeting that had been in progress for two hours.

The three main criteria on which the Travel Agent selects stopovers are: (1) the length of the stopover itself, (2) the nature of the stopover event, and (3) the distance travelled. If the user spends more than a certain number of minutes at a location, this is considered significant on its own. If a meeting was taking place there, this is considered memorable even if the user joined the meeting for only a short time. If neither of these was the case, but the user travelled a significant distance to be at a particular location, that on its own justifies inclusion of the episode. The

Travel Agent therefore requires two additional types of information not present in the badge data files: meetings attended by the user, which it obtains from the Quorum Spotter, and a floor-plan of the building giving distances between pairs of locations. These enable it to build a list of significant stopovers, each specifying a start and stop time, a location, and a pointer to an attendance record if appropriate.

Diary Episode Builder

A further stage of processing is carried out to transform the Travel Agent's stopover list into a list of episodes suitable for inclusion in the diary. As will be seen, Pepys diaries provide a continuous sequence of episodes, from which the user can see what Pepys thinks she or he was doing at any time between the first and last sighting of the day. The stopover list, on the other hand, has gaps in it caused by travel between stopovers or by other activity excluded because it failed to meet the stopover criteria. These gaps can easily be accounted for, but the resulting list is very detailed, often including insignificant entries such as 40 seconds spent going from one location to another.

The main roles of the Diary Episode Builder are to fill in the gaps in the stopover list and then to reduce its level of detail by scanning through the list repeatedly, looking for particular patterns. Gap-filling is done by inserting a period alone, if the stopovers before and after were at the same location, or a period of travel if they were not. Detail-reduction involves replacing sequences of two or more elements of the list by a single, new element. The sequence is retained as a sub-list of the new element so that the details can later be included in the diary. Figure 3 shows an example of pattern-matching by the Diary Event Builder.

alone in 2nd floor pod from 13:04 to 13:08	13:04	In 2nd floor pod [4 mins]
attending event in 2nd floor pod from 13:09 to 13:34	13:08	Gone from 2nd floor pod [1 min]
alone in 2nd floor pod from 13:34 to 13:35	13:09	Attended discussion in 2nd floor pod; with Tim [25 mins]
alone in Smith's office from 13:35 to 13:40	13:35	Mostly in meetings in office [37 mins]
attending event in Smith's office from 13:43 to 13:53	13:35	In office [4 mins]
alone in Smith's office from 13:53 to 13:54	13:40	Gone from office [3 mins]
attending event in Smith's office from 13:54 to 14:12	13:43	Meeting in office; with Alice [29 mins]
alone in Smith's office from 14:12 to 14:13	14:13	Attended event in 2nd floor pod; with Tim [11 mins]
attending event in 2nd floor pod from 14:13 to 14:18	14:24	Attended event in Commons; with Tim, Fred [4 mins]
alone in 2nd floor pod from 14:18 to 14:20	14:28	In and out of event in Watson's office; with Fred,Tim [1hr 10m]
end of travel at Watson's office from 14:20 to 14:21		
attending event in Kitchen from 14:21 to 14:22		
attending event in Kitchen from 14:22 to 14:23		
alone in Commons from 14:23 to 14:24		
attending event in Commons from 14:24 to 14:26		
alone in commons from 14:26 to 14:27		
attending event in Watson's office from 14:28 to 15:39		

Fig. 3. Pattern matching by the Diary Episode Builder. The left column shows stopovers, the right column shows the final output after pattern matching.

Diary Composer

The final stage of Pepys is the composing and mailing of diaries. Several alternative approaches were considered, including graphical presentation techniques laying out episodes along a time line. There was no single internal format, however, that could have been received by all badge wearers at their workstations, which included Suns running Xerox Lisp and Unix, and Xerox 6085 workstations running Xerox Lisp, Cedar and ViewPoint. Hardcopy was considered as a distribution medium, but this would have required daily manual intervention.

Pepys therefore distributes diaries as plain text files via electronic mail. The program runs every morning at 4:00 a.m., reading the entire log of EuroPARC users' data for the previous 24 hours. Diaries are also distributed to badge-wearers at PARC, where logs are also maintained; the program prepares these diaries at 2:00 a.m. GMT to minimise the network load caused by accessing the logs from EuroPARC. The diary consists of the hierarchical list of episodes generated by the Diary Event Builder, pruned to a level of detail specified by the user as one of his or her preferences. Other user-settable options include formatting of time and names, inclusion of summaries, and inclusion of comment fields into which the user can type a description of each event. An example of a Pepys diary, showing comment fields partially filled in, is shown in Figure 4.

Accuracy of Episode Descriptions

The ultimate goal of the Pepys project, and the AIR project in general, is to provide users with an interactive tool which can be used for activity-based information retrieval. In order for Pepys to be used as an interactive retrieval tool, it is necessary that the episode descriptions used by Pepys match those in the users' retrieval requests. One of the first steps required, therefore, is to evaluate the episode descriptions generated by Pepys, and to rectify any errors found in these descriptions. Although more research is required to provide a better understanding of how people describe episodes in their working lives, the project reported here represents the first steps in designing such an interactive retrieval tool.

Interviewing Pepys Users

Pepys has been run on data collected at both Xerox PARC in California and at Rank Xerox EuroPARC. Shortly after the distribution of diaries had begun at PARC, several Pepys users were interviewed, and these interviews were videotaped. Users were first asked to recollect the events of the previous day, and then they were shown their Pepys diaries. After reading their diaries, several users remembered events that they had previously forgotten. However, it was clear that there were some inaccuracies in the episode descriptions in the diaries. For example,

31-Oct-90 Pepys:EuroPARC:RX Diary for Tuesday, October 30, 1990

Date: October 31, 1990 9:11:20 am GMT
From: Pepys:EuroPARC:RX
Subject: Diary for Tuesday, October 30, 1990
To: Little:EuroPARC:RX
Reply-To: Pepys:EuroPARC:RX

Summaries for Tuesday, October 30, 1990

Met in Nathan's office at 15:08 with R. Hatton, W. Nathan [41 mins]
Met in Commons at 16:06 with B. Andrews, M. Morton, R. Hatton [6 mins]
Met in Wright's office at 16:57 with P. Wright [3 mins]
Met in Little's office at 17:12 with I. David, P. Wright [45 mins]
Met in Little's office at 17:58 with P. Wright [15 mins]
Met in Little's office at 18:50 with W. Nathan [6 mins]

2h 10m with others = 43 percent
2h 38m alone = 53 percent
8 mins travelling = 3 percent

4h 57m total

Diary for Tuesday, October 30, 1990

14:14		In office [50 mins] **Writing paper**
15:04		In and out of event in Nathan's office; with W. Nathan, R. Hatton [45 mins] **discussing paper**
15:50		In office [10 mins] **Reading E-Mail**
16:00		In Conference room [4 mins] **checking video set-up**
16:05		Attended part of event in Commons; with B. Andrews, M. Morton, R. Hatton [7 mins] **Comment**
16:13		Mostly in office [44 mins] **Comment**
16:57		Attended event in Wright's office; with P. Wright [7 mins] **Comment**
17:04		Looked in on event in Morton's office; with I. David, M. Morton [1 min]
17:05		Mostly in office [2 hr 3m] **Comment**
	17:05	In office [5 mins]
	17:11	In event in office; with P. Wright, I. David [1h 2mins]
	18:13	In office [36 mins]
	18:50	Meeting in office; with W. Nathan [13 mins]
	19:03	In office [5 mins]
19:09		In 2nd floor rear area [2 mins] **Comment**
19:11		Last seen

v1.13

Fig. 4. An example of a diary generated by Pepys. The first six lines show the standard header added by the electronic mail system; following these are a summary of meetings and a breakdown of time spent; the final section is the diary itself, with comments (in bold) being added by the user on receipt of the diary.example, several users commented that short events were not necessarily unimportant and should not be ignored. Some users were also unsure about what the different episode descriptions meant (e.g., 'event' versus 'meeting', etc.).

several users commented that short events were not necessarily unimportant and should not be ignored. Some users were also unsure about what the different episode descriptions meant (e.g., 'event' versus 'meeting', etc.).

Monitoring Feedback from Pepys Users

Additional detail on the accuracy of episode descriptions was obtained by monitoring feedback from Pepys users at EuroPARC. Users were encouraged to comment on the information contained in their diaries. Of the 26 badge-wearers at EuroPARC, 17 receive Pepys diaries and responses were obtained from just over half of these users. Several users complained about inaccuracies, mainly in the records of their attendances at meetings. Some users also commented on being included as attendees of meetings when they had only passed through the area where a meeting was being held. After analysis of the comments and complaints received from the Pepys users, it was discovered that some of the inaccuracies were caused by the incorrect placement of receivers in some of the rooms in the building, and some other inaccuracies occurred within Pepys itself. Errors in the placements of receivers were corrected, and various changes to the Pepys algorithms were made as a result of the feedback from Pepys users.

Estimating the Accuracy of Episode Descriptions

To get a quantitative estimate of the overall accuracy of the episode descriptions in the Pepys diaries, a sample of seven of one of the authors' (MAE's) diaries was evaluated. Because the definition of an episode varies depending on the logged events which make up the episode, this estimation of accuracy is quite rough. For the purposes of this estimation, an episode is defined as one time-stamped major entry in a diary (sub-levels under the major entry are not included). To be classified as 'accurate', the following must be true: (1) the starting time of the episode must be correct (within 5 minutes); (2) the duration of the episode must be correct (because of the summation over events that occurs in the Pepys software, the duration of the episode was deemed correct if it was within 5 minutes of the actual duration); (3) the location of the episode must be correct; (4) the description of the episode (i.e., meeting, discussion, gone from, in office, etc.) must be accepted by the author as a reasonable description of that episode; and (5) for events involving other people, all badge-wearers present at the event must be included.

A total of 95 episode descriptions occurred in the sample of seven diaries. Of these, 79 were accurate descriptions using the criteria listed above. This gives an overall accuracy of the Pepys diaries of 85%. Over half of the inaccurate descriptions (9 of 16) were due to not all badge-wearers being listed as present at the event. This inaccuracy is caused by some people at EuroPARC not consistently wearing their badges. Six of the remaining inaccurate descriptions were episodes of the type 'gone from'. This episode description is sometimes quite misleading, particularly when an exit and subsequent re-entry into the building are obscured by the description. One inaccuracy was due to the length of a partial attendance at a meeting being recorded as being for 10 minutes, when in fact it lasted less than one minute.

Overall, then, the level of accuracy in the Pepys diaries is very high. In fact, if the cases where not all badge-wearers were listed as attending an event are eliminated, the overall accuracy goes up to 90%. This is a reasonable adjusted estimate because nearly all of these inaccuracies are due to individuals failing to wear their badges 100% of time; they are thus not caused by errors in the Pepys algorithms themselves.

Summary of Problems

The inaccuracies in the episode descriptions are the results of the following problems:

(1) Although nearly all personnel at EuroPARC have been issued badges, not all people wear their badges consistently. Some of the social effects discussed earlier in this paper have contributed to some people not wearing badges. Descriptions of episodes involving personnel not wearing badges will necessarily be inaccurate (e.g., 'time spent alone' could be time spent with a non-badge-wearer; meeting rosters may be incomplete, etc.).

(2) Some people wear their badges in non-optimal positions (on hip pockets), where the emissions from the badges can be obscured by clothing or pieces of furniture.

(3) The system can 'lose' people for a variety of reasons in addition to those mentioned in (1) and (2), for example, when someone leaves the building for a brief period. Different reasons for these lost-badge events are very hard for the Pepys algorithms to recognise.

(4) Accurate episode recognition requires an understanding of how people describe episodes in their working lives. Little work has been done on this in the past, and a more thorough understanding is required.

(5) Some of the Pepys algorithms are incorrect, partly due to the problems mentioned above, and partly because the Pepys algorithms were initially designed for the sparse badge system installed at PARC and do not take full account of the complete coverage of the badge system at EuroPARC.

These problems are currently being addressed by ongoing work on the AIR project. The badges themselves are being redesigned, and this should improve the reliability of signal detection. Some of the Pepys algorithms are also being changed to deal with 'lost' badges. More research is being undertaken to understand how people describe episodes in their working lives, and this research should suggest changes to the Pepys algorithms which will make the generated episode descriptions more accurate, and thus more meaningful.

Research is also under way to conduct a comparison of the use of Pepys at several sites, and to see whether this bears out earlier experience with the Locator. Already some similarities have been observed, such as the concern over public versus private information, and the tradeoff between utility and these privacy concerns. The decision to collect badge data into a single log, and to issue diaries from a central service, appears to have led to a view of Pepys as a 'public' system, and of the log files as 'public' files. Designing Pepys as a personal tool, drawing on a private log file, might have produced a different user response. Users appeared very uncertain, at the outset, about the possible benefits of receiving diaries; this may explain why approximately one third of EuroPARC's badge-wearers did not ask to receive them. Lack of perceived utility may have heightened concerns about public access to location data. More applications based on the Active Badge System are being pursued, and as these applications are introduced, there should be an increase in the benefits associated with wearing badges.

Conclusion

The project reported here was exploratory, and in great part served as a learning exercise. When the project was started, it was not known that the recognition of episodes from location data would be such a major issue. Not only were there several false starts in achieving this episode recognition, but those episodes that were eventually generated were not accurate in all respects. One focus of our future research will, therefore, centre on evaluating and refining the accuracy of the episode descriptions generated by Pepys.

Even though there is still a great deal to be learned about how episodes are described, a number of important things have been learned. Although the diaries present only a fairly coarse-grained description of events, several novel uses of the diaries have been observed. For example, several visitors, who have received diaries for the time of their stay at EuroPARC, have used the information in the diaries to write up their trip reports. Other people have used the information to help in preparing overtime forms or in writing their own personal diaries. Still other people have commented that the diaries were useful in reminding them of meetings and also of possible commitments made during those meetings.

Many people have also suggested enhancements which should serve to make the diaries more useful. For example, several people have suggested adding known calendar events (e.g., tea, seminars, etc.) to the diaries; adding more finely-grained information to the diaries has also been suggested. For example, including details of telephone calls and of informal conversations have both been suggested, and these and other monitoring techniques are currently being pursued (Lamming & Newman, 1991).

Within the AIR project as a whole, there are two major areas of work which are currently being pursued. The first concerns investigations which will help us to understand the social effects of the technology, and thus to increase the acceptance and the perceived benefits of the technology. The second area of work is concerned with understanding more about how people's working lives are structured, and what sorts of activities people can and cannot remember about their working days. This information will then help to develop and enhance applications like Pepys to make them more useful in retrieving information about work-related activities.

Acknowledgement

We wish to thank Pierre Wellner, Lawrence Butcher, Dan Swinehart, Bart Kinne, Mike Molloy, Ian Daniel and Roy Want for their contributions to designing and building the badge system on which Pepys depends. We are grateful to Mark Weiser for his support of the initial Pepys software development at PARC, and to Bob Anderson for supporting the subsequent research at EuroPARC. Many Pepys users at PARC and EuroPARC provided valuable comments and interviews. During the preparation of this paper, Richard Harper provided valuable comments on analysis of social impact. We are also grateful for advice received from Allan MacLean, Sara Bly, Phil Barnard, Debra Bekerian and Jerry Elkind.

References

Beard, D., Palaniappan, M., Humm, A., Banks, D., Nair, A., & Shan, Y-P. (1990): "A visual calendar for scheduling group meetings", *CSCW '90 Proceedings*, October 1990, pp. 279-290.

Buxton, W., & Moran, T. (1990): "EuroPARC's integrated interactive intermedia facility (IIIF): Early experiences", *Proceedings of IFIP WG8.4 Conference on Multi-User Interfaces and Applications*, Heraklion, Crete, September 1990.

Harper, R., Lamming, M.G., & Newman, W.M. (1991): "The locator: an experiment with active badges", *EuroPARC Technical Report*, in preparation.

Lamming, M.G. (1991): "Using automatically generated descriptions of human activity to index multi-media data", *IEE Colloquium on Multi-Media Communications and Applications*, February 1991, pp. 5/1-5/3.

Lamming, M.G., & Newman, W.M. (1991): "Activity-based information retrieval: Technology in support of human memory", paper submitted for publication.

Newman, W.M. (1990): "Interacting with Ubiquitous Systems." Invited paper, Eurographics '90 Conference, Montreux, 1990.

Smith, S., Glenberg, A.M., & Bjork, R.A. (1978): "The influence of environmental context on recall and recognition. *Memory & Cognition*, vol. 6, no. 4, 1978, pp. 342-353.

Thimbleby, H., Anderson, S., & Witten, I.H. (1990): "Reflexive CSCW: supporting long-term personal work", *Interacting with Computers*, vol. 2, no. 3, 1990, pp. 330-336.

Want, R. (1990): "The active badge location system", *Olivetti Research Laboratories Report*, The Old Addenbrookes Site, 24a Trumpington St., Cambridge, England CB2 1QN, 1990.

Proceedings of the Second European Conference on Computer-Supported Cooperative Work
Bannon, L., Robinson, M. & Schmidt, K. (Editors)
September 25-27, 1991, Amsterdam, The Netherlands

Organizational Memory

E. Jeffrey Conklin
Corporate Memory Systems, Inc., USA

Susan Leigh Star
Department of Sociology and Social Anthropology, Univeristy of Keele, UK

Panelists:

Liam Bannon, University of Amsterdam, The Netherlands
John Bowers, University of Manchester, UK
E. Jeffrey Conklin, Corporate Memory Systems, Austin, Texas, USA
George Por, Organizational Learning Systems, Berkeley, California, USA
Susan Leigh Star, University of Keele, UK

This panel session brings together a diverse group of people to explore the concept of organizational memory. Closely related to organizational learning, organizational memory is the property of organizations that provides continuity and learning. Organizational memory is not just the aggregate of the memories of the organization's members -- it is a social phenomenon.

The panel session explores the phenomenon of organizational memory from the following perspectives:

1) Technology. How can CSCW augment organizational memory? CSCW applications currently focus on augmenting the process, i.e. communication and coordination. Do these alone provide the basis for organizational memory? What else is needed to make the memory effective? Organizational memory is

currently weak on remembering rationale -- the reasoning behind the artifacts and events. Can CSCW help capture this "why" information?

2) Social science. "Scaling up" our understanding of cognitive processes from individual to organizational involves conceptualizing problems of communication and interpretation of representations, as well as understanding the nature of joint work at creating those representations. What happens, for example, when a representation is created by one person and used by another? Or passed a long distance between many sites? Also, representing group and distributed cognition processes often deletes the work of making and maintaining representations, or fails to pick up informal or devalued work processes associated with them. Can we "restore the work" in discussing organizational cognition? Finally, what is the status of "cognitivism" -- the application of cognitive models to organizations.

3) Management. Why is organizational memory a buzzword in management circles now? In particular, what is the relationship of organizational memory to the "learning organization" (e.g. as described in Peter Senge's The Fifth Discipline)?

Proceedings of the Second European Conference on Computer-Supported Cooperative Work
Bannon, L., Robinson, M. & Schmidt, K. (Editors)
September 25-27, 1991, Amsterdam, The Netherlands

Boosting Connectivity in a Student Generated Collaborative Database

Douglas R. Ward
Centre for Applied Cognitive Science
Ontario Institute for Studies in Education, Toronto, Canada

CSILE is an educational knowledge-media system with which students collaborate to produce a database that encompasses most of their academic work. It is intended to promote the building and exploration of connections between ideas. Keywords are used as the basis for connecting students' notes. A CSILE database constructed by grade 5-6 students was analysed. Although students tend to use few keywords per note, the texts of their notes contain substantial and consistent domain vocabularies. A simulation was conducted of a form of procedural facilitation which would expose this phenomenon to students and significantly boost connectivity in the database.

Introduction

Trends in the development of educational computer applications are shifting from the use of computers as surrogate teachers, toward systems which facilitate student-centered "knowledge-building" through the construction and exploration of computerized knowledge bases, often through co-operative or group study efforts. One such application, CSILE (pronounced see-sil), has been studied in a school setting for five years. This *Computer Supported Intentional Learning Environment* is an educational knowledge-media system with which groups of students collaborate to construct a database of text and graphical "notes" about the topics they are studying (Scardamalia, Bereiter, McLean, Swallow, & Woodruff, 1989; see Figure 1).

CSILE is intended to facilitate deep learning and knowledge structuring by its student users as they conscientiously contribute to the database's content and structure, as well as explore the contributions of others. The contributions of groups of students working on related problems or topics need to become linked in some way so that the students can become aware of and come to understand and utilize each other's ideas in their knowledge-building endeavours. Keywords are a simple mechanism for achieving this integration, because they can provide both a simple summary of notes' contents as well as an index for searching to retrieve related notes.

Figure 1. Screen from the CSILE program showing sample notes that the user is writing (top) and reading (bottom) following a search of the communal database.

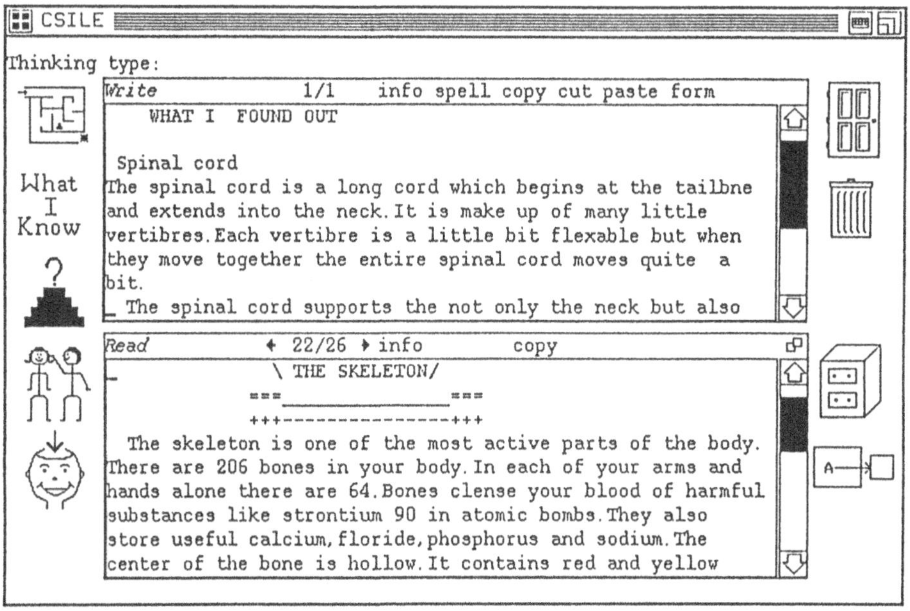

CSILE attempts to support communal knowledge integration by allowing students to make and explore connections between notes. Notes can be considered *connected* if they share keywords; a search for all notes with keyword "X" retrieves a collection of notes which presumably have something important in common (i.e. they are all about "X"). It is desirable to have a substantial amount of connectivity in the database, and for the user-interface to contribute to the user's sense of connectivity between notes. Efforts to retrieve connected notes should be rewarded by the return of notes which show what users' peers are thinking and writing on subjects of interest. A highly connected database will provide greater opportunity for this.

Studies of information retrieval systems suggest that there are generally serious problems with keywords as a means of accessing information from databases. Furnas, et al. (1983) point out that imprecision in the way humans name and refer to objects might lead to reduced performance in retrieval tasks. Random pairs of people were shown to use the same word for an object only 10 to 20 percent of the time. The usual implication of this is that users of a database cannot be very confident that they are retrieving a large proportion of relevant documents, and a small proportion of irrelevant ones; it is often difficult to anticipate the exact keywords used by the system designers or database indexers.

The traditional solution to this problem has been to restrict keyword indexes to a small set of valid descriptors. This has been shown to improve precision in meaning by increasing consistency of keyword use between indexers and users (Tinker, 1966). However, this is only suitable in applications where domain vocabulary is already standardized among database users. In the case of students building a CSILE database, knowledge from any domain might be contributed, so it would be impossible to anticipate what keywords might best be included in a restricted set of descriptors.

Another way to overcome the problem or imprecise keywords in information retrieval systems is to allow an object to be identified by many not necessarily unique words (Furnas et al., 1983). In related studies, Gomez et al. (Gomez & Lochbaum, 1985; Gomez, Lochbaum, & Landauer, 1990) demonstrated that retrieval success can be improved if the number of different names for a data object is increased. It might be expected that large index vocabularies could become awkward and ambiguous, with many objects sharing the same keywords, but the rich indexes generated by allowing "unlimited aliasing" in these studies were seen to facilitate retrieval without imposing any obvious human performance cost.

The design of CSILE is directed toward students *constructing*, rather than just exploring or retrieving information from a database of their collective knowledge. So, although it is clear that enriching keyword indexes in CSILE databases might improve retrieval success, the problem of how to get student users of the system to generate and assign these useful keywords to their notes remains. Skills of assigning and searching by keywords are neither presupposed for students using CSILE, nor do the students receive any specific instruction to develop these skills. The overall design challenge in CSILE is to provide *procedural facilitation* (Scardamalia & Bereiter, 1984; Scardamalia et al., 1989) for students to structure and elaborate their own individual and group knowledge. The CSILE user interface should support the efforts of students and foster appropriate and effective use of keywords, without presuming the skills of an expert database user, and without providing any substantive help which would direct the content of students' notes.

The version of CSILE used during the course of this study required students to assign at least one keyword before any note could be stored. Students could either select from a scrolling list of all keywords used in the database, or type one which may or may not be in the list. No other assistance was provided for the selection of keywords. To retrieve information stored in each other's notes, students formulated Boolean search statements based on keywords, authors, topics, or other criteria, through a simple "point-and-click" dialogue. The notes returned by searchers were displayed, one at a time, in a "read window".

This paper reports on young students' use of keywords as a mechanism for building and discovering connections between pieces of the collective knowledge base. Based on observed, sub-optimal patterns of keyword usage, two methods of procedural facilitation are suggested. A simulation verified that keyword standardization and enrichment processes could be valuable in boosting connectivity in the database in a way that could promote the integration of student knowledge.

Analysis of Keyword Usage

A CSILE database, generated over nine months by two grade 5-6 classes (age 10-11), was examined for this study. CSILE was used as a regular part of learning activities in the classrooms, and the topics represented include many of their units of study. A total of 1893 student-generated text notes were captured and analysed, along with system-generated transaction logs of student activities with the system.

Results and Discussion

Although it is possible to assign several keywords to each note, only one is required before a note can be stored. In 57.5% of the notes examined, only one keyword had been assigned (see Figure 2a). The maximum number of keywords per note was 10, although fewer than 10% of the notes had more than 3 keywords. Some students probably would not bother with keywords at all if they were not required, but others have indicated in interviews that they liked to put more keywords on their notes so that more students would read them. Some students seemed to appreciate the value of good keywords in note retrieval and building connections in the database.

Figure 2. (a) Frequency distribution of notes by number of keywords. (b) Frequency distribution of keywords by commonness. (The commonness of a keyword is the number of notes to which a keyword has been assigned.)

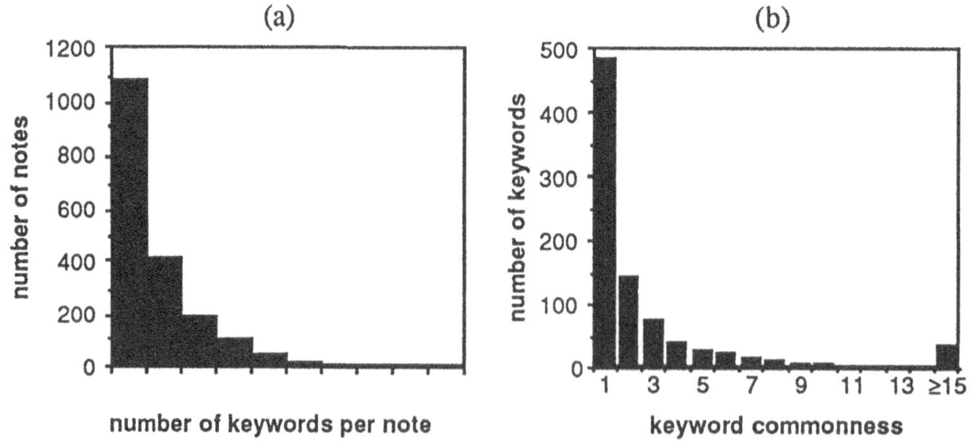

Of the 892 different keywords used, 54.3% were assigned to only one note; thus, most keywords were very uncommon in the database (see Figure 2b).

Although the most common keyword was assigned to 256 notes, only 3.8% of the keywords were assigned to 15 or more notes. There are several possible reasons for students not assigning the same keyword to multiple notes. The interface may provide disincentives to do so in that it is difficult and time-consuming to scroll through over 800 terms to find an applicable keyword. Students often create "private" or unique keywords to act like "file names" for their own use in retrieval, not thinking in terms of others retrieving their notes. The reasons for uniquely identifying one's own notes with keywords might be more apparent to the students than those for connecting one's note to other notes by assigning common keywords.

Most of the students' keywords could be identified as vocabulary relevant to the knowledge domains under study. The keyword list is not an exhaustive lexicon of any domain, but the terms students chose are certainly relevant to their fields of inquiry. There are, however, two main problems with the keywords students had invented. First, many phenomena reduced the potential for the formation of keyword connections due to a lack of standardization of terms: slight variations in spelling, case, punctuation, and abbreviation, unnecessary suffixes (e.g. "-ed", "-ing", "-s"), and the addition of articles (e.g. "the...", "a...") or pronouns (e.g. "my..."). There were many cases where a single term could have stood in the place of several independently entered "versions" of the same keyword. This is certain to reduce the potential for notes to share keywords. The second problem was with terms having little semantic value in describing the contents of a note. Unfortunately, some of the most common keywords fell into this category: "comment", "vocabulary", "book review", "junk", "plan", and "question". Although these keywords suggest something about the type of knowledge represented in the note, they do little to indicate specific information. There were also numerous examples of uncommon keywords which did not seem to indicate their notes' contents. In all, 282 keywords out of 892 were identified as problematic in either of these two main ways.

A simple measure of connectivity was generated to indicate the richness of the keyword connections the students had built into their database. Each keyword in a given note may connect that note to few or many other notes, depending on the keyword's commonness. The total number of other notes with which a given note shares one or more keywords is a measure of how connected that note is. Connectivity across the whole database is described in Figure 3 as a frequency distribution of numbers of keyword connections per note.

A large portion of the database (37.5% of all notes) had fewer than 10 keyword connections per note due to the frequent use of uncommon keywords. As many as 9% of the notes were completely unconnected. On the other end of the distribution, 13.5% had 250 or more connections due to the use of very common keywords, often in combination. Because the most common keywords were mainly not indicative of note contents (the second problem noted above), and the better keywords were less common, the amount of connectivity which might be of any use to students in retrieving related notes is really quite small.

Figure 3. Frequency distribution of number of keyword connections per note.

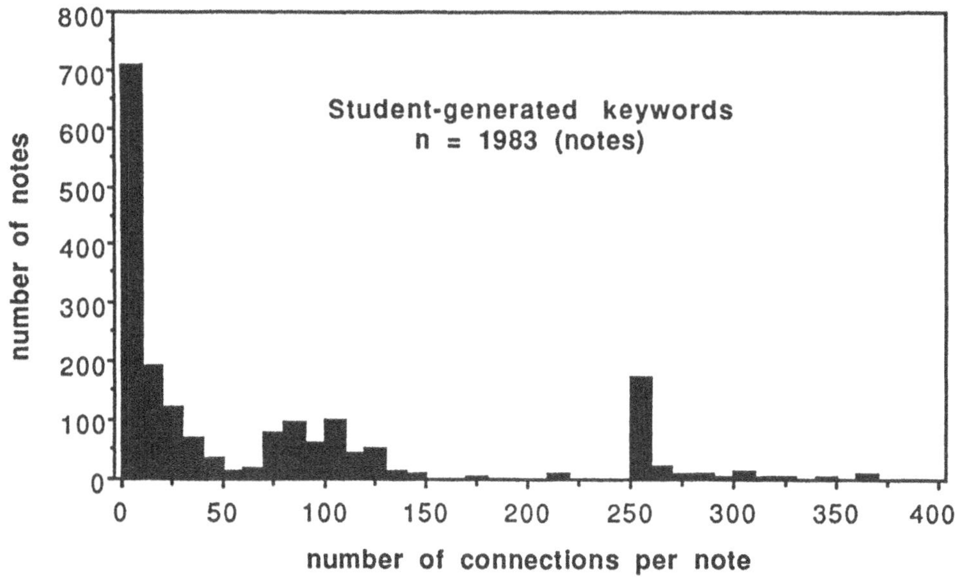

Out of 5514 searches conducted by students over the period of construction of the database, only 20% use a keyword as a search term. Keyword searches which either return very few or very many notes don't facilitate the discovery of interesting relations between notes. Without keywords providing a major role in information retrieval, it is likely that they have little apparent function to many students. In fact, students tended to pay very little attention to keywords. To view the keywords and other note information, the user is required to open a special "info" window; this was done for less than 8% of the notes which were viewed in the read window.

Simulation of a keyword enrichment facility

Based on the previous analyses, it was possible to suggest two simple forms of procedural facilitation which might eliminate some of the identified problems with students' keywords, as well as increase the connectivity in the knowledge base. First, the computer could suggest modifications to new keyword entries to help students *standardize* their keyword vocabulary without any substantive interference in the keyword selection process. Second, a keyword *enrichment* facility could suggest additional keywords for each note, based on the overlap of textual contents of notes with the user-generated keyword list, without creating any new keywords.

The use of these facilities has been simulated, *a posteriori*, on the students' own database.

Keyword Standardization

In order to eliminate problems of the lack of standardization of keyword form as described above, the following "soft" rules were applied:

- encourage correct spelling
- encourage singular words
- encourage root words (no suffixes)
- discourage extraneous punctuation
- discourage pronouns and articles
- discourage numerals
- ignore case
- discourage "invalid" words (as determined by teachers or designers)

As a form of procedural facilitation for real users, it would be important that these rules be instantiated as suggestions by the computer of an alternative keyword when a "problem" keyword is entered, so that the user could retain ultimate control over the choice of keywords. For the simulation, however, it was assumed that users would accept all suggested alternatives, and changes were applied to all instances of the 282 problem keywords.

Keyword Enrichment

It was hypothesized that many of the keywords which represent domain vocabulary would actually appear in the texts of more notes than those to which they had been assigned as keywords. If these terms were assigned as keywords, there should be an increase in the number of keywords per note, commonness of keywords, and overall connectivity through the database. This would be instantiated by having the computer suggest additional keywords at the time of creation or modification of a note, or later as an updating process. Either way, the user should be able to accept or reject the computer's suggestions. For the simulation, though, it was assumed that users would accept all suggested additional keywords.

The corrections and eliminations of problematic keywords were specified manually by creating a list of changes which were to be made. A computer program then effected the changes in the database. Because some "invalid" keywords were deleted from notes, some notes were left without any keywords. These notes were discarded from the following analyses, because it could not be determined what alternative keyword the student author might have assigned. This reduced the total number of notes analysed to 1392.

Following this process, a computer program scanned the text of every note, comparing each word with the main list of keywords (those which had been standardized). Where matches were found, the keyword was assigned to the note, generating a new database with standardized and enriched keywords. The following analyses compare this keyword-enriched database to the same notes in their unaltered form.

Results and Discussion

The unaltered database of 1392 keywords contained a total of 865 different keywords. After the standardization process, there were 24% fewer (656). The median commonness increased from 1 to 5 notes per keyword. The proportion of keywords used only once fell from 55.0% to 23.9%, and the proportion used 15 or more times increased from 3.4% to 27.1%. The enriched keywords had an improved likelihood of being shared by multiple notes.

The number of keywords per note also increased dramatically. Whereas the unaltered notes had no more than 10 keywords and a median of 2 per note, the enriched notes had as many as 35 keywords, with a median of 6. The proportion of notes with only one keyword fell from 44.3% to 6.8%. The data confirm the hypothesis that many of the keywords representing domain vocabulary are actually used within the text of students' notes more often than assigned as keywords. It is potentially very empowering to make this phenomenon visible to students, so that they know that other students are contributing information related to their own notes, and that the keywords are a means of accessing those related notes.

Figure 4. The distribution of connectivity after keyword enrichment.

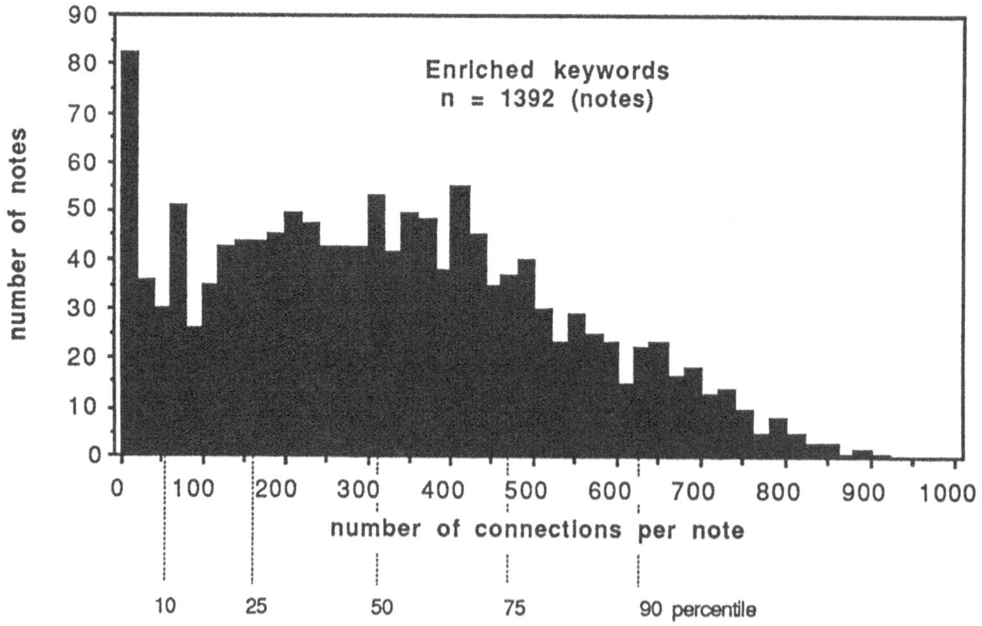

The median level of connectivity increased from 8 to 315 connections per note (see Figure 4). Only 0.8% of the notes remained completely unconnected, 3.7%

had fewer than 10 connections, and 5.9% had more than 20. A statistical comparison of the connectivity distributions before and after enrichment is based on the null hypothesis that if both connectivity distributions are the same, it can be assumed that equal numbers of notes from each set of connectivity scores will fall within any range of percentile scores from the combined distribution. Table I shows percentile scores of the combined distribution, and numbers of notes from each independent distribution which fall within each range of the combined percentile scores. A Chi-square test for homogeneity of the distributions shown in table I indicates that the two distributions do not contribute equally to their combined distribution ($\chi^2 = 1848$, df = 5; $p < 0.001$). Connectivity was radically increased by the enrichment process.

The *a posteriori* simulation of keyword enrichment might have exaggerated the potential to improve connectivity over the evolution of a database. The first notes produced on a topic will not gain as much from the enrichment facility as later notes, because users have not yet provided the domain-relevant keywords with which to cross-reference their notes. The fact that students create keywords as they create their notes remains a strength of the system, however. If a process for updating keyword connections to older notes is available as new keywords are created, these estimates of connectivity are tenable.

Table I. Frequency of notes in each of the unaltered and enriched connectivity distributions falling within the ranges of certain percentile scores from the combined distribution.

combined percentile *score*		10th *2*	25th *7*	50th *48*	75th *315*	90th *509*
Unaltered	301	716	249	126	0	0
Enriched	20	28	78	571	418	277

Conclusions

For CSILE to meet its objectives as a communal knowledge-building environment, students need to consciously utilize some mechanism for creating and discovering connections between their collective ideas. Keyword connections might form the basis of such a mechanism, but an examination of unaided keyword usage has revealed several critical problems. Students tend to assign one or very few keywords to each note. They tend not to re-use the existing keywords from their own and others' notes, creating new ones instead, even when similar keywords already exist. Many keywords have little value in terms of describing notes' contents. These facts combine to create a database with very low connectivity. This may explain the relative infrequency of keyword searches.

It should be beneficial in CSILE to facilitate an increase in the number of keywords assigned to each note by suggesting keywords which other students (or the same student at other times) felt were important descriptors of other notes. This would not only increase the probability of retrieving a given note through a keyword search, but boost the connectivity amongst the notes, as demonstrated by our simulation.

The advantage of providing this sort of procedural facilitation to students using CSILE goes beyond simply improving information retrieval performance. Students using the current version of CSILE do tend to use important domain vocabulary as keywords for their notes, but they do not benefit from the potential for building meaningful connections between their notes. If students can be informed that several other notes have a keyword which is in their note, the decision to assign the keyword becomes a decision to build connections between notes in the database. This should contribute to the sense among the student users of constructing a collaborative knowledge base, rather than merely entering personal notes into a public database.

Automatic full-text indexing could increase connectivity in the database as much or more, but enriched keyword indexing is expected to have greater benefits for student users. Analysis of expert on-line searchers reveals that expertise in information retrieval stems largely from experience, and a familiarity with the vocabulary and contents of a database (Oldroyd, 1984). CSILE users are in the advantageous position of searching within a database of their own creation. Awareness of the content of the communal database can be enhanced by keyword enrichment suggestions at the time of creation and storage of notes. Connections may more profitably be explored through searching if users are more familiar with each other's keywords, and this will in turn expose the students to more of the database. The intentional construction of an integrated knowledge base can only be enhanced as users become more familiar with the contents and vocabulary of their database, and aware of connections among their contributions.

Enrichment of keyword complements of students' notes can radically *increase* connectivity, but can it really *improve* connectivity? An optimal level of connectivity would exist if there were keyword connections between all notes which really have related contents, and none between those which do not. An increase in connectivity would be an improvement only to the extent that keywords assigned to multiple notes point to related concepts in those notes. It is possible to imagine many cases where either the creation of poor keywords or the poor application of facilitated enrichment would yield levels or sorts of connectivity which might not profit the builders of a large database. Further research will reveal whether implementation of the suggested procedural facilitation in the CSILE user interface will improve the construction of integrated student knowledge bases.

References

Furnas, G. W.,Landauer, T. K.,Gomez, L. M., & Dumais, S. T. (1983). Statistical semantics: Analysis of the potential performance of key-word information systems. *The Bell System Technical Journal*, *62*(6), 1753-1803.

Gomez, L. M., & Lochbaum, C. C. (1985). People can retrieve more objects with enriched key-word vocabularies. But is there a human performance cost? In *Proceedings of Interact '84* (pp. 257-261). Amsterdam: North Holland.

Gomez, L. M.,Lochbaum, C. C., & Landauer, T. K. (1990). All the right words: Finding what you want as a function of richness of indexing vocabulary. *Journal of the American Society for Information Science*, *41*(8), 547-559.

Oldroyd, B. K. (1984). Study of strategies used in online searching 5: differences between the experienced and the inexperienced searcher. *Online Review*, *8*(3), 233-245.

Scardamalia, M., & Bereiter, C. (1984). Development of strategies in text processing. In H. Mandl,N. Stein, & T. Trabasso (Eds.), *Learning and Comprehension of Text* (pp. 379-406). Hillsdale, NJ: Lawrence Erlbaum Associates.

Scardamalia, M.,Bereiter, C.,McLean, R. S.,Swallow, J., & Woodruff, E. (1989). Computer-supported intentional learning environments. *Journal of Educational Computing Research*, *5*(1), 51-68.

Tinker, J. F. (1966). Imprecision in meaning measured by inconsistency of indexing. *American Documentation*, *17*, 96-102.

Acknowledgements

This article reports on only a small part of the CSILE project. The development of software and provision of hardware to design and implement CSILE is made possible by support from Apple Computer, Inc., External Research Division.

The author wishes to acknowledge the support of Marlene Scardamalia and the entire CSILE research and development team for sharing their resources to make this research possible. In particular, thanks go to Jim Hewitt for his tracking and analysis programs. Thanks also to Charles Laver and Jim Webb who teach at Huron Public School, and the Grade 5 and 6 students who contributed their time and knowledge to this study. The author is also indebted to Bob McLean and others who proof-read and commented on versions of this article.

Proceedings of the Second European Conference on Computer-Supported Cooperative Work
Bannon, L., Robinson, M. & Schmidt, K. (Editors)
September 25-27, 1991, Amsterdam, The Netherlands

A Model for Real-Time Co-operation*

Flavio DePaoli
CEFRIEL-Politecnico di Milano, Italy.

Francesco Tisato
Dip. di Scienze dell'Informazione-Università di Milano, Italy

Abstract

This paper introduces a general model for both specifying and designing conferences. A major goal of the model is to be useful at both the specification and the design stage.

The model follows an object-oriented approach. It is based on the different *roles* played by *groups* of conference attendants, and describes conference behaviour in term of *role changes*. Groups are defined at different abstraction levels. Specific activities (multiplexing of data streams, floor-control for a conversation, overall conference management) are driven by *coordinators*. They encapsulate different aspects, such as: device- and media-dependencies, application-dependent behaviours and user oriented strategies. Coordinators can be combined in a hierarchical control structure.

1. Introduction

In a cooperative environment users interact via information sharing. As pointed out in Garcia-Luna-Aveces(1988), there are three basic ways of sharing information. (1) Message sharing: users interact via mailing systems. (2) Data sharing: users interact via shared data bases. (3) Application sharing: users interact with the same application program at the same time.

The two former interaction styles are basically asynchronous. Whenever a user needs to interact with another, it sends a message or updates the database. This has no immediate effect on the workspace of the second user which will later accede asynchronously to the shared information. There are no strong timing requirements;

* This work is partially supported by Olivetti Systems and Networks.

possibly just events' ordering has to be ensured. Put another way, user's workspaces are "individual" and loosely connected.

The latter interaction style is basically synchronous, since a user must perceive the effects of other user's actions in "real time", i.e. in an ordered way and within a negligible delay. This leads to the concept of "shared workspace" (Ishii, 1990).

The shared application gets input streams (e.g., voice, video and data) from some workstations, manipulates them, and delivers them to all the connected workstations. The user does not care whether the application is implemented by shared or replicated processes (see Crowley(1990) for a detailed architectural discussion). In the following we denote by *conversation* the activities performed by users while (logically) sharing an application, and by *conference* a collection of one or more related conversations.

It is worth noting that the application sharing model is general enough to include several kinds of conversations. In particular, video and voice interactions can be modeled as conversations where the shared application just plays the role of a multiplexer, without semantically processing the incoming data streams.

There are several requirements for a conference environment. First, *floor-control* must be ensured by a suitable discipline which may depend both on application's semantics and on user's interaction styles. Second, floor-control strategies must be orthogonal to device- and media- dependent issues. Third, several conversations with (possibly) different floor-control disciplines must be coordinated in a unique conference framework. Fourth, it must be possible to control properly the overall conference set-up and behaviour. Finally, a smooth transition between individual and shared workspaces must be ensured. That is conferees must be able to use the same tools (editors, spreadsheets, and so on) as in a stand-alone situation (Ishii, 1990).

The above requirements suggest that shared applications must be layered to keep the kernel of the application separated both from floor-control issues, and from multiplexing and control of single-medium data streams. Moreover, a hierarchical organization allows the definition of modular-shared applications to be used both as insulated conversations and in a coordinated multi-conversation conference.

Conference aware applications (i.e., applications which explicitly take into account that they are shared) can be designed according to these guidelines. Moreover, a clean separation between applications and floor-control mechanisms allows us to "augment" stand-alone applications with conference mechanisms without modifying the applications themselves.

This paper introduces a general model for both specifying and designing conferences. A major goal of the model is to be both understandable to the end-user and suitable as a basis for an architecture. In other terms, the same paradigm should be used both at the specification stage (where user visibility is the key issue) and at the design stage (where focus is on the architecture).

The proposed model is based on the different *roles* played by *groups* of conference attendants and describes the conference behaviour in term of *role changes*. The role of an attendant defines the actions he/she can perform (e.g., to speak, listen, or both). Events that are significant in terms of floor-control correspond to role changes. A group collects all the attendants that play the same role. Ultimately, floor-control actions are modeled via movements of attendants between groups.

Specific activities (multiplexing of data streams, floor-control for a conversation, overall conference management) are driven by *coordinators*. Coordinators encapsulate device- and media-dependencies, application dependent behaviours and user-oriented strategies. They can be combined in a hierarchical control structure. An object-based approach is possibly the most suitable for achieving modularity and reusability (Korson, 1990) (Meyer, 1988). A coordinator is defined as an object whose interface provides a set of groups and primitives to modify group memberships.

Section 2 gives an overall description of the model. Section 3 introduces the logical structure of a coordinator and discusses how coordinators can be put together into a hierarchy. Section 4 sketches the current implementation status and future developments.

2. The cooperation model

2.1. The user view

From the user's point of view the basic difference between a stand-alone activity and a conversation is that in the former case there are no distinct roles (for example, the same person is both the application manager and the application user at the same time), while in the latter case each user may play different roles according to floor-control strategies.

Let us consider a single-user word processor: it gets commands (such as *cut* and *paste*) as well as input data (typed characters) from the unique user, and delivers the output data to the same user. If the same word processor is shared, we may want to introduce some floor-control rules. For example, to state that when a user is writing the other users cannot write, but they see the typed text on the screen. Users must be able to issue, in addition to the standard commands of the word processor, extra commands that allow the control of the floor according to specific strategies.

In the general case of a conference commands for the overall conference set-up and control are also needed. It is worth noting that (1) application commands deal with the behaviour of the application as "stand-alone", (2) conversation commands deal with the cooperative strategies related to a single conversation and (3) conference commands deal with overall conference management. This "separation of concerns" seems to be useful both because it corresponds to the user's model of

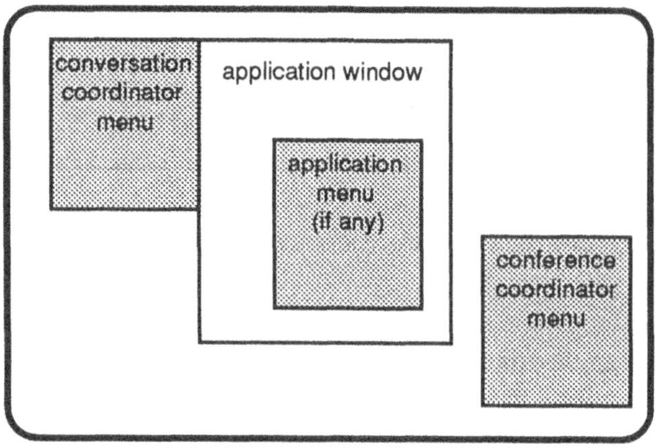

Figure 1. An example of user interface

the conference and because it can be easily mapped into the internal architecture.

Such a scheme is reflected in the menu based interface sketched in Figure 1. It shows a conference that includes a single conversation. Three menus are displayed. First, there is the conference menu. Examples of commands dealing with the overall behaviour of the conference are: join (or leave) the conference, start an application, terminate the conference.

A second menu provides commands related to conversation management. Some of them depend on the floor-control policy for the conversation. Other commands may be more general. Examples of such commands are: I want to write, I have finished writing, suspend the application, iconize the window.

The application menu (if any) belongs to the application and is affected neither by the conference nor by the conversation policy. In the case of a word processor, we may think in terms of the usual commands, such as cut, copy, paste.

Each conference attendant may have different menus enabled at different times according to his/her current role. For example we may state that only the currently writing user can use the application menu, and that not-writing users cannot execute the command *I have finished writing*.

2.2. Roles and Groups

A conference, viewed as a human activity, is characterized by the roles played by the conferees. The abstract concept of role is modeled via groups. The key idea is to introduce a group for every role and to describe the conference evolution by describing how users move from one group to another. This allows us to model the structure and the behaviour of a conference without dealing with the actual number and identity of the conference attendants.

Let us examine a simple example. In a word processor-based conversation there are basically two roles: writers and readers. A writer can both issue data and commands to the shared application, and see screen changes. A reader can just observe the changes on the screen. Let us assume a "one-writer-many-readers"

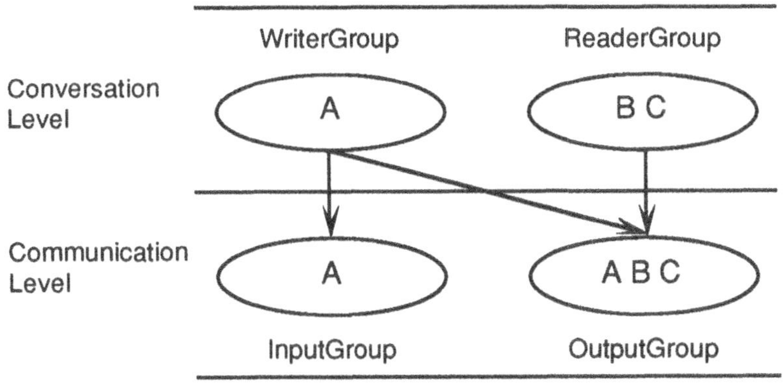

Figure 2. Example of group description

policy: this means that at any given time only one user can play the role of writer. On the other hand, all users except the writer are readers.

This situation is modeled by defining a WriterGroup and a ReaderGroup. The writer belongs to the WriterGroup, and all the readers belong to the ReaderGroup. If a reader becomes the writer, the old writer leaves the writer's group and becomes a reader.

The above is an abstraction representing the logical behaviour of the users. In general, a cooperative activity can be modeled at different levels of abstraction. In particular, if we look at the physical interactions, the users may play two more concrete roles: provide the inputs or get the outputs. Therefore we introduce a new level (we call it "communication level") characterized by two groups: the InputGroup, i.e., the group of users whose input channels are enabled, and the OutpuGroup, i.e., the group of users whose output channels are enabled (note that groups are, in general, not disjoint).

The mapping between the two levels is ensured by a (partial) mapping from conversation level groups into communication level groups, as shown in Figure 2. The meaning is that whenever a user is member of WriterGroup at the conversation level, he/she must be member of both InputGroup and OutputGroup at the communication level. In the same way, when a user is a member of ReaderGroup at the conversation level, he/she must be member of OutputGroup at the communication level. Thus floor-control actions (i.e., group changes) at the conversation level can be mapped into control actions at the communication level.

Figure 2 illustates the above example. At the conversation level the group membership of users A, B and C is driven by the floor-control strategy. At the communication level the group membership of users A, B and C is defined by the group mapping rules. Thus, A is a member of both InputGroup and OutputGroup while the other users are members only of OutputGroup. This means that the writer can type characters on the keyboard and read what he/she types on the screen, while the readers can only read what the writer is typing.

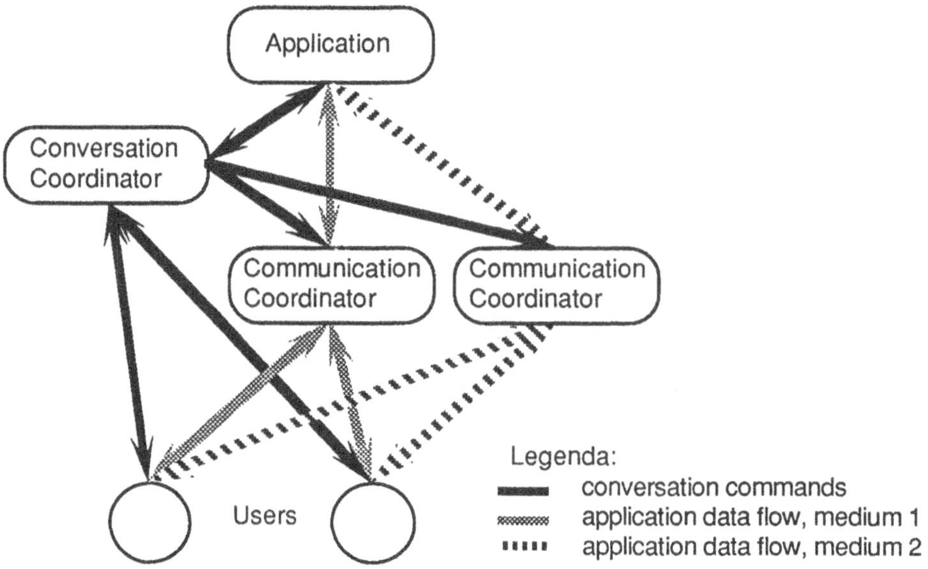

Figure 3. Object-based model of a conversation

2.3. An object-based model

The concepts above describe a cooperative activity from the user's point of view. In the following they are mapped into the architecture of the system supporting the cooperative activity.

The model introduced so far describes a cooperative activity at different levels of abstractions in terms of groups, movements of users between groups, and group mappings between levels. Since concepts and activities are similar across the levels, the system architecture is based on a general class of objects: the *coordinators*. A coordinator is defined as an object whose interface provides a set of groups and primitives for modifying group memberships. Coordinators encapsulate device- and media-dependencies, application-dependent behaviours and user-oriented strategies. They can be combined in a hierarchical control structure.

A conversation is managed by means of three object classes, as shown in Figure 3: the application, a *conversation coordinator* and some *communication coordinators*. The conversation coordinator implements the cooperation rules by interpreting commands generated either by the users or by the application. When the application is not conference aware, there is no flow of information between coordinator and application. The conversation coordinator controls the communication coordinators, which in turn control the actual exchange of information (data and commands) between users and application.

The presence of several communication coordinators reflects the requirement of dealing with different media. A communication coordinator works as a multiplexer that provides a device independent interface for the control of a single-medium data

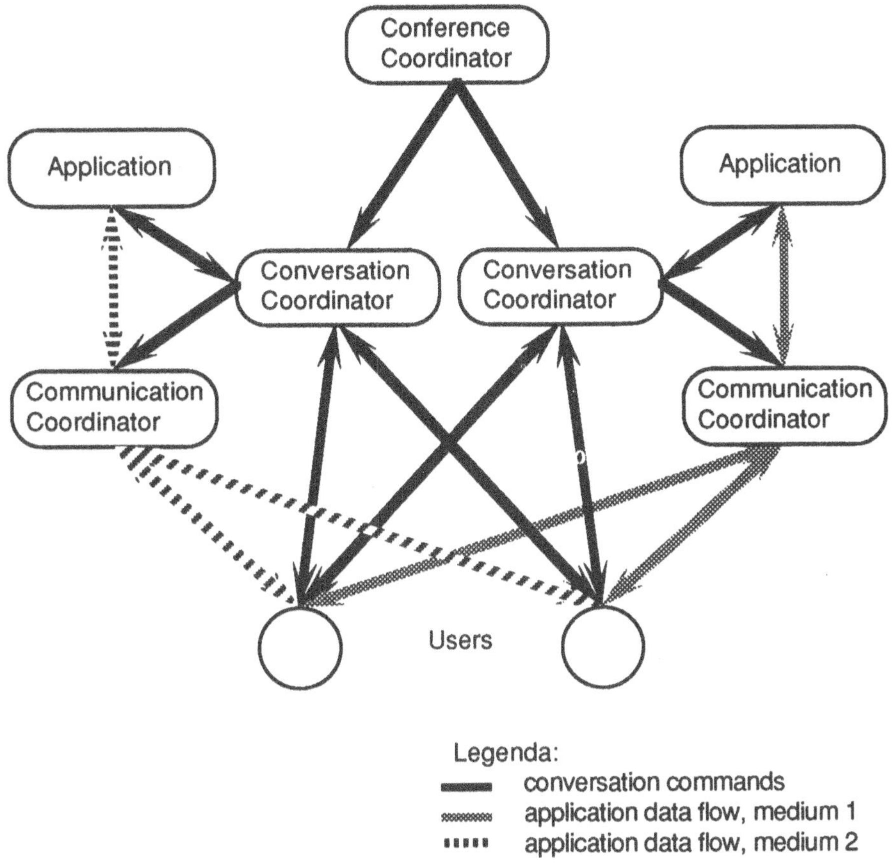

Figure 4. Object-based model of a conference

flow. Communication coordinators are generic with respect to the physical environments: networks with different speed or supporting different media, workstations with different hardware, operating systems, UIMSs or devices.

The model is based on "policy/mechanism separation": in the example above the communication coordinators provide media-dependent mechanisms for multiplexing and demultiplexing data streams, whereas the conversation coordinator provides media-independent floor-control policies.

The above scheme can be extended to overall conference management, possibly with several conversations, by introducing a higher level *conference coordinator* as shown in Figure 4. It is typically in charge of setting up the conference and controlling users when joining and leaving the conference. It controls the conversation coordinators by issuing proper commands. As we shall discuss later, this implies that some conversation commands are no more available to the users.

2.4. Media dependency: communication coordinators

Media dependency is encapsulated by communication coordinators, which behave as multiplexers with the task of providing the physical connections between users and applications. A communication coordinator is a software module based on specific hardware and software platforms. For example, if both graphics and voice are managed, there could be a graphics coordinator using sockets on top of Ethernet and a voice coordinator exploiting a telephone switching system.

Note that different coordinators provide the same interface even if they are based on different platforms. In fact, all multiplexers have the same description in term of roles and groups. Only three groups are needed to describe a generic communication coordinator: input group, output group and connected group. A user belonging to the input group is able to issue data to the shared application, while a user belonging to the output group is able to receive data from the shared application. The connected group collects all the users that are connected to the communication channel even if they are temporarily not active. This is what happens when a telephone user diverts a phone call: for a while he/she is temporarily disconnected from the audio channel, but he/she is still connected to the switching system.

3. Specification of coordinator behaviour

3.1. Groups and commands

The external interface of a coordinator is specified by means of two basic elements: (1) the *groups* it manages, and (2) the *commands* it is able to execute. As will become clear later, it would be more correct to talk of *public commands*. In the following, whenever no ambiguities arise, we shall use "commands" as a shortcoming for "public commands".

The actions a coordinator performs are ultimately movements of users among groups. It seems reasonable to introduce three basic commands which allow us to control the dynamic evolution of a generic coordinator, i.e., all the possible role changes of a user:

join (U,G);
leave (U,G);
select (G);

where U is a generic user and G is a generic group. Join(U,G) makes the user U member of group G; leave(U,G) removes U from the group G.

Select(G) returns a member of the specified group G. It is a deferred function in on object-oriented terminology, as it is not defined once and for all. In fact, it may have different definitions in order to support different strategies for user selection.

3.2. Invariants

Though the above three general commands are supported by any coordinator, their execution is bound to fulfil some *invariants*, i.e., consistency rules that must always be satisfied to ensure that the cooperative activity managed by the coordinator does not produce incorrect situations.

We introduce a semi-formal notation to specify the invariants.

U **is_in** G;
U **is_not_in** G;

denote that U is or is not a member of group G respectively. The operator *implies* (=>) can be used to impose constraints on user's memberships. The expression:

U **is_in** G1 => U **is_in** G2;

means that if U is a member of group G1, then U *must be* also a member of G2. More information about membership rules can be done by defining the cardinality of a group G with an expression of the form:

G *operator expression*;

where *operator* is a logical operator (=, ≠, >, ≥, <, ≤) and *expression* is an integer expression. Of course, for every group G holds the rule: # G ≥ 0.

For example, let us specify the invariants for a conversation coordinator whose groups are:

In_room: the group of users in the (virtual) conference room;
Speakers: the group of users who are enabled to speak;
Listeners: the group of users who can listen.

The coordinator invariants are

U **is_in** Listeners => U **is_in** In_room;
U **is_in** Speakers => U **is_in** In_room;
U **is_in** Listeners => U **is_not_in** Speakers;
Speakers < 2;

meaning that (1) a user must be in the room in order both to speak and listen, (2) Speakers and Listeners are group representing disjoint roles and (3) there may be no more than one speaker.

3.3. Commands execution

A command triggers the execution of a sequence of actions that modify the internal status of the coordinator. Actions are expressed in terms of basic *private commands* which implement elementary operations on groups and users. Since the invariants cannot be violated, the invocation of a (public) command may lead to different situations: (1) the command can be executed in a straightforward way by a private command, (2) the command execution implies some extra actions (i.e., sequences of private commands) in order to fulfil the invariants, (3) the command cannot be executed at all. Note that the execution of a public command must be atomic to avoid time-dependent errors.

Three possible public commands for our example coordinator are:

join (U, In_room)
join (U, Speakers)
leave (U, In_room)

Let *Insert* (U,G)/*Extract* (U,G) be private commands that modify the coordinator status by inserting/extracting user U into/from group G, and *Select* (G) be a private command that returns the identifier of a user belonging to group G (the selection policy depends on application issues). The execution of the above commands can be specified as follows:

Command	Execution

join (U, In_room)	**begin**
	    Insert (U, In_room);
	    return true
	end;

join (U, Speakers)	**begin**
	    if U **is_in** In_room **then**
	        begin
	        if #Speakers > 0 **then**
	            begin
	                X = *Select* (Speakers);
	                Extract (X, Speakers)
	            end;
	            Insert (U, Speakers);
	            return true
	        end
	    else return false
	end;

leave (U, In_room)	**begin**
	    if U **is_in** Speakers
	        then *Extract* (U, Speakers);
	    if U **is_in** Listeners
	        then *Extract* (U, Listeners);
	    if U **is_in** In_room
	        then *Extract* (U, In_room);
	    return true
	end;

The public command **join** (U, In_room) can be executed anyway.

The public command **join**(U, Speakers) can be executed only when user U is already "In_room". Moreover, if there is already one speaker, suitable extra actions must be performed in order to fulfil the invariant #Speakers<2. A user X must be *select*ed and *extract*ed from the Speakers group (the selection is trivial in this particular case). The extraction of X from the "Speakers" group leaves him/her in the "In_room" group. After these actions U can be *insert*ed into the "Speakers" group.

The execution of the public command **leave**(U, In_room) must ensure that user U is *extract*ed from all the groups he/she belongs to.

Commands should be presented to the user via a suitable interface (see Section 2.1) which may also provide atomic macro-commands. A macro-command could be

switch (U,V)

whose meaning is that users U and V must exchange their roles (U is speaking, gives the floor to V and becomes a listener). A possible expansion for this command is

leave (U,Speakers)
leave (V,Listeners)
join (U,Listeners)
join (V, Speakers).

It is up to the reader to look for more clever expansions of such a macro.

3.4. Coordinators control hierarchy

A coordinator is defined by its groups and its public commands. The effect of a public command is to move users between groups by performing suitable sequences of private commands. The previous discussion dealt with a "stand-alone" conversation coordinator receiving commands from the users. As shown in Figure 3, even in this simple situation there are at least two levels of coordinators: the conversation coordinator and the controlled communications coordinators. In general, as shown in Figure 4, a conference consists of a hierarchy of coordinators. A coordinator at a given level is connected via commands to the lower level ones.

Private commands (namely *Insert* and *Extract*) at a given level are implemented by invoking public commands (namely **join** and **leave**) of lower level coordinator(s) according to group mapping rules like those shown in Figure 2. Accordingly, the definition of a coordinator includes the definition of the coordinators it controls and the mapping from the groups it defines into the groups defined by the controlled coordinators.

This mechanism allows us to collect coordinators designed as "stand alone" into a hierarchy, and to map easily abstract roles supported by high level coordinators into more and more "concrete" roles supported by the lower level ones. Note that

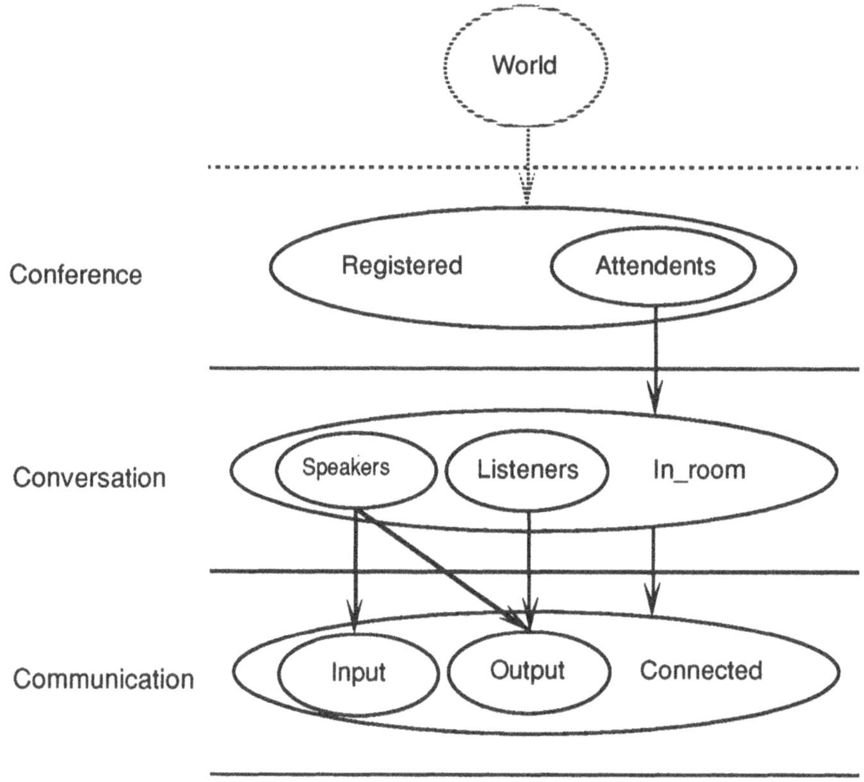

Figure 5. A membership table

groups, invariants, commands and mappings are abstract concepts expressed in a system- and media-independent way. Of course, the iteration stops at the bottom level, that of communication coordinators, whose *Insert* and *Extract* private commands are implemented in terms of system- and media-dependent features. The model is highly modular: a communication coordinator does not need to know what kind of floor-control is supported by the conversation coordinator it is serving, a conversation coordinator does not need to know anything about the conference coordinator and so on.

3.5. Hierarchy and user commands

As soon as coordinators are connected in a hierarchy, a question arises: which commands are visible to the users? It appears that, if a coordinator, say C1, is under control of a higher level one, say C2, then commands of C1 are used by C2 to implement its internal commands (i.e., group changes) according to the group mapping rules. Commands issued by a user directly to C1 cannot violate such rules, otherwise C2 looses the actual status of the system.

A straightforward solution is to impose the rule that a user can issue commands to the topmost coordinator only. A more flexible solution can be devised by looking at the example of Figure 5. The table describes a conference where there are some

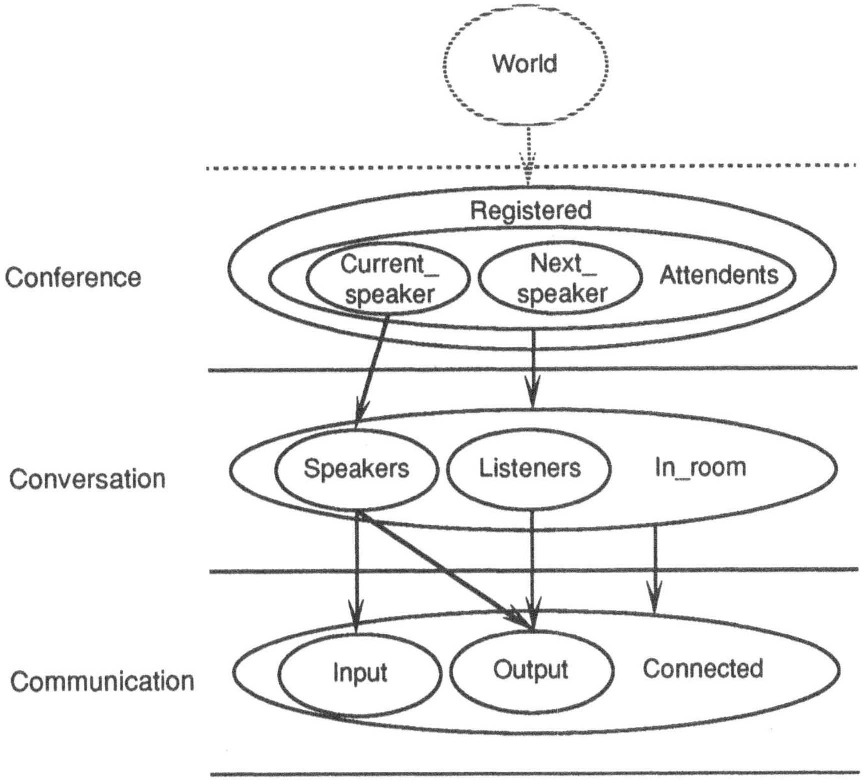

Figure 6. Another membership table

people that have registered (registered group), but not all part of them are actually attending the conference (attendance group). All people that are attending the conference are in the conference room (in_room group). One of them is the speaker, while all the others can be listeners (we consider the possibility that an attendant is not listening, maybe reading the proceedings). The lowest level illustrates the actual communication among attendances: all people are connected to the communication system (connected group), but only the speaker can actually speak (input group) while all the listeners and the speaker can listen. It physically means that the speaker's input channel is open, while the output channel is open for both speaker and listeners.

The arrows illustrate the mapping between groups of two different levels. Let us examine the conversation level (the conversation coordinator has already been discussed in a previous section). The membership of the "In_room" group is controlled by the conference coordinator: every user that belongs to the "Attendants" group is also a member of the "In_room" group. As a consequence, the application commands issued by the users cannot modify the memberships of the "In_room" group. Instead, the "Listeners" and "Speakers" groups are not controlled by the conference coordinator. This means that the users can freely move into and from such groups. In other terms, at the conversation level the only commands available to the users are **join**(U,Speaker), **leave**(U,Speaker),

join(U,Listener), and **leave**(U,Listener), while commands like **join**(U,In_room) and **leave**(U,In_room) can be issued only by the conference coordinator.

Figure 6 illustrates a different situation: the conference coordinator controls the floor taking by imposing that the member of its "current_speaker" group is the member of the "Speakers" group of the conversation coordinator. In this case, the commands **join**(U,Speaker) and **Leave**(u,speakers) are no longer available at the conversation level.

The above examples illustrate that when a coordinator is included into a hierarchy, some of its commands are issued by the higher level coordinator, while the remaining commands are still available to the users. More precisely the only commands available to the user at a given level are those that do not affect the membership to groups controlled by the higher level on the basis of group mapping (i.e., groups with incoming arrows in the figures).

4. Conclusions and future work

The model has been devised as a generalization of Conference Toolkit, an experimental conference system presented in (Bonfiglio, 1988). It provided the basic mechanisms for the implementation of a communication coordinator. In this paper the basic ideas of Conference Toolkit are extended in two ways. First, we define a general model for the description of a conferencing activity by introducing the concepts of role and group. Second, we generalize the concept of coordinator and define how coordinators can be combined into a hierarchical structure in order to design the architecture of a conference control system. The model allows us to define complex cooperative environments by composing basic building blocks and by introducing specific user-oriented policies.

The paper deals basically with specification issues. A set of prototype coordinators has been implemented and has been tested to build several conference control systems implementing different strategies. The prototypes, designed in an object-oriented style, are currently running exploiting X-Windows in a Unix environment.

The experimental activity allows us to conclude that the proposed approach is worthwhile. We have been able to build with a limited effort conferencing systems supporting different cooperation strategies, and to integrate standard X-Windows applications into them.

On-going work is related to the implementation of a set of communication coordinators for non-standard media (voice and video). We are also implementing a set of reusable standard coordinators supporting widely used floor-control strategies and overall conference management strategies. Such coordinators will be collected into a library managed by a semi-automatic tool supporting their composition.

References

Bonfiglio, A., Malatesta, G. and Tisato, F. (1988): "Conference Toolkit: A framework for real-time conferencing", Proc. EC-CSCW 89, September 88, pp 303-316.

Crowley, T., Milazzo, P., Baker, E., Forsdick, H. and Tomlinson, R. (1990): "MMConf: An Infrastructure for Building shared multimedia application, Proc. Conference on Computer-Supported Cooperative Work", ACM SIGCHI & SIGOIS, Los Angeles, October 1990, pp 329-342.

Garcia-Luna-Aveces, J.J., Craighill, E.J. and Lang, R. (1988): "An Open-system Model for Computer-Supported Collaboration", In Proc. 2nd International Conference on Computer Workstations, IEEE, March 1988, pp. 40-51.

Hishii, H. (1990): "TeamWorkStation: Towards a seamless shared workspace", Proc. Conference on Computer-Supported Cooperative Work, ACM SIGCHI & SIGOIS, Los Angeles, October 1990, pp 13-26.

Korson, T. and McGregor, J.D. (1990): "Understanding Object-oriented: a Unifying Paradigm", Communications of the ACM, 33,9, September 1990, pp. 40-60

Meyer, B. (1988): *Object Oriented Software Construction*, Prentice-Hall.

Scheifler, R.W.and Gettys, J. (1986): "The X Window System", ACM Transaction on Graphics, 5, 2, April 1986, pp. 79-109.

Stroustrup, B.(1986): *The C++ Programming Language*, Addison-Wesley.

Proceedings of the Second European Conference on Computer-Supported Cooperative Work
Bannon, L., Robinson, M. & Schmidt, K. (Editors)
September 25-27, 1991, Amsterdam, The Netherlands

Questioning Representations

Mike Robinson and Liam Bannon
Centre for Innovation & Cooperative Technology, University of Amsterdam, NL

Abstract. The role of models in the design of computer systems to support interpersonal and cooperative work is examined. It is argued that the current generation of models over-emphasise determinism at the expense of interpretation in the work process. It is further argued that there are many cases in which designs pass between many different professional groups (office workers, managers, analysts, designers, programmers). Each of these groups has its own worldview and specialised language, and hence they are termed "semantic communities". When designs pass between semantic communities, something is lost and something is gained -- but the objects on which each community works are not commensurable. The distinct objects of work (office problems, analyses, designs, programs) do not map onto each other, and cannot be mutually tested using simple true/false criteria. This is termed a problem of "ontological drift", and arises whenever several distinct semantic communities work on the "same" system. It is suggested that the disparity so often observed between design expectations and the ways systems are actually used is therefore quite normal. Current efforts are directed at eliminating the disparity. We suggest that a more fruitful approach might be to accept that the final determination of a system rests with the users. In the long run this might give rise to different types of design principles than those used at the moment. In the short run, even the consciousness of this perspective could make significant differences to design dialogues and attitudes to "users".

Introduction

The use of abstractions and modeling is ubiquitous in the development of computer-based systems for office work. A variety of methodologies have been developed to advise on how to perform such activities and ensure some veridicality between the model and actual work practices[1] -- with mixed results, as witnessed by

1 Including at least the following: SADT (Ross & Schoman, 1977); Structured Analysis (Yourdon,

the results of evaluations of such systems in the workplace[2]. While some simply argue for more powerful representational forms, and more resources to be provided to the systems analysts and designers, there has been a growing awareness that the problem is not simply one of forms or resources, but more fundamentally, of an inappropriate concept of what is "captured" in the model. Rather than viewing the models embedded in designs as implementable accounts of work processes, they should be conceived as heuristic devices that provide resources on particular occasions for particular groups of people. [3]

Our concerns developed while investigating the recent spate of design models that have been proposed for modelling group communication in the CSCW arena. Our investigation has three strands:

- a number of critical points on the theoretical grounding and practical use of models of people and work in the design of systems and applications to support cooperative and, more generally, interpersonal work processes;
- a developing account of the analysis, design, implementation, and use process in CSCW (and, more generally, computer support for interpersonal work).
- application of the critique to clarify the design process, analyse current applications, and identify some ways of improving CSCW system design.

This paper will concentrate on the second strand: an account of the design-to-use cycle. This is intended to capture some of the problematics and difficulties of design. It is *not* intended to be a full critique of current design models, or to provide pointers for improvement. The latter will be the subject of further papers.

Some Comments on Models and Modeling

Our goal is to develop an analytic case against an objective reality that can be usefully "captured" in a model and subsequently used as a sufficient basis on which to develop a computerized system. Our critique relies on the centrality of *interpretation* in the conduct of work[4], and also on the fact that the development of computer-based applications requires the collaboration or involvement of a variety of distinct communities -- workers with different skills, analysts, developers, programmers, etc. This necessary heterogeneity poses a number of problems which cannot be removed simply by ensuring good "communication" between the differing groups. The issue is more fundamental, arising out of the different practices of the groups and the essential incommensurability of their world views and language.

1982); OPSL (Zisman, 1977); ICN (Ellis et al, 1980); OAM (Hammer & Sirbu, 1980); and JSD (Jackson, 1983).

2 See reviews by Auramaki et al (ms) and by Schmidt (1990b).

3 in the sense that Suchman (1987) sees plans as resources for action

4 See, for instance, Berger & Luckmann, 1967, Latour & Woolgar, 1979, Wynn, 1979, Suchman & Wynn, 1984, Gerson & Star, 1986, Suchman, 1987.

A distinction between the nature of *description* and that of *interpretation* is relevant. Here, we wish to focus on practical issues, without detailing the philosophical discourses on realism vs. constructivism. A view of modelling that sees it as merely description of an accepted reality, or an abstraction of it, can lead to serious difficulties. Accepting that there is a sense in which all description is really interpretation (see Geertz, 1973) causes us to be more careful in ascribing veridicality to our models. Models are then seen as interpretations, as constructions, which for some purposes, under certain conditions, used by certain people, in certain situations may be found useful, not true or false. We thus see the modelling process as one of reframing rather than describing or abstracting.

We will now look at some examples with these distinctions in mind. For purposes of illustration, we will use activity/role models from some recent CSCW work. We intend to do a more thorough investigation of a comprehensive set of models in a later paper. As our example here we will refer to the specific group communication models cited in Hennessy, Benford and Bowers (1989) . The intent of these European projects (COSMOS, AMIGO MHS+, AMIGO Advanced, and MacAll II) was to create "abstract models of groups communication" and to address "critical limitations" in existing services. We hope that the similarity to other CSCW models will be apparent, and that the outline of our general doubts can be gleaned from this limited case. Our specific concern was the way the concepts of "role" and "activity" are defined and used. Each time the term "role" appears in the examples below, one may ask whether it is intended as a description, as an interpretation, or as an element in a self-contained design dialogue that is independent of any office reality.

Example 1: Notes on COSMOS

"**Actions** -- These are divided into exchanges , which are elementary communicative acts involving at least two participant roles and usually one object; and encapsulated actions (EA's) which do not involve any exchange (eg. creating objects)

Rules -- these define the conditions under which actions can occur"

Roles -- these are agents who initiate actions. A role may be played by an individual user, a collective, or an automated process"

Conditions -- these are expressions, resolving to true or false, which define the context in which rules are triggered."

Example 2: Notes on MacAll

"During the performance of an activity, people are assigned to roles, and they follow the rules associated with those roles. Messages are created, and their rules direct their transfer between workspaces. When a message arrives at a workspace, the workspace notifies the appropriate role instances that a new message has arrived, and one of the role instances processes the message according to its rules."

Example 3: Notes on Amigo Advanced

"**Roles** -- Within each activity, a set of role classes is defined. Each member of the group must be associated with at least one role that is an instance of one of these classes. The class definitions include the functions that instances of this class of roles may perform or request to be performed, and the message object types that can be sent or received."

"**Rules** -- These are used to define how each role is expected to behave during the execution of an activity."

In these examples there is a strong logico-mechanistic, or deterministic picture, consistent with the goal of machine implementation. Complementing this, in many CSCW papers, there is an absence of reference to specific office situations, or to the many sociological and anthropological studies from which the central notion of "role" is derived. This provided us with a catalyst for an initial set of comments.

* There is a constant temptation for designers to confuse the models with an underlying reality.
* The models impose an ordering on people and or events, often unilaterally.
* The models are difficult for "users" to understand and thus
* preclude people from appropriating and re-working the model in situations of use.
* The models do not define their basic concepts adequately.
* Emphasis appears to be on model form and elegance over actual coverage and practicality or usefulness.
* Emphasis is on "determinism" at the expense of "interpretation" in work processes.
* The models embody an inappropriate correspondence theory of truth, and thus
* make the untenable assumption of a specifiable, one-to-one, decontextualized relationship between an instruction and the action that satisfies it.

Our first attempt to understand the design process, and our notes on role and activity models, resulted in a simple diagram shown in Figure 1.

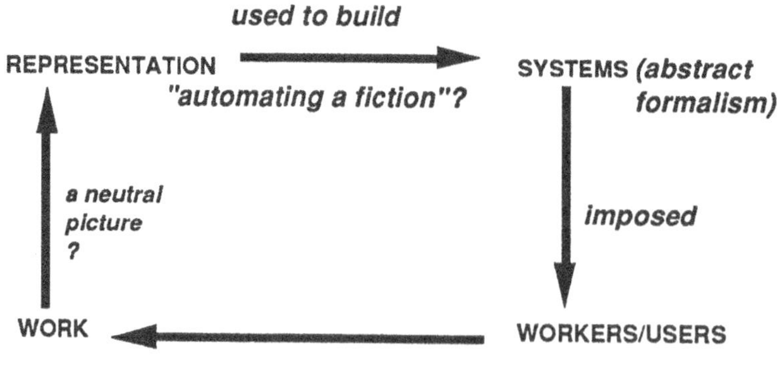

Figure 1: A sketch of some steps in the design-use cycle.

Here we attempt to summarise our understanding of a process that moves from a situation in the world to a representation, then to an implementation of the representation in a computer-based system, and finally to the re-entry of the computerised representation into the original workplace.

This understanding links several quite distinct perspectives. The language of work is abstracted in a language of representation, useful to analysts. This is transformed again into an abstract formalism, chosen for its usefulness to the system implementers. The resulting system is then imposed on workers/users, taking a critical perspective, and changes the nature of the work that the representation was built on. This is a cycle that has clear potential for catastrophic change via a positive feedback loop.

Apart from this obvious danger, Figure 1 suggests to us that there are aspects that need further exploration. The role of interpretation needs a larger place. The different groups involved in the design process need to be clarified. Following from this, the type of interpretation made by each of these groups also needs exploration.

Comments on Interpretations & Communities

Interpretations

Here we would like to suggest that the concept of a dialectical movement between an *object of interpretation* and *interpretation itself* can assist in understanding the problems and may be useful in designing applications. There are two central points. The first is that *all work involves interpretation.* This is often easiest to see when a misinterpretation happens. For instance:

> "On being informed by her postmaster that she need no longer include "R.F.D.2" in her address, a Westport matron we know informed Bonwit Teller, among others, of the fact. Her next bill from Bonwit was addressed to:
>
> Mrs. Hillary Jones
>
> Eliminate R.F.D. 2
>
> Westport, Conn." (Goffman;1974)

Even success in carrying out supposedly "low level" clerical tasks can be seen as having almost miraculous interpretive qualities. For example, Goffman (ibid) observes how infrequently secretaries, when taking shorthand, record as part of the text words that were meant as comment on it, especially given the subtlety of the cues which differentiate on-record and off-record streams.

Goffman is suggesting a different conception of role. A "role", for instance "secretary", is a way of stating what someone is doing with respect to other people in the same social milieu. When such as label becomes useful in the work context, it slides (often imperceptibly) into being seen as a description. This does not raise problems when it is used *in the context* in which it arose. A problem does arise when the "role" in question does not originate with the group in question, and ceases to be the property (or part of the ontology) of the original actors (see the earlier CSCW examples). Making sense of each other and the work situation is not given *a priori*. This is admirably caught in the following quote from McDermott, Gospodinoff, & Aron (1978).

> "In addition to sharing knowledge about each other, and whatever it is they are doing together, actors .... *struggle* to make sense of each other and *do work* to help generate the kinds of recognisable contexts for common sense to be achieved from one moment to the next. As Garfinkel .... has pointed out often, the problem facing people in interaction is never simply one of shared knowledge or overlapping interpretive grids. No matter how much people know in common, they must still work at constructing the environments that their mutual knowledge leads them to expect, and any relaxation of this effort can have disastrous consequences. People never know know exactly how to make sense of each other. "

This introduces the second point: *knowing a person's "role" is rarely sufficient in order to understand what is happening in work interactions*. The actual interaction is achieved moment by moment, with respect to a local context, which cannot be determined in advance. Reducing the complexities of such interactions and ignoring the local negotiations required to perform the work leaves one with a gloss on the work process. This may be adequate at one level for certain descriptive purposes, but becomes positively disruptive if it is viewed as adequate to support the ongoing work process as the framework of a computer system. In such cases the actual way work is accomplished is not supported through the system, leading to ways of working around the system that have been documented by Gasser (1986).

Communities

The creation of computer artefacts almost invariably involves cooperation that crosses group, professional, and subcultural boundaries. The difficulties of working in situations where several groups have different practices, traditions, and working objectives are well known. Different groups, professions, and subcultures embody different perspectives. They communicate in different "jargon". Much of this cannot be translated in a satisfactory way into terms used by other groups, since it reflects a different way of acting in the world (a different ontology and epistemology). Distinct groups of this sort will be referred to as semantic communities.[5]

Recent efforts within the systems development process to emphasize the importance of good communicative practices between these differing semantic communities attest to the difficulties that are experienced. The problem is not resolved by promoting the necessity of open communication -- since this assumes the different

---

5 This is a term coined to describe a distinction of importance, but the term itself should be regarded as tentative. It has affinities to other concepts such as "communities of practice" or the feeling of "we".

groups can be framed in a single semantic world. The meaning of terms is not transparent across groups, for example:

> "...each functional department has its own set of meanings for key terms....Key terms such as *part, project, subassembly, tolerance* are understood differently in different parts of the company" (Savage,1987, cited in Schmidt,1990a)

In such a situation the task of the systems analyst is not simply "getting it right", as there is no clear "right" answer. As Gerson and Star (1986) note:

> "No representation ..... is either complete or permanent. Rather any description is a snapshot of historical processes in which differing viewpoints, local contingencies and multiple interests have been temporarily reconciled."

In order to understand how representations (in particular the idea of "role" discussed in the CSCW designs earlier) come to be reified[6], the concepts of *interpretation* and *semantic community* have been introduced. The interplay of these two concepts leads us to a third important concept that will be discussed next, which we shall call *ontological drift.*

Ontological drift

This is the shift in meaning that can occur when knowledge artefacts (maps, designs, models) move between semantic communities. The process starts when the *object of an interpretation* and the *interpretation itself* change places. This "flipover" (Robinson, 1990) has been noted by several authors. In the activity of authoring:

> "Talk about dividing the labor of writing is likely to include plans for the paper (Kraut et al., 1987). Writers, however, do not "execute" plans in the same sense that programs do. Instead, writers use a plan as a resource in deciding what to do while they are writing (cf. Agre & Chapman, 1989). Often, the partially completed product plays an important role in the process: ***the partially completed product becomes part of the task environment and constrains the subsequent course of the design*** (Flower & Hayes, 1981; Kaufer et al., 1986)." Neuwirth et al. (1990) [our emphasis]

Here it is clear that the paper is, at first, an interpretation of a plan. The flipover happens when parts of the paper that are written become the object that the authors interpret in the subsequent parts of the paper.

A similar observation is made by in a discussion of of how groups work with symbols they create on the whiteboard they can all see in Xerox PARC's COLAB:

> ".... whiteboard items hold a dual status as elements *in* the conversation and elements that may be conversed *about*." (Tatar et al. , 1991)

Such flipovers in the process of writing (and discussion) are often useful and creative, reflecting developing moments in the understanding of a subject matter on the part of the authors. Similar flipovers in the process of software creation are often positively dangerous. This is because the process almost invariably happens *between,* rather than within, semantic communities (office workers, managers, ana-

---

6 ie. Interpretation and self-contained dialogue replaced by simple "description".

lysts, designers, programmers, customers). In the process of writing, the authors can always recapture their original intentions in their plan by throwing away the draft text that is acting as a new constraint on them. However, when the divide between communities is crossed, such a recovery is no longer possible.[7] The interpretation of one community becomes an object for interpretation by another -- but the original object of interpretation is lost in transit. There is nothing to refer back to. The original interpretation has been established as part of a different "reality" (object of interpretation) in the new group.[8]

Figure 2 [9] illustrates the problem of software development in a humorous but instructive fashion. Successive elaborations (interpretations) usually occur at an ever increasing distance from the basic need and use situation. When a feasibility study is passed to analysts, *it is convenient to assume that it is a veridical map of the work process*. The cartoon illustrates that a specification which respects the entities and relationships in the analysis is naturally assumed to apply to the work situation. We and the cartoon question this. In the end there may be no relationship between the ontology and epistemology of the artefact and that of its intended use situation. When such a situation arises, the people doing the work may respond in a variety of ways. For instance, Mackay (1990) in a field study notes that "a number [of users] spent a significant amount of time retrofitting new "improved" software to be like the old familiar software. Some avoided using the software altogether." Less commonly, but interestingly, recipients may invent their own uses that are outside the original design intentions.

---

7 We concentrate here on an exploration of what happens when "models" move between groups -- the discontinuities of meaning based on discontinuous realities termed ontological drift. None of this should be taken to imply that there is a stable "reality" within groups and communities. Here it is a common experience that meanings, emphases, and significances are mobile and negotiable. But this is a drift of an ontology, not a drift between ontologies. The emergence of new readings within a community may even exacerbate the gap between communities, making one community even more opaque to another.

8 *A note on the epistemology of ontological drift:*

A major point here is that we should acknowledge our own perspective in talking about different semantic communities and ontological drift.... where are we speaking from? who *sees* ontological drift? are we asserting some vantage point on the moon where all human problems can be seen objectively? The answer is that the ideas are inferred from problems we have seen when one group attempts to utilize the terms, distinctions, or artifacts of another group.... From particular cases, which, once spotted, can often be resolved, we infer a general situation that is much more intractable.

The status of the inferred construct is that of a fairytale. It would be naive in the extreme to believe on the one hand that there is a "warp" in the transit of representations between groups that precludes the applicability of a correspondence theory of truth -- and yet to claim that the construct that denotes this inherently mysterious process can itself be testable or measurable.

Ontological drift, like "phlogiston" or "paradigm", is a structuring metaphor that may play a useful role in design dialogues. It is not, to use one of Gregory Bateson's metaphors, an attempt to count the number of bats in a Rorschach inkblot test. The question is not whether there *are* "ontological drifts", but whether positing the concept gives a new or richer handle to understand the problem of mismatch between user needs and designed systems.... ie. is it "useful" as distinct from "true"?

9 adapted from a worn and much copied cartoon whose origins are lost to us in the mists of time.

Figure 2: Some products of ontological drift......

One of our initial comments on design models was that: "there is a constant temptation for designers to confuse the models with an underlying reality." The comment now appears too simplistic. There are *several* "realities" to be taken into account. The objects of the work of each community are not usually related to the (commonsense) underlying office reality at all. Each deals with an object that may be several "flipovers" from the work process.

First there are interpretations of a work situation produced by those who do (or who are responsible for) the work. These interpretations are not the work itself, or even a description of it. They are provisional hypotheses produced in a particular dialogical context. While they remain in their original context, connected to the hands-on experience of getting the work out by the end of the day, they are constantly subject to reconstruction.

"Oh, did I say that? Well really what happens is ...."

When the analysts take away their notes on these interpretations, and start to explore the inner connections and structures, the interpretations have been reified. They have to be "fixed" or it would not be possible to work with them. But this does not make them into veridical descriptions. The first "flipover" has happened. When the notes cross the boundary between the two semantic communities of office workers and systems analysts, the living connection to the original work process is lost. The notes become the object of interpretation in a different work process -- that of producing analyses.

Another "flipover" happens when the finished analysis is passed onto the design community. The analysis loses its status of provisional interpretation of notes, memories, doubts, and intuitions, and becomes a "fixed" object on which the design work can be performed. A further discontinuity occurs when the analysts pass their model on to the programmers.....

Our account causes us to revise another of the initial comments on design models. We said: "the models do not define their basic concepts adequately." This creates an illusion that design may be improved by better definitions. There is an assumption that a definition can "drop through" all the semantic communities to a common core. This may simply not be possible. Definitions may be quite adequate in their own communities, but do not translate or transfer between communities. The question is not one of adequate definitions in each domain, but of how these definitions might relate to each other. In other words, it may be a dangerous illusion to believe that models (especially those that have crossed semantic boundaries) can "correspond" with "reality".[10] We are squarely in the area of Wittgenstein's (1963) language games. The question is not how to verify propositions. The essential problem is how to *integrate activities that are taking place on different ontological foundations.*[11] The question is one of competence rather than truth.

Some Further Issues and Questions

The analysis sketched above has lead us into a number of interesting areas, and we will mention a couple that we are currently pursuing. One is a review of the various design methods that have been developed; the other is a reflection on how the is-

---

10 related to our earlier comment that "the models embody an inappropriate correspondence theory of truth".

11 "If a lion could talk, we would not understand him" (Wittgenstein, 1963: 223) nicely illustrates the extremes of different ontological foundations. In practice we would expect to find complex relations of intersection and differentiation among the multiple ontologies in question.

sues raised here might be better taken into account in the design process itself. Let us take these in turn.

Design Methods

It appears possible that the wide range of design methods can be understood as responses to different perceptions of the underlying phenomenon of ontological drift. The following paragraphs are initial pointers to work that might be done in this area in the future, and should not be taken as arguments or analyses.

* "Don't see the problem....."

The assertion, implicitly or explicitly, of a correspondence theory of truth in complex system design can be taken as a symptom that the issue of ontological drift is simply not recognised. It would be interesting to know whether, and under what circumstances, *any* system based on this assumption has been accepted as useful!

* "Make unifying dictionaries....."

It is most uncommon for epistemological and ontological premises in the design process to be examined, but the problem can often be sensed. A symptom of this is when designers attempt to provide a set of tight definitions that are assumed to transcend the differences between semantic communities. This is frequently a hopeless task, as noted earlier, since it ignores the interpretive processes illustrated in the Figures. A definition may be appropriate and work well in its own ontological domain -- but will not "drop through" onto the different ontological domains. Nevertheless, definitional structures proposed by methods that use successive formalisms (eg. Jackson's (1983) Structured Design) may work well in situations where ontological drift is low -- but this is not an assumption that can be generally made, especially where CSCW applications are concerned.

* "Bring the users closer to the designers...."

The strongest sense of the dangers of ontological drift can probably be found among researchers and developers within the broad church known as the Scandinavian Tradition. Here we find a serious diversity of attempts to "involve users", and thus, in our terms, bring about some closure on the process of ontological drift. For instance, Pelle Ehn (1988:116) says:

> "If designers and users share the same form of life it should be possible to overcome the gap between the different language-games. It should at least in principle be possible to develop the practice of design so that there is enough family resemblance between a specific language-game of design and the language-games the design of the computer artefact is intervening in. A mediation should be possible."

Typically, work such as this engages in a struggle to recognise and legitimate the semantic diversity of different work communities and to link "end-users" (and hence the living work situation) into all phases of the design cycle. Some of the practical problems experienced in this endeavour relate to the difficulty of maintaining *both* a recognition of distinct semantic communities *and* of evolving systems based on user correction mechanisms.

* Bring the designers closer to the use situation

Another response to the problem is the endeavour to make designers more appreciative of the nature of the work they are supporting with information systems. Such an approach, with its problems and prospects, is explicitly considered by Curtis et al. (1988). Their paper is a critique, and response to the lip service commonly paid to the idea that analysts and designers *should* understand the business they are currently working on. Recognizing these difficulties, and providing resources for more serious efforts to bring them closer to the work process would be an improvement -- but it is not clear that such efforts would avoid the dilemmas mentioned in the previous paragraph.

* Structural coupling

If it is accepted that the mix of problems concerning interpretation, different semantic communities, and the limited applicability of classical scientific verification procedures do raise major difficulties, then the complex conceptual apparatus elucidated by Maturana (1988) might be useful. In particular his idea of "structural coupling" might be used in design as it explicitly pays attention to different ontologies in action, and of interchanges between them. To date, the one major attempt to embed this framework in systems (the CO-ORDINATOR -- Winograd & Flores, 1986) has been the subject of much dispute and criticism (eg. Grantham & Carasik, 1988; Robinson, 1991).

Design Research

Switching now from design methods to design research issues, the process of ontological drift leads to an expectation of discontinuity, surprise, and unanticipated use of designed computer systems. While such experiences are endemic, they have rarely been subject to close examination or welcomed. Our approach argues for more sympathetic attention to be paid to these important phenomena. This is already beginning within CSCW -- for instance, Mackay's field study (1990) on the use of rules in prototypes of Information Lens; Tatar et al. (1991) on conversational disruptions in COLAB; Bullen & Bennett (1990) on the highly selective appropriation of features from a welter of office coordination tools. Faced with the "creative misuse" of designed artifacts, we are exploring what it would mean to undertake design work with a more paradoxical and self-critical expectation of "unanticipated use".

One particularly exciting area for further research lies in the exploration of "turn taking" and its support in CSCW systems. This complex yet universal aspect of human interaction, resting as it does on a mix of procedures, conventions and moral orders offers an interesting nexus for the concerns of many disciplinary communities within CSCW. Further, the gaps between current protocols implemented in meeting support systems, diverse workplace social conventions, and ethnomethodological analyses of conversational flux seem prima facie examples of ontological discontinuity. This offers the possibility of examining the clash between embedded and enacted conventions, and the differences between premeditated support for work, and the facilitation of unanticipated use.

Conclusion

We have attempted to develop an analytic case against the implicit belief in a "reality" that can be usefully "captured" in a model, and used as a sufficient basis for the development of computerized systems to support interpersonal work processes. The process of interpretation and reinterpretation is central, not just to the work practices of offices, but to the work of analysis, design, and implementation. The passing of work between different semantic communities, each with their own ontologies, epistemologies, and conventions; each interpreting and recontextualising the products of other communities, generates a phenomenon we term ontological drift. There is no simple correspondence or mapping between analyses, designs, implementations, and the flux of work into which systems are placed. Better definitions have a role within semantic communities, but do not address the issue of the discontinuities that arise when models cross semantic boundaries. Here the problematic is one of integrating activities that take place on different ontological foundations.

It is suggested that closure is imposed on the process of ontological drift by those who end up using (or not using) the system. It is inherent in the process of ontological drift that the type of closure achieved cannot be anticipated with any certainty. If this is not taken into account in the design dialogues, the final outcome may come as a nasty surprise to all concerned. If it is taken into account, even in broad terms, expectations of the nature and results of the design process may change considerably.

Acknowledgements

The Authors would like to thank the ECSCW-91 reviewers, colleagues in the EC COTECH Working Group 4, E. Rønby Pedersen and J. Grudin for comments.

References

Agre, P. & Chapman, D. (1989) What are plans for? MIT AI Memo 1050a, MIT, Oct. 1989.

Auramaki, E, Hirschheim, R. & Lyytinen, K. (draft ms.) Modelling Offices in SAMPO: A Comparison and Evaluation with OSSAD and ICN.

Berger, P. & Luckmann, T. (1967). The Social Construction of Reality. Harmondsworth, UK: Penguin.

Bullen, C. & Bennett, J. (1990) Learning from user experience with groupware. In Proceedings of Conference on Computer-Supported Cooperative Work, CSCW '90, October, Los Angeles, CA, pp 291-302.

Curtis, B., Krasner, H., & Iscoe, N. (1988) A Field Study of the Software Design Process for Large Systems. Communications of the ACM, 31 (11), 1268 - 1287.

Ehn, P. (1988) Work-Oriented Design of Computer Artifacts. Stockholm: Arbetslivscentrum.

Ellis, C.A., Gibbons, R., & Morris, P. (1980) Office Streamlining. In N. Naffah (ed.) Integrated Office Systems - Burotics. Amsterdam: North Holland.

Fikes, R.E. & Henderson, D.A. (1980) On supporting the use of procedures in office work. In Proceedings of the 1st Annual AAAI Conference, Stanford University, CA, August, 1980, 202-207.

Flower, L. & Hayes, J. (1981) The pregnant pause: An enquiry into the nature of planning. Research in the Teaching of English, 15: 229-243, Oct. 1981.

Gasser, L. (1986) The integration of computing and routine work. ACM Transactions on Office Information Systems, 4,3, 205-225.

Geertz, C. (1973) Interpretation of Cultures. New York: Basic Books.

Gerson, E. M. and Star, S. L. (1986) Analyzing due process in the workplace. ACM Transactions on Office Information Systems, 4, 3 (July 1986), pp. 257-270.

Goffman, E. (1959) The presentation of self in everyday life. New York: Anchor.

Goffman, E. (1974) Frame Analysis. New York : Harper Colophon.

Grantham, C.E. & Carasik, R.F. (1988) The Phenomenology of Computer Supported Cooperative Work. Interpersonal Software, Berkeley, CA.

Hammer, M. & Sirbu, M. (1980) What is Office Automation? In Proc. First Office Automation Conference, Atlanta, Georgia. March.

Henessey, P. , Benford, S. & Bowers, J. (1989) Modelling Group Communication Structures: Analysing four European projects. In Proceedings of the First European CSCW '89 Conference, Part Two, Gatwick, UK, pp. 406-420.

Hewitt, C. (1986) Offices are open systems. ACM Transactions on Office Information Systems, 4, 3, 271-287.

Jackson, M.A. (1983) System Development. Englewood Cliffs: Prentice-Hall.

Johansen, R. (1988) Groupware: Computer Support for Business Teams. New York and London: The Free Press.

Johnson, B., Weaver, G., Olson, M., & Dunham, R. (1988) Using a computer-based tool to support collaboration: A field experiment. In Proceedings of Conference on Computer-Supported Cooperative Work, CSCW '86, Austin, Texas, pp. 343-352.

Latour, B. & Woolgar, S. (1979) Laboratory Life: The Social Construction of Scientific Facts. Beverley Hills: Sage Publications.

Mackay, W. (1990) Users and Customizable Software: A Co-Adaptive Phenomenon. Doctoral dissertation, Sloan School of Management, MIT.

Mackay, W.E., Malone, T., Crowston, K., Rao, R., Rosenblitt, D. & Card, S. (1989) How do experienced Information Lens users use rules? ACM CHI '89 Proceedings, Austin, Texas, 211-216.

Malone, T. W., Grant, K. R., Lai, K.-Y., Rao, R., and Rosenblitt, D. (1987) Semistructured messages are surprisingly useful for computer-supported coordination. ACM Transactions on Office Information Systems. 5, 2 (April 1987), pp. 115-131.

Malone, T. W., Grant, K. R., Turbak, K. R., Brobst, F. A., and Cohen, M. D. (1987) Intelligent information sharing systems. Communications of the ACM, 30, 390-402.

Maturana, H.R. (1988) Ontology for Observing: The Biological Foundations of Self Consciousness and The Physical Domain of Existence. In Proc. Conference on Texts in Cybernetic Theory, American Society for Cybernetics, Felton, CA. Oct. 18-23.

McDermott, R. , Gospodinoff, K. & Aron, R. (1978) Criteria for an ethnographically adequate description of concerted activities and their contexts. Semiotica 24, 3, 4, 245-275.

Neuwirth, C.M., Kaufer, D.S., Chandhok, R. & Morris, J.H. (1990) Issues in the design of computer support for co-authoring and commenting. In Proceedings of Conference on Computer-Supported Cooperative Work, CSCW'90, Los Angeles, CA pp. 183-195.

Robinson, M. (1990) Computer Supported Cooperative Work & Informatics for Development. In Proc. INFORMATICA '90. Havana. February.

Robinson, M. (1991) Double level languages and co-operative working. AI & Society, 5, 34-60.

Ross, D.T. & Schoman, K.E. (1977) Structured Analysis for Requirements Definition. IEEE Transactions on Software Engineering. Vol. SE3. No.1. January.

Savage, C.M. (Ed.) (1987) Fifth Generation Management for Fifth Generation Technology (A Round Table Discussion), Society of Manufacturing Engineers, Dearborn, Michigan.

Schmidt, K. (1990a) Analysis of Cooperative Work: A Conceptual Framework. Risø National Lab Report M-2890.

Schmidt, K. (1990b) The Procrustes Paradigm. (Working Paper) COTECH WG4 Meeting: CEC Brussels, Nov.

Suchman, L. & Wynn, E. (1984) Procedures and problems in the office. Office: Technology and People, 2.

Suchman, L. (1983) Office procedures as practical action. ACM Transactions on Office Information Systems. 1, pp. 320-328.

Suchman, L. (1987) Plans and Situated Actions. Cambridge: Cambridge University Press.

Tatar, D. , Foster, G. & Bobrow, D. (1991) Design for conversation: Lessons from Cognoter. International Journal of Man-Machine Studies, 34, 185-209.

Victor, F. & Sommer, E. (1989) Supporting the design of office procedures in the DOMINO system. In Proceedings of the First European CSCW '89 Conference, Gatwick, UK, pp.148-159.

Winograd, T. & Flores, F. (1986) Understanding Computers and Cognition. Reading, Mass: Addison-Wesley.

Wittgenstein, L. (1963) Philosophical Investigations. Oxford, Basil Blackwell.

Wynn, E. (1979) Office conversation as an information medium. Unpublished Ph.D. dissertation. University of California, Berkeley, CA.

Yourdon, E. (1982) Managing the System Life Cycle. New York: Yourdon Press.

Zisman, M.D. (1977) Representation, Specification, and Automation of Office Procedures. PhD dissertation, Dept of Decision Sciences, The Wharton School, Univ. of Pennsylvania, PA.

Proceedings of the Second European Conference on Computer-Supported Cooperative Work
Bannon, L., Robinson, M. & Schmidt, K. (Editors)
September 25-27, 1991, Amsterdam, The Netherlands

Speech Acts or Communicative Action ?

J.L.G. Dietz
University of Limburg, The Netherlands
G.A.M. Widdershoven
University of Limburg, The Netherlands

Abstract

Systems for supporting communication in organizations should be founded on a theory of language and communication. A well-known theory for this purpose is speech act theory, developed by Austin and Searle. Flores e.a. used this theory for the design of THE COORDINATOR. Speech act theory however has some serious shortcomings which are brought to the fore by Habermas. His examination of Searle's theory leads to the development of an alternative theory: the theory of communicative action.
In this paper both theories are described to the extent considered necessary to discuss the shortcomings of the speech act theory and to show the superiority of the theory of communicative action. In addition the consequences of the latter for the design of communication supporting systems are revealed by a critical discussion of the fundamental assumptions and the practical design of THE COORDINATOR.

1. Introduction

There is a growing awareness that linguistic theories are relevant for the design of information systems, particularly for communication supporting systems. Pioneer work in this area has been done by Lyytinen and by Winograd and Flores. Lyytinen has developed an 'action-based model' of information systems (Lehtinen & Lyytinen, 1986), (Auramäki, Lehtinen & Lyytinen, 1988). This model is based on speech act theory. Winograd and Flores also refer to speech act theory (Winograd & Flores, 1986). Flores e.a. used this theory for the design of a communication supporting system, called THE COORDINATOR (Flores, Graves, Hartfield & Winograd, 1988).

Speech act theory has been developed mainly by Austin and Searle (Austin, 1962), (Searle, 1969, 1979). The theory of speech acts starts from the assumption that the minimal unit of human communication is not a sentence or other expression, but rather the performance of certain kinds of language acts, such as requests and promises. E.g. the communication of a request by a speaker (S) to a hearer (H) is an attempt by S to get H to do something. This communication is called successful if H does perform the requested act.

Speech act theory has been commented upon by many linguistic philosophers. One of them is Habermas (Habermas, 1981, 1988). He sees the importance of Searle's approach in that he considers language as a means for coordinating action. He critisizes Searle however for overlooking the orientation of the partcipants. In the example given, Searle does not distinguish between the situation in which H performs the requested act because he wants to evade sanctions, and the situation in which he does so because he accepts the validity of S's claims in a rational way. According to Habermas, communication succeeds only when H does what is requested because he considers the request to be valid. When he does not accept the validity claim of S, the communication has not eo ipso failed but can be continued by negotiating about the validity claims.

In this paper we will discuss Habermas' critique of Searle, and show its relevance for the design of communication supporting systems. We focus on Habermas' recent work, contrary to e.g. Lyytinen and Klein (Lyytinen & Klein, 1985) who, in discussing the relevance of critical theory for the design of information systems, primarily use the earlier work and therefore do not make explicit the divergences between Habermas and Searle.

In section 2 we summarize Searle's speech act theory. Section 3 gives an outline of Habermas' theory of communicative action. The critique of Habermas on Searle is discussed in section 4.

In section 5 we elaborate on this critique in discussing the characteristics of THE COORDINATOR, meanwhile drawing the major consequences of Habermas' theory for the design of communication supporting systems. We show that a change from speech act theory to the theory of communicative action has practical implications, since it calls for alterations of the conversation structure of THE COORDINATOR. Section 6 summarizes the main conclusions of the study.

2. Searle's speech act theory

This section contains a summary of Searle's speech act theory. It is based primarily on the analysis developed in (Searle, 1979), which is a major improvement of the earlier work as described in (Searle, 1969). Starting from the seminal essays of Austin (Austin, 1962), Searle developes a well founded theory of speech acts. One of his contributions is the sharp distinction between a particular speech act and the words used in some language to express it. It appears that every speech act can be expressed in many ways. By doing this Searle transcends the level of particular languages and places speech act theory at the level of language in general.
In order to classify speech acts, Searle applies three primary dimensions. These are the illocutionary point, the direction of fit, and the sincerity condition.
What is meant by the *illocutionary point* of a speech act can best be explained by defining the point of some types of acts. The point of a request, for example, can be specified by saying that it is an attempt to get the hearer to do something. The point of an assertion is that it is a representation of an actual state of affairs. The point of a promise is that it is an undertaking of an obligation by the speaker to do something.
The *direction of fit* of a speech act regards the relationship between the propositional contents and the referred world. Some illocutionary points are directed at getting the contents (the words) to match the world, others at getting the world to match the words. Assertions are in the former category, promises and requests are in the latter. Searle cites an excellent illustration of this distinction which refers to the situation of a shopper in a supermarket who selects items according to his shopping list. This shopper is followed by a detective who writes down everything the shopper takes. When the shopper leaves the shop, both have identical 'shopping' lists, but the function of the two lists is different. The detective's list has a word-to-world direction of fit (as do statements, descriptions and assertions); the shopper's list has a world-to-word direction of fit (as do requests, commands and promises).
Lastly, the *sincerity condition* of a speech act is defined as the psychological attitude of the speaker to the propositional contents. In case of an assertion e.g., he expresses the belief that the contents is true. In case of a request for an action, the speaker expresses a want that the hearer performs the action, and if a person promises to perform an action, he expresses the intention to do it.

On the basis of these three dimensions, Searle then proposes the next classes of speech acts (as usual the speaker is denoted by S, the hearer by H, and the propositional content by p):

Assertives.

Examples of assertives are 'It is raining' and 'There is a horse in the hall'.

The illocutionary point of the members of this class is to commit the speaker to the truth of the expressed proposition. The direction of fit is word-to-world, and the sincerity condition expressed is 'belief that p'.

Directives.

Examples of directives are 'Can you give me the salt' and 'Close the window'.

The illocutionary point of these acts consists in the fact that they are attempts by the speaker to get the hearer to do something, expressed by the propositional content. The direction of fit is world-to-word, and the sincerity condition is 'want that H takes a course of action establishing the truth of p'.

Searle considers questions to be a subclass of directives, since they are attempts by S to get H to answer, i.e. to perform a speech act.

Commissives.

Examples of commissives are 'I promise you to take the horse away' and 'I will be there'.

Commissives are those speech acts whose illocutionary point is to commit the speaker to some future course of action. The direction of fit is world-to-word, and the sincerity condition is 'intend to act such that p becomes true'.

Expressives.

Examples of expressives are 'I apologize for stepping on your toe' and 'I congratulate you on winning the race'.

The illocutionary point of this class is to express the psychological state specified in the sincerity condition about a state of affairs specified in the propositional content. In expressives there is no direction of fit. In performing an expressive, the speaker is neither trying to get the world to match the words nor the words to match the world The case is rather that the truth of the expressed proposition is presupposed. There are several possible sincerity conditions expressed in the performance of the speech acts in this class. The propositional content ascribes some property to either S or H. This property is not necessarily an action: next to 'I congratulate you on winning the race' one can also say 'I congratulate you on your good looks'

Declaratives.

Examples of declaratives are 'I appoint you umpire' and 'The ball is out'.

The illocutionary point of a declarative is that its successful performance guarantees the correspondence between the proposition p and the world. The state of affairs expressed by p is brought into existence by merely declaring it to exist. Because of this peculiar character of declaratives the direction of fit is both word-to-world and world-to-word. There is no sincerity condition.

Searle distinguishes a particular subclass of declaratives, which he calls assertive declaratives. The speaker of an assertive declarative may logically lie because he makes a factual claim. The second example above is a member of this class.

3. Habermas' theory of communicative action

Searle's theory, as summarized in the previous section, is a source of inspiration for many linguistic theorists. One of them is Habermas, who has taken Searle's theory as the starting point for the development of his so-called 'Theory of communicative action' ('Theorie des kommunikativen Handelns') (Habermas, 1981).

Central to Habermas' philosophy is the distinction between strategic and communicative action. When involved in *strategic action*, the participants strive after their own private goals. In doing so they may either compete or cooperate, depending on whether their goals oppose each other or rather coincide. When they cooperate, they only are motivated *empirically* to do so: they try to maximize their own profit or minimize their own losses.

When involved in *communicative action*, the participants are oriented towards mutual agreement. The motivation for cooperation therefore is not empirical but *rational:* people respond e.g. to requests because they presuppose that these requests can be justified. The basic condition for communicative action is that the participants achieve a common definition of the situation in which they find themselves. This consensus is reached by negotiations about the validity claims raised (Habermas, 1981, I, p.25 ff).

In any speech act the speaker S raises three claims: a claim to truth, a claim to justice and a claim to sincerity. The claim to *truth* entails that S contends to represent the factual contents of the speech act as they are. The claim to *justice* regards the adequacy of the projected interpersonal relation between S and H. The claim to *sincerity* entails that S is genuine in the performance of the speech act. With regard to the propositional content of a speech act, Habermas distinguishes between three worlds of reference: the objective world, the social world and the subjective world. The claim to truth refers to the objective world, the claim to justice refers to the social world of the participants, and the claim to sincerity refers to the subjective world of the speaker.

The hearer H may agree or disagree on each of the three validity claims. When H agrees on all claims, the speech act succeeds. In principle, each of the claims can be questioned. When H disagrees on a claim, S is bound to provide an account for the claim. They now go into a negotiation about the validity of the claim, resulting in a definite agreement or a definite disagreement, or a decision to enter into a discussion about the presuppositions. Habermas distinguishes between a theoretical discussion of claims to truth (the objective world) and a practical discussion of claims to justice (the social world). With respect to the subjective world Habermas posits that the participants must be able to demonstrate the sincerity of their expressions, i.e. the authenticity of their feelings.

The distinction between strategic and communicative action is related to the distinction between perlocutionary and illocutionary acts. Perlocutionary effects definitely belong to the realm of strategic action, whereas communicative action requires that the participants only have illocutionary goals. The relation between the two pairs of concepts is however not completely parallel, as will be shown hereafter.

Perlocutionary effects can only be produced if one of the participants deceives the other. These effects are said to belong to the area of *latent* strategic action. Strategic action which does not produce perlocutionary effects is called *overt*. When a speaker S acts strategically in an overt way, he tells H precisely what he expects H to do. If H acts accordingly, he does so because he understands what has been said. The coordination in this case is brought about by illocutionary means. It follows that the use of illocutionary means does not discriminate between strategic and communicative action. An additional condition is needed for communicative action, viz. the use of critisizable validity claims.

Habermas illustrates the distinction between overt strategic action and communicative action by comparing imperatives and commands (Habermas, 1981, p. 400 ff). An imperative is based on a claim to power. Let us take the expression 'I <u>want</u> you to stop smoking' as an example. The speaker expresses by means of this sentence a personal will. If the person to whom this message is addressed stops smoking, he does so because of fear for sanctions. Contrary to this, a command refers to a normative background. An example of a command would be 'I <u>ask</u> you to stop smoking'. Such an act can only be successful if it is based on a validity claim. In the case of the example there might be regulations which do not allow for smoking in the particular situation (a classroom, a non-smoking compartment of a train, etc.). A command does not need additional sanctions in order to be accepted; it will be accepted because the claims are considered valid. The conclusion is clear: only those speech acts to which the speaker assigns critisizable validity claims do motivate the hearer on their own to accept the speech act offer, and only because of this foundation do they become the mechanism for effective coordination of action (Habermas, 1981, p.409 ff).

Habermas' comparative analysis of strategic and communicative action on the one hand, and of perlocutionary and illocutionary acts on the other hand, leads to a classification of speech acts which differs from Searle's (Habermas, 1981, p. 435 ff). His taxonomy is based on one dimension only, namely the dominant claim put foreward by the speaker (we use latin words in order to avoid confusion with the class names of Searle's taxonomy):

Imperativa.
Examples of imperativa are 'Shut up' and 'I want you to stop smoking'.
S aims at a change of state in the objective world and attempts to let H act in such a way that this change is brought about. The dominant claim is the power claim. The denial of an imperativum thus normally means the rejection of the power claim.

Constativa.
Examples of constativa are 'It is raining' and 'There is a horse in the hall'.
S asserts something about the state of affairs in the objective world. The dominant claim is the claim to truth. Denying a constativum thus normally means that H contests the claim to truth.

Regulativa.
Examples of regulativa are 'Close the window, please' and 'I promise you to take the horse away'.
S refers to a common social world, in such a way that he tries to establish an interpersonal relation which is considered to be legitimate. The dominant claim is the claim to justice. The denial of a regulativum therefore normally means that H contests the normative justice of the claim.

Expressiva.
Examples of expressiva are 'I apologize for stepping on your toes' and 'I congratulate you on winning the race'.
S refers to his subjective world in such a way that he discloses publicly a lived experience. The dominant claim is the claim to sincerity. Denying an expressivum thus normally means that H doubts the sincerity of S in expressing himself.

4. Habermas' critique of Searle's theory

Acccording to Habermas Searle's most important contribution to speech act theory lies in the fact that he considers language as a means for coordinating non-strategic action. Searle points out rightly that this coordination is not brought about by perlocutionary effects, but only by illocutionary effects. He critisizes Searle however for failing to see the principle which underlies this kind of coordination, and which explains successful communication. This principle is the orientation of the participants towards mutual agreement.

Because Searle overlooks the orientation towards mutual agreement, he is incapable to distinguish between power claims and validity claims (Habermas, 1981, p. 430 ff; 1988, p. 136 ff). He considers communication primarily as an interaction between persons who try to let one another perform actions. A speech act thus succeeds if the course of action aimed at is taken. In this ontology it is impossible to distinguish a situation in which H acts because he wants to evade sanctions from one in which he responds according to the demand of S because he accepts the validity of S's claims in a rational way. Otherwise said, Searle's theory is incapable to distinguish between empirical and rational coordination of action.

The central point of Habermas' critique however is that Searle fails to reveal what really makes a speech act work. This mechanism is the critisizability of the validity claims, stemming from the orientation of the communication towards mutual agreement, and giving rise to negotiations about the claims made. It is particularly because of this weakness in Searle's theory that his taxonomy is not rigid enough.

On the one hand it misses several important distinctions. One of these is the distinction between speech acts which are based on power claims and speech acts which are based on validity claims (or speech acts proper). Another one is the distinction between speech acts which express a claim to justice (such as promises) and those which express a claim to sincerity (such as intentions).

On the other hand, Searle overlooks that both requests and promises express claims to justice, since they both regulate interpersonal relations. In consequence, Searle's taxonomy is less theoretically founded and therefore more arbitrary than that of Habermas. Figure 1 illustrates the differences between the two taxonomies.

The columns in the matrix represent the classes of Searle's taxonomy. The rows represent those of Habermas' taxonomy; the dominant claim of each class is added at the end. The hatched rectangles represent the similarities between the two taxonomies. So, the constatives of Searle conform to the constativa of Habermas. Searle's directives conform partly to imperativa and partly to regulativa, dependent on the dominant claim. An expression of will is a typical 'imperative' directive;

typical 'regulative' directives are requests and commands. Likewise, the commissives of Searle conform partly to regulativa and partly to expressiva; a typical 'regulative' commissive is the promise, whereas the intention is a typical 'expressive' commissive. Habermas' regulativa thus encompass partly Searle's directives and commissives, and entirely Searle's declaratives.
The first row (imperativa) is separated from the other rows by a bold line in order to illustrate that the imperativa are not genuine communicative acts.

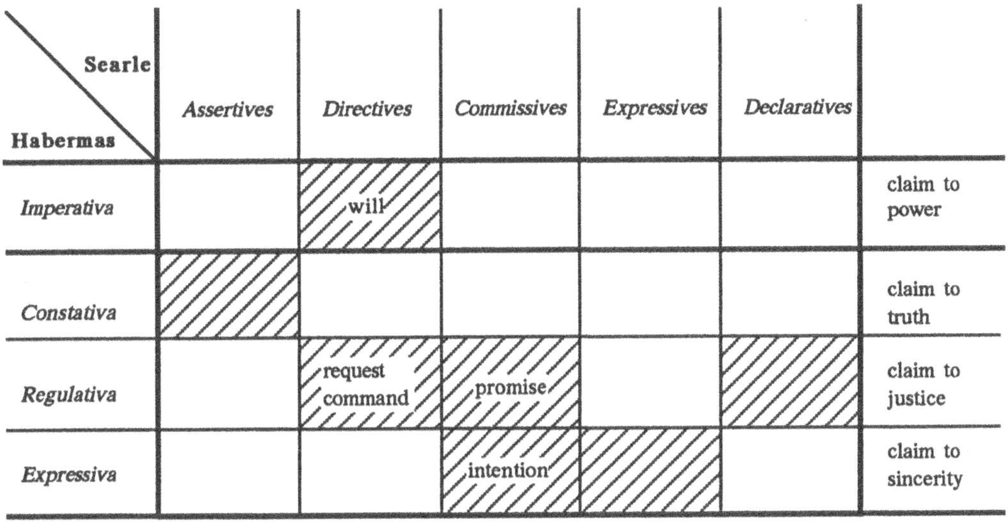

Figure 1. Comparison of Searle's and Habermas' taxonomy of speech acts.

5. Consequences for design

Habermas' critique of Searle and his alternative taxonomy of speech acts has consequences for the design of systems which are meant to support human interactions in organizations. Habermas' ontology differs from Searle's, stressing the fundamental importance of orientation towards mutual agreement, and the primary role of regulative speech acts in the coordination of action. Consequently, a design based on Habermas' theory will differ from one which is based on Searle's theory. THE COORDINATOR, described in (Flores e.a., 1988), is an example of the latter, and we suggest that this system is in need for revision on several points.

In the approach of Flores e.a., communication is defined as an exchange of speech acts. The authors consider conversation to be a ' social dance of bringing forth conditions of fulfillment, commitment to fulfill them, and completion' (Flores e.a., 1988, p. 160). They do not specify which kind of orientation of the participants is required in order to make such a dance succeed. No distinction is made between an orientation towards profit and an orientation towards mutual agreement. Therefore, it is not possible to distinguish between empirical and rational coordination of action *on theoretical grounds.*

From the examples given it is clear that THE COORDINATOR is meant to support conversations in which the participants are not empirically but rationally motivated. However, since their theoretical apparatus is not fit to specify the conditions of rational coordination of action, they run into two problems.

Firstly, they are not able to tell exactly what makes a speech act succeed, and consequently what kind of mechanism THE COORDINATOR does support.

Secondly, they are not able to exclude empirical coordination on principal grounds. Since they evidently do not want to include strategic action, they have to exclude this kind of action in a rather arbitrary way. By relying on Searle, Flores e.a. are not able to exclude imperatives right away. In order to guarantee that the system is not used in strategic ways, they have to build in safeguards. So they say that THE COORDINATOR only works well in situations in which overall interests are shared and in which the parties recognize that honest dealings with one another will be the best for their common benefit (Flores e.a., 1988, p. 168). In this way the shortcomings of Searle's theory are repaired, but the result is neither very elegant nor totally satisfying: the assumption of shared interests is not principal but ad hoc. Also, this restriction is neither necessary nor sufficient for communicative action and rational coordination. According to Habermas it is very well possible to act communicatively without shared interests, and to act strategically with shared interests. Not the sharing of interests but the orientation towards mutual agreement is the basis for communicative action and thus for the design of communication supporting systems.

On the basis of Habermas' theory these problems can be solved in an elegant theoretical way. According to this theory a communicative act succeeds because the validity claims which it entails, are accepted. A communication supporting system thus must provide facilities to negotiate these validity claims. In particular, it must be possible to distinguish between a claim to power and a claim to justice with regard to directives (cf. figure 1). We suggest therefore that this possibility is added to the conversation menu of THE COORDINATOR. It is very important that the hearer has the possibility to find out whether he is involved in an imperative act or in a regulative act, since the course of the conversation in these cases may differ largely.

Flores e.a. concentrate on the speech act types request and promise. They admit that there are other relevant types, but these are not taken into consideration. From Searle's theory it is not clear why the emphasis should be put on directives (such as requests) and commissives (such as promises). In Habermas' theory this is evident: both are subtypes of the type regulativa, which is the type that deals with all interpersonal relations. It is thus nothing more than natural that the other speech act types do not have a central position in the design. However, this is not on principal grounds, whereas Habermas' theory provides the right arguments to justify this exclusion.

Little attention is given to possible disagreements about the propositional contents of requests and promises, and to the sincerity of the participants. We propose to replace the notion of 'dance of request and promise' by the more fundamental notion of 'dance of regulativa'. In a *dance of regulativa* the claim to justice plays a dominant role. However, it is always possible that a regulativum is denied for its propositional contents or its sincerity. In that case the cognitive and expressive elements become prominent. Thus, a dance of regulativa does not exclude arguments about cognitive and expressive matters. Therefore, there should be room for these topics also in communication supporting systems. We suggest that the possibilities to raise the question of truth and the question of sincerity are added to the menu structure of THE COORDINATOR.

As a practical implementation of the remarks made above, we propose a structure for the conversation in response to a request as exhibited in figure 3. For the sake of comparison, the structure of this type of conversation in the THE COORDINATOR is shown in figure 2. This structure is reconstructed from figure 2 in (Flores e.a., 1988, p.161) and the explaining text. For the sake of brevity we have left out the trivial paths of 'Acknowledge', 'Free-Form', and 'Interim-report'.

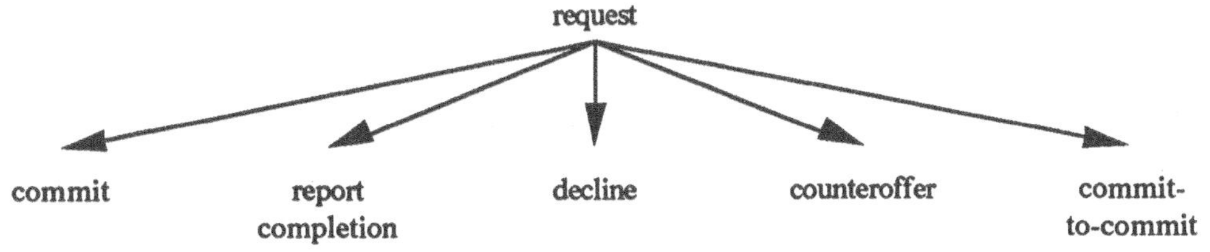

Figure 2. Request conversation stucture in THE COORDINATOR.

The paths of 'counteroffer' and 'report completion' from figure 2 seem to be missing in figure 3. However, they are only dealt with in a different manner. The 'counteroffer' is considered to be just a way of declining, while 'report completion' is covered by 'disagreement on possibilities and priorities': if something is already done, it is no more possible to do it.

In case of a decline, the parties may enter into a negotiation on the claim to justice or the claim to truth (or on both) in stead of just ending the conversation. A decline is an illustrative example of a situation of break-down, as discussed in (Winograd & Flores, 1986).

Negotiation on the claim to justice may result in exposing that the speaker in fact made a claim to power, and thus only issued an imperativum. Next, negotiation on the claim to truth may result into re-ordering the priorities of pending requests.

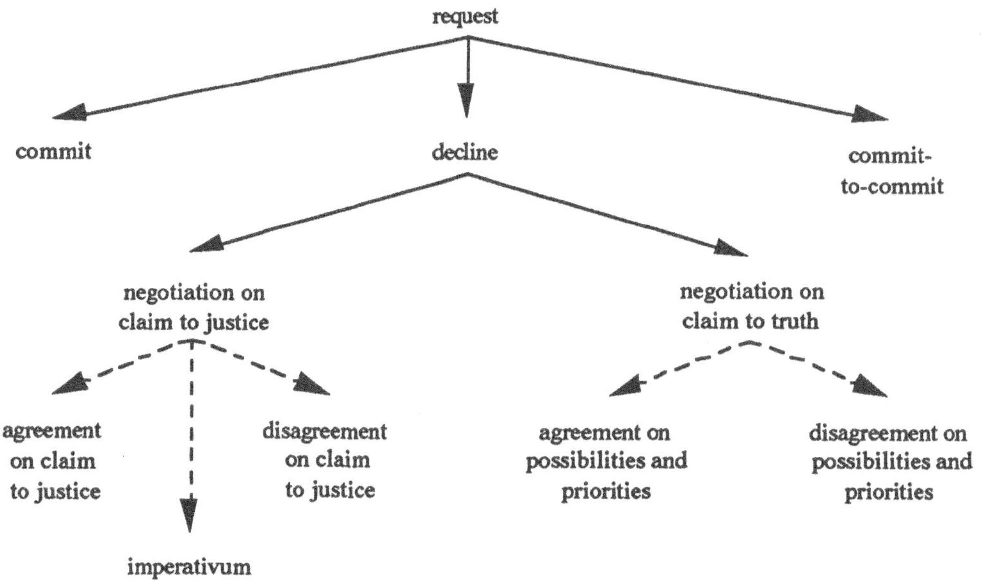

Figure 3. Suggested request conversation structure.

Lastly, Flores e.a. remark that THE COORDINATOR is only suited for organizations in which the role structure is stable, and not a matter of ongoing negotiation. Some negotiation can be allowed, but it should not be the primary concern of the bulk of the interactions (Flores e.a., 1988. p. 168). In our view this requirement is too restrictive. Successful communication is not dependent on stable roles, but on the possibility to ask for justifications of anything, including the existing role structure. This means that the role structure can be questioned whenever thought necessary.

According to Habermas, communication always requires a common background or 'life world' of the participants, which consists of common knowledge, shared institutions and mutually known competences. Part of this 'life world' can always be negotiated in the course of a communication. Furthermore, since the 'life world' is at the same time the basis for and the outcome of communicative action, none of its parts is principally excluded from negotiation and debate.
If communication is conceptualized as a process of negotiation about the situation, based on the exchange of validity claims, coordination is ensured by the orientation towards mutual agreement. In this case there is no need for stable role structures; the communication process itself makes sure that interpersonal relations become clear and that people are engaged and motivated to cooperate.

6. Conclusions

From the discussion in the previous sections it follows that Habermas' theory of communicative action has consequences for the design of communication supporting systems at three different levels.
Firstly, it provides us with an ontology which may serve as a foundation for design, specifying the fundamental mechanisms which have to be supported. On this level we propose to replace the notion of exchange of speech acts by that of rational coordination of action through the exchange of validity claims.
Secondly, it specifies under what conditions communication supporting systems are successful. On this level we suggest that one does not need the requirements of shared interests and stable role structures, but only an orientation towards mutual understanding.
Thirdly, Habermas' theory has consequences for the design itself. On this level we suggest that the focus should be on the regulativa, thus on directives, commissives and declaratives. The design should be such that it allows for detection of expressions of will (imperativa) in distinction from requests and commands (regulativa). From the point of view of Habermas it is evident that negotiation also entails cognitive and expressive elements; therefore these elements must also be taken into account. As regards the design of THE COORDINATOR, we suggest that the menu be adapted in order to include the possibility to detect imperatives and the possibility to introduce cognitive and expressive topics of communication.

References

Auramäki, E., Lehtinen, E., Lyytinen, K. (1988), 'A Speech-Act-Based Office Modeling Approach', *ACM TOIS*, vol. 6, no. 2, 1988, pp. 126-152.

Austin, J.L. (1962), *How to do things with words* , Harvard University Press, Cambridge MA.

Flores, F., Graves, M., Hartfield, B., Winograd, T. (1988), 'Computer Systems and the Design of Organizational Interaction', *ACM Transactions on Office Information Systems*, vol. 6, no. 2, april 1988.

Habermas, J. (1981), *Theorie des kommunikativen Handelns*, Erster Band, Suhrkamp Verlag Frankfurt am Main.

Habermas, J. (1988), 'Bemerkungen zu J. Searle's 'Meaning, Communication and Representation'', *Nachmetaphysisches Denken*, Suhrkamp Verlag Frankfurt am Main, 1988.

Lehtinen, E., Lyytinen, K. (1986),' An Action Based Model of Information System', *Information Systems*, vol. 13, no. 4, 1986, pp. 299-318.

Lyytinen, K., Klein, H.K. (1985), 'The Critical Theory of Jurgen Habermas as a Basis for a Theory of Information Systems', in Mumford, E. e.a. (eds.), *Research Methods in Information Systems*, North-Holland, 1985.

Searle, J.R. (1969), *Speech Acts* , Cambridge University Press, Cambridge.

Searle, J.R. (1979), *Expression and meaning*, Cambridge University Press, Cambridge.

Winograd, T., Flores, F. (1986), *Understanding Computers and Cognition: a New Foundation for Design* , Addison-Wesley Publ. Comp.

Proceedings of the Second European Conference on Computer-Supported Cooperative Work
Bannon, L., Robinson, M. & Schmidt, K. (Editors)
September 25-27, 1991, Amsterdam, The Netherlands

The concept of activity as a basic unit of analysis for CSCW research

Kari Kuutti
Department of Information Processing Science, University of Oulu, Finland

Abstract

CSCW research has had problems in selecting the basic structural and functional unit for the analysis of work. For convenient location of the computer support, some meaningful intermediate whole should be defined between the individual and the organization. The concepts of 'team' and 'group' are intuitively understandable, but somewhat weak for serious analysis.

This paper suggests that the concept of 'activity' from Activity Theory could fill the gap, and compares the properties of the activity concept with the needs of CSCW research. A classification of work support types based on the concept of activity, is produced in order to demonstrate its potential usefulness.

1. Introduction

One of the most fundamental questions of research is the selection of the basic unit of analysis. One should be able to delineate the object of research and to draw a boundary between the object and the background, and one should be able to find an entity in which all the threads of research can be conveniently connected. In many cases this is really a trivial task and not worth mentioning, especially if we stay within a well-defined tradition, but in a new, emerging research area the definition of the "real" object of research may be a major challenge, a driving force behind the long development of the whole field (the history of science contains many examples of this kind). A new research field emerges because there exist phenomena which do not fit nicely within the existing frameworks and are difficult to comprehend within existing research traditions. Because the old frameworks are not adequate, new ones have to be established. Usually there are several different approaches to grasping the "essence" of the field, however, and thus the early times may be quite confusing.

As a new research field, CSCW (Computer-Supported Cooperative Work) may be suffering just this kind of syndrome, for to legitimate its efforts an unique object should be delineated theoretically - and all the better if a corresponding entity could also be easily recognized in practice. This has not been an easy or trivial task, we do not yet have an adequate and universally accepted definition for the concept of "cooperative work", for example, although there certainly has been no lack of attempts to produce one.

This paper suggests that a lesser-known concept — that of activity — from a lesser-known research tradition — Activity Theory — might be useful for defining the basic research unit in the CSCW area. The paper is organized as follows: Section 2 contains a short overview of attempts to define the unit in recent CSCW research and some properties required of this unit, section 3 presents the concept of activity with some background regarding Activity Theory, and section 4 contains a comparison between the needs of research and the properties of the concept of activity. The usability of the concept of activity is demonstrated by producing a classification of work support types based on the structural properties of an activity.

2. Attempts to define the object of research in CSCW

Groupwork and teamwork

What is the 'cooperative work' which is to be supported by computers? The most common answer has been 'work of a group', e. g. "CSCW has emerged as an identifiable research field focused on the role of the computer in group work" (Greif 1988, p. 5), "One definition for it might be 'software for a group'. Another is 'computer-supported cooperative work.'" (Tazelaar 1988) or "CSCW looks at how groups work and seeks to discover how technology (especially computers) can help them work." (Ellis et al. 1991). Although this may intuitively sound acceptable, it is based on a naive view of groups: "In most cases the term 'group' is used in this connection without any clarification as if it had some clear, widely accepted meaning. Unfortunately, (...) this is not the case." (Lyytinen 1990, p. 6, footnote). Johansen (1988) uses instead of group the term 'business team', which is less ambiguous, and he even justifies it by referring to on-going development in business work[1]. He does not elaborate the concept towards a more analytical conceptual tool, however.

Other attempts

Besides these 'intuitive' efforts there have been some other attempts, mostly based on distinguishable external features of the work to be supported (e.g. Sørgaard 1987) or 'design metaphors' (like tool, shared material, communication medium etc.). The difficulties in defining the term "CSCW" or the corresponding research field have been notified by many recent authors, however, e. g. Bannon et al (1988), Bannon & Schmidt (1991), Lyytinen (1990) and Suchman (1989). The term has been found to be vague, redundant or undifferentiable from traditional systems, even erroneous. On the other hand, some onerous attempts to overcome these defences, e. g. Sørgaard (1987), have been evaluated as too restrictive e.g. by Bannon et al. (1987) and Lyytinen (1990).

Sørgaard's work is worth a closer examination, because the author — inspired by a perspective of greater democracy in working life — really takes pains to delineate a special kind of work in terms of the nature of the task. Sørgaard suggests that CSCW has the following attributes: it has a shared goal, it is non-competitive, it is not hierarchically organized and it is relatively autonomous. Despite his effort, the result remains somewhat elusive: "Pure cooperative work is hard to find. Cooperative work can be an aspect in many organizations ... " (Sørgaard 1987, p.721).

Bannon & Schmidt (1991) make a radical departure from the use of the external features of cooperative work or design metaphors as starting points for a definition. They presents their view briefly as follows: "Cooperative work is constituted by *work processes that are related as to content*, that is, processes pertaining to the production of a particular product or service". (pp. 5-6).

Lyytinen (1990) uses structuration theory as developed by Giddens to analyze work and the role of CSCW applications. This apparently gives a firm foothold and the paper is rich in interesting avenues for further exploration. According to Lyytinen, structuration theory sees the work process as a social structure, con-

---

[1] I agree with Johansen that there is a change going on in work organization and new, formerly exceptional work organization forms are now becoming more and more common. I have also suggested, in Kuutti 1989, that the rise of CSCW may be connected with this development. The elaboration of this theme is beyond the scope of the present paper, however.

structed continuously by 'human agents' and possessing a detailed internal structure. He puts special emphasis on the formation of social structures in interactions and thus on the role of CSCW applications both as a medium and an outcome in the formation of the work process. Lyytinen's definition of 'cooperative work' comes close to that of Bannon and Schmidt presented above.

Suchman (1989, 1991) suggests that use of the term CSCW implies more a shift in the perspective adopted by designers than actual change in technology, and emphasises a couple of fundamental aspects of work: that practice is always fundamentally social and that it is always mediated by artifacts.

Tentative synthesis

Would it be possible to find a 'lowest common denominator' for different definitions expressed above and still maintain an acceptable delineation of the research field? If we define CSCW as *work by multiple active subjects sharing a common object and supported by information technology,* we can obviously cover a great part of recent research and still be able to draw acceptably clear boundaries around the object of it.

The key element is naturally the definition of 'active subjects' or 'human agency' in Giddens' terminology: "Agency refers to the human being's capability for doing things and to the volitional character of his action, i.e. that any individual could act differently at any phase in a given sequence of conduct" (Lyytinen 1990, p. 10). This existence of active subjects gives us a means for delineating CSCW from "traditional information systems", where predetermination of work sequences by the system is the normal case. On the other hand, a common *object of work* is clearly different from a shared goal (criticized as being too restrictive) or shared material (criticized as being too loose). Negotiators may have opposite goals, but they have a common object, a problem space. Database users may share material, but the objects of their work need not have anything common. Also, a community which shares a common object of work can always be delineated in practice, whatever the contributions of the different participants may be.

Besides the basic definition, there are additional needs expressed by different researchers which should be fulfilled by the basic unit of CSCW research. Bannon & Schmidt (1991), Lyytinen (1990) and Suchman (1989, 1991) all agree that: 1) Work is mediated by artifacts and the basic unit should have this aspect too. 2) The unit should allow considerations of socially constructed meanings and cultural aspects of a work situation. 3) Work and the means for it are continuously reconstructed, and thus the unit should be suitable for studying transformation and development.

A couple of other basic needs could also be emphasized: 4) To assist accurate analysis, the unit should have a detailed internal structure (Lyytinen 1990). 5) It should also be possible to consider topics of control and conflicts within the unit (Kling 1991).

What kind of concept could fulfil all these different needs? There is a school of social thinking, Activity Theory, whose basic concept of *activity* seems to suit this purpose quite well. It will be explored in more detail in the next section.

3. Activity Theory and the concept of activity

Background

Activity Theory may be the only school of social thinking which has originated in the Soviet Union and has been able to gain a foothold in the western world, too. The theory has three main historical sources. One is the 18th and 19th century classical German philosophy from Kant to Hegel, in which the concept of activity was first introduced, another consists of the writings of Marx and Engels, who also elaborated the concept of activity further, and the third source is the Soviet cultural-historical school of psychology, founded by Vygotski, Leontjev and Lurija. Although the concept of activity as a scientific tool was first formulated within Soviet psychology, it has gained users all over the world, and it has been found useful and adaptable for the analysis of other disciplines such as education, the social sciences, cultural research, anthropology, work science etc. The activity theory "school" has just become organized, the First International Congress on Activity Theory having been held in Berlin in 1986, and the Second Congress in Lahti, Finland in 1990. From 1988 on there has also existed a journal - the Multidisciplinary Newsletter for Activity Theory.

Broadly defined, Activity Theory is a philosophical framework for studying different forms of human praxis as developmental processes, with both individual and social levels interlinked. Although the framework is still more an agenda for a research programme than a 'complete' theory, the conceptual tools developed thus far have promising qualities. Three of the key ideas of Activity Theory can be highlighted here: activities as basic units of analysis, the historical development of activities and internal mediation within activities.

Activities as basic units of analysis.

The behavioural and social sciences have always suffered from a dichotomy between the individual and the social. If one uses a social system as a unit of analysis, there are problems in maintaining human agency. If one studies individual actions, there are problems in maintaining contextuality. Social systems in general are too big and messy to be used as contexts, but actions without context are often meaningless. On the other hand, arbitrarily selected contexts (like those in many lab studies) do not help much in theory building.

The solution offered by Activity Theory is that there is a need for an intermediate concept — a minimal meaningful context for individual actions — which must form the basic unit of analysis. This unit — better defined and more stable than just an arbitrarily selected context, but also more manageable than a social system — is called an activity. Because the context is included in the unit of analysis, the object of our research is always essentially collective, even if our main interest lies in individual actions. The concept of activity is elaborated further in the next section.

History and development.

Activity Theory claims that activities cannot be really understood without seriously analyzing the historical development which has led to their present state. The activities themselves and their elements are under continuous development, and this development is not linear or straightforward but uneven and discontinuous. Because of the unevenness of the development process, different contradictions will emerge between the elements of an activity and between different activities in systems of activities, and the resolving of these contradictions is a major developmental task. The different forces and contradictions can be uncovered only through a historical analysis, and without a knowledge of these there can be only blind attempts to guide the development.

Mediation.

A key concept is that the relations within an activity are not direct ones, but they are mediated by different artifacts, e. g. instruments, signs, procedures, machines, methods, laws, work organization forms, accepted practices etc. These artifacts have been created and transformed by people during the development of the activity itself and carry with them a particular culture — historical remnants of that development. Therefore artifacts actually are not "given" and they should be never treated as such. "The idea is that humans can control their own behaviour — not "from the inside", on the basis of biological urges, but "from the outside", using and creating artifacts. This perspective is not only optimistic concerning human self-determination, it is an invitation to make a serious study of artifacts as integral and inseparable components of human functioning." (Engeström 1990a, p. 12.).

The concept of activity

The following contains a short description of some of the properties of the concept of activity. Because of the scope of the theory and the space limitations of this paper, the description is a somewhat superficial one and some topics are just mentioned[2].

As noted earlier, the basic idea is that there exists a "fundamental type" of context, which is called an activity. It is meaningless to study essentially human qualities using a smaller object of research, because without that basic context one cannot grasp the essence of the phenomenon.

The activities in which humans participate are the basic units of development and human life, and thus form a foundation of the study of all contextuality. Activities — an individual can participate in several at the same time — have the following properties:

- an activity has *a material object* [3] and activities can be distinguished according to their objects. The transformation of the object towards some desired state or in some direction motivates the existence of an activity.
- an activity is a *collective phenomenon.*

---

[2] For those with a deeper interest, (Kuutti, in press) contains a more comprehensive introduction to Activity Theory (AT) and also relevant bibliographical references. (Bødker, in press) in the same volume considers AT from a more practical (Information Systems) viewpoint. (Engeström 1990b) studies the use of AT in different empirical research settings.

[3] The term 'material' must be understood as in Marxist philosophy, for it has a different meaning in Marxism from that used in everyday language. It does not mean only touchable "things", but everything objective which exists independent of individual consciousness. Thus the Marxist definition also covers processes, relations, shared concepts, meanings etc. and is far broader than the everyday use of the term.

- an activity has an active *subject*, who understands the motive of the activity. This subject can be individual or collective. Not all participants involved in an activity necessarily understand the motive of the activity in which they are participating or even recognize the existence of it. In this case they are not active subjects of the activity.
- an activity exists in *a material environment* and *transforms it.*.
- an activity is a *historically developing* phenomenon.
- *contradictions* are the force behind the development of an activity.
- an activity is realized through conscious and purposeful *actions* by participants.
- the relationships within an activity are *culturally mediated.*

Y. Engeström (1987) has made an attempt to establish a simple structural model of the concept of activity and culturally meditated relationships within it.

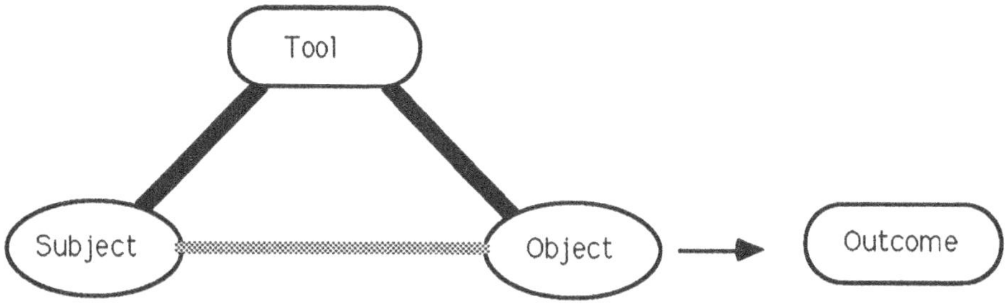

Figure 1: Structure of an individual, mediated action

Cultural mediation is dealt with in Engeström's model by replacing binary relationships with mediated relationships. This is carried out by introducing a third, intermediate term which carries with it the cultural heritage of the situation. Thus the central relationship — that between the *subject* and the *object* of an activity — is mediated by a *tool* into which the historical development of the relationship between subject and object thus far is condensed. This simple structure is not adequate to fulfil the needs of a consideration of the systemic relations between an individual and his environment, however, and thus Engeström adds a third main component, namely *community* (those who share the same object of activity). Thus two new relationships are formed: subject-community and community-object. Both of them need also a mediating member and thus we have the following structure (Figure 2):

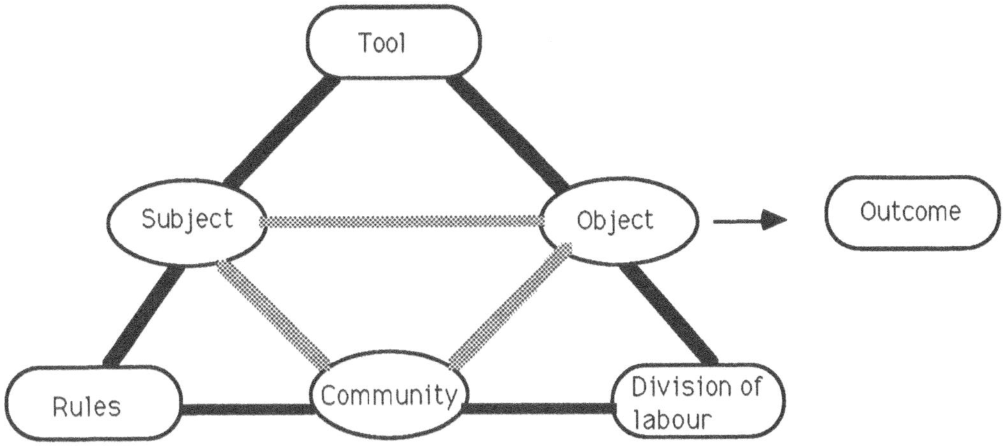

Figure 2: Basic structure of an activity

This systemic model — which according to Engeström is the simplest possible in terms of a unit of analysis— contains three mutual relationships between subject, object and community. The relationship between subject and object is mediated by tools, that between subject and community is mediated by *rules* and that between object and community is mediated by the *division of labour*. Each of the mediating terms is historically formed and open to further development. In fact, the corresponding mediating members are continuously being reconstructed during the existence of an activity. This development is not a smooth, and linear one, however, but uneven and discontinuous, driven by various contradictions.

People generally participate several parallel activities in their work, home and social life. An IS development project for a departmental application, for example, can obviously be described as an activity. It has a collective subject — the development group — which uses a development methodology as a tool in order to transform an object — the working practice to be improved. There is a community which shares the object: at least the manager of the department and those workers whose work will be affected, and there is a set of explicit and implicit rules controlling the relationship between the subject and the community: administrative procedures, accepted work practices, union regulations etc. There is also a certain division of labour in transforming the object: what the development group is expected to do, what is the role of departmental manager, the role of the workers etc.

At the same time there is another activity, in which the subject is the leader of the development project, his or her tools are project management tools and the object is the successful completion of the development project itself. The community consists of the members of the project group. Again, there is a certain — but different — set of rules and division of labour.

We can imagine a third connected activity, where the subject is the departmental manager, who is using the whole project as a tool to alter the power structure of the organization for his or her own benefit. The community is the set of his or her peer managers and upper administration, and again a body of rules and a division of labour can be found.

Thus real life situations always feature an interconnected web of activities which can be distinguished by their objects. Participation in these interconnected activities, having very different motives, can cause tensions and distortions (e. g. the position of the departmental manager in the example).

Besides this overall 'external' structure, activities also have a hierarchical inner structure. Activities consist of *actions* or chains of actions, which in turn consist of *operations*. This hierarchical structure has been found useful for analyzing the relationship between a person and a computer system at the human-computer interaction level (Bødker 1989), but it is not elaborated any further here.

One very important feature is that activities have a double nature. There is both an external and an internal "side" to every activity. The subject and the object of an activity are in a reciprocal relationship with each other. On the one hand, the subject is transforming the object — and on the other hand, the properties of the object penetrate into the subject and transform him or her. A person's internal activity assimilates the experience of society in the form in which it manifests itself in the corresponding external activity. Thus Activity Theory rejects the notion of static mental models and assumes that cognition is a situated process. The internal side of an activity is again not elaborated any further here.

This rough outline of the structure of an activity will be examined against the needs of CSCW research in the next section .

4. The potential of the concept of activity in CSCW research

The concept of activity as a basic unit of analysis

It is easy to see that the concept of work activity fits exactly with the tentative definition of the basic unit of work to be supported. The concept allows analysis to span from the individual to the organization-wide level and even broader, but it is far more flexible than the concept of formal organization. On the one hand, it is possible to study formal organizational units as activities – to the extent that a community of active subjects sharing the same object can be found. In most traditional, hierarchical organizations the formal borders of the organization do not necessarily fit nicely together with the activities, because often only the managers of the organizational units are 'active subjects', who use their units as tools in striving after their goals. Thus the activities found at the traditional organization level are mostly only managerial ones, and other people are treated as wheels in the organizational machinery, invisible in activity analysis. On the other hand, the concept of activity makes it easy to cross any departmental, organizational or geographical border – only inclusion among the active subjects sharing a object is relevant.

How well does the concept of work activity suit the other needs of CSCW research in analyzing given work settings? Let us compare it with the needs listed in section 2.

1) Mediation of work by artifacts is a fundamental feature of work activities. The concept of a mediating artifact – tool or instrument – is rich and also covers signs, symbols, models, theories etc.

2) Regarding the existence of socially constructed meanings and cultural aspects, there is an elaborate mechanism for how cultural features are brought into every activity by the corresponding artifacts. Apart from the tool/instrument/sign artifact immediately used in transforming the work object, there are two other groups of socially constructed artifacts, namely rules and division of labour.

3) Work reconstruction, transformation and development. From its very beginning, Activity Theory — and thus also the concept of activity — has been developed in order to study developmental processes. The reconstruction of the various artifacts is a basic feature in activities, and there is an elaborate mechanism for modelling the dynamics of this development.

4) The concept of work activity has a rich internal structure, of which only a part is described here. This should help in structurizing the work settings to be studied.

5) The ability to deal with issues of control and conflict. The concept of activity contains two different channels of control: hierarchical power structures embedded in the division of labour, and control through norms and values embedded in rules. There is also a mechanism to deal with conflicts: the developmental dynamics of activities are based on the emergence and solving of contradictions, and conflicts are regarded as surface symptoms of contradictions.

Although the present analysis has been superficial, the concept of activity is evidently a promising framework. If it is used as a basic unit of work analysis it may help us to include certain actual research needs and to find a more coherent perspective. The overall structure of an activity is used in the next section to classify different computer support types for work.

A typology of work support

Research into computer support types for CSCW has been limited, with the most common approach being simply the use of popular metaphors such as "tool", "medium" or "shared material". A "panopticon" – an instrument for increased social control (Bannon et al 1988) and a "shared knowledge or memory" (Bannon & Schmidt 1991) have also been mentioned. It is clearly difficult to locate the support and to produce good analytical descriptions of the relationship between work and information technology – although CSCW research is not alone in suffering from this inability. I have suggested elsewhere (Kuutti, in press) that one reason for this – using the Activity Theory terminology – is that information technology penetrates into every part of the structure of a work activity and changes them all. Thus the "support" is in fact inseparable from the corresponding parts.

The structure of the activity concept is used in the following to generate a classification of basic work support types in information technology (Figure 4). The classification is not specially aimed at CSCW applications, but is a broader analytical tool also suitable for studying personal computing applications and traditional information systems. In practice, applications usually cover several types. The classification of the columns is based on the main structural parts of an activity. The internal activity of the subject is (somewhat crudely) condensed here under the title 'thinking'. The rows are based on the different roles a person can have in an activity: a passive participant – not an active subject but 'a wheel in the organizational machine', an active subject working within a 'given' activity and, finally, an active developer of an activity.

Area of support

Role of a person in an activity	Instru-ment	Rules	Division of labour	Subject, 'thinking'	Object	Community
Passive	Routine automation	Control	Fixed	Triggering of a pre-determined action	Data	Separating, hiding visibility
Active	Tool	Shared meanings	Coordina-tion	Searching information	Shared material	Visible network
Expansive	Automation or tool construc-tion	Rule con-struction, negotiation	Organizing work	Learning, compre-hending	Object construc-tion	Community construction

Figure 4. A classification of basic types of work support.

As stated above, the design and implementation of any system causes changes in all the columns — and depending on application the changes may span several of the rows, too. These changes can be either intentional or accidental. It is obvious, that the first row describes the 'support' – more a replacement – given by traditional information systems, and it is best suited to Tayloristic work settings. We can claim that to some extent there already exists a partial mastery of the changes at that level – we can design and implement systems for Tayloristic work with some success (from the managerial viewpoint, at least), and with the advent of socio-technical design the designing community is learning some tricks for avoiding the worst accidents.

The second row describes the area of recent CSCW discussions - the support of active subjects working with a common object. There the degree of mastery is considerable less, and we merely know something about how to design tools for individual use. The systems designed to support some particular aspect of a work activity cause accidental changes in other aspects, too, as has already been recognized by researchers such as Grudin (1988) and Howard (1987).

The third row describes a new approach which has been emerging within the CSCW research - researchers who have become aware that the ultimate computer support for work is reconstruction of the work by creating computer artifacts for the work by workers themselves. The achievement of this will generate even bigger challenges than simply the support of active subjects. CSCW researchers with this attitude are e. g. Bannon & Schmidt (1991), Lyytinen (1990) and Suchman (1989, 1991).

The basic support types are considered in a little more detail below.

Routine automation: has been the old cornerstone of all computer applications — replacing the work of a person by automating some accurately defined routines.

Control of somebody using information technology. Counting of the customer throughput of a cashier etc.

Fixed division of labour. A computer system place the people automatically in a defined relation with others. The different work positions are strictly defined by a system -e. g. between a clerk (data input) and a supervisor (data use) etc.

Triggering. A computer system produces a triggering impulse for preplanned actions – various alarms etc.

Data. The object of the work can reside in the computer, but for passive participants it is merely 'data'.

Separation. A computer system may separate the members of a work community from each other and make them invisible.

Tool. A computer system is used to produce and transform an object. Examples: Text processing, diagram drawing etc. When used by a group, this needs a corresponding object (shared material).

Shared meanings. A computer system makes a set of existing rules and shared meanings more easily accessible.

Active coordination. A computer system helps a community of active subjects to coordinate their efforts.

Search of relevant information. A computer system enables the finding of additional information. Examples: database queries, running a ready-made spreadsheet model.

Shared material. A computer system helps several people to transform an object together by giving them access to the shared material.

Visible network. A computer system forms a network which promotes the existence and visibility of a community. Example: e-mail within an established work group.

Tool or routine construction. A computer system enables the automation of a new — not predefined — routine or the creation of a new tool for handling objects. Examples: Devising of a letter form, building a spreadsheet model, programming.

Rule construction. A computer system helps in negotiating a new set of rules for a community.

Work organization. A computer system helps in generating a new work organization.

Learning, comprehension, innovation. A computer system enables the construction of a new mental model of an object. Example: what-if analysis with spreadsheet models, visualization.

Object construction. A computer system enables a phenomenon to become a common object of work.

Community construction. A computer system helps in creating new communities or establishing new contacts. Examples: Creation of a new e-mail posting list for a new project team, using UNIX News or some other bulletin board in asking help.

Due to space limitations, no attempt has been made to locate existing CSCW applications in this classification. The classification may also be less successful in ordering existing applications than in opening up new views and generating new design metaphors. Despite the superficiality of the analysis some areas of potential support can be located which have scarely been discussed at all yet, e. g. the support of learning and object construction.

Conclusion

It is suggested here that Activity Theory offers a promising framework for CSCW research, because the concept of the activity as the basic unit of work analysis seems to meet a number of acute demands expressed by CSCW researchers. It has also been possible to generate some new design metaphors by starting out from the structure of an activity. How useful these constructs really are can be ascertained only in practical applications, however.

5. References

Bannon, L. & Schmidt, K. (1991) CSCW: Four Characters in Search of a Context. In J. M. Bowers & S.D. Benford (eds.) *Studies in Computer Supported Cooperative Work.* North-Holland/Elsevier, Amsterdam.

Bannon, L., Bjørn-Andersen, N. & Due-Thomsen, B. (1988) Computer support for cooperative work: an apparaisal and critique. In Bullinger, H. J. (ed.) *EURINFO 88*, Nort-Holland, Amsterdam.

Bødker, S. (in press) Activity Theory as Challenge to Systems Design. In Nissen, H.-E., Klein, H.K. and Hirschheim, R. (eds.) *Information Systems Research Arena of the 90's*. Elsevier/Norh-Holland, Amsterdam, 1991.

Ellis, C. A. & Gibbs, S.J. & Rein, G.L. (1991) Groupware; some issues and experiences. *Communications of ACM*, vol. 34, n:o 1 (Jan 1991), pp. 38-58.

Engeström, Y., (1987). *Learning by expanding*. Orienta-konsultit, Helsinki.

Engeström, Y. (1990a) Activity theory and individual and social transformation. Opening address at the 2nd Intl. Congress for Research on Activity Theory. Lahti, Finland, May 21-25, 1990.

Engeström, Y (1990b) *Learning, Working and Imagining.Twelve Studies in Activity Theory*. Orienta-konsultit, Helsinki.

Greif, I (Ed.) (1988) *Computer-Supported Cooperative Work: A Book of Readings*, Morgen Kaufman, San Mateo, California.

Grudin, J. (1988) Perils and Pitfalls. *BYTE* December 1988, pp. 261-264.

Howard, R. (1987) Systems Design and Social Responsibility: The Political Implications of "Computer-Supported Cooperative Work". *Office, Technology and People*. vol. 3 n:o 2, pp. 175-187.

Kling, R. (1991) *Cooperation and Control in Computer Supported Work*. Manuscript. Dept. Information and Comp. Sci., Univ. California, Irvine.

Kuutti, K. (1989) The Impact of Work Development on Information Systems. In *Scandinavian Research in Information Systems*, vol. 1 no 1, pp. 165-176.

Kuutti, K. (in press) Activity Theory and its applications in information systems research and design. In Nissen, H.-E., Klein, H.K. and Hirschheim, R. (eds.) *Information Systems Research Arena of the 90's*. Elsevier/Norh-Holland, Amsterdam, 1991.

Leont'ev, A. N. (1974) The Problem of Activity in Psychology. In *Soviet Psychology* vol. 13 no. 2 pp. 4-33.

Lyytinen, K. (1990) *Computer-Supported Cooperative Work - issues and challenges. A structurational analysis*. Manuscript. Univ. of Jyväskylä, Dept. Computer Science.

Suchman, L. (1989a) Notes on computer support for cooperative work. Working paper WP-12, Univ. Jyväskylä, Dept. Computer Science.

Suchman, L. (1991) Understanding Practice: Video as a Medium for Reflection and Design. In J. Greenbaum & M. Kyng (eds.) Design at Work: Cooperative Design of Computer Systems, Lawrence Erlbaum , Hillsdale NJ.

Sørgaard, P. (1987) A cooperative work perspective on use and development of computer artifacts. In Järvinen, P. (ed.) The Report of the 10th IRIS seminar. Acta Universitatis Tamperensis ser B vol 27, University of Tampere.

Tazelaar, J. M. (1988) Editorial for the section "In depth: Groupware", *BYTE*, Dec 1988, p. 242.

Proceedings of the Second European Conference on Computer-Supported Cooperative Work
Bannon, L., Robinson, M. & Schmidt, K. (Editors)
September 25-27, 1991, Amsterdam, The Netherlands

Being Selectively Aware with the Khronika System

Lennart Lövstrand
Rank Xerox EuroPARC, United Kingdom

Khronika is an event browsing and notification system that attacks the problems of information overload and information distribution for a wide range of information sources. It implements a shared network server that manages a database of general *events*, personal *event daemons*, and automatically generated *notifications* that are distributed over time. It supports both traditional search and retrieve operations as well as automatic notifications and combinations of both. Together, these two modes complement each other. The first provides a way for the user to actively find out about past, present, or future events; the second causes the system to automatically deliver notifications about pending events of interest. This means that a user can find information when she or he wants to know about it, and be automatically told when she or he needs to know about it.

Intro: A Morning in Leo Lagavulin's Life

It was a cold and dreary day in East Anglia, United Kingdom. "Just as usual," Leo Lagavulin sighed to himself as he was walking over the damp, grassy field towards his office at Rank Xerox EuroPARC. As he approached the back entrance, a subtle click could be heard as his presence was detected and the door unlocked. Leo entered, and inside the warm lobby a disembodied voice greeted him (with a slight Swedish accent): "Good morning, Leo. You have 25 new messages waiting for you. Don't forget your meeting with Margaret Macallan and Oliver Oban at 11:00 this morning. The coffee level is 5 percent." "Damn, someone has forgotten to refill the coffee machine again," Leo muttered as he climbed the stairs to his office on the 4th floor. As he entered his office, he ignored the voice as it came back and told him: "You have had visitors: Bob was here at 09:12." Leo sat down in front of his workstation and looked down at the two main windows — one with his 25 new messages (it would have been 125 in the old days), and one with the week's schedule neatly laid out on a time diagram with the events in which he had registered interest clearly marked. As he started reading his first message, his office started shaking with a thunderous sound from speakers hidden in the ceiling. Leo hastily reached out to turn down the volume — he had left it on an appropriate blues level from last night's late working session — and looked out of his window at the light rain that had just started falling. From his workstation, he could hear the distinct "thud" that indicated that even more mail was coming in as he was sitting there. Leo took a deep breath and proceeded with the chores of the day.

Overview

The main motivation behind the Khronika project is to increase peoples' awareness of what is going on around them over time by improving the effectiveness in which event information is dispersed in a work community. We see this problem as mainly characterised by *information overload* and *information distribution.* By "information overload" we mean the problem of a recipient receiving far too much information — and often irrelevant information at that — than he or she has time to process. The second, "information distribution" problem comes from the difficulty for a sender to correctly identify the appropriate recipients of a message. If the distribution is too narrow, there will be those who will never have a chance to receive it; if it is too wide, the effects of the previous problem will be increased instead. Finally, information about events is intrinsically time dependent: information that arrives too late or too early may be worse than no information at all.

Our solution is to introduce the notion of a networked *event notification service* that receives information about events from various clients, stores it in a database, and ultimately delivers notifications to those interested. Events range in size from "conferences" (days) and "meetings" (hours) to momentary events generated from automatic sensors (no duration). The connection between events and notifications is achieved by means of pattern-action based personal *event daemons* that monitor the event flow and generate notifications when triggered by a matching event. These notifications perform certain tangible actions, such as producing sound effects, synthesised speech, X11 popup windows, or automatically sending electronic mail messages according to the user's personal preferences.

A central notion behind Khronika is that of separating the senders' and recipients' responsibilities by making the system act as an intermediary *information channeller.* With Khronika, senders are only responsible for entering the information and keeping it up to date in case of changes. Instead of having the sender identify the recipients, the recipients themselves "teach" the system about what kind of events they are interested in and how they would like to be told about them. Khronika then automatically notifies them at appropriate times before the event is due to occur, thus obviating the need to manually remember the events at the right moments.

The Problem

A large amount of information is bombarding us every minute, yet something feels amiss. A lot of this "information" is unwanted and undesired, and in fact a serious hindrance to the normal function of our daily life in that by its sheer mass it hides the information we actually *are* interested in. Other pieces of information arrive too early or too late to be of any use or fail to reach us completely, either because we didn't know where to look for it or because nobody thought of sending it in our direction.

If we look at the situation in terms of standard communications theory, we can describe it as one in which a *sender* is transmitting a *message* to a (set of) *recipient(s)*. This gives us a vocabulary for describing the problems.

Information Overload

The first problem can be described as arising from the recipient receiving far too many or complex messages than he or she has capacity to process. This is known as the *junk mail phenomenon* [Denning-82].

The standard way around this problem is to apply various filtering methods, with the state-of-the-art solution today still being that of acquiring an information processing tool known as the *personal assistant*.[1] Unfortunately, these are hard to come by and often unaffordable to the ordinary individual.

Other solutions involve computerised filtering systems which usually operate on the recipient's electronic mail messages and perform actions such as sorting them into folders according to author or subject. A prime example is the *Information Lens* system [Malone-87], which implement rule-based *agents* that perform sorting, flagging, and deletion operations on a user's messages as they arrive in his or her mailbox, or even before that, by means of a redistribution mechanism known as the *Anyone* server. Users send messages to the Anyone server instead of directly to individual recipients or distribution lists; the server then runs all the potential recipients' rules and decides based on these who will receive the message. The Information Lens also promotes the use of additional header fields on messages for selection and processing, something that is carried forward in *Object Lens* [Lai-88], where the messages themselves have been turned into collections of general objects.

Spatial Information Distribution

A second problem concerns the difficulties senders have in correctly identifying the appropriate recipients for messages. With traditional communications systems, such as telephone, letters, or indeed electronic mail, it is up to the sender to decide in advance on exactly who will be receiving the message. If too few recipients are chosen there will be those who will never know of the message's existence despite potential interest. On the other hand, if it is sent to too many, the problem of information overload will be increased instead.

A primitive solution is the common *distribution list*, which allows the sender to free herself or himself from names of recipients and rather think in terms of topic categories. This has several problems, however, including (1) multiplexing a single channel for a multitude of different messages, (2) not supporting any notion of memory, which means new recipients cannot access old information, and finally (3) burdening the sender with being responsible for the physical transmission.

---

[1] Human.

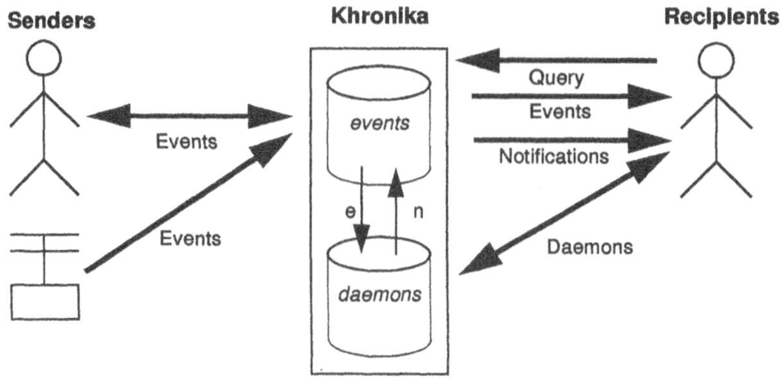

Figure 1. Schematic Overview

Electronic conferencing systems, such as KOM [Palme-84] or USENET [e.g. Spafford-87], remedy this by supporting multiple channels, one for each discussion topic, and by retaining a limited database of past messages so that newcomers don't enter a total void. However, while they often support a limited amount of filtering, they typically do not provide much help for navigating in their information spaces, nor do they automatically inform recipients about new information.

Temporal Information Distribution

A dimension often disregarded in electronic mail and conferencing systems is that of *time*, yet much information is intrinsically time dependent. A message about a seminar becomes fairly uninteresting after the seminar has happened. Similarly, although being told too soon is perhaps better than too late, one is likely to forget meetings if the only notification comes far in advance of the actual event. Clearly, the *act* of informing should be linked with the *time* most relevant to the contents of the message.

Zephyr [DellaFera-89] is a notification system that perform real-time redistribution of incoming messages to subscribing recipients. It uses a ⟨*class, instance, recipient*⟩ triple to dynamically match the classification of the message with possible interested recipients. In addition to providing an on-line interactive messaging facility, the system also handles such tasks as informing users about new mail, systems going down, locating users, etc. However, the system has no memory about the past, nor can it deal with future events. This means that if a recipient is unavailable when the message is sent, it will simply be lost.

The Khronika Solution

As illustrated in Figure 1, Khronika implements a shared *event notification service* that receives information about events from a number of different sources and provides a database of events with both manual browsing capabilities and automatic notifications to interested users. Another look at how event information may be handled in a work community will help in understanding how it operates and is used.

Placing the Recipient in Control

The model behind Khronika is that of clearly separated roles and responsibilities of the sending and receiving agents with the Khronika server itself in the middle as an *information channeller*. The sender of an event message might be the person hosting a seminar series, or the administrator that manages the community's calendar. It may also be a computer program that senses some internal or external sensors, and, as a result, posts an event whenever their state change.

With Khronika, it is the responsibility of the sender to enter the information and keep it up to date in case of changes, no more. Specifically, it is *not* the sender's job to find out who might be interested in the information that he or she is entering; that is up to the potential recipients to specify. This means that the problem of a sender having to identify the recipients of a message is avoided by transferring the task to the recipients themselves — with the aid of Khronika.

On the other side of the system, the recipients have two ways of receiving event information. One is by manual browsing, which directly corresponds to the traditional database search and retrieve operations found in other systems. This allows the interested user to find out about future, present, and past events that match the user's query. Information can presented either in list form or graphically as temporal fields in a weekly calendar.

The other way of receiving information is by means of automatic notifications, which are controlled by the user's personal event daemons. These make the system an active partner in keeping the user aware about what is going on. Users receive notifications by specifying a description of the events they are interested in and when and how they would like to be told about them. For example, a user interested in a particular seminar series might submit a daemon that looks out for events in this series and delivers synthesised speech notifications ten minutes before each seminar is due to begin.

The Triumphant Triumvirate: Events, Daemons, and Notifications

The three entities at the core of Khronika are the *events*, *event daemons*, and *notifications*. Events are at the foundation of the system and denote discrete real-world events of varying duration. For example, an event might be a one-hour seminar, a person visiting for two weeks, or even a proposed call for going to the pub in five minutes. Events are represented by sets of attribute/value pairs and describe objects positioned in a class hierarchy. They are usually presented as forms resembling structured header lines from email messages (see Figure 2). Certain attributes are well-known to the system, such as an event's time or class, while others carry untyped information specific to the class.

ID: 0x281a74ef; Owner: Chalmers; Status: Pending
Ctime: 2-Jun-91 13:39:51; Mtime: 2-Jun-91 13:39:51

Class:	Seminar
Time:	12 June, 12:30 for 1 hour
Speaker:	Graham Button & Wes Sharrock
Title:	Code as Artifact
Host:	Matthew Chalmers
Location:	EuroPARC Commons

ID: 0x2815e210; Owner: Loughnane; Status: Pending
Ctime: 26-Apr-91 16:19:50; Mtime: 12-Jun-91 09:19:22

Class:	Visitor
Time:	16 June to 3 July
Name:	Sara Bly (PARC)
Host:	Bob Anderson
Location:	Room 1.6

Figure 2. Sample Events

Event daemons map a user's personal interests, as expressed by a set of constraints, onto notification templates. Both constraints and templates are currently represented by inactive event objects, although work on a richer constraint specification language is underway. As with the events themselves, event daemons are presented as pairs of attribute/value forms to the user.

Whenever a new event is entered to the system, existing daemons are given a chance to trigger; likewise, when a new daemon is added, it is first compared with all existing events. Triggering occurs when an event matches the search pattern of a daemon and will cause a notification to be spawned as a new event scheduled at the time specified by the daemon's notification relative to the matched event. Thus, if user A enters a seminar event for 14:00 on Friday and user B has a daemon looking for seminars with a 15 minute warning, B's daemon will trigger and schedule a notification for 13:45 the same day.

Notifications are structurally identical to the events themselves, except that they cause some action to be performed by Khronika. For example, when a seminar event occurs, the only thing that happens within Khronika is that it is flagged internally as having started. On the other hand, when a speech notification is due to happen, Khronika will call the appropriate implementation routine performing synthesised speech, in this case a remote procedure call to a networked speech server.

Khronika as a Semiformal System

Khronika can be seen as a semiformal system, as described in [Lai-88] who defines it as a computer system having the following three properties:

1. It represents and automatically processes certain information in formally specified ways.
2. It represents and makes it easy for humans to process the same or other information in ways that are not formally specified.
3. It allows the boundary between formal processing by computers and informal processing by people to be easily changed.

The design of Khronika as a semiformal system means that:

- Users can register informal information with little cognitive overhead; and
- This information can still be made available for computer processing, in our case filtering and automatic actions.

All entities in Khronika are described by the same frame-like structure of named attribute/value pairs. Some attributes apply to all objects, including unique ID, owner, access list, class, and time. Other attributes are dependent on the class itself, e.g. a seminar might have a speaker, a title, and a host, while a visitor event might be endowed with a name, a location, and special requirements. Only the globally applicable attributes are interpreted by Khronika, the others are meaningful only to the human reader and his/her agent, the event daemon.

In the current version, daemon based filtering can be accomplished using a combination of three basic operations: by time interval overlaps, by subclass inclusions, and by substring matches. The first two are specific to the time and class fields, while the last one applies to all other fields; in particular, to the class specific fields.

Although the class hierarchy itself is currently fixed on a server-wide basis, users can create what are effectively new classes simply by adding new fields to already existing ones. These are treated in exactly the same way as other class dependent fields, i.e. totally ignored by the system internally, but available for human inspection and daemon matching. For example, there exists a class called *personal*, which has no fields. A user wanting to record a dentist appointment could bring up a form based on the personal class and start adding fields called (say) "type" and "location," with values like "dentist-appointment" and "Mill Road Surgery," respectively. Daemons could then be specified to notify the user when encountering events with "type: dentist-appointment" fields.

Time

Time is a difficult notion to handle in this sort of system. Computer operations concerning time tend to be very formal and distinct while our everyday usage tends to be relaxed and relatively fuzzy. For example, what is "Thursday afternoon" supposed to mean to the machine? Our approach has been to implement a comprehensive date and time parser for common English expressions and to extend the standard UNIX™ notion of second based offsets from January 1, 1970 to tuples of the same denoting the beginning and duration (or end) of an interval. This allows us to handle constructs such as "tomorrow" or "this week" as well as a seminar that might be expected to be on at "3pm today for one hour". This may not solve all our problems, but at least gives us something that is more appropriate to deal with than "31-Jan-91 17:55:35".

Another problem is the difference in date denotations between Europe and the United States. For example, "1/2/91" may mean either February 1st or January 2nd depending on the user's cultural background. Also, such simple phrases as "this

UNIX is a trademark of AT&T Bell Laboratories.

week" take on a meanings depending on whether the user believes that weeks begins on Sundays or Mondays. By default, our date parser returns an error on ambiguous representations, asking the user to rephrase the expression. Alternatively, a flag can be set to force dates to be parsed with a European or US interpretation.

Manual Browsing vs. Automatic Notifications

Khronika supports two distinct modes of delivering information to recipients: query based listings and automatic notifications. The query facility gives a static view of the event database at the moment the user searched it. It is typically implemented by an interface which asks the user for an event pattern and then presents the result in a list browser.

As discussed before, the notification mechanism is implemented using event daemons and provide a way of automatically informing the user about interesting events. The daemons can be accessed in the same way as the events themselves, primarily by using an event browser-like application.

Together, the two modes complement each other in that one provides a way for the *user* to actively find out about past, present, or future events, while the other shifts the initiative over to the *system's* side, delivering notifications to the user without any further interaction necessary from the user's side. This means that users can find information when they *want* to know about it, and can also be automatically told when they *need* to know about it.

Recently, we have also been exploring interfaces that use an aggregate of the two modes to produce an *active view* of a selected subset of the database. This is achieved by making the interface dynamically create a daemon with a callback notifier that will inform the interface whenever any new, matching events are posted or any changes are made to already displayed events. Among other things, this makes an excellent *active calender* that always is up to date with the latest events.

Shared Access vs. Privacy Control

While there are many benefits to reap from a shared server approach, we must also recognise the individual's requirement for integrity and privacy. Access control has been extensively explored in the area of file systems [e.g. ITS public access, TOPS-10 access patterns, TOPS-20 user groups, UNIX access bits, NORD-10 friend lists], but no single solution appears to be a superset of the others. With Khronika, we wanted to avoid the complexities of a fully fledged group protection system and settled instead on what we thought of as a relatively bare minimum: read access of events are controlled by an explicit access control list and write (change/delete) access is limited to the event's owner. The access control list is just another field of the event (or event daemon), which lists the users who may retrieve the event or otherwise be told about its existence. If left blank, it defaults to "everybody," meaning that every user of the system is allowed to see it. By this we hope to be able to promote automatic sharing of events like public seminar announcements, but still make it possible to keep private meetings and appointments accessible to only a limited number of people.

Khronika as an Environmental Interface

An area which we recently have started exploring is that of Khronika as an interface between the user and his physical environment. There are already several automatic event generators which either monitor external sensors, such as the active badge system [Lamming-91, Newman-91, O'Shea-91] or the weather server on the roof of the building, or internal processes, such as email deliveries or electronic A/V connections. In fact, one of the very first uses of Khronika was that of delivering audible notifications whenever a video connection was opened to a user's camera using *iiif*, the EuroPARC audio/video switching service [Buxton-90]. To achieve this, we modified the switch server to post an iiif feedback event whenever a connection was set up or disconnected. To this was added a set of connection/disconnection daemons for each user that generated appropriate sound notifications on connection events. The effect was that each time someone glanced at another person, that person would hear the sound of a squeaky door opening as the connection was set up. This allowed them to be immediately aware that someone else could see them. When the connection eventually was disconnected, the virtual door would slam shut, indicating that the watching person had left. Modifications to this included versions where the name of the connecting person would be spoken aloud as well as various popup panels and other display devices.

We now have sensory agents and corresponding daemons in use for a number of different types of automatic events. For example, the author, just like the mythical *Leo Lagavulin*, receives new mail notifications by means of a discreet thumping sound and is told about rainy weather by a mighty thunder clap.

The Sights and Sounds of Khronika

It is fair to say that of the available notification actions, *sound* remains as one of the most popular ones. Sound effects of various kinds are currently used to indicate both sensory events as described in the previous section, as well as impending meetings and seminars, etc. For this to work in an office environment, great care has to be devoted both to the technical facilities that make these ubiquitously available as well as to the design of the sounds themselves. Khronika currently supports digitised sound cues delivered over the EuroPARC A/V network or produced directly on the user's workstation. This means that sounds can be played virtually everywhere in the building, including workstation-less offices and meeting rooms. The design of the sounds themselves are described in [Gaver-91], where he also gives examples of other systems using sound for collaboration.

On the visual side, notifications can be made to generate X11 message windows (or indeed any other X11 window or UNIX action) that appear on the user's screen.

These can be made to stay until dismissed by the user, or to go away automatically after a predefined time. For non-workstation notifications, limited support exists for sending video pictures over the A/V network, but it would be a SMOP* to set up a server that would render a text message as a still video frame and transmit it a selected monitor.

Bridging the Gap

In summary, our intention with Khronika as an environmental interface is to try and *blur* the boundaries between computational and real-world events. This is achieved partly by providing a general mechanism that unifies both worlds into one event space, and partly by providing ways of making the resulting events tangible in the human-perceptible world.

Usage Experience

At the time of writing, Khronika has been in continuous use at EuroPARC for over a year. Of the lab's staff of 20-25 people, the majority use Khronika to receive notifications of common events, but only half of these are using all its facilities including the sending part.

Although there have yet not been any formal usage studies, our informal experience is very positive. There have been several cases in which users reported that they received unexpected, but welcome, reminders about events that they were unaware of or about which they had forgotten. In another interesting case, the system became unavailable for a short while and people started expressing concern because they didn't feel like they knew what was going on around them anymore.

Khronika as an environmental interface was an unexpected success. It is now used by a number of people to provide new mail indications and A/V feedback for a variety of connection types as well as the more frivolous rain sound. Khronika is also used directly as a sound generating server by other EuroPARC projects, such as the Portholes and the Activated Active Badge systems, because of its simplicity of use and ubiquitous reach.

Of course, there have been problems too. One of the most difficult ones has been to try and find a balance between the informality of free text and the formality of structured records in describing and representing the events. If they are too structured, it becomes too difficult for people to translate real world events into Khronika events; if they are too "loose," it becomes impossible to do anything meaningful with them. The current solution is more of a working compromise than anything else, and one future direction would be to investigate alternative representations further.

The current method of using a predefined static set of event classes also clearly needs to be changed. While too many classes can cause chaos and confusion, too few

* "Small Matter Of Programming"

is like force-fitting the world into your personal shoebox [sic]. We need some way of organising the event space in a form which can evolve, yet maintain its meaning and have a simple structure.

Finally, Khronika is currently not very good at supporting one-shot reminders, i.e. reminders for individual events. While daemons may be made to trigger on only one specific event, posting a daemon just to create a simple reminder is a bit awkward and unintuitive. Also, while events themselves are automatically removed after a given time, there is no garbage collection for daemons, so they require manual deletion when they become obsolete.

Conclusion

In this report, we have described how Khronika implements a shared event notification service that receives information about events from a number of different sources and automatically delivers notifications at the appropriate times to users interested in the information. By acting as a repository for past, present, and future scheduled events, it supports search and retrieval operations that allow users to interactively inspect the database using different kinds of browsers. Its event daemons let users specify patterns of events about which they would like to be notified, and determine how and when notifications are to occur. This architecture promotes clearly separated roles and responsibilities for the sending and receiving agents, with Khronika itself in the middle as an information channeller.

While calendrical events still make up the core of the system, we have recently started exploring other event types and sources, such as those automatically sensed by electronic agents, leading to blurred boundaries between computational and real-world events. With automatic event sensors and people posting events, we are able to transform information about the environment to a form which can be processed and acted upon by the computer. Likewise, we are carrying events internal to the computer out to the real world by making them, or more correctly, traces of them, tangible by means of human-perceptible sights and sounds.

Acknowledgments

The author would particularly like to thank Thomas P. Moran, formerly director of EuroPARC, now at Xerox PARC, for setting him on this fruitful track and for being a rich source of good ideas and suggestions. Allan MacLean at EuroPARC and Austin Henderson and Sara Bly at PARC have also given a lot of useful input as well as having been an invaluable source of enthusiastic support. Both Bill Gaver and Paul Luff helped considerably with many useful suggestions and corrections to this manuscript; any grammatical errors still lingering are entirely at my own fault. Finally, this report would not be complete without a warm thank-you to Nadia, who has spent many lonely evenings at home while I obsessively worked long and late hours.

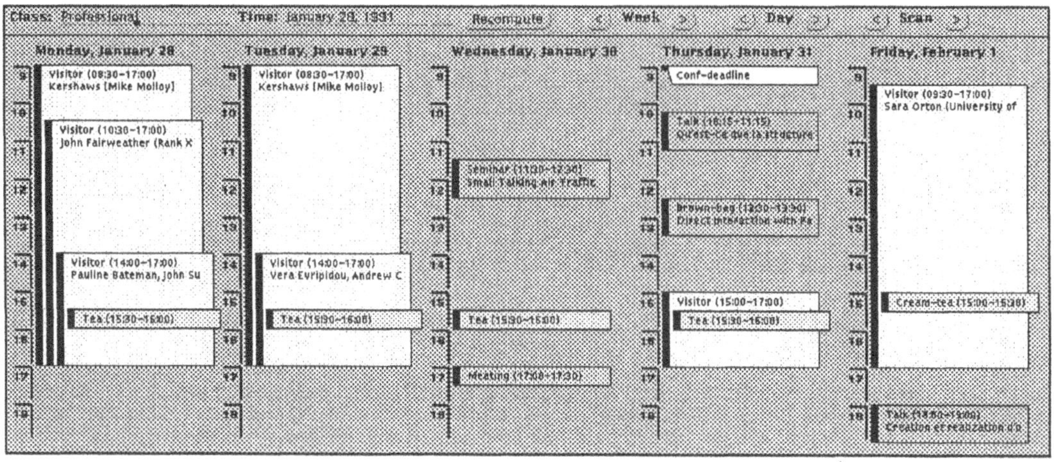

Figure 3. The XKhBrowser Interface

Implementation Description

The current version of the Khronika server is written in about 10,000 lines of C code and runs on a Sun 4/60 under SunOS 4.1.1. Clients, i.e. user interfaces and automatic event generators, communicate with the server using the SunRPC remote procedure protocol over TCP/IP. Several different suites of client interfaces exist; two using graphical user interfaces (Interlisp-D and X11) and one teletype based one:

Interlisp-D	A browser for events and event daemons; An editor for events and event daemons; Buttons for entering specific events and event daemons; Modifications to the Lafite mail system to post newmail events
X11	*xkhron*, a simple XView/Scheme based search and update tool; *xkhweek*, an experimental active update weekly browser; *xkhbrowser*, a graphical weekly browser with colour coding and proportional temporal layout (see Figure 3)
UNIX	*khputevent, khgetevent, khlistevents*: programs for storing, retrieving, and listing events; *khputdaemon, khgetdaemon, khlistdaemons*: ditto for event daemons; *khgetclass, khlistclasses*: ditto for event classes; *khmkevent, kheditevent, khmkdaemon, kheditdaemon*: shell scripts for interactively creating and editing events and event daemons.

There are currently four different automatic event generators:

khabc	Transfers events from the EuroPARC Active Badge system.
khbiff	Periodically checks if users have received new mail.
khiiif	Listens for connection information from the A/V switch server.
khweather	Periodically polls the EuroPARC weather server for its status.

References

Buxton, W. and Moran, T. (1990): "EuroPARC's Integrated Interactive Intermedia Facility (iiif): Early Experiences," *Proceedings of the IFIP WG8.4 Conference on Multi-User Interfaces and Applications*, Heraklion, Crete, September 1990.

DellaFera, C. A., Eichin, M. W., French, R. S., Jedlinsky, D. C., Kohl, J. T., Sommerfeld, W. E. (1989): *The Zephyr Notification System*, Project Athena, 1989.

Denning, P. J. (1982): "Electronic Junk," *Communications of the ACM*, vol. 25, no 3, pp 163-165, March 1982.

Gaver, W. W. (1991): "Sound Support for Collaboration," *Proceedings of the European Conference on Computer Supported Collaborative Work*, 1991.

Lai, K-Y., Malone, T. W., Yu, K-C. (1988): "Object Lens, 'A Spreadsheet' for Cooperative Work", *ACM Transactions on Office Information Systems*, vol. 6, no 4, October 1988.

Lamming, M. and Wellner, P. (1991): *The EuroPARC Active Badge Service*, forthcoming report from Rank Xerox EuroPARC.

Malone, T. W., Grant, R. G., Lai, K-Y., Rao, R., Rosenblitt, D. A. (1989): "The Information Lens: An intelligent system for information sharing and coordination," in M. Olson (ed). *Technological support for work group collaboration*, 1989.

Newman, W., Eldridge, M., Lamming, M. (1991): "PEPYS: Generating Autobiographies by Automatic Tracking," *Proceedings of the European Conference on Computer Supported Collaborative Work*, 1991.

O'Shea, T., Lamming, M., Chalmers, M., Graube, N., Wellner, P., Wiginton, G. (1991): *Perceptions and Expectations of Ubiquitous Computing: Experiments with BirdDog, a Prototype Person Locator*, submitted to ITAP-91.

Palme, J. (1984): "You have 134 unread mail! Do you Want to read them now?," Computer Based Message Services, *IFIP Proceedings*, 1984.

Spafford G. (1987): "USENET Software: History and Sources", recurrent article in *news.admin* and *news.announce.newusers*, USENET, 1987.

Proceedings of the Second European Conference on Computer-Supported Cooperative Work
Bannon, L., Robinson, M. & Schmidt, K. (Editors)
September 25-27, 1991, Amsterdam, The Netherlands

Participation frameworks for computer mediated communication

Marina Jirotka   Paul Luff   Nigel Gilbert

United Kingdom

This paper is concerned with the development of a more complex view of the analysis of social interactions in CMC systems. There is an apparent paradox in findings of previous studies of text-based CMC which may be due to the nature of this type of communication for it requires users to orient to two models: conversation and text. This is illustrated by showing the detailed analysis of instances of interactions on a particular CMC system. By utilising the notion of feedback and exploring its function in conversation, we emphasize the need for a more refined view of the relationship between speaker, hearer and feedback. We draw on Goffman's analysis of social encounters and offer a preliminary view of the contributions that participation frameworks and production formats can make to CSCW.

> "Feedback - sending back to the user information about what action has actually been done, what result has been accomplished - is a well known concept in the science of control and information theory. Imagine trying to talk to someone when you cannot even hear your own voice, or trying to draw a picture with a pencil that leaves no mark: there would be no feedback."
>
> Norman 1988 p 27

Introduction

The concept of 'feedback' is recognized as an important feature in the design of interactions between computer systems and their users. In a range of interfaces, from those based on natural language to those that manipulate objects on the screen, efforts have been made to ensure that users' actions have an immediate and obvious effect. At the natural language end of this range, Hayes and Reddy (1983) examine human conversations in order to outline the requirements for graceful spoken and text-based interaction between users and computer systems. One component they identify is 'robust communication' - 'the set of strategies needed to ensure that a listener receives a speaker's utterance and interprets it correctly' (p 233). Hayes and Reddy list three problems of robust communication. First, the listener may not receive the message. Second, the listener may receive the message but may not be able to interpret all or part of it. Third, the listener may receive the message but interpret the message incorrectly. From examining conversations, Hayes and Reddy identify five strategies which could be expressed as forms of feedback - implicit confirmation, implicit acknowledgement, explicit indications of incomprehension, echoing and fragmentary recognition. Natural language systems should conform to one or more of these strategies if interactions with them are to be 'graceful'.

In direct manipulation systems, feedback is displayed through changes in the behaviour of objects (Hutchins, Hollan and Norman 1986). This supports the 'feeling of acting on the objects themselves' and allows for 'the modification of actions even as they are being executed'. By continually showing the state of the system, users feel they are directly acting on the object on the screen and the computer, as an intermediary, is removed from perception.

The aspects of feedback described above relate to design principles derived from studying single users interacting with a computer. There must also be equivalent notions of feedback in multi-user situations. However, the notion of feedback at once becomes more complex as users now not only require feedback from their own computers, but also from other systems on the network and other users. An analogous issue is feedback in conversation. This is often performed through turn-taking, where an interaction emerges in a turn-by-turn manner, each party displaying an understanding of the other's prior utterance. Feedback in conversation is also displayed through the use of 'backchannelling' procedures, that is 'ums', 'uh huh's' and nods intended to convey to the speaker that the listener is attending to what is being said (Duncan and Fiske, 1977). Verbal and non-verbal responses have been termed collectively as back-channel behaviours (Yngve, 1970)

In text based computer-mediated communication (CMC)[1] there seems to be an assumption that the interaction is similar to a conversation. Recently several researchers have examined different forms of CMC. Most of these have concentrated on the way that users give and take turns. Bowers and Churcher (1989) review previous work on electronic mail and computer conferencing and show that there are apparently contradictory claims for these types of communication. Severinson Eklundh (1986) suggests that electronic mail is based

---

1 Bannon (1986) reviews a range of computer systems that could be considered to support communication which includes single computer systems, shared file systems and electronic mail. In this paper we will be begin by concentrating on a system that is primarily intended to support text-based synchronous communication.

around a three-part turn structure while Hiltz (1977) claims that turn-taking has little influence on computer conferencing. Bowers and Churcher (1989) show that in fact two-part turns appear to predominate in computer-mediated conversations, yet the nature of turn-taking is different in this medium to that of conversation. Although computer-mediated conversations may be locally managed, Bowers and Churcher state that not all computer-mediated communication is conversational. Instead, CMC consists of a mixture of local and global structure with conversation-like turns occurring within globally managed episodes.

McCarthy et al (1990) explore a 'minimal' synchronous electronic conferencing system. They suggest there are four generic communication tasks to be supported by any communication system: synchronising communication, maintaining conversational coherence, repairing conversational breakdown and maintaining shared focus. They take various approaches to discourse and conversation from the social sciences to show problems encountered by the users of their system. In particular, they suggest that 'users abandon a strict turn system' and some interactions are 'different from well-ordered, turn-based, conversation'.

In his examination of CMC, McIlvenny (1990) sets up a framework based on Suchman (1987) whereby he records pairs of users at each end of a communication link. He introduces notions of transience, permanence, turn-construction, monitoring and 'double dialogues'.

In common with McCarthy et al. and McIlvenny, we focus on a synchronous CMC system. However, our system was intended for facilitating private interaction between sub-groups of users. All users were linked into a conferencing telephone system, but because anything they said over the telephone was audible to everyone, private, person to person interactions had to be communicated through a text-based medium on the computer screens. By examining details of instances of interactions on this system, we develop the notion of feedback in terms of the nature of the participation of the users. From this we offer some recommendations for the design of this type of application and for CSCW systems in general.

The Paradox in the Nature of CMC

The work mentioned above appears to suggest a paradox in the nature of computer-mediated communication. When the participants are both geographically dispersed and their communication is asynchronous, their conversational interaction is 'locally managed and structured around adjacency pairs' (Bowers and Churcher 1989). However when their communication is synchronous, 'users abandon a strict turn system' and 'interleave adjacency pair parts in an apparently unconventional way' (McCarthy et al. 1990). These results seem surprising as it would be expected that the synchronous nature of a computer-mediated interaction would increase its similarity to 'conversation'. This paradox may be due to the way these studies have compared CMC to conversation using 'findings' of Conversation Analysis such as 'adjacency-pairs' and yet have overlooked some of the basic assumptions from which they were derived. For example, McCarthy et al. compare an interaction with question-answer adjacency pairs and yet attempt to describe these questions and answers in terms of 'illocutionary force', a notion from Speech Act theory (Austin 1962, Searle 1969, but c.f. Levinson 1983).

In this paper we will begin to show some of the complexities of applying the notion of 'feedback' taken from studies of other types of communication systems to CMC. It is too simplistic to view the interaction as switching between speaker and hearer, with one participant responsible for providing 'feedback' to the other. It is also necessary to decompose the nature of the rôles of speaker and hearer in a social encounter. By drawing on Goffman's analysis of social encounters we will offer a preliminary view of the contributions that participation frameworks and production formats can make to CSCW.

An Example of Text-Based CMC

In order to explore the paradox mentioned above, we will describe and explicate details of instances of synchronous CMC. The data for this investigation consist of logs and recordings of groups using a networked program. Users were given the task of playing several campaigns of a networked version of DIPLOMACY. (Hewitt, Wilbur and Gilbert 1991). DIPLOMACY is a game of skill normally played on a board on which is drawn a schematic political map of Europe as it was in 1901. Each player acts the part of a country and aims to conquer the rest of Europe. The merit of this particular game is that players are unlikely to win if they act on their own; to conquer other countries they need to form alliances. A computerised version of this game must be able to support the dynamic formation and dissolution of groups of players.

A prototype networked version of DIPLOMACY has been implemented using SUPERCARD[2] and HYPERAPPLETALK[3]. In the networked application, there are several windows available to players: a map of 1901 Europe which represents the current state of play; a window to set up negotiations, that is, to select countries with whom to negotiate; a text window in which to communicate privately with other allies; a trial map for members of a negotiating group to display possible moves; and a text field in which to type movement orders at the end of a campaign.

Players have several channels of communication open to them; all players are connected by an audio link conference call, subgroups of players can communicate through a text field which is private to the subgroup, and subgroups also interact through the trial map. This analysis will concentrate on audio recordings of the telephone link and logs of the contributions to the text field.

---

2 SUPERCARD is a personal software toolkit produced by Silicon Beach Software.

3 HYPERAPPLETALK is a local area networking library that is produced by the Apple Corporation

Conversational Organisation of CMC

As Bowers and Churcher (1989) and McCarthy (1990) suggest, CMC does appear to possess similar interactional features to conversation. In the following instance, two parties France (F) and England (E) begin a negotiation in the text field.[4]

(1) England :12:07:17 pm Sun, Aug 19, 1990

((F selects England on negotiate card
and then presses the talk button))
((E selects 'Yes' on the dialogue box))
F : How about forming an alliance
E : Yes
F : You could head up north and north central
europe and I could go for south and south
central europe
E: OK - so which countries exactly would
you require my support for?
F: As germany and italy are neutralshould
be easy to take them

France's "How about forming an alliance" (line 4) both initiates a topic and makes an offer to England. In accepting, England's "Yes" (line 5) appears to recognise the previous utterance as an offer. Similarly, France's next statement (lines 6-8) displays a recognition of England's acceptance. At the same time, France offers a suggestion for a possible strategy. Again, England's "OK" recognises and accepts France's suggestion (lines 9). Following this, England asks a question (lines 9-10) which France answers (lines 11-12).

The interaction, therefore, appears to proceed in a turn-by-turn manner, each participant displaying their understanding of the other's prior statement and advancing the context for the next statement. The parties are 'locally managing' the interaction.

In Hayes and Reddy's (1983) terms, the turns in fragment (1) are instances of graceful and robust communication. A listener implicitly confirms and acknowledges that he has received and interpreted the speaker's utterance. However, it is important to note that this confirmation and acknowledgement occurs in and through the next 'message'. As in conversation, the participant's roles within this type of interaction do not simply switch between 'speaker' and 'listener' (see Levinson 1988) nor is one participant solely responsible for 'feedback' to the other's utterances. Instead, it is through the turn-by-turn character of interaction

---

4 The data are an exact replication of what the users typed into the text field. Each new contribution appears in the recipient's text field only when a user presses the return key. This is shown in the transcripts by prefacing each contribution by the first letter of the country the user is playing. It is possible for one player to send consecutive contributions.

that the participants display their understandings of the state of the interaction (cf. Heritage 1984).

Further examination of instances of data reveal other similarities between the organization of talk and the organization of CMC, particularly in the way interactions commence (cf. openings, Schegloff and Sacks 1973) and topics within the interaction change (cf. preclosings, Schegloff and Sacks 1973, Button 1987).

Textual Organisation of CMC

In the preceding section we outlined the ways in which it appears that a structure based on turn taking emerges from the negotiation. However, this assumed a similarity between turns of talk and typed utterances. Sacks, Schegloff and Jefferson (1974) formulate an ordered set of rules for the allocation of the next turn in a conversation. These are applied at transition-relevance places (TRP) within a turn. If at a TRP the current speaker does not select a next speaker and no hearer self selects, the current speaker may continue. Thus, in broad terms, participants in a conversation have to monitor continually the production of a turn for possible points of completion. In the following fragment France and England are negotiating[5].

(2)

E:	France - I'm still here, but considering your offer. I'm not sure that you might gain all the advantage by taking Germany (the black bit, whatever that is!) But as long as I can be assured of your support going into Russia and down into the grey and orange bit beneath (I'm not too good at Geography!)	E: It's a problem remembering what countries are F: Press on the main map to find out what the names are
E:	OK, I just had a look at the map again. Your strategy seems ok.	
F:	the grey and orange bit is austria so be careful as Mary is austria	

If we want to maintain the idea that turns in this interaction are similar to turns of talk, then there are TRPs at line 8 where England continues her turn and at line 10 where France self selects. Yet, France's turn does not appear to relate to what is immediately prior, for it refers back to the first part of England's turn (lines 7-8).

It does seem to be the case that France is orienting (lines 11-12) to a TRP after line 8, but both the size of England's contribution (lines 1-8) and the time it takes to construct, delay a response from France. In fact, England's contribution does not appear to be designed as an interactional component. Although speakers in a

5 In this instance, the text the users type appears in the left hand column and their conversations on the telephone conference call appear in the right.

conversation can hold the floor for a long time, they tend either to preface packages of talk with some sort of initiator or the turn emerges through several TRPs. Neither of these appear in lines 1 to 8; rather England's contribution appears as a recognisable piece of text (e.g. she brackets part of the text).

Because of the design of the system, France is unable to monitor England's turn as it is produced. More pertinently, close coordination of speaker turns in conversation relies on speakers positioning the start of their turn immediately after the prior turn. France's failure to do this results in England continuing her turn. This is due to the nature of this type of text based CMC. Neither participant is able to monitor the production of the other's utterances and therefore cannot fully coordinate the production of their own.

One way of characterising this passage is in terms of two models of interaction, text and conversation. The users are combining devices from each model in the course of the activity. This has implications for design of CMC systems. For example, McCarthy et al (1990) have proposed 'quick response mechanisms' that might be useful in coordinating the interaction, such as 'I agree' or 'OK' buttons. Although these devices may be useful for 'receivers' of messages, they assume that users are orienting to the interaction as a conversation. But if users are constructing their messages as pieces of text, even if, as McCarthy et al suggest it appears as it is typed, coordination of the use of these devices with the text might still be problematic.

In conversation, it may seem that 'feedback' is performed as each turn displays an understanding of the prior. This relies on participants monitoring talk as it is produced and tying in talk into another's turn. In text-based CMC these activities are more difficult; monitoring is performed by reading, and coordination is by tying one's typing to another's both spatially and temporally. Furthermore, any analysis also rests on a rather crude characterisation of 'interaction' as individuals intermittently switching rôles of speaker and hearer.

Participant Framework and Production Format

Goffman (1981) criticises a view commonly held of the simple dyadic relationship of speaker to hearer in a conversation. In this view, only two individuals are involved and the rôles of speaker and hearer are interchanged as they pass turns back and forth to one another. He argues that this is insufficient for the analysis of social encounters. He goes on to decompose first the notion of 'hearer' and then of 'speaker' by examining the status of participants in a social encounter[6]. First, there

6 Goffman (1972) describes an encounter as involving, for participants 'a single visual and cognitive focus of attention; a mutual and preferential openness to verbal communication; a heightened mutual relevance of acts; an eye-to-eye ecological huddle that maximises each participant's opportunity to perceive the other participants' monitoring of him' (p.19)

is the official status of a *ratified participant*. Ratified participants can either be *addressed* or *unaddressed*. In two party interaction, one of the parties will be addressed and in multi-party interaction it will often be the case, at least in periods of the encounter, that one party is addressed leaving others unaddressed. *Unofficial participants* to an interaction can still be listening: either as *overhearers* or as *eavesdroppers*. As Goffman puts it, "a ratified participant may not be listening, and someone listening may not be a ratified participant". He then continues by outlining the relations between these rôles, examining the interaction at the time that one party is speaking. He argues that one can describe the rôle and function of all the other members in the social gathering in relation to the speaker. On an individual level, the relation of each member to the speaker's utterance is that member's *participation status*. At the level of a gathering, the relation of all the members to the speaker's utterance is the *participation framework*.

When considering the notion of speaker, Goffman suggests three further categories. First, the *animator*, a category similar in kind to that of recipient, someone who produces the utterances. Second, the *author*, someone who selects 'the sentiments that are being expressed and the words in which they are encoded'. Third, the *principal*, someone who is actually committed to the words that are spoken. Commonly, the term 'speaker' implies the case where all three categories are taken together. However, individuals can recite other people's words and can speak 'for someone else'. They can also switch between these rôles even during the course of producing an utterance. The *production format* of an utterance is its relationship as it is produced to these three categories. Levinson (1988) attempts further clarification of both 'reception rôles' (cf. participation framework) and 'production rôles' (cf. production format), by introducing further categories with finer distinctions. Also, Goodwin (1981, 1984) has revealed the ways that in face-to-face interactions participants display and manage their differing participant statuses to one another through their gestures, gaze and talk.

Goffman's production formats and participation frameworks and related, recent developments by Levinson and Goodwin have direct implications for CSCW systems. In determining the requirements of a CSCW system, the notion of production formats and participation frameworks can be useful for examining the practices of people working in real world environments. For example, Heath and Luff (1991a), using this as an analytical device, have revealed the details of the nature of communication and collaboration in a complex technological environment. In a London Underground Control Room, a controller talks to an operator of a train (an addressed recipient) while his talk is also available for public announcers (unaddressed recipients) to monitor. In a study of a similar type of operations room, Goodwin (1991) develops the notions of 'overhearers' and ratified participants in an environment where operators use a range of technologies and monitor each others' talk and activities, yet sit 'back-to-back' rather than 'face-to-face'.

In addition, there are implications for the design of CSCW systems. A 'speaker' may expect a different nature of 'feedback' from a ratified addressed participant than from an unaddressed one. Meanwhile, both addressed and unaddressed participants may provide feedback, changing their respective statuses. Thus, CSCW systems that aim to be sensitive to the range of user rôles in an interaction must provide facilities for users to monitor others' activities, to display that monitoring to others and to allow for shifts in the participation status of users in that interaction.

Multi-party CMC

In previous sections we have analysed instances of synchronous CMC where communication takes place between two participants. We concluded that although there may be similarities between the organisation of talk and the organisation of CMC, problems with this view arise when the notion of feedback as monitoring and coordination is incorporated. We have emphasised that feedback is more difficult to give when monitoring can only be performed by reading and coordination can only be performed by typing. In multi-party CMC, as might be expected, monitoring and coordination become even more complicated. In the following excerpt Turkey, Austria and Russia are still negotiating[7]. Just prior to this fragment, Austria has selected Russia and Turkey to negotiate with.

(3)

R: Turkey what do you suggest?
T: austria to italy, turkey to bulgaria, russia to
germany, ok?
A: Fred do you think it wise to give Russia all
that power, I'll take Germany, probably Italy is
less strategic Russia to take Scandinavia and
Turkey to come through Rumania to Italy
T: ok by me
A: Do you want to try moves
R: Yes, show me some moves baby!!!

All the users appear to be full participants in the interaction and, as in (1), the interaction appears to be organised in a turn-by-turn fashion, each turn displaying an understanding of the prior. Nevertheless, such an interaction would be unusual in a conversation as the participants select the next contributors by identifying them by name; Russia in line 1 and Austria in line 4. By selecting 'Turkey' as the next, Russia not only addresses Turkey but also explicitly does not address Austria. Similarly, when Austria identifies 'Fred', Turkey is addressed and Russia is not. Although all users are participants in the interaction, they do not each have the same status in it.

---

7 Turkey is played by Fred.

When Austria selects Russia and Turkey for negotiation both Russia and Turkey become ratified and addressed participants in a three party interaction. The other players, France and Germany, become unratified participants. By identifying Turkey, Russia selects Turkey as the next speaker and also transforms the participation framework (line 1). Turkey becomes the addressed participant and Austria the unaddressed participant. At this point, Russia's message is available for monitoring by both ratified participants. As an addressed participant, Turkey responds to Russia's question with a suggestion for next possible moves (line 2). Again, there is a shift in the participation framework. Austria remains an unaddressed participant, but Russia now becomes the addressed participant. By Austria contributing (line 3) she moves from being an unaddressed participant and by selecting Fred (Turkey) as the next speaker at the beginning of the turn, the participation framework changes once more, Russia becoming the unaddressed participant. Turkey responds to Austria's statement and there is yet another shift in participation statuses. By examining the contributions to the communication in fragment (3), we can see the way that a participation framework can be transformed throughout an interaction. The interaction is sensitive to these changes, and shifts are displayed not only after a contribution has been made but also within a contribution.

In instances 1, 2 and 3 participants gained a ratified status because their negotiations were carried out within a shared but 'private' communications window. However telephone links connecting all players on a conference call allowed participants to have a different status, that of 'overhearers'. In fragment (4), France is carrying out a negotiation with England, while Austria, Russia and Turkey are carrying out another, separate negotiation.[8]

(4)

	F: Got to go into the sea first
A: If france is talking about moving the fleet we must defend Italy, over to you Steve	
R: Why?	

In this instance, Austria appears to overhear the talk between France and England on the telephone, an encounter in which she is not a ratified participant. She then displays her overhearing to the participants on her encounter, also selecting (Russia) as the next speaker.

Viewing CMC as a participation framework appears to be a useful way of describing the details of the moment-to-moment interaction as it unfolds from the point of view of each user. Further work is necessary to apply Goffman's analysis to CSCW, but it should provide a better starting point than characterising interactions between users as speakers and hearers 'switching' control of the floor between them. It will also be necessary to utilise recent theoretical and empirical

---

8 The contributions in the shared window are transcribed in the left column and talk on the telephone conference call is transcribed on the right.

developments to Goffman's framework (e.g. Goodwin 1984, Levinson 1988). Although this type of analysis appears to apply most to systems where users collaborate through text or speech, it could also apply to systems that involve direct manipulation of objects. In these it is also necessary to identify the various participating rôles of the users and the ways their actions can change format through their production.

Conclusion

We have shown an apparent paradox in the findings of previous studies of text-based CMC. Users appeared to have problems orienting to turn-taking in synchronous communication whereas asynchronous communication was found to be structured around turns. This paper suggests that this paradox may be due to the nature of this type of communication for it requires users to orient to two models. We have shown that users do indeed design contributions as interactional units and that other participants appear to display an understanding of these as such. However, we have also shown that users design contributions as pieces of text. The confusion of these two tasks appears to lead to interactional difficulties.

The notions of participation framework and production format have also begun to inform the design of systems to support collaborative work. Heath and Luff (1991b) in their study of video-mediated interaction reveal some of the interactional asymmetries of the medium. They suggest that these asymmetries, by rendering nonverbal behaviour relatively ineffective, can allow users to remain insensitive to the demands of others in an office environment. As users may have to cope simultaneously with the demands of being an addressed participant in an interaction and having to use a range of technology, the insensitivity of the medium may facilitate rather than undermine collaborative work. Furthermore, they suggest that developments in multi-media technology could be towards letting users control their own visual availability and the accessibility of the co-participant. In other words, allowing users more control over their participation status and allowing this to change throughout an interaction. Other developments in CSCW appear to be directly related to issues in participation frameworks and production formats. For example, Greenberg (1990) describes an interface that gives feedback on whether users have control of the floor, want control of the floor or are just observing. This could easily be developed to take into account other participation statuses. But more importantly, devices must be designed which take into account the way a participation framework emerges turn by turn and the way a production format transforms within a turn.[9]

---

9 It may be interesting to consider electronic mail and other forms of CMC in terms of a production format. For example, changes in category from author to animator (or 'forwarder') may be marked in contributions to electronic mail.

We have begun to show some of the complexities of applying the notion of 'feedback' taken from studies of other types of communication systems to CMC. It is too simplistic to view the interaction as switching between speaker and hearer, with one participant responsible for providing 'feedback' to the other. It is also necessary to decompose the nature of the rôles of speaker and hearer in a social encounter. By drawing on Goffman's analysis of social encounters we have offered a preliminary view of the contributions that participation frameworks and production formats can make to CSCW. These include: the analysis of the requirements for systems to support collaborative work, the analysis of users interacting through these systems and ultimately the design of systems which support different participation rôles within an interaction.

Acknowledgements

We would like to express thanks to members of the TMPI project; those at Queen Mary and Westfield College, Betty Hewitt and Sylvia Wilbur and from British Telecom Research Laboratories, Alastair Rogers and Keith Dickerson. We would particularly like to thank Christian Heath for his support and advice. And last but not least many thanks to all the people who came to play DIPLOMACY.

References

Austin, J. (1962): *How to do things with words.* Oxford University Press, Oxford.

Bannon, L. J. (1986): " Computer-mediated Communication", in D. A. Norman and S. W. Draper (eds.):*User-Centered System Design*, Lawrence Erlbaum Associates, Hillsdale NJ, pp. 433-452.

Bowers, J. and Churcher, J. (1989): "Local and global structuring of computer mediated communication: developing perspectives on CSCW in Cosmos", Office: Technology and *People*,Vol. 4, no. 3, pp. 197-227.

Button, G. (1987): "Moving Out Of Closing" , in G. Button and J. R. E. Lee (eds.):*Talk and Social Organisation* , Multilingual Matters, Clevedon and Philadelphia, pp. 101-151.

Duncan, S. and Fiske, D. W. (1977): *Face-to-face Interaction.*, Lawrence Erlbaum, Hillsdale, N.J.

Goffman, E. (1972): *Encounters,*. Penguin, Harmondsworth.

Goffman, E. (1981): *Forms of Talk,* Blackwell, Oxford.

Goodwin, C. (1981): *Conversational Organization: Interaction Between Speakers and Hearers,* Academic Press, London and New York.

Goodwin, C. (1984): Notes on story structure and the organization of participation, in J. M. Atkinson, and J. C. Heritage (eds.): *Structures of Social Action: Studies in Conversation Analysis,* Cambridge University Press, Cambridge, pp. 225-246.

Goodwin, M. H. (1991): "Announcements in Their Environment: Back-to-Back Interaction in a Multi-Activity Work Setting", Xerox PARC Working Paper, Xerox PARC, Ca.

Greenberg, S. (1990): "Sharing views and interactions with single-user applications". In *COIS '90: Proceedings of the Conference on Office Information Systems*, Boston, April 1991.

Hayes, P. and Reddy, D. (1983): "Steps Towards Graceful Interaction in Spoken and Written Man-machine Communication", *International Journal of Man-machine Studies*, Vol.19, pp. 231-284.

Heath, C. C. and Luff, P. (1991a): "Collaborative Activity and Technological Design: Task Coordination in London Underground Control Rooms", in this volume, the *Proceedings of ECSCW '91*, Amsterdam, September 1991.

Heath, C. C. and Luff, P. (1991b): "Disembodied Conduct: Video Communication and Collaborative Work", in *Proceedings of CHI '91*, New Orleans, April -May 1991, pp. 99-103.

Heritage, J. C. (1984): *Garfinkel and Ethnomethodology*. Polity Press, Cambridge.

Hewitt, B., Wilbur, S. and Gilbert, G. N. (1991): "Truth, Lies 'n Negotiation". *Colloquium on CSCW: Computer Supported Cooperative Work*. Institution of Electrical Engineers, London, March 1991.

Hiltz, S. R. (1977): "Computer Conferencing: assessing the social impact of a new communications medium", *Technological Forecasting and Social Change*, Vol. 10, pp. 225-238.

Hutchins, E. L. , Hollan, J. D. and Norman, D. A. (1986): "Direct Manipulation Interfaces", in D. A. Norman and S. W. Draper (eds.):*User-Centered System Design*, Lawrence Erlbaum Associates, Hillsdale NJ, pp. 87-124.

Levinson, S. C. (1983): *Pragmatics*, Cambridge University Press, Cambridge.

Levinson, S. C. (1988): "Putting Linguistics on a Proper Footing: Explorations in Goffman's Concepts of Participation". In P. Drew and A. Wootton (eds.):*Erving Goffman: Exploring the Interaction Order* , Polity Press, Cambridge, pp. 161-227.

McCarthy, J.C., Miles, V.C., Monk, A.F., Harrison, M.D., Dix, A.J. and Wright, P.C. (1990): "Using a minimal system to drive the conceptual analysis of electronic conferencing", University of York Technical Report.

McIlvenny, P. (1990): "Communicative Action and Computers: re-embodying Conversation Analysis?" In P. Luff, G. N. Gilbert and D. M. Frohlich (eds):*Computers and Conversation* , Academic Press, London and New York, pp. 91-134.

Norman, D. A. (1988): *The Psychology of Everyday Things*. Basic Books, New York.

Sacks, H., Schegloff, E. A. and Jefferson, G. (1974): "A simplest systematics for the organisation of turn-taking for conversation", *Language*, Vol. 50, pp. 696-735.

Searle, J. R. (1969): *Speech Acts : An Essay in the Philosophy of Language*. Cambridge University Press, Cambridge.

Schegloff, E. A. and Sacks, H. (1973): "Opening up closings", *Semiotica*, Vol. 7, pp. 289-327.

Severinson Eklundh, K. (1986): "Dialogue Processes in Computer-Mediated Communication: A Study of Letters in the COM System", Linkoping Studies in Art and Science, Linkoping.

Suchman, L. A. (1987): *Plans and Situated Actions*. Cambridge University Press, Cambridge.

Yngve, V. H. (1970): "On getting a word in edgewise", *Papers from the Sixth Regional Meeting of the Chicago Linguistic Society*, Chicago Linguistic Society, Chicago.

Proceedings of the Second European Conference on Computer-Supported Cooperative Work
Bannon, L., Robinson, M. & Schmidt, K. (Editors)
September 25-27, 1991, Amsterdam, The Netherlands

Sound Support For Collaboration

William W. Gaver

Rank Xerox EuroPARC, England

Shared work often involves fluid transitions between relatively focussed collaboration, division of labour, general awareness and serendipitous communication. This leads to a tension in the design of software systems meant to support shared work: focussed collaboration implies the need to coordinate people's views of work objects, while division of labour requires individual control over views. A similar tension exists in the office environment as well: group engagement in the workplace depends on a shared context, but individual work is facilitated by privacy and freedom of action. Auditory cues have the potential to reduce these tensions because graphics and sound can provide two independent ways to present and obtain information. I illustrate the potential of sound in collaborative systems with observations drawn from two systems: the ARKola simulation, which explores the effects of sound on collaboration within a workstation environment; and EAR, in which auditory cues are used to increase general awareness of events and encourage group engagement within the workplace itself. These examples suggest useful functions sound can play in collaborative systems.

Introduction

The shift from computer systems that support a single user working alone to those supporting a group of users working together is a profound one. It leads to a consideration of the ways people work together in the everyday world and possible ways to extend and support their interactions. Perhaps more importantly, it suggests that the unique capabilities of computers should be embedded more firmly in ordinary work practises, so that the distinctions between the world of the computer and the workaday world are blurred (Moran & Anderson, 1990).

Developments in collaborative systems are promising, but if traditional models of human computer interaction seem to assume that we work in isolation, the new model sometimes seems one of people spending the totality of their working lives in meetings. To date, most software systems designed to support shared work seem aimed at supporting relatively intensive periods of collaboration – for instance, in meetings (Mantei, 1988), creating structured outlines (Ellis et al., 1988), or simultaneously developing documents (CSMIL, 1989).

But just as most people don't work alone at all times, nor do they always work together. Often people are merely aware of each other – aware of others' presence, perhaps their activities and progress. Occasionally people meet randomly in the course of day to day work, and these meetings are serendipitously fruitful, as when casual conversation leads to some question being answered or a longer term collaboration being started. And even when collaborating, people often divide their labour, meeting one another to share results and plan the future. Only occasionally do we actually join and work together closely on the same task.

People shift from working alone to working together, even when joined on a shared task. Building systems that support these transitions is important, if difficult. One promising approach is to embed collaborative software in a larger system of audio and video interconnectivity that allows people to be virtually co-present even if not working closely with one another (e.g., Buxton & Moran, 1990; Root, 1988; Goodman & Abel, 1987). Such systems have had some success, but it also seems important for such transitions to be supported by software systems themselves.

In this paper, I discuss the potential for auditory cues to support relatively casual and serendipitous forms of collaboration, both in software and office environments. First, I explore the movement between awareness and focussed collaboration, and discuss the reasons auditory cues seem appealing for support of smooth transitions in the degree of engagement on a common task. The potential of auditory cues is illustrated with examples from two systems that use sound to support collaboration. The first example comes from the ARKola bottling plant simulation, which explores the effects of auditory cues on a collaborative task in a workstation environment. The second system, called EAR (for Environmental Audio Reminders), is a system in which sound helps users maintain awareness of one another and events within the workplace itself. These two examples complement one another in focussing on the effects of auditory cues on collaboration in the workstation environment and the more general office environment; together they point the way towards many possible future developments.

Moving among ways of working

Figure 1 is a simple representation of the complex process of working together. Although simplistic, it provides a useful orientation to the extremes of the experience. Four major landmarks are indicated here. Underlying all is *general awareness*. This is a pervasive experience, one of simply knowing who is around and something about what they are doing: that they are busy or free, meeting or alone, receptive to communication or not. Awareness is necessary for all collaborative work, but the degree to which its focus is shared varies. An intense sharing of awareness characterizes *focussed collaboration* – those occasions in which people work closely together on a shared goal. Less is needed for *division of labour*, that common work practise in which a shared goal is divided and component tasks addressed separately. Finally, more casual awareness can lead to *serendipitous communication*, in which people realize the potential for productive work through chance encounters.

People move among these ways of working together along many trajectories. Simple awareness may lead to serendipitous communication, which in turn may lead to division of labour or focussed collaboration. Alternatively, a period of focussed collaboration may be followed by a division of labour. All of these forms of working together are likely to be important at one time or another in a shared project; supporting fluid movements among them is an important goal for collaborative software.

Yet the design of systems with the flexibility necessary to support many styles of shared work is not an easy task. One problem seems to be the tension between the need to maintain a common focus for collaborators and the desire to allow individuals freedom to work on their own. Bellotti et al. (1991) make this tension explicit in a Design Rationale based around studies of a shared editor (cf. MacLean et al., 1989). Two of the criteria they identify as pervasive in the choice of design

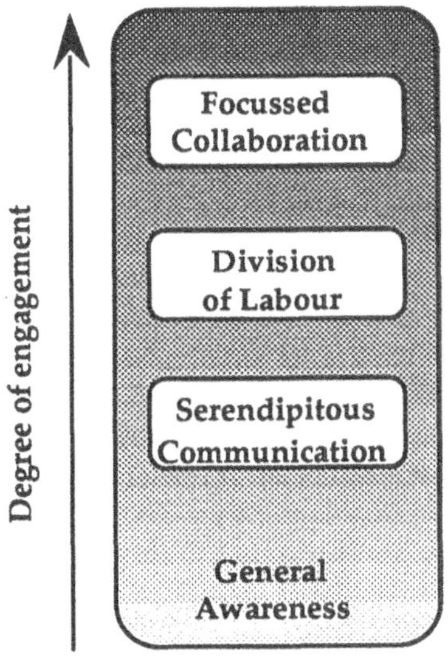

Figure 1: Shared work involves fluid transitions among focussed collaboration, division of labour, serendipitous communication, and general awareness (which supports them all).

options are the seemingly contradictory ones of "maintaining shared work focus" and "allowing individual work."

In the design of shared software systems, the tension between shared and individual work is reflected in issues concerning the degree of control over work objects afforded users. Individual work is supported by giving people complete control over their view of a work object: over its screen placement, the parts of it made visible, their appearance, etc. But shared focus is supported by *reducing* individual control over their view. From this perspective, focussed collaboration is most likely to occur when all participants can be assumed to be viewing the same thing. Although enforcing an identical focus on a given task may be helpful for supporting focussed collaboration, it is likely to hamper the smooth flow to other, less close forms of shared work (Bellotti et al., 1991).

Similar issues arise in offices, where the shared contexts necessary for group engagement compete with the privacy needed to concentrate on individual work – it is difficult to get work done when constantly in meetings about work. Providing ubiquitous audio-video interconnectivity may encourage awareness, but one must monitor a video screen at the expense of attention to one's work. Using video windows on a workstation is only a partial solution, since they must vie for valuable screen real-estate with other graphical tools.

In sum, systems which seek to support both shared work and individual flexibility suffer from the need to compete for control over the same display resources and limited visual attention. Clearly these issues can be dealt with by increasing the size and number of displays and relying on the time-honored panacea of social control. In this paper, however, I suggest that sound can provide a valuable alternative to vision as a means of providing the contextual information that allows free movement among more and less intense forms of collaboration.

Auditory icons and collaborative work

There are a number of reasons to think that sound has the potential to complement visual displays in supporting the transitions between focussed collaboration and more casual and separate forms of shared work. Primary among these reasons is hearing's status as a distance sense secondary only to vision. By distance sense, I mean that we are able to listen to information about events at a distance. Just as we can see a tree fall from far away, so can we hear it. We hope, on the other hand, neither to feel or taste the falling tree; and though we may smell it the experience is not likely to provide us with much useful information.

Because we can listen to as well as look at distant events, we can divide information about computer events between the two senses. On the one hand, we may provide redundant information about an event, so that we can both see and hear it. More interesting, we can disassociate the two, so that we may hear what we don't see.

Hearing also complements vision in that listening to an event does not necessarily interfere with the maintenance of a visual focus on another event. As I write this, for instance, I might hear a colleague walk by my office. The sounds of footsteps, doors opening, etc., provide information about what is going on around me, but I can nonetheless maintain my focus on my work. This should carry over quite well to collaborative systems, so that individual control can be granted users while sufficient cues as to the activities and whereabouts of others are still available. By splitting information about a shared workspace between sound and vision, we may reduce the tension between the desire to maintain a shared focus and that of allowing individual work.

Of course, no matter how attractive sound may be as a medium, it must be able to convey relatively complex information about events if it is to be useful. Clearly a collaborative system relying on the beeps and buzzes currently used in computers to increase awareness of colleague's activities would entail too high a cognitive overhead to provide valuable support to users (not to mention the irritation it would cause). It is not only necessary that sound complement vision, but that it provide information in subtle and intuitively obvious ways.

I have been developing a strategy for using sound to convey complex information that is based on the ways people listen to events in the everyday world (Gaver, 1986). From this perspective, we listen not to sounds and their attributes (such as pitch, loudness and timbre) but rather to events and theirs (e.g., footsteps, force and size). *Everyday listening* refers to the experience of listening to events. Taking this experience of listening as primary allows the development of a framework for analyzing and manipulating sounds that is based on attributes of events rather than the parameters of sound *per se*. These attributes, in turn, may be mapped to attributes of computer events, giving rise to *auditory icons*. Auditory icons are environmental sounds (like taps, scrapes, etc.) designed to convey information by analogy with everyday sound-producing events.

Auditory icons have several appealing qualities as a method of providing feedback about events. First, sound as a medium is a valuable way to provide information that is not constrained to a single location (e.g., I can hear a sound without facing my computer monitor). Second, non-speech audio is often less distracting, less susceptible to masking, and more efficient than is speech. Third, everyday sounds can often be mapped more closely to the events they are meant to represent than can musical sounds. Finally, auditory icons can be designed to present information in an almost subliminal way – just as we are likely to get a great deal of information without conscious attention from the sounds of colleagues working, so can auditory icons convey a great deal of information without being overly distracting.

Experience with systems employing auditory icons has suggested that such cues can be useful for individual work (Gaver, 1989). In particular, sound can convey information about events and objects that is difficult to convey visually – for instance, about the timing of events or the nature of interactions – as well as information that is inconvenient to present and obtain visually, for instance about the progress of relatively long lasting processes. Finally, informal experience with sound in a large-scale, collaborative system called SoundShark (Gaver & Smith, 1990) suggests that sound can support general awareness of collaborators' whereabouts and activities.

What I am suggesting, then, is that a smooth flow from focussed collaboration to division of labour can be facilitated by using well-designed auditory icons to increase awareness of activities and events. In the next two sections, I expand and support this notion by detailing experience with two collaborative systems which employ auditory icons. The first is the ARKola bottling plant simulation, a system in which sound provides cues designed to aid users collaborating in a workstation environment. The second is EAR, a system that uses designed audio cues to support awareness of events and activities within the entire work environment.

The ARKola bottling plant simulation

The ARKola bottling plant is a simulation designed expressly to explore the functions of auditory cues in complex, collaborative software systems. The simulation was developed to serve as a domain for testing that would satisfy a number of constraints:

- We hypothesized that sounds would aid in monitoring multiprocessing systems, so many simultaneous processes should be involved in the task.
- Sound should enable people to track hidden or invisible events, so the task domain should be too big to entirely fit the computer screen.
- Auditory cues are likely to be most evidently useful when tasks are demanding, so we wanted a task that was simple to understand yet difficult to perform.
- We expected sound to affect collaboration, and so wanted a task that would encourage shared work.
- Finally, we wanted a task that would seem natural and engaging for participants, so they would not be bored or confused during our studies.

The ARKola simulation seemed to fulfill these requirements quite well. We stress, however, that though this simulation may seem more representative of video games or process control tasks than of traditional workstation domains, we believe it shares many features with – and thus our results are relevant to – more traditional domains. Although we were interested in testing several functions for auditory icons within this environment, for the purposes of this paper I focus primarily on aspects directly relevant for collaborative work (for a more complete description of this work, see Gaver et al., 1991).

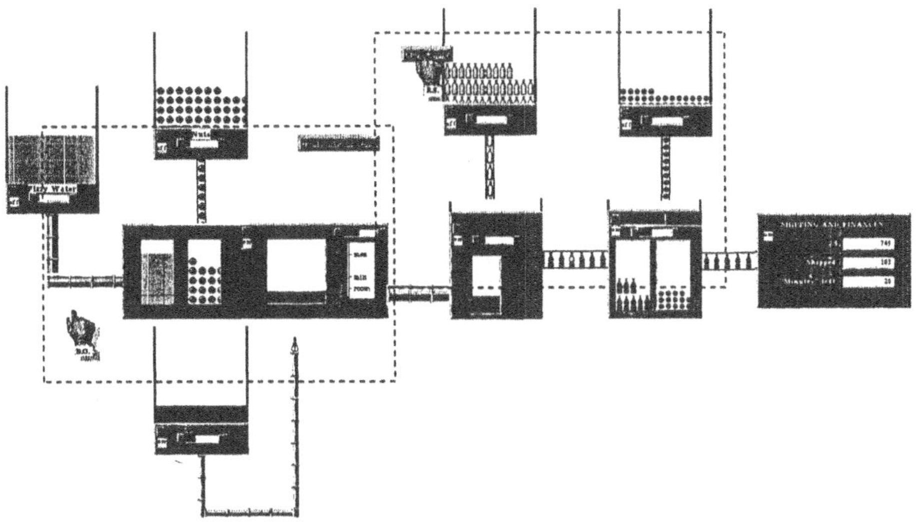

Figure 2: The ARKola bottling plant simulation. Nine machines mix, cook, bottle, cap, and count bottles of simulated cola. Mouse-driven hands are used to move and press buttons, control machines, etc. Dotted rectangles show the approximate extent of the view each user could have of the plant. (This figure is approximately one-fifth actual size.)

The plant, shown in Figure 2, consists of a virtual assembly line for producing a simulated softdrink. Users control the plant using mouse-driven "hands" to activate machine controls and to move and activate "buttons" which order new supplies or repair broken machines. Completed bottles of cola add funds to a virtual "bank account" at the end of the line; buying supplies or repairs deplete funds. The goal of participants, then, was to make money by producing as much cola as possible as efficiently as possible.

The simulation was implemented in SharedARK, a collaborative version of the Alternate Reality Kit (Smith, 1987); thus the simulated softdrink was called ARKola and the plant named accordingly. SharedARK, a fascinating environment in its own right, was used here as a foundation for developing the visual appearance and actions of the plant and participants' interactions with it.

Feedback about the status of the plant was provided by visual and auditory cues. Supplies could be heard as they moved along: cooking cola burbled, the capping machine clanged, and wasted supplies crashed and spilled audibly. Although some attempt was made to equate the information presented audibly with that displayed graphically, the purpose of the experiment was not to compare the two media in terms of effectiveness, but rather to understand their different characters.

The bottling plant was designed to be too large to fit on a computer screen, so each participant could only view part of the plant at a given time. However, participants could move their view by "sliding" their screen over the plant. Thus people could coordinate their views to work with a shared focus, or use separate views and divide their labour.

Observing collaboration on the plant

We observed eight pairs of people using the system for two one-hour sessions apiece; one session with and one without auditory feedback. Half the participants had auditory feedback on their first sessions and half did not. Partners worked on the system from different offices in the building, working together in the "same" factory shown on different workstations and communicating via a two-way audio and video link. Figure 3 shows the experimental set-up for the two offices.

We collected video-taped data upon which we based our observations of plant usage both from the subjects' audio-video links and from cameras pointing at each of their screens. Our observations are informal, relying mainly on occasions when participants explicitly referred to the sounds. We were able to cull a number of suggestive examples of the use of sounds. We take our data, then, as providing hypotheses for further testing and exploration.

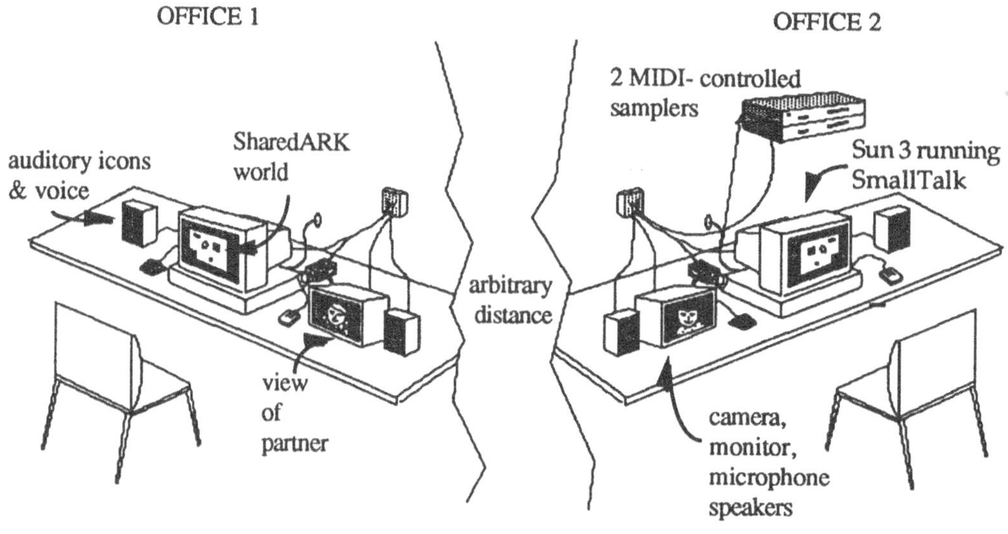

Figure 3. Setup for the ARKola experiment. Subjects worked in separate offices, collaborating on the ARKola simulation and communicating via an audio-video link. Data was collected from their camera and from cameras pointing at the computer screens.

Collaboration in the ARKola Simulation

We were struck with the great degree to which participants divided the labour of running the system in this study. We had not expected this, but our observations indicated that division of labour was encouraged by the design of the simulation. The plant divides rather neatly into two halves, with the four machines on the left (which produce cola) connected to the five on the right (which bottle and cap it) by only one pipe. In addition, the operation of the cooking half did not depend on bottling at all, while incoming cola was buffered by the bottling machine, reducing time dependency on the cooking half. Because the two sides were relatively independent, then, and because there was only one connection between them, each could be run without much care for the other – though of course successful performance on the task itself required that both sides be well run.

The tendency for participants to divide the task was made apparent by the large amounts of time that they spent using different views on the system. After an initial period during which the partners would usually wander over the plant together in order to orient themselves to the machines, they almost always separated and seldom shared views again. (For instance, participants M. and H. made this explicit. M: *"Maybe this is a good strategy, actually, to look after half of the world each..."* H: *"Yes, then we can... keep an eye on machines and see them break straight away."*) This division of labour was also made evident in their conversations. Although each would comment to the other about events and progress on their respective sides of the plant, longer conversations in which the two would collaborate on solving a problem were relatively rare.

The addition of auditory cues seemed to change this pattern of division of labour to a noticeable extent. Although subjects still maintained separate views to a great degree, their conversations seemed to reflect a greater degree of concern for events on their partner's side. (For instance, in one tape E is working on the cooker half and P on the bottling half. P remarks on a sound made by a machine on the other side of the plant: *"Isn't that the fizzy water that's leaking?"* E: *"I don't think it's leaking... I think it's just going into the tank."* Caps start spilling on P's side. P: *"Ok, I'm losing, uh..."* E: *"That's the caps."* P: *"caps..."* P turns off cap dispenser.) While joint problem-solving was relatively rare without sound, it became common with auditory feedback.

The ability for both partners to hear events seems to be the key to sounds' effect on their collaboration in this task. Running the ARKola simulation was relatively demanding, requiring constant attention to the state of supply hoppers and the flow of materials through the plant. Leaving one's area of responsibility was risky in that some disaster was liable to occur; without auditory feedback this would go unnoticed until one's return. Because partners could not see each others area of the plant, joint problem-solving required verbal descriptions of plant status and made problem solving much more difficult for the distant partner. Each participant tended to focus on his or her own responsibilities, without the possibility of direct awareness of other events.

Auditory feedback allowed users to be aware of parts of the plant that were not visible on the screen or at the focus of their visual attention. Thus participants could refer directly to sounds from their partner's half of the plant and hear problems occurring in areas on which they were not focussing. (For example, when bottles started breaking on T's side of the plant, his partner, S, said: *"Bottles are breaking!"* T: *"Where?"* S: *"I don't know, but they're breaking..."*) Being able to hear the status of the plant also reduced the risk of venturing to other areas of the plant. If problems did occur during one's absence, they were likely to be heard. In providing a new dimension of reference for partners running the plant, auditory cues seemed to ease the transition between division of labour and collaboration in this system.

Of course, the sounds we used were not without their problems. Care was needed to ensure that the auditory feedback was loud enough to be heard without preventing conversation, for example – though this is not a difficult task, it is a crucial one. In addition, designing the sounds to work together so that all could be heard was quite demanding (see Gaver et al. 1990 for a description of our approach to this problem). Finally, some of the sounds were more effective than others. Most notably, when a supply hopper ran out of supplies its sound simply stopped. We had expected that participants would notice the cessation of sound and refill the hopper; instead the sound's absence often went unnoticed. Nonetheless, the majority of sounds seemed informative and useful to subjects.

In sum, the auditory feedback used in this system had important effects on participants' collaboration. Sound provided a new dimension of reference for subjects. By increasing ways to maintain awareness it smoothed the transition between division of labour and focussed collaboration. Being able to hear the status of offscreen machines allowed a dissociation of focussed visual attention and more general awareness, so that each participant could have an area of primary responsibility and still join together to solve problems.

It is important to stress that we expect these findings to be relevant to a broad range of shared software, not just the sort of process control simulation described here. As systems become more powerful, they are increasingly likely to demand the scheduling and control of simultaneous tasks which are often hidden or invisible – and collaborative as well. The ARKola simulation was designed as it was precisely to embody these features in a self-motivating task domain, so that our results would be broadly relevant.

Our observations of the ARKola simulation in use are indicative of the potential for auditory cues in collaborative software systems. Such cues can also support awareness of events and activities beyond the computer in the encompassing workplace. I explore these possibilities in the next section.

Ambient audio in the workplace

A great many collaborative activities take place in the office environment, ranging from relatively formal meetings to more casual encounters. Just as there is a tension in collaborative software systems between enforcing a shared focus and allowing individual activities, so are there tensions in the workplace between encouraging group engagement and providing for individual work. As with collaborative software, group engagement in the workplace depends on a shared context – meeting rooms, open spaces, and established office hours. But individual work is facilitated by individual control over the environment – private offices, work at home, or work during off-hours.

In the everyday world, this tension is mitigated to some degree by the naturally-occurring auditory environment. We often listen to ambient sounds in the workplace in order to maintain awareness of our colleagues' activities. As I write this, for instance, I can hear automobiles and buses pass by on the street below, people walking by outside my office, and the sudden roar of the copier machine being used. As with collaborative software, these sounds may provide the sorts of awareness useful for moving in and out of close collaboration. For example, hearing Paul enter his office next door may prompt me to ask him about some project of mutual interest. Hearing the murmur of voices from outside my office may encourage me to join in an informal discussion with my colleagues. Hearing nearby events in the building can support casual awareness of others or indicate ongoing meetings, whether serendipitous or formal.

Hearing events in the workplace can draw us into them; but in large buildings many will go unheard. In addition, many potentially relevant events don't make informative sounds. For instance, hearing Paul leave his office may tell me he is unavailable, but not whether he is going to a meeting, to fetch some coffee, or to the pub. And of course, naturally-occurring sounds can be irritating, as sounds of the rush of traffic, the roar of the copier, and the blare of Paul's stereo often are. Such sounds are annoying because they are not informative or relevant: Noise is uninformative sound. In general, the ambient audio environment of the workplace can be useful, easing the tension between group and individual work. But sound can also pose problems: not all events may be heard, some important events may not make sounds, and the sounds events do make may be annoying.

EAR: Environmental Audio Reminders

For the past year and more, we have been using a system at EuroPARC which allows us to design informative ambient audio environments in our workplace. Called EAR, for Environmental Audio Reminders, this system triggers short, unobtrusive audio cues which are transmitted to offices around the building in order to inform people about ongoing events or to remind them about upcoming ones. Using this system, we can smoothly expand the naturally-occurring office ambience so that we can hear events out of earshot, and events which don't ordinarily make sounds. This work can be seen as moving auditory icons out of the workstation and into the world, so that the working environment itself becomes the interface. From this perspective, the strategy guiding the use of sound to facilitate collaboration in workstation environments can be applied to the overall work environment as well.

The EAR system relies on two interesting features of EuroPARC's environment. The first is a data-base of events called Khronika (Lövstrand, 1991) which allows a wide range of events to be browsed, edited and indicated by various cues. Khronika controls the generation of audio cues which are routed to speakers in particular rooms by the second system, a computer-controlled audio-video network (Buxton & Moran, 1989). The net result of this environment is that events generate designed audio cues that can be heard remotely.

As with the design of auditory icons for workstation environments, two design constraints are important in shaping the auditory cues used in EAR. First, the sounds must be semantically related to the messages they are meant to convey. This is achieved by using sampled environmental sounds that are either causally or metaphorically related to their referents. The second constraint is that they be acoustically shaped to avoid distraction and annoyance. Our strategy for creating unobtrusive sounds has been guided by work on designing sets of auditory alert sounds of appropriate perceived urgency (Patterson, 1989). For instance, most of the sounds we are designing have relatively slow onsets, which means they do not startle or distract listeners but instead slowly emerge from the natural auditory ambience of the office. In general, we try to maintain a balance between designing auditory cues that have clearly recognizable semantic content and designing them to be acoustically appropriate.

EAR in action

EAR is used to play audio cues which support casual awareness of one another, indicate opportunities for casual (and perhaps serendipitous) communication, and inform us about more focussed and formal events in our working environment. For instance, meetings are signalled by the sound of murmuring voices slowly growing in number, ended by the sound of a gavel. The sound interrupts individual work discreetly, reminding the listener about a prior engagement to join with other members of the lab. We view teatime, on the other hand, as an opportunity for informal communication. Each afternoon people in the building are invited to take tea by the sound of boiling water, followed by sounds of pouring water and spoons stirring in teacups. This sound serves as a more gentle reminder to those of us concentrating on our work that we might want to join our colleagues. Finally, sounds have evolved to indicate even very informal meetings. For instance, in the evening one of us is likely to trigger the pub-call, which plays the sounds of a pint being poured in a background of people talking and laughing.

These sounds serve as unobtrusive yet effective announcements of events in the workplace. They don't interrupt ongoing work, and can easily be ignored (though meeting sounds are likely to be heeded). Because they are stereotypical versions of the sorts of sounds we might hear around the building every day, the auditory cues used in EAR provide an effective and intuitive way to call people together and keep them informed of events around the building.

The EAR system also uses a number of auditory cues to indicate events in the electronic environment. For instance, the arrival of email can be accompanied by the sound of several pieces of paper falling on a surface, like letters falling through a mail slot. Other auditory cues are valuable in maintaining our awareness of the status of our audio-video network. This network allows people to connect their monitors to cameras around the building to gain a sense of "virtual co-presence" with distant colleagues. Because there is no visual indication when somebody accesses the signal from a camera (and video symmetry is not enforced), a pervasive sense of monitoring might be expected to result. But the EAR system allows audio feedback about connections, so that when somebody connects to my camera I hear the sound of a door creaking open; when they disconnect I hear the door shut. These simple audio cues provide invaluable feedback about the state of the audio-video network and seem to bolster feelings of privacy control to a significant degree. In addition, they can serve to tell us about a wider context of activities than is revealed by the network alone. For instance, auditory cues are used to distinguish the purpose of an audio-video connection: Different sounds indicate "vphone" calls; casual, one-way glances; and camera accesses by our framegrabber service.

Many of the sounds we use in EAR may seem frivolous because they are cartoon-like stereotypes of naturally-occuring sounds. But it is precisely *because* they are stereotyped sounds that they are effective. Using sounds that mimic those made by actual events means that the mapping between the information to be conveyed and the sound used to represent it can be quite close, and thus easy to learn and remember. While the sounds we use must be introduced to new users, they are quickly understood and seldom forgotten. It seems unlikely that more "serious" sounds – such as electronic beeps or sequences of tones – would be as effective at providing information in an intuitive and subtle way.

Like the sounds in the ARKola simulation, the cues about our electronic environment indicate computer events without demanding visual attention. But because the primary purpose is to provide cues about events in the workplace, the system has the further effect of bringing the two environments closer. The workstation is no longer the sole source of information about the electronic environment; instead electronic events are made an integral part of the general environment.

EAR is an installed system, constantly evolving to reflect our current needs and opinions about the auditory cues. Thus we have taken a strategy of "evaluation by use," in which cues which do not seem useful or which are annoying are discarded or redesigned. Generally this evolution has involved the introduction of subtle variations between cues. For instance, soon after the door-opening sound was introduced to indicate camera accessing, new sounds appeared which differentiate between short connections made by colleagues and connections made by an application which digitizes images and makes them available to colleagues overseas.

In sum, the auditory cues used in the EAR system can be unobtrusive, informative, and valuable. They serve to indicate events in the same way that they might be heard in everyday life, with the added advantage that the events cued are chosen by users. They allow us to hear distant events, or events that don't naturally produce informative noises, helping to blur the distinction between the electronic and physical environments. Perhaps most importantly, by informing us about ongoing events in the building they help to ease the transition between working alone and working together.

Discussion

The ARKola simulation and EAR system complement one another as examples of the use of auditory cues in collaborative systems. Where the ARKola simulation explored the design of auditory cues that support collaboration within the workstation environment, the EAR system demonstrates that similar principles can guide the design of useful auditory cues in the more general working environment as well. In ARKola, auditory cues were crucial sources of information, whereas in the EAR system sounds generally support a relatively unconscious awareness of ongoing events.

But though the two systems are different in many ways, parallels can be drawn in the functions auditory cues perform in each. In both the ARKola simulation and the EAR system, auditory cues make use of sound as a new medium for increasing awareness of events and activities which are not visually available. The effect of this new dimension of reference seems to be that users can simultaneously maintain visual attention on a potentially shared focus of work while remaining aware of a wider context of interest. This ability, in turn, seems to lead to smoother transitions between different ways of sharing work.

The functions auditory cues play in the ARKola simulation and the EAR system should be broadly applicable to a number of CSCW systems. The tension between maintaining a shared focus and allowing individual control over work seems common in the class of collaborative tools that allow synchronous editing of objects (Bellotti et al., 1991). Our observations of the ARKola simulation suggest that this tension may be reduced by exploiting sound as an alternative medium for presenting and receiving information. So, for instance, users of a shared document editor might hear their partners' editing operations even when such activities are offscreen. Such sounds could be useful in coordinating activities ("...it sounds like you're making major changes up there – should I hold off on this section?").

Similarly, experiences with EAR suggest that using auditory cues to communicate contextual information in the workplace itself can facilitate the flow of engagement among colleagues. For example, just as EAR allows us to hear activities in distant parts of our building, so might users of systems supporting virtual co-presence hear activities in distant environments. Such sounds could provide a natural means for indicating potentials for casual or focussed engagement by conveying contextual information which might otherwise be lost.

I have shown in this paper some of the functions sound can perform in collaborative systems. But it should be stressed that our work on the use of auditory cues to facilitate collaboration has only just begun. Both the ARKola simulation and EAR are suggestive, but neither is definitive; the potential of sound as an intuitive, unobtrusive medium for communication promises to be much richer than either of these applications can show.

Acknowledgements

The ARKola study was done in collaboration with Randall Smith and Tim O'Shea; the EAR system with Lennart Lövstrand. I thank Allan MacLean for his many insightful comments on this work, and give particular thanks to Victoria Bellotti and Paul Dourish for many helpful discussions about the nature of sharing.

References

Bellotti, V., Dourish, P., & MacLean, A. (1991). From users themes to designers DReams: Developing a design space for shared interactive technologies. EuroPARC/AMODEUS Working Paper RP6-WP7.

Buxton, B., & Moran, T. (1990). EuroPARC's Integrated Interactive Intermedia Facility (IIIF): Early experiences. *Proceedings of the IFIP WG8.4 Conference on Multi-user Interfaces and Applications*, Heraklion, Crete, September.

CSMIL (1989). ShrEdit: A multi-user shared text editor: Users manual. Cognitive Science and Machine Intelligence Laboratory, The University of Michigan.

Ellis, C., Gibbs, S., & Rein, G. (1988). Design and use of a group editor. MCC Technical Report Number STP-263-88.

Gaver, W. W. (1986). Auditory icons: Using sound in computer interfaces. *Human-Computer Interaction*. 2, 167 - 177.

Gaver, W. W. (1989). The SonicFinder: An interface that uses auditory icons. *Human-Computer Interaction*. 4 (1).

Gaver, W. W., & Smith, R. B. (1990). Auditory icons in large-scale collaborative environments. *Human-Computer Interaction – Interact'90.* D. Diaper et al. (eds.) Elsevier, North-Holland.

Gaver, W. W., Smith, R. B., & O'Shea, T. (1991). Effective sounds in complex systems: The ARKola simulation. *Proceedings of CHI 1991*, New Orleans, April 28 - May 2, 1991, ACM, New York.

Goodman, G., & Abel, M. (1987). Communication and collaboration: Facilitating cooperative work through communication. *Office: Technology and People, 3* (2), 129 - 146.

Lövstrand, L. (1991). Being selectively aware with the Khronika system. In the Proceedings of ECSCW'91, Amsterdam, The Netherlands.

MacLean, A., Young, R., & Moran, T. (1989). Design Rationale: The argument behind the artifact. *Proceedings of CHI'89: Human Factors in Computing Systems,* April 30 - May 4, Austin, Texas, 247 - 252. New York: ACM.

Mantei, M. (1988). Capturing the Capture Lab concepts: A case study in the design of computer supported meeting environments. *Proceedings of the Conference on Computer-Supported Collaborative Work.* Portland, Ore., September 1988, 257 - 270.

Moran, T. P., & Anderson, R. J. (1990). The workaday world as a paradigm for CSCW design. *Proceedings of CSCW 90* (Los Angeles, U.S., October 1990).

Patterson, R. D. (1989). Guidelines of the design of auditory warning sounds. *Proceedings of the Institute of Acoustics 1989 Spring Conference. 11* (5), 17 - 24.

Root, R. (1988). Design of a multi-media vehicle for social browsing. *Proceedings of the Conference on Computer-Supported Collaborative Work.* Portland, Ore., September 1988, 25 - 38.

Smith, R. B. (1989). A prototype futuristic technology for distance education. *Proceedings of the NATO Advanced Workshop on New Directions in Educational Technology.* (Nov. 10 - 13, 1988, Cranfield, U.K.)

Smith, R. B. (1987). The Alternate Reality Kit: an example of the tension between literalism and magic. *Proceedings of CHI + GI 1987* (Toronto, Canada, April 5 - 9, 1987) ACM, New York, 61 - 67.

Proceedings of the Second European Conference on Computer-Supported Cooperative Work
Bannon, L., Robinson, M. & Schmidt, K. (Editors)
September 25-27, 1991, Amsterdam, The Netherlands

CSCW: Discipline or Paradigm?

A sociological perspective

John Hughes, Dave Randall and Dan Shapiro

Department of Sociology and Centre for Research in CSCW, Lancaster University, UK

We argue there is still much confusion about what is meant by cooperative work, and therefore what is meant by CSCW. It does not arise simply where more than one person is involved, and other attempts to delimit the field do not succeed. Since all work is socially organised, it would seem that all work potentially falls within the CSCW domain. If so, then (i) it would not be confined to a particular class of system ('groupware'); (ii) it would not be a small specialism but would extend virtually throughout system design; and (iii) its interdisciplinary character would affect large areas of its contributing disciplines. We defend these consequences, and argue that CSCW is therefore more akin to a paradigm shift for its contributing disciplines than a particular subdiscipline in itself. We also consider not what CSCW *is* but *how it has arisen* in terms of a political economy - the interests of researchers, funding institutions and clients - and a set of ideologies. This sets out a position for contributing disciplines, but leaves open the detailed content of interdisciplinary relations.

CSCW has now acquired considerable momentum. It has engaged the interest of researchers in both academic and commercial environments, gained the attentions of commercial think-tanks, systems houses and service providers, and raised hopes and spirits among potential users/victims. But what is it? This will soon, if it has not already, become a tiresome question, but we think it still worth another round or two. We would not have dared to venture it if we were not also involved with 'real' CSCW at the coalface (Harper et al, 1991; Ackroyd et al, forthcoming; Harper at al, forthcoming).

Attempts to define CSCW

Most practitioners, we think, get by with assuming three semi-articulated characteristics of CSCW. First, that it involves settings where two or more people interact with each other through a computer. Second, that it is to do with a particular class of system to service such settings (perhaps not just groupware, but something along those lines). Third, that it is interdisciplinary. We will not be proposing that there is any one right answer, and there is something to each of these characteristics, but for a sociological participation they pose some interesting problems.

Multiple users: multiple disciplines

It seems obvious that cooperation can only be taking place where more than one person is involved. It must therefore be appropriate to consider this as a distinct class of activities or situations, which may call for distinct techniques and design principles to address them. It is this which is calling into being the distinct discipline or subdiscipline of CSCW. We could think of this model as involving a *spatial* or *territorial metaphor* for the division of labour between areas of academic research. Each speciality would be said to cover a particular 'terrain'; these specialities may, in principle at least, be cumulative in contributing to the sum of scientific knowledge; although there will, of course, be fuzzy edges where they abut and where disciplinary affiliation is unclear.

This model can also accommodate the *interdisciplinarity* which is one of CSCW's strongest features. Because CSCW involves cooperative relations in organisations, system design is likely to be improved by consulting those whose speciality it is to study organisational forms, functions and behaviours. On the 'map', therefore, CSCW can be placed on the boundaries of computer science, sociology, organisational and management studies, perhaps even anthropology; not to mention older HCI concerns which already place it on the boundaries of psychology, linguistics and ergonomics. The task - daunting because of the strangeness of some of the bedfellows but attainable in principle nevertheless - is therefore to constitute a new discipline or subdiscipline by 'bounding' a territory where they overlap while seeking to dissolve some of the demarcation lines within that territory. Meanwhile, *other* areas of computer science and system design continue relatively untouched.

From a sociological perspective, however, the notion of 'cooperative work' is a puzzling one, both in the sense of there being a distinctive class of collective work, and of there being a distinctive class of work which is 'helpful' or 'harmonious'. We rather consider that *all* of work is - ie can helpfully be analysed as - socially organised. We say more about what this means below, but at its broadest it involves the claim that it makes no more sense to consider 'work' as individual than to consider language as individual: they cannot exist outside of a collective context. This not only widens the scope of a sociological approach to work but also calls into question the spatial metaphor of interdisciplinary relations. As it happens, the distinction between one and more than one participants is already familiar because it has often been proposed - along the lines of the spatial metaphor - as the means of establishing a disciplinary division of labour between psychology and sociology. A classical illustration of this would be in contrasting sociological and psychological treatments of a phenomenon such as 'aggression'. On the basis of the spatial metaphor, psychology would be invoked to explain why a man picks a fight in a bar, while sociology would be invoked to account for wars. But there is also a quite different model - a 'searchlight' metaphor, perhaps - in which each discipline offers a competing explanation and perspective on the *same* terrain of phenomena. That is, psychological perspectives might account both for a fight in a bar and for war (and for football hooliganism in between) in terms of instincts, or mental states, or triggers for violent behaviour; while sociological perspectives might account for the same things in terms of the social settings and circumstances in which violence can be forbidden, condoned or expected, or in terms of structured conflicts of interest. Of course, both can attempt to reconcile their explanations, explore common ground and renounce a disciplinary imperialism: no psychologist, for example, would in everyday life try to account for the Gulf War in only these terms, and similarly for sociologists. The point, however, is that the methods and premises of their disciplines will press them towards one kind of account rather than another, and one cannot know in advance how much of a challenge to those methods and premises an attempt at reconciliation may pose. Hence this impacts directly on another tacit assumption of CSCW, that 'classical' HCI, grounded primarily in psychology, was appropriate and adequate for 'individual' systems but is no longer sufficient for collective ones.

It is, nevertheless, true that all work, however complex the interactions it involves, is carried out by individuals. It may therefore make sense, as one approach to the analysis of work (though not as an 'essentialism' of how work arises), to consider the ways in which work processes are 'individuated' - that is, translated into things that persons can do. Various 'mechanisms of individuation' are possible, including organisational forms, the decomposition of work, and of course particular technologies. Hence one could say that there is a *social* process of the *individuation* of work, in which CSCW offers a radical intervention.

Characteristics of the work process

Of course, there have not only been casual and tacit assumptions about CSCW, but also very carefully considered attempts to delineate the field (eg Bannon & Schmidt, 1991; Schmidt, 1991a). These have tried various means to constrain its range and make it manageable, beside the distinction between single and multiple users (Bannon & Schmidt, 1991, p. 5). Schmidt, for example, proposes that we treat cooperative work as that which is *related as to content.* From this he draws the subordinate distinctions that cooperative work is different from social interaction at work in general; that it relates to production and not consumption; that it requires some organisational form; and involves deliberate rather than accidental relations (1991a, p. 10). Useful as these distinctions are, we think they also encounter interesting difficulties.

Schmidt argues that,

> Cooperative work, as used here, is constituted by *work processes that are related as to content*, that is, processes pertaining to the production of a particular product or type of products. Cooperative work, then, is a far more specific concept than social interaction in the system of work in general. The concept pertains to the sphere of production. It does not apply to every interaction pertaining to the running of, say, a company. (1991a, p. 10, o.e.)

As a prescription for a *concept* of cooperative work this has much to recommend it. Problems arise, though, when we ask in concrete terms what the work process is and how it is to be discovered, since units or aspects of the work process bear no 'flags' with which to identify themselves. It is (as Schmidt agrees) not confined to the organisation, it is certainly not congruent with the organisation's official model of itself, it spills over into endless ramifications of connections and sub-connections. *Practitioners* will be only partially conscious of these relations and only partially able to report them accurately and succinctly. We cannot, therefore, simply ask practitioners to relate these matters to us. If the *researcher* is to trace them, then on what basis? An obvious choice presents itself of following either the *logic of the task*, or the *network of the group*. If the former, then the researcher will be powerfully drawn into idealisations of task processes which reflect his or her existing perspectives and which govern the way in which activities are ruled to be 'pertinent' or 'peripheral' for the task. The result will certainly be limited and may often be 'wrong'; that is, that designing on the basis of these judgements will in the event prove disruptive of the tasks in hand. The latter - the network of the group - is initially attractive because it appears to offer a more empirical approach to the problem: the researcher can *observe* the interactions that really do take place with a minimum of preconceptions about what they must be. The difficulties here, though, are that interactions spill over into each other in an even more uncontrolled way than tasks do. Without some way of categorising them in relation to function and purpose the results are unusable. But if they are so categorised then all the problems of task analysis re-emerge. What is more, some task relations, particularly of the 'coordination' kind (Schäl and Zeller, 1990), may take place without interaction at all.

Of course, in a sense this is simply what social research is like, and one has to cope with it without undue carping. In investigating the world of work, the complexities and unboundedness of tasks and of interactions simply exist and one must try and make sense of them. The key point, however, is that this is *a part of* the job of analysis, not a prior means of defining and constraining the field so that research can be more efficiently focussed and coherent.

This similarly affects the proposal that cooperative work can be confined to that which is deliberate rather than accidental, and does not spill over into social interactions in work in general. Take the not entirely frivolous example of colleagues who meet regularly in the bar at lunchtime but never exchange a single word related to their work. Yet the relationship established and reinforced in this way would certainly affect the way in which they provide work services for each other at other times. More plausibly, of course, in bars, coffee breaks, and indeed in the office and on the factory floor, conversation will slide constantly and barely discernibly between being work and non-work related. Hence the CSCW projects which aim to support informal interaction do indeed have a point (eg Fish et al, 1990).

Without wishing to labour the point, one could say that there are also difficulties with the distinction between *production* which is organisationally related and *consumption* which is mediated by the market. The social construction of markets and their negotiated and 'imperfect' character are central in debates in institutional economics (Williamson, 1975; Granovetter, 1985) and in sociological discussions of the 'modes of governance' of economic sectors (Schmitter, 1988). In the language of these 'governance' debates, it is, at the least, necessary to consider the ways in which hierarchical, networked, and corporatist forms modify the operation of markets. More mundanely, 'pure' markets can certainly be supported by technological arrangements of a potentially 'cooperative' kind, eg stock exchange dealing systems.

We would argue, therefore, that these and other attempts do not succeed in any practically relevant sense in reducing the entirety of socially organised work to some smaller subset to which we can confine our attentions for the purposes of CSCW. None of this is to deny that there are tasks which *can* be relatively solitary, such as painting a room or word-processing a document. That is, within socially organised work there will be greater and lesser degrees of complexity (though this too will be quite hard to discern). With respect to this we would, however, add: (a) that this is nevertheless a relative distinction and not an absolute one; (b) that it involves a somewhat constraining model of the activity which is quite historical, eg as soon as we are able to, we support collective authoring, common printing, various modes of despatching a paper, etc; and (c) that these examples appear so prominent, significant and ubiquitous precisely because that is where systems have seemed 'obvious' and have fitted well. Once away from this rut, the world of 'individual' work may look much smaller. Nor does this approach deny that work can usefully be analysed in terms of types of cooperation. Schmidt (1991a), for example, proposes that cooperation takes place sometimes for augmentation and sometimes for differentiation of capacities and tasks, for the discount of biases and the integration of perspectives, etc; while Schäl and Zeller (1990) propose a distinction between coordination, collaboration and co-decision. What we are contesting, rather, is any view that there is a mass of 'individual' tasks that have been relatively well served by computer support but that there is now a separate set of 'cooperative' tasks for which we need to derive specialised techniques for computer support. We maintain that all work is (amongst other things) socially organised; that most significant tasks are *complexly* social; and that it is largely for this reason that they have sometimes been poorly served by computer systems.

What conclusions should be drawn from these difficulties in circumscribing the field? If it does not seem possible to do this then one may begin to wonder whether CSCW is a coherent topic at all. We propose two ways forward. One, which we consider later, is to continue to seek some coherence for the field. The other, which we consider now, is to try to account for the field, not in terms of *what it is* but instead in terms of *how it has arisen.*

The development of CSCW

In accounting for how CSCW has arisen we do not intend, and would not be qualified, to give a history. We mean rather to consider in quite a speculative way the forces that have motivated participants and pressed them in some directions rather than others. We can broach this in terms of, on the one hand, a political economy and, on the other, an ideology of CSCW. We will also consider some substantive issues which have formed a context for its development. Taken together, these should help to explain how the social organisation of work in general has been translated into particular types of design.

Political economy

We can distinguish three main 'parties' to the development of CSCW: researchers, funding institutions, and clients. Obviously these can overlap, eg clients can employ researchers. Among researchers we can currently distinguish three main disciplinary affiliations: computer science, HCI, and sociology. These must be understood broadly: HCI to cover a range of psychological and ergonomic approaches; sociology to cover organisational and management studies, anthropology, etc.

Among researchers in computer science and HCI the development of CSCW can be understood as a reaction to the relative failure of systems to provide the anticipated levels of support in various work contexts (Grudin, 1988). That in turn does not exist in a vacuum. Buyers and users of computer-based systems have arguably entered a new phase of expectations. In the recent past they may have been simply terrified or overawed or implacably sceptical. Now, many are more critical in requiring systems to accommodate to them in ways which they find useful. That has forced a reappraisal of the basis on which systems are designed. It is also, perhaps, a response to a certain disenchantment with aspects of computer science such as AI, which carried the highest profile and expectations in the early '80s.

So far as sociological participation is concerned, an earlier generation of research which criticised the failure of computer-based systems to recognise that work is socially organised, suddenly found itself pushing at an open door in a remarkable convergence of concerns and interests. This has produced what is (except, perhaps, for management studies) a most unfamiliar situation in which the interdisciplinary participation of sociologists is being actively sought and generously funded. The field is not yet widely enough known for this to have turned into a gold-rush, but that cannot be far off.

Funding institutions can be divided into public sector agencies, and large corporations which fund some basic research, either integrated with their general research effort or devolved to separate 'think tanks'. All of these are now under more pressure to justify their expenditures. CSCW has been able to present an attractive combination since it offers - and may even yet deliver - to make use of significant theoretical departures to break a log-jam in providing services which will enhance efficiency and competitiveness. CSCW has also succeeded in becoming a field in which the US, Europe, and increasingly Japan are in competition.

'Clients' for the most part still do not consist of end users, but software and hardware houses who wish to develop products incorporating the new design philosophy, and service providers such as telecommunications organisations for whom this could offer a new and intensive class of business. They will naturally be tempted to look for quick results, and to 'oversell' new products. When it comes to developing CSCW systems for use in real organisations then some difficult dilemmas are likely to emerge. We mentioned above that for us the notion of 'cooperative work' is a puzzling one, both in the sense of there being a distinctive class of collective work, and of there being a distinctive class of work which is 'helpful' or 'harmonious'. The emphasis in sociology has rather - and perhaps excessively so - been the reverse: to view organisations as sites of multiple structured and overlapping *conflicts* of interest and practice which are, nevertheless, just as much socially organised as cooperation. That means that on top of the practical problems of the analysis of organisations, there will always be the problem of *which* aspects and interests to 'support'. The senior management of an organisation, who hold the reins in terms of ordering and specifying a system, will naturally be resistant to any suggestion that the real social organisation differs from the official model. Yet if they want a CSCW system at all it will be precisely for the power which the recognition of this organisational complexity can release. Practical and political problems for the designers of systems are therefore inevitable, since they will have to confront sponsors with the official 'lies' about their organisations!

However, there is also a broader sense of the political economy of the relationship between clients and CSCW systems, which stems from arguments about qualitative changes in the world of work. Recent theories of reorganisation and technical change have developed around notions of 'flexible accumulation' (Aglietta, 1987; Piore and Sabel, 1984; Atkinson, 1986). In these accounts a contrast is drawn between 'Fordism' and 'post-Fordism' as systems, or regimes, of production. Fordism, in the ascendancy from the early years of this century until roughly the 1970s, involved the mass production of relatively standard commodities, with the production line as its archetype. But it also involved a regime of mass consumption of those standard commodities. The true novelty of the system lay not just in the Taylorist methods of work decomposition and supervision, but in the fact that, for the first time, the consumers of these mass products were broadly the same people as their producers, rather than capital or luxury goods produced for élites by the toiling masses.

Post-Fordism - though the theory comes in different versions (Bagguley et al., 1990, pp. 18-26) - denotes the breakdown of this 'virtuous circle' of production. It is assailed partly from within, as the production line system meets its limits of efficiency and increasing resistance; and partly from without, as the demands of consumers move beyond the standardised mass commodity. The response of producers is claimed to be, on the one hand, the development of more specialised, innovative, differentiated and prestigious goods and services, sold into 'value-added' niche markets (Bourdieu, 1984). On the other hand, the structure of production also changes, being organised into smaller, more autonomous and responsive units capable of rapid shifts in what they produce and the processes by which they do so. This in turn is achieved through 'flexibility' (Atkinson, 1986). First, flexible technology, and particularly information technology, which allows relatively small runs of frequently changing goods and services to be delivered at high efficiency. Second, functional flexibility, whereby in place of the old demarcations and specialisations, workers are expected to exercise initiative in deploying a range of skills to suit the demands of the moment. Third, numerical flexibility, by which firms employ a 'core' of these valuable multi-valent workers, and a 'periphery' of low-skill staff who can be hired and fired to suit changing conditions. And fourth, subcontracting, allowing firms to externalise peripheral functions and distribute risk.

There is a deep ambivalence in the debates as to whether these developments mark a further turn in exploitation and the dominance of capital, or a broader societal development to which capital is forced to respond, with at the least mixed fortunes for labour, and a newly acknowledged position for the consumers of goods and services (Harvey, 1988). The emerging 'information society' is dependent on new kinds of computer system, and CSCW could be seen as an archetype of such developments. More concretely, to survive these transformations work organisations require support from advanced information systems that can facilitate the coordination of distributed decision making. This is illustrated by the efforts in the area of Computer Integrated Manufacturing to integrate formerly separated functions such as design and process planning, marketing and production planning, etc.; and by the efforts in the area of Office Information Systems to facilitate and enhance the exchange of information across organisational and professional boundaries (Schmidt, 1991b).

Given this overall context, there are two points of departure for the designers of CSCW systems. First, there are those areas of organisational life where the need for sophisticated computer support is felt most acutely, and where there are therefore market pressures and opportunities. However, since awareness of CSCW has not really penetrated amongst 'end-user' clients, that is not a category which yet exerts much force. There are indeed pressures in both public and private sectors to turn to computer systems as panaceas for problems, sometimes as little more than icons of modernity and purpose; but these do not as yet produce a demand for CSCW as opposed to any other kind of system. That, perhaps, is why designers are freer to take the second point of departure, namely the tools and problems that they already have. It will, as it were, always be easier to 'start from here'. Some tools have been discovered almost by accident to have CSCW properties - email is the most obvious example (Fafchamps et al., 1991) - and they form the basis for more deliberate development. It has often been remarked that CSCW developments betray a certain reflexivity in reflecting the work problems that their designers themselves experience - supporting either co-located or distributed design meetings, for example! That is an appropriate start, but will eventually prove too limited a sphere. It will always be the case, however, that existing techniques will impose a framework and limitations on design, which is why it is no bad thing for the 'strict constructionists' to have their head (Bannon & Schmidt, 1991, p. 7), at least as one avenue of development.

There is certainly no other sense, from our point of view, in which some categories of work are appropriate for computer support while others are not. 'Computer supported cooperative work' makes no more sense as a category than 'paper supported cooperative work'. This is not only to make the obvious point that a computer is (just) a tool. Rather, it is that both would be similarly absurd as a means to contain or define a set of work activities. Hence, just as focussing on *cooperative* work is not a means to delimit the field of CSCW, nor is focussing on *computer supportable* work.

Ideology

Ideologies in relation to CSCW cannot be divorced from a political economy since ideologies are not just independent and stable world views, but fluid constructions and rationalisations in a changing context. Academic disciplines justify themselves in various ways, but common to them all, of course, is the entertainment, game and career of intellectual activity. Those aspects of computer science that are concerned with designing systems for users have also an ideology of service: contributing to the capacity for creation and production (and sometimes - in terms of funding rather often - for destruction). For HCI such a notion is necessarily central. Sometimes that involves a more critical notion of service which is concerned about *who* benefits from systems and what uses they are put to; others are content to follow a market-led notion of utility. When systems seem to be failing, that is a problem for either version.

In the face of such limitations, turning to other disciplines is one avenue to explore, and it is very striking how desirable 'interdisciplinarity' has become in the eyes of public and private sponsors of research. One could see this in part as a response to a new climate of accountability, in which the need to deliver real solutions has produced a certain radicalism of approach. It must also, no doubt, relate to the depoliticisation of social science in the 1980s. Whatever the causes, this implies a renewed faith in the 'unity of all the sciences' which, as we have suggested, has its ideological aspects too (Anderson et al., 1989). There are also variations in ideological climate which have real effects on the development of CSCW. For example, Scandinavian experiments in forms of civil society and mixed economy have been reflected in a 'human relations' emphasis in organisational and political structures in which labour movements, broadly conceived, have been much more empowered; though these have come under sustained pressure in the 'market' decade of the 1980s (cf. Lash and Urry, 1987). This has also been reflected in the topics considered suitable for research funding and the criteria applied in evaluating them. Bowers and Benford (1991a, p. 313) point to what one might term a distinctive 'Scandinavian school' of CSCW, which is concerned to develop design methodologies which are themselves cooperative and participatory, which respect existing skills, and which can play a role in promoting workplace democracy (Ehn, 1988; Hellman, 1989; Bødker and Grønbæk, 1991; and see the contributors to Bjerknes et al., 1987).

Organisational change and design transparency

All this, however, leaves untouched what is perhaps the most fundamental question, namely why, if organisations are so complex and impenetrable, it is only now that an interdisciplinary approach seems so necessary. Since technological changes have been continuously taking place in organisations, this amounts to asking what it is that makes computer-induced change different, and why a computer system need be treated differently than any other tool. We argue that a combination of two features helps to explain this.

The first is the organisational *dynamics* of the introduction of computer-based systems. It is hard enough to generate an adequate picture of how an organisation functions, but even that is not sufficient. The intention of introducing a system is not to reproduce exactly the situation that was there before but to change and, hopefully, improve it. The purpose, as Schmidt puts it, is 'therapeutic' (1991a, p.

5). Even if that were not the aim it is still inevitable that there will be major changes in the way that tasks are carried out. In Winograd and Flores' terms, 'design is ontological' (1986; Bowers and Benford, 1991a, p.313). Introducing a system is to throw a stone into the pond of the organisation. However, that in itself does not amount to a difference between computers and other technologies since any major technological innovation can be expected to have such effects. The most that can be said - and it relates to debates of more than a century's standing about technological determinism in accounting for social change - is that some technologies are more 'powerful' than others. That is, they can seem to offer such huge advantages (from the perspective, at least, of some of those involved) that it is 'worth' the wholesale disruption of organisational forms and practices which they entail. That could be applied historically to the development of a centralised power source as a major factor in calling into being the factory system, and it could be applied to the role of the mainframe in centralising a whole range of functions which have since, with further technological change, been re-distributed.

The second and we think more distinctive feature is to do with the way in which technological change is accommodated. Members of organisations exercise great ingenuity in putting to work the human and material resources that they find to hand to serve their purposes - which may not, of course, be fully congruent with the formal purposes of the organisation. When changes are introduced people quickly learn their characteristics and discover how to get the best out of them. In this process of familiarisation, adaptation and 'old-handing', they use their knowledge and experience to modify what they can to suit them, and work around the rest. There is always, therefore, a substantial gap between the design or concept of a machine, a building, an organisational plan or whatever, and their operation in practice, and people are usually well able to effect this translation. Without these routine informal capacities most organisations would cease to function.

When computer systems are introduced people do the same. They explore the system's characteristics and turn them to use as best they may. The problem, however, is that there is a large difference, amounting we think to a qualitative difference, in the extent to which users are able to understand *how* a computer system functions so that they can tune it to suit them, by comparison with most of the other artefacts - including other technological artefacts - with which they have to work. This links to 'transparency' in system design and indeed to the whole notion of an interface. Since users *cannot be expected* to understand what the system is *really* doing, in algorithmic terms, in carrying out functions, these must nearly always be presented in terms of a metaphor. This process of protecting the user from knowledge of the operations of the system is, of course, precisely what is meant by 'transparency', though this is clearly a misnomer since in fact it is *opacity* which is the service delivered to the user. It is very hard to see how this problem can be addressed, but the effect is to make users significantly less empowered in relation to the technology and to limit the ways in which they can exercise ingenuity in old-handing the equipment. They are, in effect, uniquely at the mercy of the skill of the designer in constructing the metaphor for the interface, in a way which anticipates all the needs which may arise in practice. That is a task which designers will not usually be in a position to fulfil, and certainly not when working alone.

Discipline or paradigm?

We have argued so far that it does not make sense to define CSCW in terms of interactions with a system involving more than one user, or by specifying some particular characteristics of the work process, or in relation to a particular class of technology. That also, therefore, casts into doubt notions of CSCW as a particular discipline, or sub-discipline, or interdisciplinary combination of subdisciplines. It need not be a great surprise that clear defining features are hard to find, since CSCW is still in large measure a discursive phenomenon. That is, it is not a 'thing' in the real world which must therefore have features waiting to be discovered and then deciphered. It is, rather, a set of theoretical and practical proposals (as well as a set of practices) which have, as we have suggested, an ætiology, a political economy and various ideologies, but not necessarily any formal coherence or consistency. It could therefore be quite mythical to consider either that it must have a hidden coherence to be unearthed, or an 'essence' that can be derived from first principles and then prescribed.

We have, nevertheless, argued that there is a real substantive context in which computer-induced organisational change is qualitatively different from other technological change in ways that make interdisciplinary contributions relevant if not essential. Our view is simple but with far-reaching consequences, namely that CSCW should be viewed not as a specialised subdiscipline but as a general shift in the perspective from which computer support systems - *all* computer support systems - are designed. It would be excessive to label this a paradigm shift in the full Kuhnian sense (Kuhn, 1970), but the term paradigm may not be out of place. It involves recognising and gradually incorporating the view that functions in organisations do not exist in abstract but are - for anything short of full automation - borne by human agents embedded in complex social and interactional settings, which crucially modify the nature and operation of the 'functions' they have in their charge. Any attempt to treat that as pure system is bound to go wrong.

If we are proposing CSCW as a paradigm change for computer science, then how should sociology be affected? Sociology (and, of course, its associated disciplines) has, so far, been presented in a 'service' role for CSCW, in supplying the specialised knowledge of work and of organisations which it needs. This yields three related problems. First, it is hard to see why, other than financially, such a role should be of interest, since it would seem to involve just 'plugging in' existing knowledge and perspectives rather than original intellectual work. But, secondly, the discipline may not in fact stand up very well to the test of having the perspectives and analyses that it proposes incorporated into designs for support systems in the real world, since they were hardly developed in the first place with such an end in view. That is, it may have some difficulty in delivering on the territory it has staked out. And thirdly, if this confrontation is to produce a change in paradigm for computer science, then why should sociology be immune?

We think that taking CSCW seriously does indeed pose a real challenge for sociology. Much of the sociology of work, for example, makes empirical claims which are testable and operationalisable in principle, but it has hitherto been unclear how it could be tested, and indeed there has been little interest in doing so. It is unlikely, for example, that some of the simplistic claims of the earlier followers of Braverman's work on the labour process could have survived an attempt to put them in place. Hence substantial changes in the discipline should be expected, and indeed are necessary for its contribution to be useful. Sociology should be well able to accommodate such changes, since thoroughgoing shifts of theoretical emphasis occur quite frequently within the discipline. Since the mi-1980s many former theoretical certainties have been swept away. Amongst other things, and particularly relevant for our purposes, this has called into question formerly 'obvious' distinctions between 'theoretical' and 'applied' research. A new theoretico-empirical terrain is being formed, as much in the sociology of work and organisations as elsewhere, and the interdisciplinary confrontations invoked in CSCW can be a formative influence.

We have set out a *position* for sociology in relation to CSCW, but that is not the same as setting out a *stall*. To do that would involve specifying the different perspectives within the discipline with an actual or potential contribution. In doing that, some of the difficulties we have alluded to in reconciling the perspectives of different disciplines would be reproduced on this scale too. For example, although they are superficially close, it is an entirely different thing to analyse the division of labour in the labour process, and to produce an ethnomethodological account of a working division of labour. Setting out a stall for sociology would also involve focussing in a much more business-like way on the direct contributions that could be made to systems *design*, and indeed much of our current research is concerned with making the transition from formulating critiques of existing systems to activley participating in their specification and development. Those are large issues in their own right, however, and must remain as tasks for another occasion.

Acknowledgements

In thinking about these issues we have benefited from discussions in several different groups, and particularly with our colleagues in the Centre for Research in CSCW at Lancaster University, the EC COST 14 meetings on Cooperation Technology, the ESPRIT Basic Research group on interdisciplinary theory for CSCW, and the UK CSCW Special Interest Group. We are also very grateful for the comments of three not-so-anonymous but nonetheless biting referees.

References

Ackroyd, S., Harper, R., Hughes, J., Shapiro, D. and Soothill, K. (forthcoming): *New Technology and Practical Police Work*, Open University Press, Milton Keynes.

Aglietta, M. (1987): *A Theory of Capitalist Regulation*, Verso, London.

Anderson, R. J., Hughes, J. A. and Sharrock, W. W. (1989): *Working for Profit: the social organisation of calculation in an entrepreneurial firm*, Avebury, Aldershot.

Atkinson, J. (1986): *Changing Work Patterns: How Companies Achieve Flexibility to Meet New Needs*, National Economic Development Office, London.

Bagguley, P., Mark-Lawson, J., Shapiro, D., Urry, J., Walby, S. and Warde, A. (1990): *Restructuring: Place, Class & Gender*, Sage, London.

Bannon, L. and Schmidt, K. (1991): "CSCW: Four Characters in Search of a Context", in Bowers and Benford (1991b), pp. 3-16.

Bjerknes, G. et al. (eds.) (1987): *Computers and Democracy - a Scandinavian Challenge*, Gower, Aldershot.

Bødker, S. and Grønbæk, K. (1991): "Cooperative Prototyping Studies - users and designers envision a dental case record system", in Bowers and Benford (1991b), pp. 315-332.

Bourdieu, P. (1984): *Distinction: a Social Critique of the Judgement of Taste*, Routledge & Kegan Paul, London.

Bowers, J. M. and Benford, S. D. (1991a): "CSCW and Design: Principles and Practices", in Bowers and Benford (1991b), pp. 313-314.

Bowers, J. M. and Benford, S. D. (eds.) (1991b): *Studies in Computer Supported Cooperative Work: Theory, Practice and Design*, North-Holland, Amsterdam.

Ehn, P. (1988): *Work-Oriented Design of Computer Artifacts*, Almqvist & Wiksell International, Stockholm.

Fafchamps, D., Reynolds, D. and Kuchinskya, A. (1991): "The dynamics of small group decision-making using electronic mail', in Bowers and Benford (1991b), pp. 211-224.

Fish, R., Kraut, R. and Chalfont, B. (1990): "The VideoWindow System in informal communication", in *Proceedings of the Conference on Computer-Supported Cooperative Work*, October 7-10 1990, Los Angeles, CA, pp. 1-11.

Granovetter, M. (1985): "Economic Action and Social Structure: the Problem of Embededness", *American Journal of Sociology*, vol. 91, no. 3, pp. 481-510.

Grudin, J. (1988): "Why CSCW Applications Fail: Problems in the Design and Evaluation of Organizational Interfaces", in *Proceedings of the Conference on Computer-Supported Cooperative Work*, Portland, Oregon.

Harper, R., Hughes, J. and Shapiro, D. (1991): "Harmonious Working and CSCW: Computer Technology and Air Traffic Control", in Bowers and Benford (1991b), pp. 225-234.

Harper, R., Hughes, J., Shapiro, D., and Sharrock, W. (forthcoming): *Ordering the Skies: the sociology of coordination work*, Routledge, London.

Harvey, D. (1989): *The Condition of Postmodernity*, Blackwell, Oxford.

Hellman, R. (1989): "Emancipation of and by Computer-Supported Cooperative Work", *Scandinavian Journal of Information Systems*, vol. 1, pp. 143-161.

Kuhn, T. (1970): *The Structure of Scientific Revolutions*, University of Chicago Press, Chicago.

Lash, S. and Urry, J. (1987): *The End of Organized Capitalism*, Polity Press, Cambridge.

Pioré, M. and Sabel, C. (1984): *The Second Industrial Divide*, Basic Books, New York.

Schäl, T. and Zeller, B. (1990): "A Methodological Approach to Computer Supported Cooperative Work", in *Proceedings of the Fifth European Conference on Cognitive Ergonomics*, Urbino, Italy, 3-6 September, pp. 291-304.

Schmidt, K. (1991a): "Cognitive Work: a Conceptual Framework" in J. Rasmussen, B. Brehmer and J. Leplat (eds.): *Distributed Decision Making: Cognitive Models for Cooperative Work*, Wiley, Chichester, pp. 75-109. NB: page references used here are to the version appearing as Risø National Laboratory Paper M-2890.

Schmidt, K. (1991b): "Computer Support for Cooperative Work in Advanced Manufacturing", mimeo, Cognitive Systems Group, Risø National Laboratory, DK-4000 Roskilde, Denmark.

Schmitter, P. (1988): "Sectors in Modern Capitalism: Modes of Governance and Variations in Performance", paper to the 'Markets, Institutions and Cooperation' conference, Venice.

Williamson, O. E. (1975): *Markets and Hierarchies: Analysis and Antitrust Implications*, The Free Press, New York.

Winograd, T. and Flores, F. (1986): *Understanding Computers and Cognition: A new foundation for design*, Ablex, Norwood, NJ.

ECSCW '91 Small Workshop Abstracts

1) Small changes that make a big difference

2) Whither GDSS in CSCW?

3) CSCW Design Methodologies

Proceedings of the Second European Conference on Computer-Supported Cooperative Work
Bannon, L., Robinson, M. & Schmidt, K. (Editors)
September 25-27, 1991, Amsterdam, The Netherlands

ECSCW '91 Small Workshops

Small changes that make a big difference

Organiser: Mikko Korpela

The workshop focuses on how CSCW technologies and applications can have the widest implications on the everyday work of large groups of people, with simple modifications or additions to existing technologies and practices.Where to find voluminous work procedures in which even a slight improvement would have a big effect? How to analyze existing cooperative practices in order to find gaps in the computer support for them? How to build on existing technologies, how to "keep it simple"? Simply, how to make "CSCW for the people"?

Joan Greenbaum
City University, New York, USA.

Most people see changes in the computer world as events that occur very rapidly. But those of us in the computer field know that in the day-to-day practice of developing computer systems, as in most practices, changes are slow, and in fact quite small. Our work is not to bemoan the fact, but rather to celebrate some of the changes taking place and to point to areas where further small, inexpensive and uncomplicated changes can to take place. We emphasize the importance of using workshops and group interaction methods to help system developers act as facilitators in enabling people in workplaces to talk about their work and their expectations about future systems.

Scandinavian approaches to systems design include a wide range of strategies for people who use computers and computer system developers to work cooperatively towards making decisions about computer support. These strategies stress the importance of understanding the nature of work and the organizational setting. The applicability of the Scandinavian approaches in the United States is still open for discussion. Our focus is on an American consulting project where a variety of workshop techniques were used to help staff members in the organization to better articulate their need concerning desktop hardware and software. We would like to use this example to demonstrate ways that workshops "break the ice" in opening up organizational discussions, and also raise fundamental questions concerning differences between the needs of management and the needs of the staff.

Mike Hales
Brighton Polytechnic, England

This contribution refers to a model for human centred ('HC') development of information systems in bureaucratic organisations - the Information Systems Use (ISU) design model. A main function of the model is to underline that HC systems development is not simply a matter of 'participation'. The contribution will discuss weaknesses of a merely participatory definition of HC, referring to an office technology case study in local government.

Starting from the assumption that it is possible and necessary to design *use practices,* as distinct from technology systems, the ISU model identifies three design dimensions: participative structures and styles for design practices; jobs and careers, attending to equal opportunity issues; management roles and development programmes in skills required to manage HC development.

All this involves challenges to the established order of bureaucratic institutions. In other words, *effective design is political.* There is nothing intrinsically 'small' about this kind of design activity. But the approach is associated with smallness in two ways: the scale of the technology involved, to produce major changes, may be small (e.g. 'appropriate' or low-tech technology); attention to details is essential - stylistic and cultural matters that enable marginalised groups and individuals to appropriate some of the technology-related action, in order to establish and assert their own needs.

Maisa Antti-Poika
Peijas-Rekola Hospital, Finland

In Finnish hospitals and health centers, thousands of people work cooperatively daily, more or less supported by shared computerized Medical Records, ordering laboratory tests and returning test results by computer, and so on. In a Finnish district hospital and a primary health center, small extensions to the "shared-database CSCW" were used to enhance cooperation.

Technically, changes to existing systems were small. Standard electronic mail is used as a tool to transfer patient referrals from the general practitioners to the specialists (from health center computer to hospital computer), to facilitate electronic consultation within the hospital, and to communicate lab orders and results. The electronic orders and referrals have dramatically speeded up patient-related communication between different health care units. Electronic requests for additional information have decreased "unnecessary" appointments (i.e., need for patients to travel), and enabled new forms of interaction between hospitals and health centers.

To nurses and doctors, both external and in-house consultation has increased, and they spend a lot of time replying to consultation requests. Nurses have to do more indirect care, through "computerized paper work", compared to the situation before. Apparent savings in costs and travelling, together with more cooperation amongst the staff, were achieved by minor extensions. Privacy hazards, excessive computer work, and the complexity of the overall system are potential risks. More attention is needed to this kind of "everyday CSCW".

Mikko Korpela
University of Kuopio, Finland

Feminist research has shown how important it is to use the viewpoint of specific people with faces, histories, gender, ethnicity, and class. In assessing technology like CSCW, one should ask how well it promotes the basic needs of specific groups of people. On a global scale, the most useful technology would serve low-class women of the Third World in their daily struggle for a better life. Conversely, the least useful technology goes where the money is, as *CSCW Toys for the Rich White Boys*. Looking at CSCW applications represented in various conferences, there is a lot of multi-hyper-giga technology, some goodies for the designers themselves, and just a few pieces of technology for the "Middle-Income White Working Women". Not much of it has anything to offer to the majority of humankind.

Simple electronic mail, for instance, would be very useful in a context of poor telephone lines, bad roads and slow mail. It would not perhaps be used by the "Poor Black Working Woman" herself, but facilitate services she and her children need. E-mail technology is, however, designed for an environment where each node has a systems administrator. Small changes are needed to make it robust enough for developing-country use. But who is interested if one can develop costly hype for those who can pay?

Whither GDSS in CSCW?

The following set of position statements are the basis for a small workshop discussion on Group Decision Support Systems.

Joost Zuurbier

Twente University, The Netherlands

GDSS Design: The first decision support systems (DSS) date back to the '60's. In the seventies, there was an awareness of management problems not covered by systems like EDP and MIS. The first comprehensive text on the subject was published in 1978 by Keen & Scott Morton. Since then more and more DSS applications have evolved thanks to developments in hardware (PC's) and software (fourth generation languages). A number of interesting empirical studies on the effectiveness of DSS were conducted. Design was given less attention. Most writers focus on system construction, which is a technological viewpoint. A recent research program, now becoming known as the Delft School in organisational analysis and DSS design, focused on the design process to be supported. The hard core of the program consists of an analysis and design method. Many successful single user and group DSS applications were developed as part of the protective belt around this hard core.

The Delft School favours the use of process models. This views the tasks as mechanical processes. No attention is given to connections with the informal system. We think these can be made by doing a semantic analysis using NORMA. This leads to a description of the important business semantics.

Abhijit Chaudhury & Sukumar Rathnam

University of Massachusetts & University of Texas, USA

An Axiomatic basis for GDSS: As a method for structuring organisations the use of human groups is becoming increasingly popular. From a technology perspective there has been an explosive growth in the interest in computer systems to support group decision making (GDSS). However, when these tools have been ported to industrial or commercial organizations "*the results have so far been mixed*". In order to improve the performance of GDSS it has been felt, by the designers of these systems, that we need "*a better understanding of what business groups now do*".

The main drawback of many systems to support such multi-agent situations, the resolution of multi-conflicting goals is the result of finding compromise solutions. This paper is directed towards building process models and theories of team behaviour, during consensus formation and conflict resolution, by the use of an economic and social perspective. The motive is to model the *properties of process* by which groups arrive at a solution by the acts of bargaining and negotiation, much as people do in real life in multistage game situations, and present their use in GDSS. For such classes of problems we model the interactive group process, under very weak conditions, and derive sufficient conditions for their asymptotic resolution, and present their use in GDSS.

Elgen Grigoriev & Oleg Zhirkov
Institute "Mosproect-3", Moscow, USSR

The INVARIATRON system is a special video-acoustical environment which stimulates creative activities by means of autodialogue and the dialogue within a combined group team. INVARIATRON supposes that basic data will be kept in human memory, it is intended not to use the "system of knowledge", but to stimulate collective creative activities of specialists. INVARIATRON can be used in various fields of human activities: designing; planning; engineering.

It ensures interaction of making decisions which are realised at different levels and results in strengthening the integrity and strength of though. The development of the information object undergoes a number of stages: the preliminary structuring of reality; the formation of the purpose's structure; the generation of the object. The system's work is based on the use of invariants reflecting the objects essence.

The users of INVARIATRON system work in a studio equipped with a big projection screen necessary for displaying the actions of the groups of specialists and experts. With this some original models come into reality, such as "INVAR", "KARTOIDS", "ECONOMY QUALITY", some "KNOW-HOW", created by the authors of INVARIATRON system. As the output the user has a documented protocol or multivariant process for producing and choosing the most harmonised decisions.

Jim Bryant
Sheffield City Polytechnic, England

Paralleling the development across the Atlantic of sophisticated, computer-based environments for group decision support, here in Europe (and especially in Britain) pre-existing methodologies for process-facilitated group decision support have been enhanced by the use of newly-created computer tools. The presentation contrasts the two approaches, and provides and overview of some of the structured methodologies which have been developed in the UK in current application.

CSCW Design Methodologies

Co-organisers: Gro Bjerknes & Karl Kautz

Tone Bratteteig
University of Oslo, Norway

As a system developer I see some important differences between analysing the technical and the organizational and social basis for a CSCW system and a ``traditional'' computer system. A "traditional" computer system may function as a medium for sequential communication between human beings, whereas a CSCW system supports simultaneous communication, i.e. cooperative and communicative situations. From my point of view, the interesting features of CSCW systems are concerned with the fact that time and space are important attributes of cooperative situations.

When two or more people are working on the same task at the same time independent of their location in space, the computer system may function as a distributed support of work. A relevant analysis of work would be a description of the communicative parts of the work situation. As a tool for cooperating on a work task, the computer system should present the ``raw material'' of the work task to all the users. In addition, the system should support communication about the task, simulating features of a face-to-face communication situation (e.g.several windows, sound, video). When a group of people working on the same task shares one physical computer interface, the computer system functions as a representation of the work rather than a tool.

Gro Bjerknes and Karl Kautz
University of Oslo, Norway

General Characteristics and Specific Implementations of Cooperation --- A Study of two different Work Settings: On the basis of comparing cooperation and computer support in system development projects and in nursing, we have drawn the following conclusions :

It seems that cooperation can be discussed and described in terms of goals, organization of work, communication and overview.These factors interpenetrate in a complex way.

Moreover, we cannot expect to find two similar cooperation settings, due to the fact that there always will be local differences in goals, organization of work and communication.

This means that computers only to a small extent can support cooperation, and only if the anomalies lie in connection with information exchange and recording. Even then, it can be more beneficial to do something with e.g.- the task structure than to introduce a computer system.

For the moment we can forget about building general CSCW-systems, such as meeting systems that can be used in many disciplines or fields, as the local setting will require specific support.

Although there are no general computer systems, there may be common denominators in all cooperation settings. Knowledge of common denominators can be used for analysing cooperation settings and in this way contribute to building computer support-systems for the situated cooperation settings.

Thomas Schael & Buni Zeller
University of Technology (RWTH), Aachen, Germany and RSO, Milan, Italy

RSO developed the TicutomiNet methodology to analyze, evaluate and design cooperative networks. It is based on two of RSO's socio-technical guidelines:

i) viewing the design of a system as a never ending innovative process in an enterprise. It is composed of planning, design and field test.

ii) supporting choices for socio-technical systems on the basis of the consonance among the enterprise's model, its organization and the skills of those involved; and the appropriateness of performance characteristics of the system environment to the socio-technical system.

The methodology aims to:

i) support the description of characteristics and critical aspects of cooperative networks.

ii) identify organizational and technical key-components supporting cooperative work in the system.

iii) identify, analyze and re-design work flows in cooperative processes.

The network is analyzed as a non-permanent organizational form. The methodology helps develop a framework to analyze cooperative work and a common language among the persons involved in its application. It guides the social process during application.The final result is the design-specification for Information Systems to support different types of cooperation (coordination, collaboration and co-decision) within the workflows of business processes.The methodology has been applied in different Italian companies. Some results will be discussed in the workshop.

C. Bignoli, F. De Cindio, C. Simone, A.M. Zanaboni
University of Milan, Italy

The development process needs support, yet an a-priori defined process model is difficult for designers to follow. Our idea is that such a support should be able to understand what goes on in communications inside the design team in order to construct a map of the distributed behaviours, and to give this map back to the people involved in order to let them know the overall situation in which they cooperate. Moreover, it should be able to recognize regularities in people behaviour and to support their interactions.

Our proposal is therefore to start from communication support in order to design a software development process support, and then to integrate other specific aspects in this framework. Thus process models emerge from interactions among people according to their role, their expertise, their ability in orienting their partners and their past experience in working together.

We propose the functionalities of CHAOS (Commitment Handling Active Office System), a knowledge based system whose basic characteristic is a learning capability; UTUCS (User to User Communication Support) whose focus is the design of a conversation handler interfacing communication media other than e-mail; CHILE (Conversation Handling Individual Local Environment), which handles user defined rules to manage the communication flow on the user side.

ECSCW'91 Directory: Authors & Committee Members

Eric Andriessen
Delft University of Technology
Unit of Work and Organisational Psychology
Kanaalweg 2B
2628 EB Delft Netherlands
phone: +31 15 78 37 20
fax: +31 15 78 71 05
email: WMBPAND@HDETUD1.TUDelft.NL (BITNET)

Maisa Antti-Poika
Peijas-Rekola Hospital
Sairaalakatu 1
SF-01400 Vantaa Finland

Kazuho Arita
NTT Human Interface Laboratories
1-2356, Take
Yokosuka-Shi, Kanagawa, 238-03 Japan
phone: +81 468 59 4266
fax: +81 468 59 1054

Liam Bannon
University of Amsterdam
Centre for Innovation & Cooperative Technology
Grote Bickersstraat 72
Amsterdam KS 1013 Netherlands
phone: +31 20 525 1225 / 50
fax: +31 20 525 1211
email: bannon@ooc.uva.nl

Steve Benford
University of Nottingham
Department of Computer Science
University Park
Nottingham, NG7 2RD UK
phone: +44 602 484 848, x.3814
fax: +44 602 590 339
email: sdb@cs.nott.ac.uk

Celsina Bignoli
Dipartimento di Scienze dell'Informazione
Universita di Milano
via Moretto da Brescia 9
I-20133 Milano Italy
phone: +39 2 757 5266
email: bignoli@imiucca.unimi.it

Tora Bikson
Rand Corporation
1700 Main Street
Santa Monica, CA 90406-2138 USA
phone: 213 393 0411/7227
email: tora@rand-unix.org

Gro Bjerknes
Universitetet i Oslo
Institute for Informatiks
PO Box 1080 Blindern
N-0316 Oslo 3 Norway

Gordon Blair
CSCW Research Centre
Computing Department
Lancaster University Bailrigg
Lancaster LA1 4YR UK
phone: +44 524 65201 x.3823
fax: +44 524 381707
email: tom@comp.lancs.ac.uk

John Bowers
University of Nottingham
Department of Psychology
University Park
Nottingham, NG7 2RD UK
phone: +44 602-484848, ext. 3892
fax: +44 602-590339
email: jmb@psyc.nott.ac.uk

Susanne Bødker
Århus Universitet
Department of Computer Science
Ny Munkegade 116
DK-8000 Århus C Denmark
phone: +45 86 12 71 88
fax: +45 86 13 57 25
email: bodker@daimi.dk

Tone Bratteteig
Universitetet i Oslo
Institute for Informatiks
P.O. Box 1080 Blindern
N-0316 Oslo 3 Norway
phone: +47 2 45 34 27
fax: +47 2 45 34 01
email: TONE@IFI.UIO.NO

Jim Bryant
Sheffield City Polytechnic
School of Comp. and Managment Sci.
100 Napier st.
Sheffield S11 8HD UK
phone: +44 742 533106/159
fax: +44 742 533161

Abhijit Chaudhury
Department of Management Science
College of Management
University of Massachusetts
Boston, MA 02125 USA
phone: +1 617 287 7880
fax: +1 617 245 7173
email: chaudhur@umbsky.bitnet

Claudio Ciborra
InstituteTheseus
BP 188 Sophia Antipolis
06561 Valbonne Cedex France
phone: +33 92 945 100 or 345 100
fax: +33 93 653 837
email: ciborra@mirsa.inria.fr

Jeff Conklin
Corporate Memory Systems Inc.
3500 W. Balcones Center Dr.
Austin, TX 78759 USA
phone: +1 512 338 3562
fax: +1 512 338 3899
email: conklin@mcc.com

Fiorella De Cindio
Dipartimento di Scienze dell'Informazione
Universita di Milano
via Moretto da Brescia 9
I-20133 Milano Italy

Flavio De Paoli
Dipartimento di Elettronica
Politecnico di Milano
Piazza Leonardo da Vinci, 32
20133 Milano Italy
phone: +39 2 2399 3634
fax: +39 2 2399 3411
email: depaoli@imicefr.bitnet;
depaoli@imicef.it

Jan Dietz
Department of Informatics
Faculty of Economics and Business Administration
University of Limburg
P.O. Box 616
6200 MD Maastricht Netherlands
phone: +31 43 888 781
fax: +31 43 253 344

Peter Docherty
Institute of Management and Innovation Technology
Saltmåtargatan 13-17
PO BOX 6501
S-11383 Stockholm Sweden
phone: +46 8 736 9000
fax: +46 8 326 524
email: pmopd@hhssun.sunet.se

Marge Eldridge
Rank Xerox Limited
Cambridge EuroPARC
61 Regent Street
Cambridge CB1 2AB UK
phone: +44 223 341 500
fax: +44 223 341 510
email:
Eldridge.EuroPARC@RX.Xerox.Com

Susan Frontczak
Collaborative Tools Research and
Development Lab
Hewlett-Packard Company
3404 East Harmony Road
Fort Collins, Colorado 80525 USA
phone: +1 303 229 2569
fax: +1 303 229 2446
email: susan@hpfcda.hp.com

Bill Gaver
Rank Xerox Limited
Cambridge EuroPARC
61 Regent Street
Cambridge CB1 2AB UK
phone: +44 223 341 500
fax: +44 223 341 510
email: Gaver.EuroPARC@
RX.Xerox.Com

Nigel Gilbert
Department of Sociology
University of Surrey
Guilford
Surrey, GU2 SXH UK

Charles Grantham
University of San Francisco
42 Midhill Road
Martinez CA 94553 USA
phone: +1 415 370 1724
email: cegrant@well.sf.ca.us

Eileen Green
School of Health and Community Studies
Sheffield City Polytechnic
36 Collegiate Crescent
Sheffield S10 2BP UK
phone: +44 742 532 388
fax: +44 742 532 430

Joan Greenbaum
CUNY
341 N. Fullerton Ave
Upper Montclair, NJ 07043 USA

Saul Greenberg
Department of Computer Science
University of Calgary
Calgary T2N 1N4 Canada
phone: +1 403 220 6087
fax: +1 403 284 4707
email: saul@cpsc.ucalgary.ca

Elgen Grigoriev
MOSPROEKT-3 Institute
3 Kuznetsky Most
Moscow 103031 USSR
phone: +7 095 292 1746 / 0788;
+7 095 229 3452
fax: +7 095 292 6511 (add:
P.O.Box 011190, INVAR)

Mike Hales
Centre for Business Research
Brighton Polytechnic
Mithras House Lewes Road
Brighton BN2 4AT UK
phone: +44 273 600 900 x.2471
fax: +44 273 685 896
email:
MH55@VMS.Brighton.AC.UK

Brad Hartfield
Apple Computer, Inc.
20525 Mariani Avenue, MS: 76-2C
Cupertino, CA 95014 USA
phone: +1 408 974 0554
email: HARTFIELD@AppleLink.Apple.COM

Christian Heath
Rank Xerox Limited
Cambridge EuroPARC
61 Regent Street
Cambridge CB2 1AB UK
phone: +44 223 341 515
fax: +44 223 341510
email: heath.europarc@rx.xerox.com

and also
Department of Sociology
University of Surrey
Guildford
Surrey GU2 5XH UK

Riitta Hellman
Postdirektoratet
Plan- og utviklingsavdelingen
Dronningens gate 15
Postboks 1181 Sentrum
N-0107 Oslo 1 Norway
phone: +47 2 40 80 73 / 40 90 50
fax: +47 2 40 80 14 / 81 00 / 80 98 / 42 66 87

Elke Hinrichs
German National Research Center for Computer Science (GMD)
Institute for Applied Information Technology
Schloß Birlinghoven
D-5205 Sankt Augustin 1 Germany
phone: +49 2241 14 0 x.2442
fax: +49 2241 14 2084

John Hughes
Department of Sociology & Centre for Research in CSCW
Cartmel College
Lancaster University
Lancaster LA1 4YL UK
phone: +44 524 65201 x.4175
fax: +44 524 844788
email:
soa004@central1.lancaster.ac.uk;
shapiro@lancaster.ac.uk

Hiroshi Ishii
NTT Human Interface Laboratories
1-2356, Take
Yokosuka-Shi, Kanagawa, 238-03 Japan
phone: +81 468 59 3522
fax: +81 468 59 2332
email:
ishii%ntthif.ntt.jp@relay.cs.net

Marina Jirotka
University of Surrey
Department of Sociology
Guilford, Surrey, GU2 SXH UK
phone: +44 483 509 292
email: marina@soc.surrey.ac.uk

Karl Kautz
University of Oslo
Department of Informatics
P.O.Box 1080
Blindern N-0316 Oslo 3 Sweden

John King
University of California, Irvine
ICS Department
Irvine, CA 92717 USA
email: king@ics.uci.edu

Karl-Heinz Klein
German National Research Center for Computer Science (GMD)
Institute for Applied Information Technology
Schloß Birlinghoven
D-5205 Sankt Augustin 1 Germany
phone: +49 2241 14 0 x.2720
fax: +49 2241 14 2084

Mikko Korpela
Computing Center PL6
SF-70211 Kuopio Finland
fax: +358 71 225 566
email: korpela@uku.fi; Bitnet: korpela@finkuo

Thomas Kreifelts
German National Research Center for Computer Science (GMD)
Institute for Applied Information Technology
Schloß Birlinghoven
D-5205 Sankt Augustin 1 Germany
phone: +49 2241 14 0 x.2643
fax: +49 2241 14 2084
email: tom@f3svb.gmd.de

Klaus Kreplin
TA Research
TA Triumph-Adler AG
Fürther Str. 212
D-8500 Nürnberg 80 Germany
phone: +49 911 322 6306
fax: +49 911 322 6282
email: kk@triumph-adler.de

Bernard Kubiak
University of Gdansk
Department of Computer Science
ul. Poli Gojawiczynskiej 3A/8
Gdynia-Karwiny 81-987 Poland
phone: +48 58 510061 ext. 400

Kari Kuutti
University of Oulu
Institute of Information Processing Science
Linnanmaa
SF - 90570 Oulu Finland

Mik Lamming
Rank Xerox Limited
Cambridge EuroPARC
61 Regent Street
Cambridge CB1 2AB UK
phone: +44 223 341 500
fax: +44 223 341 510
email: Lamming.EuroPARC@RX.Xerox.Com

Henrik Lewe
University of Hohenheim
Lehrstuhl fur Wirtschaftsinformatic (510 H)
P.O. Box 70 05 62
D-7000 Stuttgart, 70 Germany
phone: +49 711 459 3238
fax: +49 711 459 2785
email: Lewe@rus.uni-stuttgart.dbp.de

Lennart Lövstrand
Rank Xerox Limited
Cambridge EuroPARC
61 Regent Street
Cambridge CB1 2AB UK
phone: +44 223 341 500
fax: +44 223 341 510
email: Lovstrand.EuroPARC@RX.Xerox.Com

Iva Lu
Department of Computer Science
University of Toronto
10 Kings College Road
Toronto, Ontario M5S 1A4 Canada
phone: +1 416 978 5512
fax: +1 416 978 4765
email: ivalu@dgp.utoronto.edu

Paul Luff
Rank Xerox Limited
Cambridge EuroPARC
61 Regent Street
Cambridge, CB1 2AB UK
phone: +44 223 341 528
fax: +44 223 341 510
email: luff.europarc@xerox.com

and also
Department of Sociology
University of Surrey
Guildford
Surrey GU2 5XH UK

Marilyn Mantei
Department of Computer Science
University of Toronto
10 Kings College Road
Toronto, Ontario M5S 1A4 Canada
phone: +1 416 978 5512
fax: +1 416 978 4765
email: mantei@dgp.toronto.edu / mantei.chi@xerox.com

Hans Marmolin
Interaction and Presentation Laboratory
Numerical Analysis and Computing Science
Royal Institute of Technology
S-100 44
S-100 44 Stockholm Sweden
phone: +46 8 790 6279
fax: +46 8 791 0930
email: hanmarm@nada.kth.se

Kathy Miner
Collaborative Multimedia Program
Hewlett-Packard Company
3404 East Harmony Road
Fort Collins, Colorado 80525 USA
phone: +1 303 229 3595
fax: +1 303 229 4720
email: miner@hpfcspm.hp.com

Leandro Navarro
Departamento d'Arquitectura de Computadors
Universitat Politecnica de Catalunya
P.O. Box 30.002
E-08034 Barcelona Spain
phone: +34 3 401 6807
fax: +34 3 401 7055
email: leandro@ac.upc.es

William Newman
Rank Xerox Limited
Cambridge EuroPARC
61 Regent Street
Cambridge CB1 2AB UK
phone: +44 223 341 500
fax: +44 223 341 510
email: Newman.EuroPARC@RX.Xerox.Com

Markku Nurminen
University of Turku
Computer Science
Lemminkaisenkatu 14 A
SF 20520 Turku Finland
fax: +358 21 329 059

Wanda Orlikowski
Sloan School of Management
Massachussets Institute of Technology
50 Memorial Drive, E53-329
Cambridge, MA 02139 USA
email: wanda@eagle.mit.edu

Jenny Owen
School of Health and Community Studies
Sheffield City Polytechnic
36 Collegiate Crescent
Sheffield S1 1WB UK
phone: +44 742 532 425
fax: +44 742 532 430

Den Pain
School of Computing and Management Sciences
Sheffield City Polytechnic
Napier Street
Sheffield S11 8HD UK
phone: +44 742 533 153
fax: +44 742 533 161

Elin Pedersen
System Sciences Laboratory
Xerox Palo Alto Research Center
3333 Coyote Hill Road
Palo Alto, CA 94304 USA
phone: +1 415 494 4756 (off.); +1 415 494 7193 (pr.)
fax: +1 415 494 4380
email: epedersen@parc.xerox.com

Björn Pehrson
Swedish Institute for Computer Science
Box 1263
S-164 28 Kista Sweden
phone: +46 8 752 1510
fax: +46 8 751 7230
email: bjorn@sics.se

Wolfgang Prinz
German National Research Center for Computer Science (GMD)
Institute for Applied Information Technology
Schloß Birlinghoven
Posfach 1240
D-5205 Sankt Augustin 1 Germany
phone: +49 22 41 14 27 30
fax: +49 22 41 14 20 84
email: prinz@fs.gmd.dbp.de (or @73.)

Kari-Jouko Raiha
Department of Computer Science
University of Tampere
P.O.Box 607
SF-33101 Tampere Finland
fax: +358 31 156 070
email: kjr@cs.uta.fi

Dave Randall
Department of Sociology & Centre for Research in CSCW
Cartmel College
Lancaster University
Lancaster LA1 4YL UK
phone: +44 524 65201 x.4175
fax: +44 524 844788
email: shapiro@lancaster.ac.uk

Sukumar Rathnam
MSIS Department
CBA 5.202
The University of Texas at Austin
Austin, Texas TX 78712-1175 USA
phone: +1 512 471 3322 / 8879
fax: +1 512 471 0587
email: sukumar@emx.utexas.edu

Christianne Ribeiro
Rua Tonelero 308/303
Copacabana
Rio de Janeiro, RJ 22030 Brasil

Mike Robinson
University of Amsterdam
Centre for Innovation & Cooperative Technology
Grote Bickersstraat 72
Amsterdam KS 1013 Netherlands
phone: +31 20 525 1225 / 50
fax: +31 20 525 1211
email: mike@ooc.uva.nl

Tom Rodden
CSCW Research Centre
Computing Department
Lancaster University Bailrigg
Lancaster LA1 4YR UK
phone: +44 524 65201 x.3823
fax: +44 524 381707
email: tom@comp.lancs.ac.uk

Andrei Roussakov
University of Amsterdam
Centre for Innovation & Cooperative Technology
Grote Bickersstraat 72
Amsterdam KS 1013 Netherlands
phone: +31 20 525 1225 / 50
fax: +31 20 525 1211
email: andy@ooc.uva.nl

Thomas Schael
RSO SpA
Via Leopardi 1
I-20123 Milano Italy
phone: +39 2 72 00 05 83
fax: +39 2 86 45 07 20 / 86 45 21 16 / 48 18 842
email: schael@vdveer.cs.vu.nl; schael@psy.vu.nl

Kjeld Schmidt
Risø National Laboratory
Cognitive Systems Group
P O Box 49
4000 Roskilde Denmark
phone: +45 42 37 12 12
fax: +45 42 37 39 93
email: Kschmidt@Risoe.dk

Stephen Scrivener
Lutchi Research Centre
Loughborough University of Technology
Loughborough, Leics., LE11 3TU UK
phone: +44 509 222 696
fax: +44 509 610 815
email: s.a.scrivener@loughborough.ac.uk

Peter Seuffert
German National Research Center for Computer Science (GMD)
Institute for Applied Information Technology
Schloß Birlinghoven
D-5205 Sankt Augustin 1 Germany
phone: +49 2241 14 0 x.2868
fax: +49 2241 14 2084

Dan Shapiro
Department of Sociology & Centre for Research in CSCW
Cartmel College
Lancaster University
Lancaster LA1 4YL UK
phone: +44 524 65201 x.4175
fax: +44 524 63 806
email: shapiro@lancaster.ac.uk (or soa004@cent1.lancs.ac.uk)

Carla Simone
Dipartimento di Scienza dell'Informazione
via Moretto da Brescia 9
I-20133 Milano Italy
phone: +39 2 7575 219
fax: +39 2 7611 0556
email: SIMONE@IMIUCCA.BITNET

Pål Sørgaard
Norsk Regnesentral
Postboks 114 Blindern
N-0314 Oslo 3 Norway
phone: +47 245 3575
fax: +47 269 7660
email: Pal.Sorgaard@nr.no

Ronald Stamper
Universiteit Twente
School of Management Studies
Postbus 217
NL-7500 AE Enschede Netherlands
phone: +31 5389 3509
fax: +31 5335 7956
email: stamper@henut5.bitnet

S. Leigh Star
University of Keel
Department of Sociology and Social Anthropology
Keel, Staffs. ST5 5BG UK
phone: +44 782 621 111 x.4041
fax: +44 782 613 847
email: soa03@seq1.keele.ac.uk

Lucy Suchman
Rank Xerox Limited
Palo Alto Research Center
3333 Coyote Hill Road
Palo Alto, CA 94304 USA
phone: +1 415 494 4340
email: suchman.pa@xerox.com

Yngve Sundblad
Interaction and Presentation Laboratory
Numerical Analysis and Computing Science
Royal Institute of Technology
S-100 44 Stockholm Sweden
phone: +46 8 790 7147
fax: +46 8 791 0930
email: yngve@nada.kth.se

Francesco Tisato
Dipartimento di Scienze dell'Informazione
Politecnico di Milano
Via Moretto da Brescia, 9
20133 Milano Italy
phone: +39 2 757 5268
fax: +39 2 761 105 56
email: tisato@hermes.unimi.it

Michel Tueni
IFATEC
3 Rue Petigny
7800 Versailles France
phone: +33 1 3902 3850
fax: +33 1 3902 1391
email: tueni@masbull.my.bull.fr

Stephen Viller
Dept. of Computation
UMIST
Sackville Street
P.O. Box 88
Manchester M60 1QD UK
phone: +44 61 200 3361
fax: +44 61 228 7386
email: viller@sa.co.umist.ac.uk

Ina Wagner
Institut fur Gestaltungs- und Wirkungsforschung
Technische Universitat Wien
Argentieniersstr. 8
A-1040 Wien Austria
phone: +43 222 58801 x.4439
fax: +43 222 65 84 53 / 505 4801

Douglas Ward
Ontario Institute for Studies in Education
Department of MECA
252 Bloor Street West
Toronto, Ontario M5S 1V6 Canada
phone: +1 416 536 7771
fax: +1 416 926 4725
email: dward@utoroise.bitnet

G. Widdershoven
Department of Health Care Ethics and Philosophy
Faculty of Health Sciences
University of Limburg
P.O. Box 616
6200 MD Maastricht Netherlands
phone: +31 43 888 377
fax: +31 43 253 344

Paul Wilson
CSC Europe
Computer Sciences House
Brunel Way, Slough
Berkshire SL1 1XL UK
phone: +44 753 73232
fax: +44 753 516178
email: wilson@cs.nott.ac.uk; paul_wilson@hicom.lut.ac.uk

Gert Woetzel
German National Research Center for Computer Science (GMD)
Institute for Applied Information Technology
Schloß Birlinghoven
D-5205 Sankt Augustin 1 Germany
phone: +49 2241 14 0 x.2648
fax: +49 2241 14 2084

Anna Maria Zanaboni
Dipartimento di Scienze dell'Informazione
Universita di Milano
via Moretto da Brescia 9
I-20133 Milano Italy
phone: +39 2 757 5266

Gerard de Zeeuw
University of Amsterdam
Center for Innovation and Cooperative Technology
Grote Bickersstraat 72
1013 KS Amsterdam Netherlands
phone: +31 20 525 1209
fax: +31 20 525 1211
email: a717gerard@hasara11.bitnet; Gerard_de_Zeeuw@ooc.uva.nl

Buni Zeller
RSO FUTURA SRL
Via Leopardi, 1
I-20123 Milano Italy
phone: +39 2 72 00 05 83
fax: +39 2 48 18 842 / 80 68 00
email: RSO.@INFOBOX

Oleg Zhirkov
MOSPROEKT-3 Institute
Department of INVARIATRON system
3 Kuznetsky Most
Moscow 103031 USSR
phone: +7 095 292 1746 / 0788; +7 095 229 3452
fax: +7 095 292 6511 (add: P.O.Box 011190, INVAR)

Heinz Züllighoven
German National Research Center for Computer Science (GMD)
Institute for Applied Information Technology
Schloß Birlinghoven
P.O. Box 1240
D-5205 Sankt Augustin 1 Germany
email: zue@gmdzi.uucp

Joost Zuurbier
Technische Universiteit Twente
Faculteit der Bedrijfskunde
Postbus 217
7500 AE ENSCHEDE Netherlands
phone: +31 53 892 141
fax: +31 53 339 885

GPSR Compliance

The European Union's (EU) General Product Safety Regulation (GPSR) is a set of rules that requires consumer products to be safe and our obligations to ensure this.

If you have any concerns about our products, you can contact us on ProductSafety@springernature.com

In case Publisher is established outside the EU, the EU authorized representative is:

Springer Nature Customer Service Center GmbH
Europaplatz 3
69115 Heidelberg, Germany

Batch number: 10762209

Printed by Printforce, the Netherlands